The Amphibians and Reptiles of Louisiana

THE AMPHIBIANS AND REPTILES OF LOUISIANA

Harold A. Dundee

*Curator of amphibians and reptiles and Emeritus Professor of Biology,
Tulane University*

Douglas A. Rossman

*Curator, Museum of Natural Science, and Adjunct Professor of Zoology,
Louisiana State University*

Illustrated by Eugene C. Beckham

Louisiana State University Press
Baton Rouge and London

Louisiana Paperback Edition, 1996
05 04 03 02 01 00 99 98 97 96   1 2 3 4 5

Designer: Sylvia Malik Loftin
Typeface: Trump Mediaeval
Typesetter: The Composing Room of Michigan, Inc.
Printed and bound in Hong Kong by Everbest Printing Co., through Four Colour Imports, Ltd.,
Louisville, Kentucky

Library of Congress Cataloging-in-Publication Data

Dundee, Harold A.
    The amphibians and reptiles of Louisiana.

    Bibliography: p.
    Includes index.
    1. Amphibians—Louisiana.   2. Reptiles—Louisiana.
I. Rossman, Douglas Athon, 1936–   . II. Beckham,
Eugene C.   III. Title.
    QL653.L6D86   1989   597.6'09763   88-12873
    ISBN 0-8071-1436-7 (cloth)   ISBN 0-8071-2077-4 (pbk.)

The outline maps of Louisiana are adapted from George H. Lowery, Jr., *The Mammals of Louisiana
and Its Adjacent Waters* (Baton Rouge, 1974).

A friend of the LSU Museum of Natural Science who wishes to remain anonymous has generously
assisted in the publication of this volume.

The paper in this book meets the guidelines for permanence and durability of the Committee on
Production Guidelines for Book Longevity of the Council on Library Resources. ∞

To my late wife, Dee Saunders Dundee, whose continual encouragement and expectation were so instrumental to the fruition of this substantial undertaking.

Harold A. Dundee

To my wife, Nita Jane Rossman, for her assistance in the field, her dedication in typing the many drafts of the manuscript, and for her constant encouragement, my contributions to this book are lovingly dedicated.

Douglas A. Rossman

Contents

CONTENTS

Preface

Provincial pride, identity, and interest are forces that lead to the production of publications such as *The Amphibians and Reptiles of Louisiana*. Animals and plants do not respect state borders; species are clearly associated with artificial boundaries only where natural geographic features coincide with political subdivisions. Yet however arbitrary our regional study might appear, we have endeavored to produce a treatise that will be useful to amateur and professional herpetologists as well as the lay public.

Louisiana's herpetofauna is highly diverse. We recognize at least 129 species, an assemblage comprising 22 salamanders, 27 frogs, 27 turtles, 14 lizards, 39 snakes, and 1 crocodilian. The list includes three species of lizard and one frog that have been introduced and established. Were we more liberal in our interpretation of what constitutes a species, we could add one salamander, and for that matter we could add one frog that we consider to exist here only in a hybrid state.

Everywhere in Louisiana people are in intimate contact with the world of reptiles and amphibians; even within the city limits of the largest city, New Orleans, one can find a good variety of amphibians and reptiles, even alligators and poisonous snakes. The abundance of some of our species has made Louisiana a paradise for commercial collectors; most of the large salamanders (*Amphiuma means*), chamaeleons (*Anolis carolinensis*), red-eared turtles (*Trachemys scripta*), water snakes (*Nerodia*), and bullfrogs (*Rana catesbeiana*) used in research laboratories are probably shipped from the state, and today, with resurgence of the alligator, Louisiana is the major domestic producer of alligator hides used for leather goods. In addition, Louisiana probably is the major U.S. producer of freshwater turtle meat.

Many books dealing with reptiles and amphibians cover the identification and natural history of the individual groups of all the species inhabiting Louisiana. But a study focusing on the state can discuss in much greater depth and detail distribution and local variation. This book includes many new observations on appearance, distribution, habitat, habits, systematics, etc., gleaned from the examination of many museum specimens and their accompanying data. Occasionally, the complexities of identifying specimens have caused us to discuss in detail our views of the taxonomy of certain species. And, of course, our repeated visits to the field have revealed many fascinating aspects of the natural history of our herpetofauna that enhance interpretations of what is known about life histories of the animals involved or that suggest the need for additional studies.

We hope this book will enrich public knowledge of the Louisiana herpetofauna, but this is only part of our objective. By alerting interested persons, we hope to stimulate further studies. The reader who peruses in totality any species account that we include should detect that very little is known of some of the most fundamental aspects of the biology of commonly seen species. One need not be a professional to go into the field and collect useful data; in fact, the secretive habits of many reptiles and amphibians prevent the professional herpetologist from making many of the needed observations. Successful collection of valuable data is the result of such factors as planning, persistence, fortuity, and knowledge of how to observe. Wise professional workers encourage amateurs and the public at large to come to them with observations and queries; we all ultimately benefit.

We do, however, add a word of caution to those interested in contributing to our knowledge. We live in an era of substantial alteration of our environment; urbanization, land clearing for agriculture, widespread use of pesticides, pollution in general, draining of swamps, digging of canals in our marshes, damming or channelization of streams, and many other human practices are reducing animal populations. Reptiles, especially, have suffered through human ignorance that leads to their indiscriminate slaughter. Students should be most judicious in their studies, depending as much as possible on mere observation, perhaps by marking animals and releasing them so that they can be seen repeatedly. Any study that requires sacrifice of animals should be well planned (multipurpose, if possible) so as to make maximum use of a minimum number of specimens. No reported extant species of reptile or amphibian native to Louisiana is known to have become

eliminated in the state, but several have been reduced to precariously low numbers or are restricted to very small areas. Thus, we plead energetically for the public to help us conserve and protect our natural heritage.

In this book, Rossman contributed the sections on the alligator, snakes, and lizards; Dundee treated the amphibians and turtles. Although we agreed to a common format, the detail needed to adequately describe the appearance of animals in the respective treatments or to summarize their habits has created some differences between the accounts, but in every case we feel that the reader has gotten the maximum amount of information that we could reasonably justify in a book of this nature. Wherever we have disagreed on an interpretation, we freely ascribe the opinion to the appropriate author.

Acknowledgments

We wish to thank the following curators of collections for granting us access to their Louisiana material: James E. Bohlke (deceased), Academy of Natural Sciences, Philadelphia; Richard G. Zweifel, American Museum of Natural History; Ray E. Ashton, personal collection; Robert H. Mount, Auburn University; Richard M. Blaney, personal collection; Wilmer Tanner, Brigham Young University; C. J. McCoy, Carnegie Museum of Natural History; Albert E. Sanders, Charleston Museum; Kraig Adler, Cornell University; Hymen Marx and Robert Inger, Field Museum of Natural History; Walter Auffenberg, Florida State Museum; Donald E. Hahn, personal collection; William E. Duellman, University of Kansas Museum of Natural History; John Wright, Los Angeles County Museum; Ernest A. Liner, personal collection; Laurence M. Hardy, Louisiana State University, Shreveport; Billy J. Davis, Louisiana Tech University; James D. Lane, McNeese State University; Ernest E. Williams, Museum of Comparative Zoology; William Palmer, North Carolina State Museum of Natural History; Neil Douglas, Northeast Louisiana University; Kenneth L. Williams, Northwestern State University of Louisiana; Larry Crain, Southeastern Louisiana University; Bryce C. Brown, Strecker Museum, Baylor University; James R. Dixon, Texas Cooperative Wildlife Collection, Texas A & M University; W. Frank Blair (deceased), Texas Natural History Collection, University of Texas at Austin; Robert A. Thomas, personal collection; T. Paul Maslin (deceased), University of Colorado Museum; Donald W. Tinkle (deceased), University of Michigan Museum of Zoology; Edmund D. Keiser (formerly) and James F. Jackson, University of Southwestern Louisiana; J. William Cliburn, University of Southern Mississippi; George R. Zug and James A. Peters (deceased), National Museum of Natural History; Larry D. Wilson, personal collection.

We are also grateful to Louisiana State University at Baton Rouge and Edward M. Simmons of the Louisiana Research Foundation for financial assistance for some of our travels to visit collections; Richard M. Blaney for photographs used to help prepare some of the illustrations; Robert H. Chabreck and Philip M. Hall for providing information on the alligator; and Edmund D. Keiser for loaning us his unpublished distribution maps of the Atchafalaya herpetofauna. We also wish to thank Dolores Gunning and Nita J. Rossman for typing the preliminary draft of the book, Nita J. Rossman for typing the final manuscript, and Mary C. Hester for her skillful copy editing. Finally, we are indebted to Robert H. Mount, Patrick A. Myer, and Kenneth L. Williams for critically reading the manuscript—in part (Myer) or in its entirety (Mount, Williams)—and offering many helpful suggestions.

PART ONE: Introduction to Herpetology

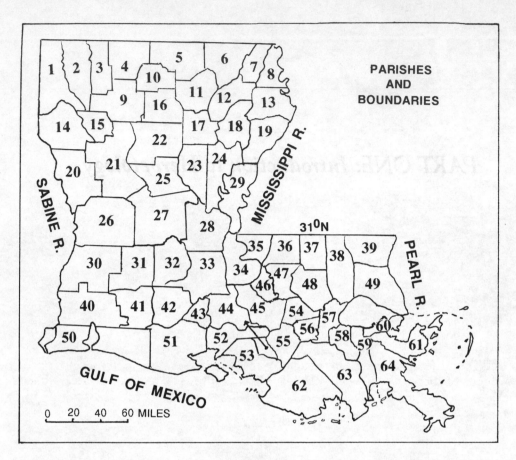

PARISHES
AND
BOUNDARIES

Acadia **42**	Grant **25**	Sabine **20**
Allen **31**	Iberia **52**	St. Bernard **61**
Ascension **54**	Iberville **45**	St. Charles **58**
Assumption **55**	Jackson **16**	St. Helena **37**
Avoyelles **28**	Jefferson **59**	St. James **56**
Beauregard **30**	Jefferson Davis **41**	St. John the Baptist **57**
Bienville **9**	Lafayette **43**	St. Landry **33**
Bossier **2**	Lafourche **63**	St. Martin **44**
Caddo **1**	La Salle **23**	St. Mary **53**
Calcasieu **40**	Lincoln **10**	St. Tammany **49**
Caldwell **17**	Livingston **48**	Tangipahoa **38**
Cameron **50**	Madison **13**	Tensas **19**
Catahoula **24**	Morehouse **6**	Terrebonne **62**
Claiborne **4**	Natchitoches **21**	Union **5**
Concordia **29**	Orleans **60**	Vermilion **51**
De Soto **14**	Ouachita **11**	Vernon **26**
East Baton Rouge **47**	Plaquemines **64**	Washington **39**
East Carroll **8**	Pointe Coupee **34**	Webster **3**
East Feliciana **36**	Rapides **27**	West Baton Rouge **46**
Evangeline **32**	Red River **15**	West Carroll **7**
Franklin **18**	Richland **12**	West Feliciana **35**
		Winn **22**

HISTORY OF HERPETOLOGY IN LOUISIANA

When herpetological collections were first made in Louisiana cannot be precisely determined because the date Europeans first visited the state is unclear in the accounts of early-day explorers. Possibly the first traveler was Cabeza de Vaca about 1528, but certainly by 1543 Hernando de Soto's expedition was in Louisiana. In 1682 La Salle came down the Mississippi River, and about 1698 Iberville also reached the Mississippi. Iberville came with Indians to the site where Bienville would found the city of New Orleans in 1718. In 1700, maps based on La Salle's and Iberville's travels appeared, and some concept of locality emerged. The earliest permanent settlement, Natchitoches, established in 1714, was difficult to reach, and most early biological visitations or collections took place in the New Orleans area after the city was founded.

Once New Orleans became established, it was a focal point for expeditions, travels, and commerce. Many animals that reached museums were labeled simply "New Orleans." We know from present-day distributions and the ecological relations of reptiles and amphibians that some of the animals certainly came from north of Lake Pontchartrain rather than from New Orleans. Thus, early accounts and descriptions of specimens that refer to "New Orleans" may in fact have been based on material taken far from the city. New Orleans was simply the only map location or shipping point at that time.

The first reference to a Louisiana specimen may be Daudin's (1803) description of an alligator from the "borders of the Mississippi." Daudin was based in Paris and hence may have obtained the specimens from early French explorers, especially because France used New Orleans as its main entry to the Mississippi Valley. But in 1808, Barton reported, "In the meanwhile, I shall only observe, that South-Carolina possesses a large four-footed Siren; and that a species (probably the very same), with four feet also, has been seen and examined by one of my pupils, in the neighbourhood of the Red-river [sic], which empties itself into the Missisippi [sic]. The Louisiana animal was three feet in length, and six inches in circumference." The pupil referred to was Dr. Peter Custis of Virginia. Thus our first definite Louisiana report refers to the salamander *Amphiuma means*.

Cuvier (1827) provided an early description of *Amphiuma means tridactylum* from New Orleans. This, based on our present knowledge, would be a Florida Parishes animal.

In 1831 Jacob Green described a salamander, *Eurycea cirrigera*, from "Louisiana, near New Orleans." That species is found in the state only in the Florida Parishes, thereby confirming our conception of New Orleans simply as a base. At that same time Green also described the tiger salamander, *Ambystoma tigrinum*, from New Orleans, but we have been able to confirm its existence in eastern Louisiana only from larvae taken in 1964 in St. Tammany Parish north of Lake Pontchartrain. Shortly after Green's report, Schlegel (1837) described a subspecies of the mudsnake, *Farancia abacura*; the source of the specimen was somewhat ambiguous, but is now considered to be Louisiana. A modest number of descriptions appeared throughout the 1800s, but none of the describers, who were working with museum specimens, were actually operating in Louisiana.

Although specimens were accumulating during the early 1800s in museums, notably at the Academy of Natural Sciences in Philadelphia and at the United States National Museum, Louisiana still had no native professional herpetologists. In 1885 a museum was begun at Tulane University. The nature of its herpetological collections in the early days are not known to us, but in 1893 George E. Beyer (1861–1926) became curator, and herpetology was among his interests. In 1900 he published a paper on Louisiana's herpetological records. Among the collections acquired during Beyer's tenure was a personal natural history collection donated by Gustav Kohn, a wealthy New Orleans citizen. Kohn's collection, presented in 1904, contained a modest number of reptiles, of which a number of mounted specimens, especially turtles, remain in the current Tulane herpetological collections.

Louisiana's first major herpetologist probably was Percy Viosca (1892–1961). Viosca, a versatile naturalist, was guided by Beyer, then chairman of biology at Tulane University. He received a B.S. at Tulane in 1913 and an M.S. degree in 1915. He became curator of reptiles, amphibians, and fishes at the Louisiana State Museum in 1915; at the same time he began a commercial venture, Southern Biological Supply Company, a source for many herpetological specimens that ultimately reached various collections, especially those at Tulane University. Viosca wrote several papers on the Louisiana herpetofauna, including periodic checklists. He also described several kinds of frogs and salamanders, sometimes using Louisiana material as type specimens.

A contemporary of Viosca was E. A. McIlhenny, originator of the famous condiment Tabasco Sauce and an avid amateur naturalist. In 1935 McIlhenny published a fascinating book, *The Alligator's Life History*, based primarily on observations made around his home at Avery Island in Iberia Parish.

The advent of intensive herpetological studies in Louisiana can be associated with Fred R. Cagle's (1915–1968) arrival as a professor of zoology at Tulane University in 1946. Cagle began to build the Tulane herpetological collections, and he initiated a graduate program that produced the first Ph.D.s in herpetology from Tulane. He wrote a number of significant papers on the systematics and ecology of southeastern U.S. amphibians and reptiles. He began accumulating data for a book on the herpetology of Louisiana, but increasing administrative duties and his promotion to a vice-presidential post in the university removed him from an active role in the Zoology Department.

During the post–World War II educational boom, many Louisiana colleges and universities added herpetologists to their staffs, and collections were begun or greatly augmented, especially at Northeast Louisiana University, the University of Southwestern Louisiana, Louisiana Tech University, Northwestern State University of Louisiana, and Louisiana State University in Baton Rouge. The many new records thus added greatly clarified knowledge of the Louisiana herpetofauna. A rather novel collection has recently been founded by Dr. Herbert Dessauer, a Louisiana State University Medical School biochemist sometimes described as the "father of herpetological biochemical systematics." The collection, housed at both the LSU Medical School in New Orleans and the LSU Museum of Natural History in Baton Rouge, provides a repository for frozen tissues that can be used for studies at the molecular level.

Although new knowledge that might be gleaned from traditional systematics and distributional studies on the Louisiana herpetofauna is becoming limited, the rich assemblage of reptiles and amphibians in the state offers a wide variety of opportunities for investigations in ecology, behavior, physiology, and molecular biology.

DISTRIBUTION OF AMPHIBIANS AND REPTILES IN LOUISIANA

The present distribution of amphibians and reptiles within the state is the result of both ecological and historical factors. Ecological conditions provide both opportunities and barriers for a species to enter an area; historical factors influence subsequent dispersal.

Major Habitats

The average amount of precipitation does not vary greatly from one part of Louisiana to another (although the southern part of the state tends to be somewhat wetter), and the state lacks any areas of high relief (elevations range from 0 to 535 feet or 163 m). Nevertheless, the different soil types, their associated vegetation, and the nature of the surface water provide sufficiently diverse habitats for the distributions of many species of amphibians and reptiles to vary across the state. Our map of major habitats of Louisiana (Fig. 1) is based on Newton's (1972:35), but is less detailed, particularly with respect to the locations of cypress forests and gallery forests. The seven regions shown in Figure 1 are briefly described below. Brown (1945:5–11) provided a more detailed discussion of these regions.

Marsh. This region has both saltwater and freshwater marshes predominantly vegetated by emergent grasses and rushes. The Marsh habitat also includes cheniers (ancient dunes or beach ridges surrounded by marsh) and natural levees, on which the live oak is the dominant tree. The Marsh provides abundant habitat for many semiaquatic species (most notably *Alligator mississippiensis*) and forms a barrier to many terrestrial species, although some are able to penetrate the Marsh along the natural levees.

Prairie. This area in southwestern Louisiana is basically a grassland, but hardwood trees (and some pines) grow in poorly drained depressions, as well as on ridges, and they form the gallery forests that border streams. The Louisiana distributions of such predominantly western taxa as the ornate box turtle (*Terrapene ornata*) and the plain-bellied water snake (*Nerodia erythrogaster transversa*) are largely confined to the Prairie.

Bottomland Hardwoods. This extensive region includes the broad floodplain forests of the Red, Ouachita, Tensas, Atchafalaya, and Mississippi river basins, as well as the much narrower floodplains of the Sabine and Pearl rivers. Before most of the bald cypress were lumbered, cypress–tupelo gum forest covered much of the area. The remainder of the Bottomland Hardwood forest was, and is, dominated by a variety of moisture-tolerant oaks, gums, willows, ash, elm, hackberry, sycamore, and cottonwood. Canebrakes are common.

Flatwoods. Two separate areas of Flatwoods occur in Louisiana, one in the southwestern part of the state and the other in the southern portion of the Florida Parishes. Historically the forest consisted of longleaf pines (now mostly "lumbered out" in the Florida Parishes) and hardwoods; open areas were and are covered by wiregrass and palmetto. Winter rains produce many standing pools in the flatwoods, which are favored breeding sites for many amphibians.

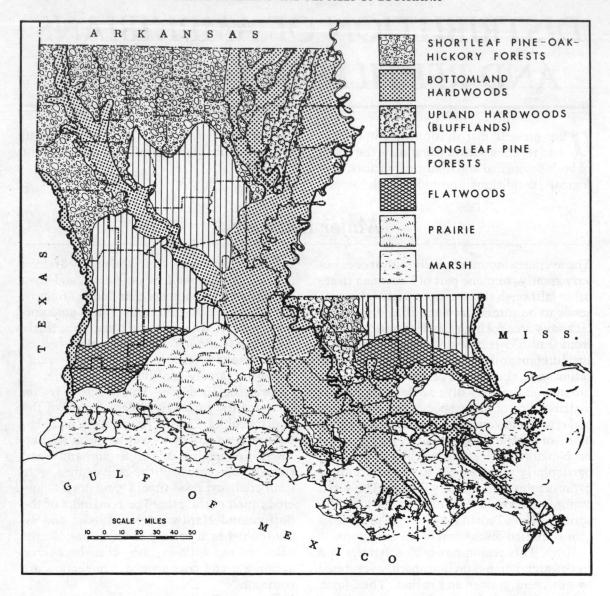

Figure 1. Distribution of major habitats in Louisiana. Based on the distribution of natural vegetation as depicted by Newton (1972: 35).

Longleaf Pine Forests. These are relatively dry upland forests on sandy soil. Pine logs and needles usually provide a rather sterile environment for the herpetologist who hunts beneath them, but road collecting at night during the warmer months of the year has proved that these forests do support a diverse herpetofauna. In Louisiana, the pine snake (*Pituophis melanoleucus* subspecies) and red-backed salamander (*Plethodon serratus*) are confined to this habitat.

Shortleaf Pine-Oak-Hickory Forests. These upland forests, dominated by pine, oak, and hickory, lie adjacent to the Longleaf Pine Forests and have a similar herpetofauna.

Upland Hardwoods (Blufflands). In these upland forests on loessial soils, the tree species are generally the same as in the better-drained parts of the Bottomland Hardwood region. Tunica Hills, a deeply dissected section of the Blufflands in West Feliciana Parish, has long been of great interest botanically. The cool, well-shaded, mesic ravines harbor species of ferns, mosses, and herbaceous plants rarely found elsewhere in Louisiana, but common in the mixed mesophytic forest of the eastern United States, to which the Tunica Hills are connected by the narrow belt of Bluffland forest in western Mississippi (Delcourt and Delcourt 1975). The only known locality of the southern zigzag salamander (*Plethodon websteri*) in Louisiana is in the Tunica Hills.

Origin of the Herpetofauna

Louisiana is, herpetologically speaking, truly a crossroads. Less than half of the state's taxa are widely distributed throughout the south-central United States. Most of the taxa are extraneous; that is, they reach one periphery of their range in Louisiana and presumably originated elsewhere. The extraneous elements of our herpetofauna appear to be of either eastern (including northeastern) or western (including northwestern) origin (Tables 1, 2). Extraneous reptiles generally have equal eastern and western representation, but as might be expected, eastern extraneous forms predominate among the more moisture-dependent amphibians, especially the salamanders. Most of the extraneous turtles are eastern, whereas a majority of the extraneous lizards and snakes are of western ori-

Table 1.   LOUISIANA HERPETOFAUNA AND PROBABLE SOURCES OF ORIGIN

INTRANEOUS TAXA[1]	EASTERN EXTRANEOUS[2]	WESTERN EXTRANEOUS[3]
Salamanders		
Ambystoma maculatum	*Ambystoma tigrinum* ($\frac{1}{2}$)	*Ambystoma tigrinum* ($\frac{1}{2}$)
Ambystoma opacum	*Amphiuma means*	*Necturus maculosus*
Ambystoma talpoideum	*Desmognathus fuscus*	*Plethodon serratus*
Ambystoma texanum	*Eurycea cirrigera*	
Amphiuma tridactylum	*Eurycea longicauda*	
Desmognathus auriculatus	*Hemidactylium scutatum*	
Eurycea quadridigitata	*Plethodon glutinosus*	
Necturus beyeri	*Plethodon websteri*	
Notophthalmus viridescens	*Pseudotriton montanus*	
Siren intermedia	*Pseudotriton ruber*	

NOTE: If more than one subspecies of a species occurs in the state, each subspecies is treated as a separate taxon. If different populations of the same taxon appear to have entered the state from different directions, each source is credited with one-half of that taxon.

[1]These taxa are widely distributed through the south-central United States, or their ranges are such that they cannot be assigned an origin outside Louisiana. Names of the categories follow Mohlenbrock (1959) and Rossman (1960).

[2]These taxa probably entered the state from the northeast, or their main distribution lies directly to the east.

[3]These taxa probably entered Louisiana from the northwest, or their main distribution lies directly to the west.

Table 1.   (Continued)

INTRANEOUS TAXA	EASTERN EXTRANEOUS	WESTERN EXTRANEOUS
Frogs and Toads		
Acris crepitans	Acris gryllus	Bufo americanus (½)
Bufo woodhousei	Bufo americanus (½)	Bufo valliceps
Gastrophryne carolinensis	Bufo quercicus	Pseudacris streckeri
Hyla chrysoscelis-versicolor	Bufo terrestris	Rana a. areolata
Hyla cinerea	Hyla avivoca	Scaphiopus holbrookii hurterii
Hyla crucifer	Hyla femoralis	
Hyla squirella	Hyla gratiosa	
Pseudacris triseriata	Pseudacris ornata	
Rana catesbeiana	Rana areolata sevosa	
Rana clamitans	Scaphiopus h. holbrookii	
Rana grylio		
Rana palustris		
Rana sphenocephala		
Turtles		
Apalone m. mutica	Apalone mutica calvata	Apalone spinifera hartwegi
Chelydra serpentina	Apalone spinifera aspera	Apalone spinifera pallida
Chrysemys picta	Deirochelys r. reticularia	Deirochelys reticularia miaria
Graptemys kohnii	Gopherus polyphemus	Graptemys pseudogeographica
Graptemys	Graptemys oculifera	ouachitensis
pseudogeographica	Graptemys pulchra	Terrapene ornata
sabinensis	Sternotherus minor	
Kinosternon subrubrum	Terrapene carolina major	
Macroclemys temminckii		
Pseudemys concinna		
hieroglyphica		
Pseudemys concinna		
mobilensis		
Pseudemys floridana		
Sternotherus carinatus		
Sternotherus odoratus		
Terrapene carolina triunguis		
Trachemys scripta		
Lizards		
Anolis carolinensis	Eumeces inexpectatus	Crotaphytus collaris
Cnemidophorus sexlineatus	Ophisaurus attenuatus	Eumeces septentrionalis
Eumeces fasciatus	longicaudus[4]	Eumeces anthracinus pluvialis
Eumeces laticeps	Ophisaurus ventralis	Ophisaurus a. attenuatus
Sceloporus undulatus	Sceloporus u. undulatus	Phrynosoma cornutum
hyacinthinus		
Scincella lateralis		
Snakes		
Agkistrodon contortrix	Carphophis amoenus helenae	Coluber constrictor flaviventris
Agkistrodon piscivorus	Coluber constrictor priapus	Coluber constrictor etheridgei
Cemophora coccinea	Crotalus adamanteus	Carphophis amoenus vermis
Coluber constrictor anthicus	Elaphe g. guttata	Elaphe guttata emoryi
Coluber constrictor	Farancia erytrogramma	Elaphe obsoleta lindheimeri
latrunculus	Lampropeltis calligaster	Elaphe o. obsoleta
Crotalus horridus	rhombomaculata	Lampropeltis c. calligaster

---

[4]If, indeed, this subspecies occurs in Louisiana.

Table 1.   (Continued)

INTRANEOUS TAXA	EASTERN EXTRANEOUS	WESTERN EXTRANEOUS
Snakes (continued)		
Diadophis punctatus	*Lampropelis triangulum*	*Lampropeltis triangulum*
Farancia abacura	*elapsoides*	*amaura*
Heterodon platyrhinos	*Micrurus f. fulvius*	*Micrurus fulvius tenere*
Lampropeltis getulus	*Nerodia sipedon*	*Nerodia erythrogaster*
Masticophis flagellum	*Pituophis melanoleucus lodingi*	*transversa*
Nerodia clarkii	*Rhadinaea flavilata*	*Pituophis melanoleucus*
Nerodia cyclopion	*Storeria dekayi wrightorum*	*ruthveni*
Nerodia erythrogaster	*Tantilla coronata*	*Regina grahamii*
flavigaster	*Thamnophis sauritus*	*Storeria dekayi texana*
Nerodia fasciata		*Tantilla gracilis*
Nerodia rhombifera		*Thamnophis proximus orarius*
Opheodrys aestivus		*Thamnophis p. proximus*
Regina rigida		
Sistrurus miliarius		
Storeria dekayi limnetes		
Storeria occipitomaculata		
Thamnophis sirtalis		
Virginia striatula		
Virginia valeriae		

gin. This result is not surprising inasmuch as snakes and lizards as a group tend to be less moisture dependent than most turtles.

The eastern extraneous taxa are largely confined to the Florida Parishes. The distributions of many reach the eastern border of the Mississippi floodplain, but others have not penetrated as far into the state. Whether these have been blocked by areas of unfavorable habitat or have had insufficient time to

Table 2.   ANALYSIS OF THE PROBABLE SOURCE AREAS FOR THE LOUISIANA HERPETOFAUNA.

Taxonomic Group	Total Taxa	Intraneous Taxa[1]	Extraneous Taxa[2]	Eastern Extraneous[3]	Western Extraneous[4]
Amphibians	49	23(46.9%)	26(53.1%)	19(73.1%)	7(26.9%)
Salamanders	22	10(45.5%)	12(54.5%)	9½(79.2%)	2½(20.8%)
Frogs and Toads	27	13(48.1%)	14(51.9%)	9½(67.9%)	4½(32.1%)
Reptiles	96	44(45.8%)	52(54.2%)	26(50.0%)	26(50.0%)
Turtles	27	14(51.9%)	13(48.1%)	8(61.5%)	5(38.5%)
Lizards	15	6(40.0%)	9(60.0%)	4(44.4%)	5(55.6%)
Snakes	53	23(43.4%)	30(56.6%)	14(46.7%)	16(53.3%)
Alligator	1	1(100.0%)	0(0.0%)	0(0.0%)	0(0.0%)

NOTE: If more than one subspecies of a species occurs in the state, each subspecies is treated as a separate taxon. If different populations of the same taxon appear to have entered the state from different directions, each source is credited with one-half of that taxon.

[1]These taxa are widely distributed through the south-central United States, or their ranges are such that they cannot be assigned an origin outside Louisiana. Names of the categories follow Mohlenbrock (1959) and Rossman (1960).

[2]Louisiana is peripheral to the main distributions of these taxa, which almost surely originated elsewhere.

[3]These taxa appear to have entered the state from the northeast, or their main distribution lies directly to the east.

[4]These taxa appear to have entered Louisiana from the northwest, or their main distribution lies directly to the west.

disperse farther cannot readily be determined in most cases. River basins, such as those of the Pearl, Bogue Chitto, Tangipahoa, Tickfaw, and Amite, may act as barriers to some taxa, but seem to have served as pathways of north-south dispersal for a number of aquatic and semiaquatic species. On the other hand, two species, *Plethodon websteri* and *Bufo americanus*, appear to have entered the Florida Parishes from the north by way of the loess-covered Blufflands.

The western extraneous forms, with a few exceptions, seem to fall into two broad categories: those taxa primarily inhabiting hill country and those mostly confined to lowland habitats. Some of the widespread taxa are dichotomized in the same way, but most occur in both upland and lowland situations.

Viosca (1944) suggested that the alluvial soil of the Mississippi basin was the chief barrier in Louisiana to east-west distribution of various amphibian and reptile species, but that the Mississippi River itself "is an excellent agency for dispersal." We acknowledge the Mississippi alluvium as one factor, but feel that he underestimated the ability of the Mississippi River and its major tributaries to act as barriers. Major, though infrequent, periodic flooding of the basin appears to us to be the primary factor rendering the area practically uninhabitable for snakes (such as *Virginia*) that do not climb well and lizards (such as *Sceloporus*) that deposit their eggs in the soil or in rotten logs and apparently do not rapidly reinvade flood-scoured forest.

COLLECTING AND PRESERVATION TECHNIQUES

Collecting

Various methods are employed to collect living amphibians and reptiles. Special techniques are sometimes needed, but all the methods are based on the basic habits, dictated by physiological needs, of the animals sought. Any natural setting offers a variety of habitat conditions, and a given species often utilizes only a particular habitat or perhaps is active only at a particular season or under limited weather conditions. Informed collectors consider these habitats and needs and are selective in how and where they attempt to find and capture specimens.

Collectors should practice conservation by collecting no more than what is needed and whenever possible returning cover objects to their original positions so that established hiding places remain useful to the animals.

Collecting tools. A device for lifting ground cover objects is essential for most terrestrial hunts. Some of the more useful devices are potato rakes or hoes, which have an L-shaped end that can be inserted under objects in place of hands. A very durable and versatile device can be made from a high-quality hoe that has the blade and shank made as one piece. The blades can be clipped off to leave an L-shaped end composed of the shank and the strong, tapered spine of the center of the blade section. This device will suffice to lift the heaviest logs or stones one can manage; it can also be used to strip bark off logs, tear logs apart, dig, rake, aid in climbing, lift poisonous snakes, or pin down squirming snakes.

For capture of smaller poisonous snakes (up to three feet long), a pair of gauze forceps, which are about a foot long, can be used after the animal is held down. For larger poisonous snakes, a pole with a noose made from a wide leather strap can be used. Commercially produced tongs about three feet long are available for snake handling. In any case, when handling a snake with a tong or noose, try to grasp it at midbody; holding it just behind the head and allowing it to thrash around may result in damage to the animal's spinal column, and it may die several days after capture.

For wary creatures such as lizards, a slender rod, like a car radio antenna, equipped with a short slipknot noose hung from one end allows the collector to approach close enough to noose the animal without "spooking" it. For the fast-running racerunner lizards (*Cnemidophorus*) or arboreal forms, one may have to resort to a .22-caliber pistol that fires dust shot. The rifling in the pistol barrel must be bored out to allow the gun to fire a shotgun-type pattern. Animals can be hit from distances of up to 40 feet; they will probably be killed, but will be intact enough to use as study specimens.

A safer way of securing lizards, often without killing them, is to use linked, heavy-duty rubber bands that can be stretched by hand and fired at the animals. Blowguns constructed of hollow aluminum tubing to fire corks pierced by needles can be very effective. The rubber-band system can be enhanced by

11

making a wooden gun, such as children use as a toy, for firing the band. The gun can be shaped like a foot-long pistol with a clothespin tacked on and reinforced by a strong rubber band attached to the rear of the handle. The band, secured in the clothespin and stretched to the tip of the "barrel," can be fired accurately for distances up to 15–20 feet and will stun many lizards.

Turtle capture may require the use of baited hoop nets or funnel traps, or barrels with ramps leading up to the barrel so that the animals can climb up to bask and then, when frightened, dive off into the barrel, where they can be retrieved.

Dip nets and seines may be needed to collect aquatic amphibians and sometimes turtles.

A flashlight or a lantern with a reflector on one side is necessary for locating reptiles and amphibians at night.

Collecting containers. Muslin cloth bags having enough depth to allow safe knotting of the bag are best. Do not use burlap—its mesh can be forced apart. In any event, always check bags to be sure that no holes have developed from contact with thorny plants or barbed-wire fences. The open end of a bag can be tucked under a belt for practical and rapid field use. This is satisfactory for harmless "herps," but never carry a poisonous snake that way—tie the bag and carry it away from your body.

Plastic bags with ties are adequate for amphibians, but not for animals that have claws.

Otherwise, as circumstances dictate, jars, buckets, minnow pails, etc., can be very useful. A strong box is needed for turtles because their claws will tear bags, but the box must have air holes. If you punch holes in a metal lid, be sure to punch outward and then flatten the jagged edges of the holes to prevent injury to yourself.

For transport of specimens in cold weather or in a car whose interior may heat up, a good insulated cooler, perhaps with a jar of ice inside for hot conditions, may be needed to protect specimens from extreme temperatures.

Safety measures. Avoid handling poisonous snakes by hand. If you use tongs be sure that you grasp the animal at a point where it cannot reach around to your hand. If you use a hook, coax the animal into a bag held open with another hook, or better yet, tie the bag open at several points onto a bush and lift the snake into the bag. Before tying the bag closed, be sure that the snake is in the bottom of the bag, then twirl the neck of the bag a couple of turns, and tie the bag above the base of the twirled section.

Do not use a forked stick to hold a snake so that you can then grasp the snake behind the head—the width of the fork may allow the snake to twist its head far enough back to bite your hand.

Never handle a dead poisonous snake carelessly; on more than one occasion, a person has been bitten and poisoned by a dead snake undergoing a reflexive contraction.

In the field never put your hand or foot under anything if you cannot see under it. When you come to a large log or stone, step on top of it, then jump clear of it; a poisonous snake might be coiled beneath the overhang of the object.

When crossing fences, especially if carrying poisonous snakes in bags, place the bags safely on the ground beyond the fence; do not climb with bags in hand.

Do not rub your eyes after handling amphibians; some of their skin secretions may prove very irritating.

Always look first. Never grab at something on the ground before you have made a quick inspection to be sure that no poisonous snake, stinging or biting arthropod, or other hazard is present.

Rationale and technique for collecting amphibians. Amphibians are often far more abundant and represented by more species in a given area than any casual observer might realize; only some of the frogs (*Rana, Acris*) associated with permanent water bodies and the conventional toads (*Bufo*) are likely to be seen. Several species of treefrogs (*Hyla*) are occasionally found clinging to windows. Tadpoles, of course, may be conspicuous in open, clear water. But generally, amphibians, because of their naked skins, are prone to desiccate if exposed to dry air or heat and thus are secretive beasts whose behavior is largely governed by the need to conserve body water. Many amphibians are negatively phototatic; that is, they avoid light, hiding in dark places under objects, in crevices, under leaf litter, in tunnels, and in other places that are protected from extremes of temperature and that tend to stay moist and humid. By day they hide, but at night, when temperatures are lower and the humidity increases, they emerge and move in the open.

Many species, however, remain hidden most of the year in underground retreats or have such low population densities that they are rarely encountered. Some species are rarely discovered, even by expert collectors, except when they come out to breed, which may occur for only a week each year, even perhaps in alternate years. In any case, the collector must find these species at the pools or streams where their eggs are laid. The collector can locate frogs and toads relatively easily by following the voices of singing males. To find salamanders that lay eggs in water, the collector must either happen onto suitable pools or must locate such sites by discovering the eggs or larvae, often well after the adults have completed their courtship and egg laying and left the pool. The same principle may apply to frogs and toads—sampling the larvae can suggest where to find the adults when the breeding season again occurs.

Amphibians usually have body temperatures lower than the ambient temperatures of their surroundings because the evaporation of moisture from the skin reduces their body temperatures. Lower temperatures produce less evaporation, which is another reason amphibians are most active at night or are at the surface only in cooler weather.

To find amphibians the collector should

1. Turn over ground cover such as stones, logs, boards, sheet metal, tar paper, fallen palm fronds, etc.
2. Strip bark from fallen logs, stumps, and standing dead trees. After being superficially examined or turned over, adequately decayed logs can be torn apart to reveal animals sheltering in insect tunnels. The same applies to stumps. If the ground beneath the log is loose and tunneled, dig into it.
3. Rake ground litter, such as leaf piles.
4. At night, when the ground is damp, look along road cuts. Salamanders often emerge from burrows and are exposed on the barren soil of the cuts.
5. Rainy periods are especially productive; cruise slowly along roads by auto and watch for amphibians hopping or crawling on the wet road. Be alert—some salamanders, such as the dwarf salamander (*Eurycea quadridigitata*), look like a pale-colored straw on the road. Always be cautious; do not impede traffic flow, and don't stop on the road if a safer pullover is available. A marker such as a cloth containing a weight can be dropped where the animal is seen so that the point of sighting can be quickly relocated after a safe stop is achieved.
6. Listen for frog voices, especially after rains, and proceed to the site where the frogs are singing. Once the sound is localized, a flashlight can be shined into the anuran's eyes; this usually keeps it immobilized until the collector can cautiously approach near enough to grab the animal. Sounds may be deceptive; some frogs are capable ventriloquists and others conceal themselves in holes or under vegetation when singing. Some frog choruses cease when a car passes, others seem to become louder. If the sound

13

ceases, wait patiently until it again commences. With practice, many songs can be imitated, and the collector's imitations may stimulate the frogs to start singing again.

7. To capture larval amphibians, the collector should run a seine or dip net toward the shoreline to reduce the possibility of the animals escaping from beneath or above the net. The best places to dip are in leaf masses or amid vegetation growing in the water.

8. Large salamanders such as *Amphiuma* are very slippery to handle and can inflict painful bites. Wear canvas gloves to collect them. Locate the animals in clear water at night, approach carefully, grab the animal, throw it onto land, and then place it in a wet bag. Sirens and mudpuppies (*Necturus*) are rather difficult to secure because they are usually concealed in holes or leaf mats or, in the case of *Siren*, in the mud. *Necturus*, especially, can be caught by bankline fishing with liver as bait. The lines must be run regularly at night.

9. Look under streetlights or yard lights at night during the warmer seasons to find toads (*Bufo, Scaphiopus*) out feeding, or locate them by slowly cruising roads at night.

In most cases, you can capture the animal by placing your hand over it. Captured animals can be carried in cloth or plastic bags containing moist soil or leaves. Do not confine frogs with toads (*Bufo*); the skin secretions of the toads may kill the frogs. Also, keep large animals separate from smaller ones to prevent the larger ones from crushing or eating the smaller. If plastic bags or other impermeable containers are used, do not confine animals for more than a day or so without changing the water within; urine secreted by the animals tends to break down and produce ammonia and other toxic gases. In all cases, try to keep the animals cool.

Rationale and techniques for collecting reptiles. Reptiles generally are not as moisture sensitive as amphibians and thus can occupy a wider range of habitats. Reptiles also prefer warmer settings and usually frequent spots where more sunlight can penetrate. Many reptiles are diurnally active and may be found basking or wandering freely in the open; others are nocturnal and hide by day under objects or sleep in sheltered places. Small snakes do tend to be moisture sensitive and are thus secretive, usually hiding under objects or appearing on the surface only in mild, moist weather. Except for aquatic turtles, water snakes, and the smallest snakes, there is little aggregation by reptiles in Louisiana. In cooler climates, denning sites may harbor numerous individuals during the winter months.

Aside from merely wandering about and carefully looking, the best ways to find reptiles are to

1. Lift ground cover objects just as you would when looking for amphibians. Strip bark from logs and stumps, tear rotted logs apart, dig in loose soil beneath logs if tunnels are present. Cover objects lying along the edges of water bodies are excellent places to find water snakes and mud snakes.

2. Search ridges in swampy ground; reptiles like better-drained ground.

3. Water snakes bask on trees and banks along water. Often they must be noosed before they escape. At night they can be approached by boat and grabbed from the branches.

4. Road cruising is especially effective on warm nights (above 75°F or 24°C), particularly from mid-May to July, for finding snakes on the prowl. Some species are most active at dawn and dusk. The best roads are those where the roadbed and adjacent land are at the same level and not divided by deep drainage ditches.

5. Aquatic turtles usually must be trapped

(see collecting tools) because they are far too wary for a collector to approach. At night, however, some river species, such as *Graptemys*, can be caught (if the water is clear enough) by using a boat to approach logs and branches in the water and easing up to the turtles, which are usually clinging just beneath the surface, then grabbing them by hand. Snorkeling and scuba diving may also be employed by day or night to approach aquatic turtles.

6. For reptiles and amphibians, pitfall traps may be dug and drift fences (low, fine mesh or sheet metal) erected to funnel the animals to the trap.

Preservation

Killing. Specimens that are to be permanently preserved for research purposes must first be killed as humanely as possible in a way that does not contort the body before the animal is fixed in the desired position. Reptiles may be killed in a closed container with ether or chloroform, or they may be drowned, ideally in warm water (about 105°–110°F, 40°–43°C) or in weak alcohol (15–20 percent). Controlled substances such as nembutal, phenobarbitol, and chloral hydrate, which are used to induce sleep, can also be used and are especially practical for turtles, which are otherwise difficult to kill. Aqueous or alcoholic solutions are injected into the animals, preferably near the heart or into the brain. Amphibians can be killed by ether or chloroform, or by immersion in weak alcohol solution (15 percent), or by immersion in warm water (100°–105°F, 38°–40°C). Anesthetics such as MS 222 and chloretone in solution can also be used, especially on larval amphibians.

Fixing. This is a process by which the tissues of the animal are dehydrated and rendered bacteria-free. The usual fixative is formalin, a solution of formaldehyde gas in water. The concentrated stock is 37–40 percent formaldehyde gas in water, which constitutes 100 percent saturation, hence 100 percent formalin. For reptiles 10 percent formalin is desirable, but for amphibians the concentration can be as low as 5 percent. Commercial formalin usually has impurities that make it acidic; a teaspoon of borax in a gallon of 10 percent formalin will neutralize the acidity and keep the fixative from hardening specimens excessively. Formalin is very potent and irritating—avoid breathing the vapor or getting the fluid into cuts on the hands. Skinks (*Eumeces, Scincella*), which have fragile tails, may be fixed in 55 percent isopropyl, 75 percent ethyl alcohol, or 10 percent formalin. There is less risk of the tail breaking off if a skink is fixed in alcohol, but such a specimen may be rather soft.

The tails and bodies of reptiles should be injected with fixative or, especially in larger animals, spaced slits should be made along the underside of the tail and body to permit access of the fixative. In turtles the feet may require injection. If injection is used, be sure to insert the needle at several points along the body. In either case, injection or slitting, press the body to expel any trapped gasses; if properly done the body will not float. In male reptiles the tail base may be pressed, or an injection made a short distance behind the vent to evert the hemipenes.

Only the largest amphibians may require injection or slitting.

Turtle mouths and salamander mouths should be propped open with a wad of paper or some cotton to permit later study of the jaw surfaces and teeth, respectively. Although not commonly employed, the practice of leaving snake and lizard mouths slightly open is also desirable.

Once fixed, the animals should be hardened for one to three days in the fixative solution. The animals are usually arranged in a fashion that allows easy measurement and observation of external features. Snakes should be coiled within a jar, taking care that the body does not fit too firmly against the walls of the container, or may be laid flat in a set of elongate concentric loops with the head in the inner loop, making sure that the total length is no greater than that which will fit the height or length of the storage container. Lizards with long tails should have the tail looped back toward the head to reduce the length of the specimen (wrapping the animal in cheesecloth is recommended to protect the delicate tail against breakage). The legs should be stretched out, the lower front limbs turned forward at right angles, and the lower hind limbs turned back and at right angles. Turtles should have the neck, tail, and limbs stretched out and arranged in normal posture. Salamanders are arranged much like lizards, except that the tail should extend straight back. Frogs should have the front limbs stretched out, with the forearm directed forward. The thighs (femurs) should extend outward at right angles to the body, and the lower hind limbs should extend backwards, with the ankles turned inward to touch each other. If specimens are placed in a shallow tray lined with paper towels and only a shallow depth of fixative added, they will harden in the arranged shape in perhaps an hour, after which the fixative level can be raised to cover the specimens. Never crowd specimens.

After fixation the animals should be washed for an additional day or two in running water or in a series of changes of water to remove excess fixative and to negate the strong odor of the formalin. Final storage is usually in alcohol (60 percent isopropyl or 80 percent ethyl for turtles, 60 percent isopropyl or 75 percent ethyl for snakes and lizards, 40–60 percent isopropyl or 60 percent ethyl for amphibians), but tadpoles and amphibian eggs should be kept in 3–10 percent formalin. Allow 5 to 10 times the specimen volume for storage fluid.

Individual animals should be tagged with waterproof paper tags or plastic or metal tags. The tags should have a number corresponding to data listed in a catalog, or the tag can have important basic details of place and date of collection and the name of the collector printed in indelible ink. Tags on specimens are tied with good-quality linen or nylon thread. A small knot should be placed about one-half inch from the tag and the free ends then tied around the waist of lizards, salamanders, and frogs, and sewn through the body of snakes and the back leg of turtles.

THE PROBLEM OF SNAKEBITE

*B*ecause poisonous snakes are not usually aggressive, taking a few simple precautions in any area where poisonous snakes are known to occur will greatly reduce the risk of being bitten.

1. Be sure to wear leather boots and long pants that hang loosely outside the boot.
2. Watch where you place your feet as you walk, your hands when you climb up banks or hillsides or turn over objects on the ground, and your backside when you sit on the ground or on a log.
3. When you cross a log, step up on it rather than over it so you can see where you are putting your feet.
4. Don't pick up any snake whose identification is even slightly doubtful.

If you encounter a snake that you think is poisonous, you are better off avoiding it than getting close enough to kill it with a stick—do not panic, just walk around it. Remember also that poisonous snakes play a part in the balance of nature and should not be killed unless they are found close to human residences—out in the woods or the swamps, just leave them alone.

If you or your partner (hiking, hunting, or fishing should always be done in pairs) is bitten by a snake, do not panic. Panicking will only speed up the circulation and reduce your ability to act calmly and quickly. Remember that although snakebite should be taken seriously, it is rarely fatal. Next, be sure the snake is actually poisonous, lest the treatment be more dangerous than the bite. If there is any doubt, kill the snake, pick it up carefully so that it does not bite you by reflex action, and bring it along to the doctor (but be sure to put it in a stout container so you do not accidentally get snagged on a fang—being

"bitten" by a dead snake could prove embarrassing as well as painful). If the snake escapes, check the bite area; if there are two deep puncture marks, the snake probably was poisonous. If there are two parallel rows of tooth marks (somewhat resembling briar scratches), the snake almost surely was nonpoisonous, and the wound should be cleaned and treated like any other scratch.

If the snake was poisonous, immobilize and calm the patient, clean the bite area, and drive the patient to the nearest hospital or doctor as soon as possible. The decision to inject antivenin should be made by trained medical personnel. If the bite is on a limb, a tourniquet can be applied between the bite area and the heart to slow the movement of the venom. If a tourniquet is used, however, be sure it is not too tight (you should be able to slip a finger under it) and that you release it completely for 90 seconds every 10–15 minutes. The traditional "cut-and-suck" technique is advocated by some authorities (Russell 1980), but only if trained medical personnel are more than 20 minutes away and only if administered within 15 minutes after the bite. Because this technique does incur the real risk of cutting a major blood vessel, it should be used with considerable caution.

Incision and suction is apparently ineffective in the case of coral snake bite (Russell 1980). Suction—without cutting—applied directly to the fang punctures may be useful in extracting some of the venom. Do not try to suck the venom out with your mouth unless it is free of cuts or sores through which the venom could enter your bloodstream. Finally, using ice or other means to freeze the bite area is definitely *not* recommended by medical authorities; you could cause serious tissue damage by doing so.

CARE OF AMPHIBIANS AND REPTILES IN CAPTIVITY

Many species of reptiles and amphibians fare well in captivity if they receive conscientious care and proper housing. Unless you plan to give a pet proper care, however, we advise against retaining reptiles or amphibians. Our native fauna is vanishing rapidly, so removing an animal from the wild only to let it waste away through neglect is unfair.

The following instructions are rather limited because care of captive reptiles and amphibians is a vast subject, and each species may have special needs. Some valuable references for more exacting details are the following:

The Care of Reptiles and Amphibians in Captivity, by Christopher Mattison, 1983, distributed in the United States by Sterling Publishing Co., 2 Park Ave., New York, New York 10016.

Reproductive Biology and Diseases of Captive Reptiles, J. B. Murphy and J. T. Collins (eds.), 1980, published by the Society for the Study of Amphibians and Reptiles. Order from D. H. Taylor, Publications Secretary, Department of Zoology, Miami University, Oxford, Ohio 45701.

Amphibians

Several important aspects of amphibian biology must be remembered if you are to keep these animals successfully. First, they have no internal temperature controls and must not be kept too warm (ideally under 75°F, 24°C) or exposed to freezing temperatures. Amphibians also have naked skins and thus desiccate easily, so they must be provided with suitably moist conditions. If you keep them outside, you must provide some sort of shelter so that they can avoid freezing in winter—either some type of mild heat source or a situation where they can retreat to a depth that freezing temperatures do not penetrate. In nature a differential usually exists between daytime and nighttime temperatures. If the animals are kept indoors, a timer plus a small light bulb can be used to provide some semblance of a natural situation and may prolong the life of your pets.

Few amphibians will reproduce in laboratory confinement. Special techniques and conditions are needed to propagate them.

Frogs and toads. Terrestrial forms may be kept in glass aquaria with moist soil for a bottom and with some sort of container of water. Toads will do best if the substrate is sandy. The best setting includes vegetation planted in the terrarium, especially for tree frogs. The terrarium must be kept moist by occasionally sprinkling the soil, and some type of ground cover object such as a small board or stone, or an opaque "hut" with an opening for access should be provided. If you use a screened top, be sure that the soil does not dry out, and, conversely, if you use a solid cover, be sure that air can circulate adequately. Always remove carcasses of dead specimens or dead, uneaten prey before they spoil. Do not crowd the animals, and be cautious about the size of the assemblage—the larger specimens may eat the smaller ones.

Most frogs and toads will thrive on a diet of worms and various insects. If the terrarium is deep enough and the specimens cannot climb the walls, the container, with a light bulb suspended above it, can be placed outdoors in mild weather. The bulb will attract flying insects, thus providing a varied diet.

Salamanders. Terrestrial forms can be kept in the same terrarium or under similar circumstances as frogs and toads, but if salamanders are kept alone, the water bowl may be omitted unless you wish to keep it as a source for humidifying the air. Again, be cautious that large and small animals are kept separately.

Salamanders feed readily on worms, slugs, small snails, adult and larval insects, or any animal small enough to capture and swallow. Some, especially large *Ambystoma*, can be taught to take small slivers of meat or bits of hamburger moved in front of the snout.

Aquatic forms can be kept in aquaria containing clean and adequately oxygenated water. Tap water is not recommended because it may contain harmful chemicals, despite the water treatment process. If you do use tap water, be sure to aerate it thoroughly first or let it stand a few days to get rid of the chlorine content. Water in the aquarium can be kept oxygenated with a small pump that can be purchased at any pet store. Provide aquatic plants, such as elodea, water hyacinth, and water lillies, so that the animals have some sort of cover and semblance of the natural setting.

Tadpoles are essentially vegetarian. You can feed them on lightly cooked lettuce or spinach. If possible, provide them with algae. If the aquarium has enough sunlight, algae can grow on its sides, and the tadpoles can scrape these algae for food. Be sure that you clean fecal residues and decaying food from the aquarium. This can be done with siphons and filters obtained from pet shops. Remember, tadpoles as a rule are going to metamorphose into froglets in a few weeks to a few months; thus they must have something, such as a brick, projecting above the water line that they can climb onto when they transform.

Salamander larvae and the large aquatic amphiumas, sirens, and mudpuppies are carnivores; they will eat worms, insects, insect larvae, small to large crawfishes, and so forth. Larval salamanders can be cannibalistic, so be cautious about the size groups kept together. Be sure that their water is kept clean and well aerated; change it periodically if you do not have a good siphon and filter system.

Reptiles

Turtles. As poikilotherms (ectotherms), turtles must avoid extreme heat or cold, but they usually like to bask in the sun until their bodies are adequately warm, then they retreat into shade, shelter, or water. When the weather is too cool for basking, they will seek shelter under objects, in burrows, or in the mud; thus any confined turtle should have the alternative situations available.

Aquatic turtles can be kept in outdoor ponds or in aquaria that provide them with the means to climb out to bask. To remain healthy, turtles need sunlight or some other source of ultraviolet light (lamps are commercially available). Calcium is essential for their good health because it is needed to construct strong shells. If a natural diet of whole animals is provided, that should suffice, but otherwise the diet can be augmented by adding mineral and vitamin supplements or ground cuttlefish shell, which can be dusted onto the food immediately before it is offered. A block of plaster of Paris placed in the aquarium water of aquatic turtles will help keep water calcium levels high.

Use siphons and filters such as are available at pet stores for fish aquaria to keep water for aquatic turtles clean. An aquarium heater can be installed to keep temperatures at 80° ± 5°F (27° ± 3°C). Box turtles or tortoises can be kept in pens with an earthen substrate, ideally deep enough to allow some burrowing. These turtles can be kept in outdoor pens if a suitable shelter (burrow, pile of leaves or straw, etc.) or heat source is provided to protect them against freezing temperatures. Box turtles and tortoises can thrive quite well wandering around your home (they will soon learn where the refrigerator is or where dog bowls are), but unfortunately they cannot be housebroken.

Food needs of turtles vary; the species accounts in this book detail the diets of each species. Pet stores sell pelleted turtle food, but natural foods such as fish, insects, snails, and vegetation should be provided as the main diet or as a supplement.

Turtles may court, mate, and reproduce in captivity. Their nests are almost invariably made in the ground; thus a deep-enough soil substrate will encourage them to propagate.

Lizards. Most Louisiana lizards can be maintained in a terrarium with a screen lid. The bottom should be covered with dirt or gravel, and pieces of bark or dead leaves for the lizards to hide beneath should be included. A small water dish should be provided, but many lizards prefer to lap droplets of water from cage vegetation, which should be sprinkled daily. Most live insects or spiders small enough for a lizard to swallow are a good food source, but if you include mealworms in the diet, be sure to first remove their heads because hastily swallowed mealworms can chew through a lizard's gut wall. Lizards should be fed daily. To ensure proper digestion, cage temperatures for both lizards and snakes should be maintained at 75°–85°F. This may be accomplished by attaching a reflector lamp to the cage lid and adjusting its position until the desired temperature is attained inside the cage.

Snakes. All but the smaller species of snakes (which may do better in terraria) can be best cared for in an aquarium with a firmly attached screen lid or in a glass-fronted wooden cage with a hinged screen lid. In either case the floor should be covered with paper for absorption of moisture and ease of cleaning, although including a small cardboard box with a hole cut in it for the snake to retreat into is usually advisable. The water dish should be large enough that the snake can coil in it to soak prior to shedding its skin, but the dish should also be heavy enough that the snake cannot tip it over. A rock, tree limb, or some other rough surface should be present to assist the shedding process. Snakes need to be fed only once every week or two, but the paper in the cage should be changed and the water dish cleaned whenever they become dirty so that conditions remain as sanitary as possible. Species that are usually fairly easy to maintain in captivity include the fish-and-frog-eating water snakes and garter snakes, the toad-eating hognosed snake, the rodent-eating rat snakes, and the rodent-and-reptile-eating kingsnakes. Most other species are too nervous, too secretive, or have too specialized a diet to make good pets. *Poisonous snakes should not be kept as pets*—the potential danger to you, your family, or your friends is simply not worth the risk.

Although keeping snakes as pets is an interesting hobby, doing a proper job of it requires time, so don't try to keep more animals than you have time to care for. Snakes maintained in overcrowded conditions are especially susceptible to disease. Should one of your snakes become sick or develop a skin infection, the most humane thing to do is to release it where you found it—the chances for self-healing are much greater in the wild than in captivity.

CONSERVATION

Through the years Louisiana's reputation for environmental protection has not been particularly good. The state has been a major commercial source of turtles, alligators, water snakes, anole lizards, amphiuma salamanders, and many other species of amphibians and reptiles. Overharvesting of any organism results in sharply decreased numbers, sometimes to the extent that too few individuals are left for replacement reproduction or to save the species from extirpation. Add to overexploitation the tremendous impacts of deforestation; monoculture forestry and agricultural practices; forest fires and deliberate burning of underbrush; general habitat alterations such as canals, urbanization, clearing for agriculture, and waste dump sites; air and water pollution; slaughter due to ignorance; and so forth, and we see that the herpetofauna must surely be greatly depleted. The histories of the bullfrog, dusky gopher frog, red-eared slider, alligator, alligator snapping turtle, and gopher tortoise are prime herpetological examples of the net result of humans' adverse effects on the environment.

We have seen federal and state laws to protect the alligator save it from extinction; state laws protect the Ouachita red-backed salamander and the tiger salamander, and federal law protects sea turtles. We have now asked that the state protect the gopher tortoise, whose western populations (including those in Louisiana) were placed on the threatened species list by the U.S. Fish and Wildlife Service in 1987. These measures will succeed only if supported by an educated public and enforced.

Why should such protective measures be applied to noncommercial species? Each living thing plays a role in maintaining the Earth's natural balance. Humans should be encouraged to study and enjoy nature's diversity, the evolutionary process, and the fascinating dimensions these add to our cultural history. If our herpetofauna, indeed our entire fauna, is to survive and flourish, we must implement basic conservation measures and set aside appreciable amounts of natural habitat. Such an approach exists for game animals; it should extend to all of Louisiana's native animals and plants.

Under "Collecting and Preservation Techniques" we recommend taking no more specimens than one actually needs. Both biology teachers and amateur and professional herpetologists need to remember that Louisiana is a relatively well-collected state, and assembling large general collections can no longer be justified. We should satisfy ourselves primarily with observing the animals and studying their biology, and not indiscriminately collect and preserve specimens.

SPECIES AND SUBSPECIES

*T*raditionally, a group of organisms capable of interbreeding among themselves but reproductively isolated from other such groups has been called a *species*. In recent years biologists have observed that some closely related species occupying very different habitats may interbreed occasionally where they come together in the contact zone between the two habitats, thus producing interspecific *hybrids*. Individuals having intermediate features occur only in the contact zone, and the adjacent parent populations exhibit only the features characteristic of those species in all other parts of their respective ranges.

Most, if not all, wide-ranging species exhibit some form of geographic variation. Color, pattern, body proportions, and meristic features (i.e., things that can be counted) each seem to be sensitive to changes in environmental characteristics such as temperature, humidity, soil type, vegetation cover, etc. When the population of a species inhabiting a particular geographic area is distinct from all other populations in one or more of the features mentioned above, it often is described as a *subspecies* and given an addition to its scientific name (e.g., the corn snake, *Elaphe guttata*, has two subspecies: *E. guttata guttata*, which occurs chiefly east of the Mississippi alluvial plain; and *E. guttata emoryi*, which occurs west of it). Adjacent subspecies interbreed freely; there is often a broad zone of intergradation between them, and the distinguishing characteristics of one subspecies frequently appear in some individuals well within the range of another subspecies.

That subspecies designations are not entirely exclusive reflects, in part, the opinion of some taxonomists that a geographically delimited population can be described as a new subspecies if 75 percent of the specimens from that population are distinguishable from members of the other population. Therefore, as many as 25 percent may not be distinguishable. For this reason, we have described subspecies boundaries and zones of intergradation in the text in fairly general terms, but have not drawn them on the species maps. Subspecies names can be applied only to populations—not to individuals—and too few specimens are available from most localities near the "edge" of the range of a subspecies to characterize the local populations with any degree of confidence.

COMMON AND SCIENTIFIC NAMES

Many species of living things are well known to laymen and have widely used common names (e.g., bullfrog) indigenous to most of the range. In other instances, the same species may have different names in different localities (e.g., black snake, black rat snake, pilot snake, pilot black snake, and chicken snake for *Elaphe obsoleta*) or several species or races that appear similar to the layperson may be called by the same common name. Scientists around the world apply a single scientific name to any given species or race; this practice leaves little doubt about the organism being discussed. Relying on common names, however, may impede communication—bullfrog in South Africa, for example, is not the same species as bullfrog in the United States. Louisianians use many local names that are alien to people from elsewhere in the country, such as "green trout" for the black bass or "sac-a-lait" for the crappie fish. The Society for the Study of Amphibians and Reptiles has issued a list of recommended common names for amphibians and reptiles that it hopes will gradually gain acceptance as standardized names for the lay public to use. The list has been revised twice and will undergo periodic updating (we do not necessarily agree with all current suggested common names). We list the recommended common name* just below the scientific name in each account, but for the convenience of the reader, we also include other common names used in Louisiana.

*We have, however, consistently emended the SSAR recommended names to reflect our contention that a hyphenated compound adjective with an *-ed* ending is preferable to a nonhyphenated compound noun used as an adjective (e.g., Black-headed Snake vs. Blackhead Snake for *Tantilla coronata*). Such compound nouns are perfectly acceptable when they stand by themselves and are not used as modifiers (e.g., Spade-footed Toads or Spadefoots). Our recommended emendation is also used to a large extent in a recent publication (1987), *Checklist of Vertebrates of the United States, the U.S. Territories, and Canada*, edited by R. C. Banks, R. W. McDiarmid, and A. L. Gardner, U.S. Fish and Wildlife Service Resource Publication 166.

PART TWO: *Identification Keys and Species Accounts*

IDENTIFICATION OF LOUISIANA AMPHIBIANS AND REPTILES

*T*here is no perfect way to identify every specimen of amphibian or reptile that comes to hand; even the experts sometimes have difficulty. Novices should read all of these introductory remarks before using the keys or species accounts in this book.

Keys are designed to facilitate identification by eliminating the need for reading all species descriptions in detail. Keys are based on the principle that specimens can be grouped according to shared characteristics. For example, a pile of hardware objects might first be separated into two piles, one composed of metal objects, the other of nonmetallic objects. The metal objects might then be divided into two piles—one that includes only objects made of iron, the other, objects made of nonferrous metals. The iron objects could then be broken into piles of threaded and nonthreaded objects. The threaded ones, say screws, could be classed according to flat heads or rounded heads, and so on, until finally some item remains as the only one in its pile and thus can be given a name. The operational principle of a key is that it gives the reader alternative choices—it either is this or is not this.

Ideally a key should work on simple alternatives, using only a single feature for each alternative (couplet) offered. Our experience is that too few features provide a high percentage of separation, and reliance on a single feature for the alternative may mislead the user, especially in regard to amphibians. We have selected, therefore, couplets that often give two or three pertinent features in the alternatives and thereby provide the inexperienced user with a high degree of confi-

dence in the choice. Sometimes a character may be rather technical for a novice, but we have tried to supplement such features with more readily determinable characters and have provided a glossary (pp. 273–77) of technical terms.

Keys are tools used to determine the *probable* identity of a specimen at hand. Once a probable identity is established, the user should turn to the species account and determine whether the specimen matches the recognition features described. If the specimen does not match the description, an error probably was made in the choice of alternatives, in which case the reader should try the key again, carefully reconsidering each alternative.

Keys are rarely based on true evolutionary relationships of animals, but ordinarily refer to conspicuous, easily seen features. A good key will enable the user to identify probably 95 percent of the animals encountered; the other 5 percent will reflect odd or miscellaneous variations that occasionally appear. For example, almost any species may produce an albino or a completely black individual, yet these are so rare that they cannot be satisfactorily incorporated into a key. Even the recognition description given in the species account cannot accommodate all variations; such data usually are found only in detailed technical works.

Our keys have been designed to assist both novice and advanced students in dealing with the Louisiana herpetofauna. With increasing experience the observer will become sufficiently familiar with the animals' "personalities" to be able to make accurate identifi-

27

cation of all but the most extreme and unusual variants.

In the species accounts, the abbreviations "TU" and "LSUMZ" refer to the her-petological collections of Tulane University and the Louisiana State University Museum of Natural Science, respectively.

KEY TO THE MAJOR GROUPS OF LOUISIANA AMPHIBIANS AND REPTILES

1. Skin naked, usually damp, or if dry-feeling then without scales or tail; bushy gills present or absent, but if not evident then tail compressed, often with vertical fins; no claws on toes   2

   Skin dry and scaly, or if somewhat damp-appearing then limbs scaled and toes clawed; tail always present, rounded in cross-section and without fins (except alligator); claws always present on toes   Class Reptilia, 3

2. Tailless, or if tailed then aquatic, with or without visible legs and with a globular body; gills visible only in newly hatched larvae

       Order Anura—frogs and toads (p. 66).

   Tailed; body elongate; two forelimbs or four legs present; bushy gills present or absent

       Order Caudata—salamanders (p. 31).

3. Legs present; body and tail elongated; tail compressed; head and snout rough and strongly pitted

       Order Crocodylia—alligator (p. 270).

   Legs present or absent; tail circular in cross section; body covered by hard or leathery shell or not shelled   4

4. Body covered with hard or leathery shell

       Order Testudines—turtles (p. 167).

   Body not covered with shell

       Order Squamata—snakes and lizards, 5

5. With or without limbs; external ear openings present; usually with movable eyelids

       Suborder Lacertilia—lizards (p. 209).

   No limbs; no external ear openings; no moveable eyelids

       Suborder Serpentes—snakes (p. 224).

Class Amphibia
Frogs, Toads, Salamanders, and Caecilians

The amphibians, a cosmopolitan group of animals, were the first vertebrates to successfully colonize the land. Their early ancestry indicates that they were derived from fishes about 400 million years ago. Their naked skins and need to return to wet places to reproduce kept them in moist habitats near water. In their early history the amphibians were favored by the presence of extensive swamplands and a mild, wet climate, and they expanded into diverse groups, one of which gave rise to the Class Reptilia. The modern amphibians share an obscure ancestry, but in any case they are dead-end groups

that represent perhaps 3,900 species. Amphibians are ectotherms; their body temperatures are variable, usually near that of their surroundings, but often somewhat cooler because of evaporative cooling due to the moist skin.

A key feature of the amphibians is that their life histories usually have two phases, a larval phase—usually aquatic—and an adult phase. Body form is usually substantially different in the two phases. After a brief to sometimes prolonged larval period, there is a rather rapid transformation, or metamorphosis, into the adult form.

ORDER CAUDATA: *Salamanders and Newts*

The approximately 350 species of salamanders, comprising 8 to 10 families, occur in a wide area of temperate North America, Europe, and Asia, but penetrate into far northern South America (primarily in the cooler mountain regions) and the Mediterranean region of Africa.

In contrast to anurans (frogs and toads), these amphibians have long tails throughout their adult and larval lives, and their bodies are elongate. The group is diverse: some have only two limbs; some are aquatic and may or may not retain external gills and fins; and some newts have rough, dry skin. Some species are secretive, subterranean dwellers except during breeding season, but most live in moist, forested regions and hide by day in holes, under litter, or under stones and logs. Some tropical species are arboreal. The larvae superficially resemble adults, but have external gills, fins on the tail, lidless eyes, and differences in the skin and in skull morphology. Because of the resemblance between larvae and adults, metamorphosis is less dramatic than in anurans. Both adults and larvae are carnivores.

Many salamanders lay gelatinous eggs in water, but most deposit the eggs in moist places on land. Several European species retain eggs within their bodies until they are ready to hatch. When eggs are laid on land or retained within the body, the larvae may have very large, bushy gills.

Primitive caudates have external fertilization comparable to that of anurans, but the vast majority of salamanders have a remarkable method of sperm transfer and fertilization. Males court the females, usually with elaborate nudgings and posturing, and eventually deposit small, stalklike structures, the spermatophores, which are produced from glands at the base of the tail. The top part of the spermatophore is a gelatinous cap containing the spermatozoa. The female picks up the spermatophore or the sperm cap with her cloacal lips, and the spermatozoa are then stored for a few days or even months in a special chamber, the spermatheca, in the roof of her cloaca. When the eggs are laid, they pass through the spermatheca and the spermatozoa are released to fertilize the eggs.

Some salamanders transform at nearly adult size, but most must grow considerably before attaining adult length.

KEY TO THE SALAMANDERS OF LOUISIANA
(includes larvae and adults)

1. No external gills   2
   External gills present   19
2. Body elongate, eel-like; limbs tiny, each with 3 or fewer toes   3
   Body not eel-like and with head distinct from neck; limbs not reduced and each with 4 or more toes   4
3. Limbs usually with 3 toes; venter markedly lighter than the dark dorsum; underside of chin with dark patch
   Amphiuma tridactylum (p. 44)

   Limbs usually with 2 toes; venter not markedly lighter than dorsum; no dark throat patch
   Amphiuma means (p. 42)
4. Nasolabial grooves present; costal grooves conspicuous; hind foot with 4 toes or 5 toes   5
   Nasolabial grooves absent; costal grooves conspicuous or not; hind foot with 5 toes   14
5. Hind foot with 4 toes   6

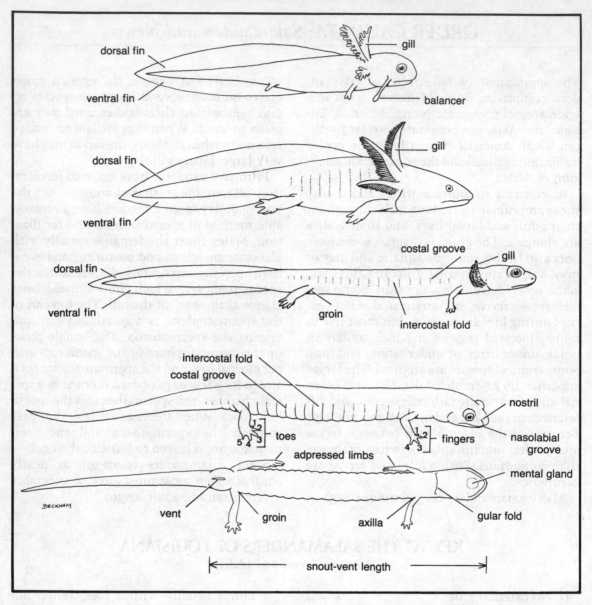

Figure 2. Structural features of salamanders: (from top to bottom) lateral views of a recently hatched pond-type larva, an older pond-type larva, and a stream-type larva; dorsolateral view of an adult plethodontid salamander and ventral view of an adult plethodontid salamander.

Hind foot with 5 toes 7

6. Belly white, marked with black spots; tail constricted near base
    Hemidactylium scutatum (p. 52)
   Belly yellow, unmarked; tail normal
    Eurycea quadridigitata (p. 51)

7. A light stripe from eye to angle of jaw;

tail keeled; tongue attached in front
    Desmognathus spp. (p. 45)
No light stripe from eye to angle of jaw; tail keeled, compressed, or rounded and tapering; tongue mushroom shaped, with central pedicel and free on all sides, or attached in front 8

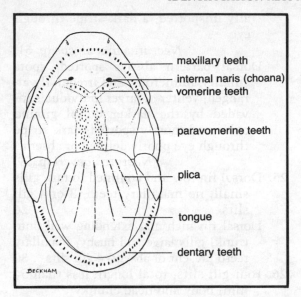

maxillary teeth

internal naris (choana)

vomerine teeth

paravomerine teeth

plica

tongue

dentary teeth

BECKHAM

Figure 3. Interior of a salamander mouth.

8. Tail rounded and tapering; tongue attached in front   9

   Tail keeled or compressed; tongue with central pedicel   11

9. Dorsal color black, with or without white or golden flecks and/or frosting; venter plain dark gray or black; costal grooves 16; adults exceed 60 mm snout-vent

        Plethodon glutinosus (p. 53)

   Dorsum usually with red, orange, or yellow stripe, or if stripe lacking, the dorsum dark gray and the venter mottled gray; costal grooves 18 or 19, rarely 17; snout-vent length less than 50 mm   10

10. Middorsal stripe, when present, with "saw-toothed" edges, the points of which correspond to the costal grooves; no reddish pigment on belly

        Plethodon serratus (p. 54)

   Middorsal stripe, when present, irregular or lobulated, but not saw-toothed nor with the lobes corresponding to the costal grooves; reddish pigment present on belly

        Plethodon websteri (p. 55)

11. Body and tail relatively stout; costal grooves 16 or more; vomerine and paravomerine teeth in a continuous series   13

   Body and tail relatively slender; costal grooves 14; vomerine and paravomerine teeth separated by a gap   12

12. Dorsum with median dark stripe; venter mottled; snout-vent length may exceed 72 mm

        Eurycea longicauda (p. 49)

   Dark median stripe absent or poorly defined; venter plain yellow; snout-vent length less than 43 mm

        Eurycea cirrigera (p. 48)

13. Iris of eye brown; dorsum with numerous black specks, each usually much smaller than the eye; venter clear, not markedly different in color from dorsum

        Pseudotriton montanus (p. 57)

   Iris of eye yellow; dorsum with fewer and larger spots, each near size of eye; venter profusely spotted and lighter colored than dorsum

        Pseudotriton ruber (p. 58)

14. Costal grooves absent or inconspicuous; skin rough or smooth

        Notophthalmus viridescens (p. 62)

   Costal grooves usually evident; skin smooth   15

15. Dorsum dark with light yellow spots or bars, or with gray or silvery bands with black interspaces   16

   Dorsum dark, unmarked or with small, lichenlike lighter markings   18

16. Color black, with crossbands of gray, white, or silvery gray, or appearing to have light-colored blotches

        Ambystoma opacum (p. 37)

   Color black or dark brown with yellow spots or bars   17

17. Dorsum with small, rounded, yellow or orange spots tending to form a row on either side

        Ambystoma maculatum (p. 35)

   Dorsum and sides with pattern of irregularly arranged yellow to olive bars, blotches, or spots

Ambystoma tigrinum (p. 41)

18. Body stocky; head large, broader than trunk; costal grooves 10 or 11

Ambystoma talpoideum (p. 38)

Body more slender; head narrower than trunk; costal grooves 14 or 15

Ambystoma texanum (p. 39)

19. No hind limbs; tail not clearly distinct from trunk; costal grooves 30 or more to vent; total length more than 35 mm

Siren intermedia (p. 63)

Hind limbs normally present except in very early stages; if hind limbs absent then total length less than 35 mm; tail distinct; costal grooves 18 or fewer to vent   20

20. Digits 3–3 or 2–2; 55 or more costal grooves (larva)   3

Digits 4–4 or 4–5; costal grooves 18 or fewer   21

21. 4 toes on hind foot*   22

5 toes on hind foot*   25

22. Dorsal fin extending onto posterior end of trunk; total length less than 80 mm   23

Dorsal fin confined to tail; total length to 220 mm or more   24

23. Total length normally less than 25 mm; caudal fin high, reaching well onto trunk; costal grooves 13 or 14

Hemidactylium scutatum (larva) (p. 52)

Total length to 77 mm; caudal fin lower and reaching only onto posterior end of trunk; costal grooves 16, occasionally 15 or 14; a dorsolateral black stripe usually present on body

Eurycea quadridigitata (larva) (p. 51)

24. Dorsal pattern of stripes, or if spotted the spots large and tending to form longitudinal dorsolateral series; venter usu-

ally unspotted; a dark stripe through eye

Necturus maculosus (p. 61)

Dorsal pattern always spotted; spots smaller, numerous, and irregularly arranged; venter of larger individuals invaded by the darker dorsal ground color and mostly spotted; dark stripe through eye poorly defined or absent

Necturus beyeri (p. 59)

25. Dorsal fin low and confined to tail; gills small; no maxillary teeth; 3 or 4 gill slits   26

Dorsal fin high and extending well onto trunk; gills large and bushy; maxillary teeth present or absent; 4 gill slits   30

26. Four gill slits; total length less than 54 mm; body and head chunky

Desmognathus (larva) (p. 45)

Three gill slits; total length may exceed 150 mm; body and head relatively elongated   27

27. Costal grooves 16 or 17   28

Costal grooves usually 14   29

28. Side with a dark or black stripe; dorsum usually with a dark midline; total length rarely exceeds 50 mm

Eurycea longicauda (larva) (p. 49)

Sides usually lighter; if dark stripe present, then a double row of light spots evident on sides; middorsal area with a light stripe, sometimes with some middorsal dark flecks arranged in a line; total length may exceed 77 mm

Eurycea cirrigera (larva) (p. 48)

29. Dorsum light brown with scattered, irregular dark flecks

Pseudotriton montanus (larva) (p. 57)

Dorsum mottled, streaked, or with large spots

Pseudotriton ruber (larva) (p. 58)

30. Side of head with dark line continuing through eye; maxillary teeth absent

Notophthalmus viridescens (larva) (p. 62)

No dark line through eye; maxillary teeth present   31

*The key is inadequate at this point to separate very young larvae that lack hind limbs, but it will ordinarily suffice for identification of most larval salamanders that exceed 15 mm in total length.

31. Costal grooves 10 or 11; dorsum with a series of large, squarish blotches (neotenous individuals may be brownish gray with small black dots); venter with median dark line

> *Ambystoma talpoideum* (larva) (p. 38)

Costal grooves 11 or more; dorsal blotches present or absent; no dark midventral line 32

32. Costal grooves 14 or 15; dorsum blotched; conspicuous lateral light line

> *Ambystoma texanum* (larva) (p. 39)

Costal grooves 11 to 13; dorsal blotches and lateral light line, if present, not distinct 33

33. Costal grooves 11, rarely 12; dorsal color uniformly dark brown or black; throat usually well pigmented

> *Ambystoma opacum* (larva) (p. 37)

Costal grooves usually 12 or 13; dorsum with small dark spots or with dorsolateral dark blotches; sometimes a dark stripe or light line along sides; ground color greenish yellow to olive 34

34. Toes cylindrical

> *Ambystoma maculatum* (larva) (p. 35)

Toes broad at base, pointed at tips

> *Ambystoma tigrinum* (larva) (p. 41)

FAMILY AMBYSTOMATIDAE
MOLE SALAMANDERS

The family Ambystomatidae occurs solely in North America from Alaska and southern Canada to central Mexico. It contains two genera and approximately 30 living species. The genus *Ambystoma* is the only one occurring in Louisiana.

Ambystoma maculatum (Shaw)
Spotted Salamander
Plate II

Recognition. A stout salamander averaging under $5\frac{1}{2}$ in. (140 mm) in total length in Louisiana, but averaging 6–7 in. (150–175 mm) and reaching 9 in. (225 mm) elsewhere; ground color bluish black, black, slate, or brownish black, with 25 to 40 rounded yellow or orange spots in two dorsolateral rows from the head to the end of the tail; belly dark grey; costal grooves 11 to 13, usually 12; toes of adpressed limbs separated by 1 to $1\frac{1}{2}$ intercostal spaces except in newly metamorphosed individuals (toes overlapping).

Similar species. The tiger salamander (*Ambystoma tigrinum*) could be mistaken for the spotted salamander, but has spots that are more irregular or elongated and that extend far down on the sides; the belly tends to be substantially lighter colored than the back. The spotted salamander has no more than one tubercle on either palm, whereas the tiger salamander has two.

Distribution. Throughout the state in pine-hardwood forests, but in the Florida Parishes, at least, not known in the pine flatwoods or in the Pearl River bottomlands (Map 1).

Taxonomic comments. No subspecies are recognized, but P. W. Smith (1961) suggested that two subspecies may eventually be recognized. Anderson (1967a) gave the most recent comprehensive account of the literature on the species.

Habitat and habits. This is a secretive species, largely subterranean, and its presence is often undetected except during the brief breeding season or when the eggs or larvae are found. Generally, the spotted salamander appears to prefer areas having soils with some clay content and a preponderance of hardwood trees.

Although common, the spotted salamander is difficult to find during most of the year

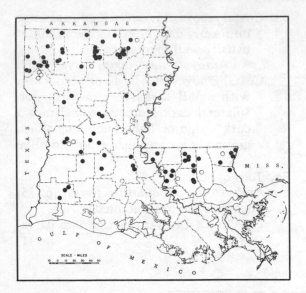

Map 1. Distribution of *Ambystoma maculatum*. Solid circles represent specimens examined; hollow circles represent museum specimens not examined or literature records.

because of its tendency to hide in rodent burrows and beneath logs and litter, or in logs. In wet stream bottomlands or in woodlands where the water table is high, however, it may be encountered in any season. The annual breeding migrations may bring large numbers of this species onto the forest floor or cause them to cross roads on the rainy nights associated with the breeding stimulus. Several hundred animals may use a single temporary water pool for breeding.

Spotted salamanders are sluggish and make little attempt to escape when discovered. Their food includes worms, arthropods, snails, and slugs. In captivity they can be trained to take worms or pieces of meat.

Reproduction. The eggs have been found as early as 1 November at Greensburg, St. Helena Parish (Viosca notes), but the main breeding period extends from late December to late February (24 February at Monroe, Ouachita Parish), the earlier activity occurring as a rule in the Florida Parishes. Unhatched eggs have been seen as late as 3 March in Bossier Parish

(Viosca notes). The breeding activities appear to be triggered by warm rains only after the first nearly freezing weather of the winter. In a given area there may be several waves of breeding activity. For example, in Livingston Parish, fresh eggs were deposited 26–27 December 1961, and in the same site newly laid eggs, apparently deposited 13 January 1962, were discovered. Eggs seen there later in January appeared to have been deposited after 13 January. In each case, a cold snap or passage of a cold front was followed by a warm rain. Breeding sites range from farm ponds, woodland depressions, stump holes, and shallow wheel ruts to roadside ditches that lack predatory fishes.

The female lays up to 300 eggs in clusters of 50 to 200 encased in a tough, clear, gelatinous material and attaches them to submerged sticks or leaves them free on the bottom.

The individual eggs and their envelopes are 5–6 mm in diameter and appear as capsules within the main jelly mass. Each jelly cluster is 37–75 mm in diameter. The eggs hatch within a few weeks, depending on temperature, and the pond-type larvae grow to a length of 40–75 mm before transforming between late March and June. Some egg masses develop a milky appearance due to invasion by fungi and fail to develop. A characteristic phenomenon in spotted salamander eggs is the development of a symbiotic alga that gives the gelatin a distinct green tinge. The oxygen produced by the algae presumably augments the growing embryo's oxygen supply, which otherwise is obtained only via slow diffusion from pond waters through the thick, insulating jelly mass.

The larvae are voracious creatures, feeding on all sorts of aquatic invertebrates, and may even be cannibalistic. The larvae are greenish yellow and have darker olive areas on the head and small dark spots on the dorsal surfaces. The spots may form an indistinct band on either side.

Newly transformed young are dark, with

scattered golden flecks on the body. The adult pattern may not develop for several weeks.

The breeding sites are shared with *Ambystoma talpoideum*, *A. opacum*, *A. texanum*, and *Notophthalmus viridescens*. Larvae and eggs must therefore be identified cautiously.

Closer monitoring of this species is needed to determine precise conditions triggering the breeding migration. Details of the postmetamorphic life history are virtually unknown.

Shoop (1967, 1968) has raised some interesting questions regarding how the spotted salamanders find the breeding sites; he has also shown that because some nongravid females go to the ponds, the migration is not merely a response to the reproductive drive.

Ambystoma opacum (Gravenhorst)
Marbled Salamander
Plate II

Recognition. A stocky salamander attaining a length of 5 in. (127 mm), but more commonly reaching 4 in. (102 mm); color bluish black with white or silvery crossbands on the back and tail giving the animal a somewhat ringed appearance; crossbands on the trunk sometimes uniting dorsolaterally to form longitudinal lines, creating an effect of black blotches on a white ground color; venter black; costal grooves 11 to 13, usually 11 or 12; toes of adpressed limbs meeting or somewhat overlapping.

Distribution. Throughout Louisiana north of the coastal marshes (Map 2).

Taxonomic comments. No subspecies are recognized, and no real attempts to study the systematics appear in the literature. Anderson (1967b) is the most recent comprehensive account of literature on the species.

Habitat and habits. The marbled salamander is a common but secretive species, most often encountered in bottomlands or in wet

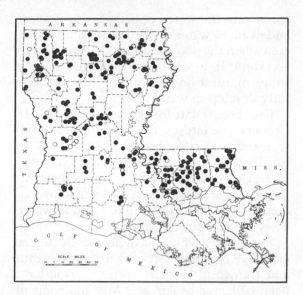

Map 2. Distribution of *Ambystoma opacum*. Solid circles represent specimens examined; hollow circles represent museum specimens not examined or literature records.

woodlands, where it is usually found under logs, boards, and debris. It tolerates surprisingly dry situations and may be found under logs at any time of the year. The species is sluggish and makes little attempt to escape when exposed.

Stomach contents in Louisiana have included large numbers of millipedes, plus centipedes, spiders, insects, and snails (Cagle notes).

Reproduction. In marked contrast to other Louisiana *Ambystoma*, this species is a fall breeder and lays its eggs on land in protected, moist depressions, usually under logs. The eggs, attended by the female, may remain for a number of weeks until rains flood the depressions, at which time the eggs hatch. If the delay until flooding is considerable, the larvae may undergo substantial development and emerge from the eggs shortly after the inundation.

Around some permanent pools (e.g., near Enon, Washington Parish) there is need to determine if the *A. opacum* might lay eggs directly into the water, or perhaps the eggs are laid near the water's edge and are simply covered when the pool expands. Thus we need to ascertain if newly deposited eggs require some maturation before they can successfully develop in water.

The earliest date for eggs in Louisiana is 25 October, the latest 4 December. Liner (1954) reported that two masses of eggs, ready to hatch, were found 18 January near Lafayette. The eggs, usually 39 to 117 in a cluster in Louisiana, are approximately 4 mm in overall diameter on land but swell to 7 mm in water. They are laid singly, but in clusters.

The larvae, which have been collected as early as 8 November, reach a length of 76 mm and transform in early spring. Larvae have been collected as late as 2 May and some of approximately 44 mm total length were collected in Evangeline Parish on 29 April, suggesting a transformation even later than 2 May. On a rainy night, 11 March 1974, large numbers of newly transformed specimens (averaging 74 mm in total length) were found crossing a road in Mississippi near the Louisiana border.

The larvae are dark brown or black, with some mottling on the lower sides. Newly transformed specimens are dark, with scattered light flecks. Adult coloration does not develop until several weeks after transformation. A specimen from Marion, Union Parish, did not have a complete adult pattern when collected on 11 June 1950.

The breeding sites of *A. opacum* are frequently utilized by other species of *Ambystoma*, as well as by other salamanders; thus several species of larvae may be found in the pools.

Ambystoma talpoideum (Holbrook)
Mole Salamander

Plate II

Recognition. A short, chunky salamander with a large head, averaging approximately 4 in. (100 mm) long, but attaining a maximum size of 4¾ in. (122 mm); dorsum dark gray, brown, or bluish black, with numerous light lichenlike markings; belly bluish gray, often with a dark midventral median stripe and longitudinally elliptical dark and light areas, especially in young and recently metamorphosed animals; costal grooves 10 (or 11 including the one above the hind limb); toes of adpressed limbs overlapping somewhat.

Distribution. Throughout much of the state, apparently in wet woodlands where hardwoods are common or where low, wet depressions are present (Map 3). This species is absent from the major river floodplains and the coastal marshes and from the southwestern terrace flatwoods and prairies. Individuals are occasionally found at times other than the winter breeding season, but an accurate mapping of the range will probably depend on collections of the larvae.

Taxonomic comments. No subspecies are recognized. P. W. Smith (1961) studied specimens from several regions and found no significant differences. The most recent com-

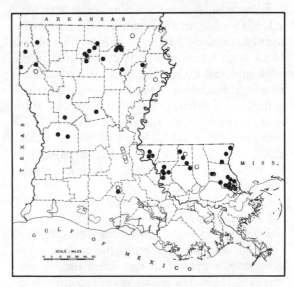

Map 3. Distribution of *Ambystoma talpoideum*. Solid circles represent specimens examined; hollow circles represent museum specimens not examined or literature records.

prehensive account of the literature on the species is that by Shoop (1964).

Habitat and habits. Like most *Ambystoma*, this species is secretive, sluggish, and usually found under logs and debris, rarely away from wet depressions or low, wet ground. It presumably feeds on worms, arthropods, and snails. Most specimens are found very close to the breeding sites.

Reproduction. Shoop (1960) studied reproductive behavior of Louisiana populations. *Ambystoma talpoideum* primarily utilizes temporary ponds and lays eggs from early December to mid-February in extreme southeastern Louisiana, usually when heavy rains coincide with cold weather. Shoop indicated that the season is 6 to 16 days long and that, unlike salamanders such as *A. maculatum*, which require a warming trend after freezing temperatures, *A. talpoideum* requires a cooling trend. Shoop did not suggest that successive reproductive waves might use the same pond, but the larval size groups seen by Dundee on 18 March 1962 at Shoop's primary study site indicated that there may have been a split breeding period. Larvae ranging from 24 to 75 mm collected 28 March 1950 in West Feliciana Parish also support the occurrence of several waves.

Hardy and Raymond (1980) presented comparative breeding data from Caddo Parish in the extreme northwestern corner of Louisiana. They reported that in a two-year study the males arrived as early as 2 December and continued to arrive in waves until 11 March; females began to arrive several days after the males and continued to as late as 8 March. Departure from the ponds began as early as 29 December and continued until 24 March. Virtually all of the emigration occurred in one night in one of the two seasons of the study. Individual animals might remain in the pond for up to 108 days.

The eggs, which number from 226 to 401, are laid in small groups of 4 to 20 enclosed in a rather soft, common gelatinous mass, often stained brown.

The distinctive larvae have a dorsal series of alternating patches of black melanophores and clusters of yellow chromatophores, a melanistic midventral line, and a low costal groove count. Transformation takes place from late April into June, although larvae taken in January 1965 transformed in the laboratory in February (Dundee 1974a). However, neoteny occurs in this species (Carr and Goin 1943; Boyd and Vickers 1963), and large larval-appearing animals therefore could be expected at any time of the year. On 12 December 1966, larvae of 100 mm total length were found in St. Helena Parish. Specimens measuring 102 mm, collected 2 February 1960 in Lafayette County, Mississippi (perhaps the same group reported by Boyd and Vickers in 1963 as being neotenic), had large pigmented vasa deferentia and small unyolked ova. Some of these animals were just transforming. Normal larvae appear to transform at total lengths of 72–82 mm. Small, presumably normal larvae, have been seen as late as 9 June in southeastern Louisiana. The conditions associated with production of neoteny in this species warrant careful analysis.

Breeding sites are often shared with other species of *Ambystoma*.

Ambystoma texanum (Matthes)
Small-mouthed Salamander

Plate II

Recognition. A medium-sized, relatively slender *Ambystoma* usually less than 5½ in. (140 mm) in total length in Louisiana, but reaching 7 in. (178 mm) elsewhere; head narrow, the mouth small; plicae of the tongue diverging from a median longitudinal groove (in other Louisiana *Ambystoma* the plicae radiating outward from the base of the tongue); color from dark slate or bluish black to brown, usually with lichenlike markings more numerous and lighter in color on the lower sides, giving a frosted appearance; venter darker than dorsum and also with some lichenlike marks; costal grooves 14 or 15; toes of adpressed limbs separated by 2 to 3½ intercostal spaces, except in newly metamorphosed individuals (toes touching).

Distribution. Statewide, but absent in the coastal marshes except where it occurs in oak-pine hammocks such as exist in the Rigolets area of southeastern St. Tammany Parish (Map 4).

Taxonomic comments. No subspecies are recognized. That geographic variation occurs in this species has long been known, yet no one seems to have published an extensive study of variation. Petranka (1982), studying the small-mouthed salamander in Kentucky and adjacent states, indicated that *A. texanum* has two forms that differ in breeding habitat, breeding habits, and in early developmental history. Because the two forms are allopatric over most of their ranges, parapatric in southeastern Indiana, and sympatric in western Kentucky, Petranka suspected the existence of a sibling species complex.

Habitat and habits. This species occurs in many habitats, even intensively cultivated areas, but is most prevalent in wet woodlands and bottomlands where hardwoods are common. It uses all sorts of ponds and ditches as breeding sites. Although secretive, the small-mouthed salamander is not infrequently encountered at various times of the year under logs in woodlands where the water table is high. Here it takes refuge in crawfish burrows, where it retreats when disturbed. It probably uses crawfish burrows for shelter in agricultural areas and grasslands. One specimen was unearthed four feet underground at Mandeville, St. Tammany Parish (Viosca notes). The food is reported to be mostly earthworms plus some arthropods.

Reproduction. This salamander may either live in wet ground adjacent to the breeding pools all year, or like typical *Ambystoma*, it may migrate from more distant breeding sites. The eggs, usually laid singly or at most

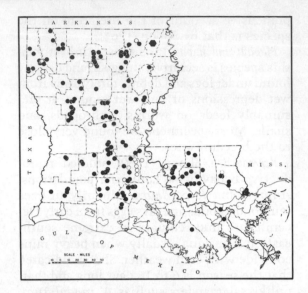

Map 4. Distribution of *Ambystoma texanum.* Solid circles represent specimens examined; hollow circles represent museum specimens not examined or literature records; a hexagon in the middle of a parish represents a literature record for the parish with no specific locality stated.

in clusters of two or three, are deposited on sticks, vegetation, and the undersurfaces of leaves on the bottom of the pool. The eggs are reported to number as many as 700; one Louisiana specimen laid 247 eggs in the laboratory (Cagle notes). The double-enveloped eggs are slightly more than 2 mm in diameter, and the outer envelope diameter is 6–6.5 mm. The spermatophores have not been described, but more than 400 were found in one 3-ft² area in St. Tammany Parish (Cagle notes). The breeding sites may be shared with *A. opacum* and *A. maculatum*, and perhaps *A. talpoideum.*

Based on our limited information on breeding dates, newly hatched larvae, fresh eggs, or spermatophores have been found from 10 December to 20 February. Transformation on 5 March and in late April suggests a rather short larval period; large larvae have been found as late as 29 April. The larvae reach at least 69 mm total length.

The larvae are dark gray or black and have

vertical light areas or spots in addition to a white stripe on each side of the body and tail. The high costal groove count is the best way to identify these larvae in Louisiana.

Ambystoma tigrinum (Green)
Tiger Salamander
Plate II

Recognition. A large *Ambystoma* reaching 13 in. (330 mm) in length but generally 7–8 in. (178–203 mm); ground color dark brown to black, with numerous irregularly spaced and formed yellow dorsal spots, sometimes coalescing on the lower sides to form extensive yellow patches or bars; venter mottled yellow on a dark grayish background; costal grooves 12, occasionally 11, 13, or 14; toes of adpressed limbs overlap; toes tapering to points rather than being cylindrical and rounded at the tips as in other *Ambystoma*.

Similar species. Ambystoma tigrinum superficially resembles the spotted salamander, *A. maculatum*, but the irregular spacing of the dorsal yellow markings and the light venter identify the tiger salamander. Tiger salamanders have two tubercles on each palm rather than one or none as in *A. maculatum.*

Distribution. The species was first reported from Louisiana in 1831 by Green, but until Rossman (1965a) and Dundee (1974a) reported newly discovered specimens, the presence of this species in the state had been questionable.

The three currently known localities (two in Vernon Parish, one in St. Tammany Parish) are in areas formerly covered by longleaf pine forests, which have since been replanted with slash and loblolly pines (Map 5). The tiger salamander is rarely found above ground, except during the brief breeding period; thus further knowledge of the distribution may have to come from sampling pools for the larvae.

An old record in the National Museum of Natural History (USNM 4709), comprising

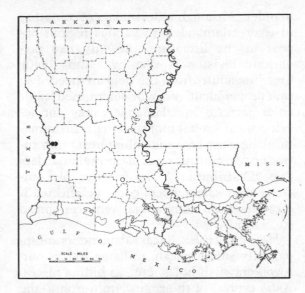

Map 5. Distribution of *Ambystoma tigrinum.* Solid circles represent specimens examined; hollow circles represent museum specimens not examined or literature records.

two specimens from Grand Coteau, St. Landry Parish, is in question. Cope (1889) mentioned those specimens, giving details of one, which he said was an "immature stage." Neither Dundee, nor at an earlier time, Viosca, encountered those specimens at the National Museum of Natural History. The validity of the St. Landry Parish record seemed to be confirmed by discovery of specimens deposited at the Northeast Louisiana State University Museum of Zoology, but Dundee (in press) discovered that these were probably escapees from a commercial venture in aquaculture of tiger salamanders, which brought in breeding stock from Oklahoma.

Taxonomic comments. Both the distribution and subspecific identity of the species in this state need to be established. Rossman (1965a) reported that the laboratory-transformed animals from Vernon Parish had patterns intermediate between those of *A. t. tigrinum* (Green), the eastern tiger salamander, and *A. t. mavortium* Baird, the barred tiger salamander. Although assessments of variation in tiger salamanders in various regions appear in the literature, the only real taxonomic revision is that by Dunn (1940). Breeding adults from the field are needed so that proper identity can be determined (adult color patterns in salamanders may not develop until several months after transformation). Because commercial interests may introduce extraneous races of tiger salamanders (see "Distribution"), the genetics of Louisiana tiger salamanders could be affected if escapees from commercial ventures spread successfully.

Habitat and habits. Tiger salamanders are apparently subterranean, utilizing rodent burrows, crawfish holes, etc., as hiding places. As is typical of the genus *Ambystoma*, the tiger salamanders move to breeding ponds in large numbers; such movements may be discovered as the animals cross roads on wet nights. Their large size and voracious habits result in a diet ranging from worms and insects to fishes, tadpoles, frogs, snakes, and nestling mice. Larvae likewise are voracious and eat virtually any kind of aquatic prey; in the plains states, especially, they may even be cannibalistic.

Reproduction. Dundee (1974a) offered a thorough discussion of the breeding season in Louisiana. The tiger salamander apparently may lay eggs from September to December. Eggs are laid in clusters of up to 100 and are enclosed in a gelatinous mass (not as stiff in consistency as that enclosing *A. maculatum* eggs); each egg is enclosed in three envelopes, the outermost 5–12 mm in outside diameter.

The larvae reach at least 125 mm in total length in Louisiana, but elsewhere may reach more than 300 mm, especially if neoteny occurs. Rossman (1965a) indicated that larvae taken in February transformed in March in the laboratory, but Dundee (1974a) reported larvae of 60–125 mm taken in Vernon Parish on 6 April. Thus the time of transformation may extend at least into late April. Young larvae may have dorsolateral paired spots on a yellowish green background and a light band along each side. Larger larvae may appear uniformly green; sometimes the lateral light line is distinct. The tapered, pointed toes are distinctive.

Pools are known to be shared with *A. talpoideum* in Louisiana; perhaps elsewhere in the state the tiger salamander will be found to use the same pools as other *Ambystoma*.

FAMILY AMPHIUMIDAE
AMPHIUMAS

The large, eel-like species of the family Amphiumidae are found only in the southeastern United States, usually at elevations of less than 500 ft above sea level. The single genus contains three living species, two of which occur in Louisiana.

Amphiuma means Garden Two-toed Amphiuma, Lamper "Eel," Congo "Eel"
Plate I

Recognition. A large, eel-like salamander commonly up to 2½ ft (760 mm) in total length, but reaching almost 46 inches (1,162 mm); two pairs of tiny, virtually nonfunctional legs, each with two toes; dorsal color dark brown to black, belly dark gray and somewhat lighter colored than the dorsum; a weakly defined black patch on the throat.

Similar species. The three-toed amphiuma, *Amphiuma tridactylum*, is characterized by three toes per limb (occasionally fewer because of injury), a much paler and thus more contrasting belly, and a distinct dark throat patch. The limbs of *A. tridactylum* are longer than those of *A. means*—the body length is 35 to 37 times longer than the forelimb compared to 44 to 50 times longer in *A. means*, and the body is 22 to 25 times longer than the hind limb compared to 31 to 34 times longer in *A. means*.

Distribution. Thus far known only from three Florida Parishes, in which this species may occur in the same ditches with *A. tridactylum* (Map 6). The ranges of the two large amphiumas are almost mutually exclusive, except in a small section of extreme southern Mississippi, extreme southwestern Alabama, and in the Florida Parishes; *A. means* may be widespread throughout the Florida Parishes.

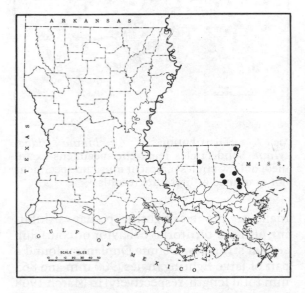

Map 6. Distribution of *Amphiuma means.* Solid circles represent specimens examined; hollow circles represent museum specimens not examined or literature records.

Taxonomic comments. No subspecies have been recognized. The most recent taxonomic study is that by Hill (1954).

Habitat and habits. Almost any type of freshwater habitat is utilized by amphiumas, but the habitats where they appear to be most abundant and are most easily found are shallow permanent or temporary ditches. Amphiumas are primarily nocturnal animals. By day they hide under debris in the water or in crawfish burrows. At night they emerge to forage for any invertebrates and small vertebrates that they can capture. The favored prey is crawfish, and any ditch that has numerous crawfish holes beneath the water level is almost certain to harbor *Amphiuma.*

During rains the two-toed amphiuma may slither overland. This salamander is exceedingly difficult to capture; its slippery, serpentine body and ability to inflict a painful bite necessitate special capture techniques. Wearing cotton gloves is advisable, and the amphiuma should be located by flashlight and approached stealthily. The animal can then be grabbed and quickly thrown onto shore, where it can be scooped up and tossed into a damp cloth bag. Individuals can be coaxed from crawfish holes by "twiddling" a slender twig within the burrow entrance. The amphiuma will snap at and follow the twig until the animal's emergence from the burrow makes capture possible.

Amphiumas have been extensively sought for biological research because their cells are exceptionally large and thus ideal for preparation of tissue study slides and for physiological studies. Fortunately, these animals have not been sought for the dinner table; their firm, white meat is comparable to frog legs in flavor, but skinning an amphiuma is so difficult that gourmets would soon be discouraged.

Parasites are frequently found in amphiumas, and several new species have been described from Louisiana amphiumas. Chandler (1923) described three trematodes, *Telorchis stunkardi, Cephalogonimus amphiumae,* and *Megalodiscus americanus* (the genus also new), and Zeliff (1932) described a new cestode, *Crepidobothrium amphiumae.*

Adult amphiumas are preyed upon by mud snakes (*Farancia abacura*), but the large size this amphiuma attains suggests that reciprocal dining pleasures might be possible. Scars found on the snakes probably are due to damage inflicted by the amphiuma's formidable jaws. Little is known of the ecology of this species. Its sympatric occurrence with *A. tridactylum* might make interesting studies in resource partitioning possible.

Reproduction. Nothing is known of the reproduction of this species in Louisiana. The long, rosarylike strings of eggs, each egg with an outer envelope diameter of 9–10 mm, have been found attended by the female in depressions under logs and rocks in damp places. The eggs presumably hatch when the depressions are flooded. Newly hatched young have gills, but the gills are apparently lost immediately after hatching. Considering Louisiana's latitude, the eggs are probably deposited from early spring to early summer. Newly hatched young are about 55 mm long, and newly transformed young may be as short as 70 mm.

Amphiuma tridactylum Cuvier
Three-toed Amphiuma, Lamper
"Eel," Congo "Eel"
Plate I

Recognition. A large, eel-like salamander commonly up to 2½ ft (760 mm) in total length, but reaching almost 42 in. (1,060 mm); two pairs of tiny, virtually nonfunctional legs, each with three toes (occasionally fewer due to mutilation); dorsal color dark brown to black, belly a much paler light gray contrasting markedly with the dorsum; a well-defined dark patch present on the throat.

Similar species. See under *Amphiuma means.*

Distribution. Statewide in all sorts of freshwater habitats, but especially abundant in drainage ditches in suburban and agricultural areas of the lower Mississippi River floodplain (Map 7).

Taxonomic comments. Goin (1938) considered *A. tridactylum* a subspecies of *A. means.* Studies by Baker (1947) and Hill (1954) concluded that the two amphiumas are distinct species. Hill indicated that 3 of 131 specimens from the Gulf Coast region were hybrids.

Habitat and habits. Amphiuma tridactylum is ecologically similar to *A. means.* Adult

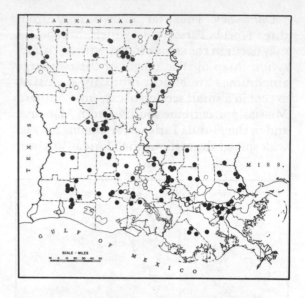

Map 7. Distribution of *Amphiuma tridactylum.* Solid circles represent specimens examined; hollow circles represent museum specimens not examined or literature records.

males are prone to fighting, perhaps exhibiting either a territorial behavior or courtship season struggles. Dennis Duplantier found a pair of large fighting males (900 mm and 865 mm total length, respectively) in March 1968 in a canal within three miles of downtown New Orleans. Although these animals must breathe principally through cutaneous gas exchange, they are forced from water by rotenone, a poison that constricts fish gills. Presumably rotenone similarly constricts the integumentary vessels of *Amphiuma.* Chaney (1951) examined 180 stomachs from amphiumas taken in the New Orleans region of southeastern Louisiana and found that crawfish constituted 52.4 percent of the contents by volume; earthworms, 24.3 percent; insect larvae, 5.6 percent; mole crickets, 4.4 percent; fish, 2 percent; grasshoppers, water beetles, skinks, spiders, and snails, 2 percent; and vegetation (probably accidentally ingested—our interpretation), 9.3 percent. In terms of percentage of stomachs containing the different items, vegetation was in 70 percent, earthworms in 52.2 percent, and crawfish in 46.7 percent. Seasonal differences in food taken reflected the availability of items such as earthworms and insect larvae. Cagle (1948a) provided an excellent account of the ecology.

Reproduction. On the basis of follicle counts in the females he studied, Cagle (1948a) reported the string of rosarylike eggs to number from 42 to 131 and average 98, but Rose (1966a), who examined larger females, indicated a potential of at least 354 eggs and an average of 201. Eggs are laid from April through early September, and the female attends the eggs. All the nests found have been in damp places, but, as with *A. means,* the gills apparently are lost immediately after hatching. Cagle (1948a) suggested an incubation period of five months. Several authors have suggested that females have biennial reproductive cycles. New hatchlings average 64 mm in total length, and transformed animals without gills are known to be as small as 60 mm. A remarkable observation appears in Viosca's notes for April to May 1937: when a female from Monroe was slit open, about two quarts of eggs with active embryos inside the egg cases were revealed. This indicates that *A. tridactylum* might potentially be ovoviviparous, a condition known in salamanders only among some European newts, a European plethodontid, and a Neotropical plethodontid.

FAMILY PLETHODONTIDAE
WOODLAND SALAMANDERS

The family Plethodontidae contains more than 28 percent of the 96 or so genera and more than 53 percent of the over 400 species of salamanders, fossil and living, known today; of the extant forms it contains more than 44 percent of the genera and 62 percent of the species. The family apparently originated in the southern Appalachian Mountains of the United States, but its representatives have spread to Canada and northern South Amer-

ica, and two species dwell in western Europe. The vast majority of species are wholly terrestrial and dwell in Latin America. All members are lungless, and transformed animals have a unique feature, the nasolabial groove, extending from each nostril to the upper lip. Louisiana has 5 genera and 10, perhaps 11, species.

Desmognathus fuscus—auriculatus
Complex
Desmognathus fuscus (Green)
Dusky Salamander
Desmognathus auriculatus (Holbrook)
Southern Dusky Salamander
Plate III

Recognition. A medium-sized to stout salamander reaching 6⅜ in. (163 mm) in length; dorsal and ventral patterns variable (see "Taxonomic comments"); face with a light line from the eye to the angle of the jaw; cheek area bulging; head outline tapering anteriorly, rounded in front; tongue attached in front, free only at sides and behind; base of the tail rounded or triangular in cross section and the posterior half or one-third of the tail angling downward relatively abruptly from dorsal keel to tip; usually 14 costal grooves between adpressed limbs; hind limbs stocky in comparison to front limbs.

Distribution. Widespread over the state but absent from the Marsh, the Prairie, the Shortleaf Pine-Oak-Hickory Forest west and south of the Red River, and the northern section of the Mississippi River alluvial plain (Map 8).

Taxonomic comments. The genus *Desmognathus* has always been a problem for systematists; its wide distribution, its extreme variability, and local isolation of many populations have complicated attempts to characterize virtually any one of the perhaps nine or more species. Valentine (1963), concentrating on Mississippi populations of *D. fuscus,* con-

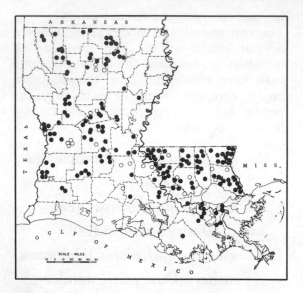

Map 8. Distribution of *Desmognathus fuscus-auriculatus.* Solid circles represent specimens examined; hollow circles represent museum specimens not examined or literature records.

cluded that two sympatric species, *D. fuscus* and *D. auriculatus,* were present. He characterized *D. fuscus* as a hillside stream dweller having fewer filaments on the larval gills than *D. auriculatus,* gill filaments white rather than pigmented, larger dorsolateral spots in larvae, adult pattern of large instead of small pale spots, and longer limbs (usually 2 to 4 rather than 4½ to 5½ costal folds lying between the adpressed limbs of large adults). *Desmognathus auriculatus,* according to Valentine, is better adapted to muddy, bottomland swamps and sloughs, as is reflected by its bushier larval gills, more reduced pattern in larvae and especially in the darkly colored adults, and shorter limbs. Folkerts (1968) reported finding intergrades between the two forms in Alabama and attributed the apparent presence of two pattern and morphological types to ecological segregation resulting from long separation of two races. Subsequent migration brought the animals into apparent sympatry but left them still adapted to restricted habitats. Means (1974)

emphasized Florida populations and corroborated Valentine's (1963) conclusions. Means' study explored additional characters, particularly dental and skeletal features, and revealed that most of the variable characters of the form called *D. fuscus* could not be effectively used for identification over the entire range. For example, New York and Louisiana populations had more in common on jaw profile characteristics than did Louisiana and Florida populations. Means' study revealed that the most useful characters in defining the two forms are adult pattern and tail morphology; Means did not use the number of costal folds between adpressed limbs as a criterion for identification.

We do not question that there are two morphological types of *Desmognathus* in Louisiana: one a ravine dweller with a light-colored, heavily patterned adult and larval dorsum, and fewer gill filaments in larvae; and the other a muckland form of dark coloration, usually having one or two rows of small, white-rimmed spots ("portholes") on the sides, and bushy gills that tend to cover the forelimb insertion in the larvae. Both forms can be found virtually side by side—the elevational separation may be as little as 2 ft.

We have not made a detailed study of the vast number of specimens available from Louisiana, but the interpretations of specimens that we have examined and those identified by others pose some notable problems. Means (1974) designated specimens from western Louisiana (Sabine Parish) and from Tyler County, Texas (i.e., south of the Red River) as *D. fuscus.* He also identified dusky salamanders from western Louisiana (Natchitoches Parish north of the Red River), from northern Louisiana (Union and Ouachita parishes), and from southeastern Louisiana (Washington and St. Tammany parishes) as *D. fuscus.* Means reported *D. auriculatus* from several of the Florida Parishes and from swampland areas south of New Orleans. The maps presented by Conant (1975) showed that *D. auriculatus* does not occur in northern Louisiana, but is the only dusky salamander south of the Red River in western Louisiana. Cook and Brown (1974) called all Texas material *auriculatus*, even specimens from Tyler County. Cook and Brown tended to use the criteria introduced by Valentine. Thus we see contrasting interpretations based perhaps on variability of valid characteristics, use of the wrong criteria, careless geographical mapping, or the problem of how a particular author interprets pattern, tail form, and so forth. From inspection of specimens at Tulane, Dundee determined that all of the animals from central, western, and northern Louisiana fall into the short-legged form, *auriculatus*; that is, they have 4½ to 5½ costal folds between adpressed limbs. Everywhere the tails of dark animals with the small "porthole" lateral spots lack the cylindrical, tapered tip Means (1974) attributed to *D. fuscus*, are strongly compressed at the posterior end and usually keeled above (at least on the last two-thirds of the length), and have a narrow light middorsal line; in other words, the tails of these animals are *auriculatus* in appearance. Animals having a patterned or only moderately dark dorsum usually have a cylindrical, tapered tail tip and hence are seemingly *fuscus*; but some with complete tails have keels and a narrow middorsal line on the tail—*auriculatus* tails. Larvae of both types, sparsely and bushy gilled, occur, and some even have pigmented fimbriae but few filaments, an intermediate condition. Thus, *auriculatus*, *fuscus*, and intermediate types occur near Minden in Webster Parish, and in the Fishville-Pollock area in Grant Parish; intermediate forms are present in Calcasieu and Bossier parishes. The Florida Parishes clearly contain both forms, as well as intermediates.

Because of such diversity in identification and interpretation, the status of Louisiana *Desmognathus* cannot be clearly resolved on the basis of currently available criteria. Karlin and Guttman (1986) used electrophoretic methods to study isozyme variation and concluded that *auriculatus* and *fuscus* are different species and that an unidentified species of *Desmognathus* of the *fuscus-auriculatus* complex exists in the Gulf Coastal Plain of Georgia, Alabama, and Florida. Their studies involved many populations of *fuscus* and indicated that southern and northern *fuscus* may be genetically differentiated, possibly at the species level, but electrophoretic data may be inconclusive. Their studies involved two populations of *fuscus* from central Mississippi and one population of *auriculatus* from the Florida Panhandle. Although they considered *auriculatus* to be not particularly closely related to the *fuscus-ochrophaeus* complex, from which *auriculatus* was presumed to be derived, they had previously reported (Karlin and Guttman 1981) that *fuscus* and *ochrophaeus* hybridize and that introgression of genes occurs in these latter species. We see, therefore, that hybridization between *Desmognathus* species can occur; thus electrophoretic evaluation of the apparent hybrids (or intergrades) from Louisiana might explain the systematic enigmas that we have described. In their 1986 report, Karlin and Guttman also noted a need to determine if *auriculatus* has undergone adaptive radiation. Such an investigation might reveal the nature of the variation seen in Louisiana *Desmognathus*.

If we are dealing with two ecologically separated subspecies, the appropriate names are *Desmognathus fuscus conanti* Rossman, the spotted dusky salamander, and *D. f. auriculatus* (Holbrook), the southern dusky salamander. If we are dealing with two species rather than two races, then extensive hybridization is occurring; if there is only one species, extensive intergradation is occurring, and subspecific designation of many individual animals is difficult.

Habitat and habits. As indicated above, the dusky salamanders occur in swampy mucklands or in ravines. They are locally abundant, especially around spring seepages, and readily discovered beneath logs and debris, especially in very shallow water or adjacent to the water. Most can be found by lifting objects partially in, or immediately adjacent to the water. When uncovered, the dusky salamander is alert and agile, running and leaping with remarkable agility, usually plunging into the water in its escape attempts. In swamplands the salamander often escapes by diving into crawfish burrows.

Chaney (1949, 1958) studied dusky salamanders in Louisiana and noted in the stomach contents a diverse array of arthropods, worms, snails, two-lined salamanders, and even individuals of their own species. The prey items included both terrestrial and aquatic species, as might be expected for a salamander that remains so close to water.

Reproduction. Chaney (1949) observed that female dusky salamanders in Louisiana lay from 7 to 36 eggs in small excavations beneath sheltering objects or in the ground in damp places from July to early September. The female broods the eggs during the month or so of development; they hatch in the last half of October and in early November. The newly hatched larvae average about 16 mm in length and are gilled. Although larvae may eventually enter water, they can develop on land, in fact, at an accelerated rate. The gills may be lost as early as January, but some larvae retain them until May. Chaney (1949) also noted that there were two types of larvae, one transforming at 12–16 mm snout-vent length, the other at 23+ mm (Valentine [1963] noted *fuscus* as transforming at 16–20 mm, and *auriculatus* transforming at 22–32 mm). Chaney suggested that the smaller larvae developed terrestrially, whereas the larger ones developed aquatically.

Rose (1966b) studied the homing behavior of some brooding female dusky salamanders in St. Charles Parish. He found that females aggressively defended their nests. If displaced along the axis of the stream where the nests were located, the females would return to their nests; if the females were displaced at right angles to the stream, their return was less likely. Females displaced with their eggs would remain with the eggs. He concluded that the females might have been familiar with their surroundings and that homing seemed more likely to occur during damp weather.

Eurycea cirrigera (Green) Southern Two-lined Salamander
Plate III

Recognition. A salamander attaining a maximum length of about 3⅞ in. (98 mm); ground color of yellow to pale orange and a dark stripe running from the eye well onto the tail on either side; dorsum often peppered with dark specks, the lower sides mottled and with a row of circular light spots; costal grooves 13 or 14, with 0 to 2 grooves between the adpressed limbs; adult males sometimes with prominent downward projections (cirri) from the upper lip below the nostrils.

Similar species. The dwarf salamander, *Eurycea quadridigitata,* superficially resembles the two-lined salamander, but has only four toes on each hind foot, rather than five toes.

Distribution. Confined to the Florida Parishes (Map 9).

Taxonomic comments. This species was long recognized as *E. bislineata cirrigera,* but Jacobs (1987) offered electrophoretic and morphological data to support its elevation to species rank. This species was described by Green (1831) from "near New Orleans." Because New Orleans was then literally the only community of note in southeastern Louisiana, it was used as a geographic designation for many organisms secured from the general area. There is no evidence that *E. cirrigera* occurs south of Lake Pontchartrain, so the type locality remains an enigma.

Habitat and habits. The favored habitats are swampy creek bottomlands, ravine seepages, and small brooks. In these habitats, the two-lined salamander may live under logs and

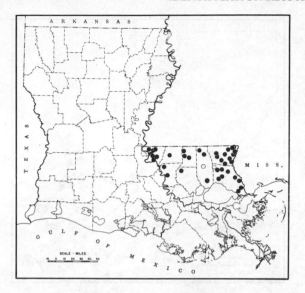

Map 9. Distribution of *Eurycea cirrigera*. Solid circles represent specimens examined; hollow circles represent museum specimens not examined or literature records.

debris at the water's edge or under slightly submerged objects, but individuals are occasionally found on adjacent slopes, well above the wet areas. Such habitats are shared with all of the native plethodontids that have aquatic larval stages.

This is a secretive species that emerges at night to forage for its food, which includes all kinds of terrestrial and aquatic invertebrates. This salamander is quite at home in water, and it may remain submerged for long periods.

Reproduction. Courtship and production of spermatophores apparently occur during the fall months in Louisiana, as evidenced by the large cirri present in males collected in the fall. Eggs, very close to hatching, were taken by F. R. Cagle on 29 and 30 January from a clear, shallow, gravel-bottomed ditch in a ravine near St. Francisville, West Feliciana Parish; some of these eggs hatched 4 February in the laboratory. The larval period is prolonged; apparently one to two years must elapse before transformation occurs.

Newly hatched larvae measure about 10.5 mm in total length. Larvae ranging from 16 to 26 mm in total length are represented in March collections, at least one group ranging from 22 to 30 mm long is known from a 5 June collection, a series with individuals from 26 to 49 mm is in a 7 September collection; but larvae over 60 mm taken in mid-January and others ranging from 52 to 65 mm taken in June indicate that the developmental period can probably last a year or more. The largest larvae measured, 73 and 77 mm (preserved specimens), were taken in March. Transformation, however, may take place in much smaller larvae, so the larval period cannot yet be definitively interpreted.

Large larvae have the dark lateral stripes well developed and resemble the adults. Younger larvae must be distinguished from larvae of several other species of plethodontids. The low costal groove count (13 or 14) distinguishes this species from *Pseudotriton* larvae. *Desmognathus* can be distinguished from *Eurycea* because the rami of the gills of *Eurycea* are long, and the laterally directed filaments are short, whereas in *Desmognathus* the rami are shorter than the filaments. In addition, *Desmognathus* larvae are chunkier animals and rarely exceed 40 mm in total length. *Eurycea cirrigera* differs from *E. longicauda* larvae in having far less black on the sides and in lacking a middorsal stripe; the larvae of *longicauda* rarely exceed 50 mm total length.

Eurycea longicauda (Green) Long-tailed Salamander
Plate III

Recognition. An elongated salamander attaining a maximum total length of 7⅞ in. (200 mm), but typical adults usually less than 6 in. (152 mm) long; tail long, often constituting more than 60 percent of the total length (may be only 50 percent in newly transformed animals); dorsum yellow or tan with a dark middorsal stripe or series of elongated spots; belly rather strongly mottled with dull greenish gray on dull yellow; costal grooves 13 or 14, with one-half to two intercostal spaces between the adpressed limbs.

Distribution. Confined to the Florida Parishes (Map 10).

Taxonomic comments. Three subspecies are recognized: the distinctive form found in Louisiana is the three-lined salamander, *Eurycea longicauda guttolineata* (Holbrook). Martof et al. (1980) referred to the three-lined salamander as *E. guttolineata*, but gave no basis for elevating it to the species level. Other authors, such as Mount (1975) and Valentine (1962), referred to intergrades of *E. l. longicauda × E. l. guttolineata* as evidence of subspecific status.

Habitat and habits. This species may be found in bottomlands, ditches, seepages of ravines, etc., and on slopes leading to bottomland swamps. This salamander freely enters water and may remain submerged for long periods. It is secretive, but when revealed in its hiding place it may scurry rapidly to escape, often entering crawfish burrows and crevices. Good places to find it are under debris piles and logs near streams and under boards and rubble of old buildings near water. Although this species is primarily nocturnal, Gordon (1953) reported individuals active on the surface in midafternoon in Florida when the sky was overcast and rain imminent. Tinkle (1952) examined the stomach contents of transformed specimens from the Florida Panhandle and found a large variety of invertebrates, especially arthropods.

Reproduction. Little is known of reproductive behavior in this species, but indirect evidence interpreted from ovarian eggs and larval growth (Gordon 1953; Bruce 1970, 1982) suggests that in coastal plain regions eggs are deposited from late autumn to early winter. Mount (1975) found several females and their eggs in early December in Alabama; the eggs were in groups of 8 to 14.

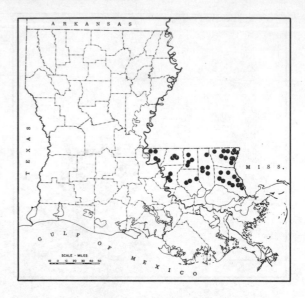

Map 10. Distribution of *Eurycea longicauda.* Solid circles represent specimens examined; hollow circles represent museum specimens not examined or literature records.

Few larvae are available from Louisiana, despite the abundance of adult animals in collections. Larvae varying from 22 to 29 mm in total length have been secured between 13 and 27 March. The only recently transformed specimens from Louisiana have total lengths of 56 mm (collected 18 November) and 34 mm (17 mm snout-vent length; collected 16 March). Not only is the latter specimen exceptionally small for a transformed animal, but the March date suggests an unusually early transformation. Bruce (1970) reviewed the published data and suggested a minimum snout-vent length of 22.5 mm (41.5 mm total length) for this race, a larval period of three to six months, and metamorphosis in late spring or summer after a late winter hatch. But in 1982 Bruce, reporting on the same populations, indicated that slower-growing individuals may overwinter, thus extending the larval period to 12 to 16 months.

The larval pattern develops shortly after the larvae hatch and strongly resembles the adult pattern, except that the middorsal stripe is poorly developed. The only larva with which *E. longicauda* can be confused is that of *E. cirrigera*, which has far less development of the lateral dark stripe, grows to greater size, and can be found in any season.

Eurycea quadridigitata (Holbrook)
Dwarf Salamander
Plate III

Recognition. A small, slender terrestrial salamander (rarely more than 3 in., or 76 mm, long); maximum length 3⅔ in., 93.5 mm, based on a preserved specimen from Jefferson Parish; four toes on each hind foot; ground color yellowish brown to brown, with a dark dorsolateral stripe on each side; some specimens having numerous black specks on the dorsum; belly and underside of the tail yellow; costal grooves usually 15 to 17, and usually 3 to 5 intercostal folds between the adpressed limbs.

Similar species. The only other four-toed terrestrial salamander in Louisiana, *Hemidactylium scutatum*, has a constriction at the base of the tail and a white venter with black spots on it.

Distribution. Statewide except absent from the coastal marshes and apparently absent from the northern Mississippi River alluvial floodplain (Map 11).

Taxonomic comments. Cope (1869) regarded *Salamandra quadridigitata* Holbrook as being distinctive enough to assign to a new genus, *Manculus.* Dunn (1923, 1926) considered it to belong to *Eurycea.* Mittleman (1967) considered the four-toed condition and the unusual tail fin of the larva as significant and applied the generic name *Manculus.* We choose to follow Wake (1966) in regarding *E. quadridigitata* simply as a specialized species of *Eurycea.*

Several races have been recognized, but have subsequently been considered to be geo-

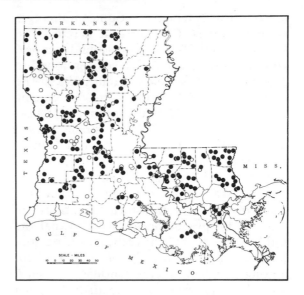

Map 11. Distribution of *Eurycea quadridigitata.* Solid circles represent specimens examined; hollow circles represent museum specimens not examined or literature records.

graphically clinal or lacking in correlation of structural features with geographic distribution—Mittleman (1967) listed proponents of the monotypic interpretation.

Habitat and habits. This is an abundant species, especially in western Louisiana, that occupies spring seeps, swampy ground, damp hardwood and pine forests, pond margins, and stream bottomlands. It is ordinarily found hidden beneath cover objects, sometimes many animals under a single log or board, but it also commonly crosses roads on rainy winter nights. Specimens on roads look like small, whitish twigs in the glare of auto headlights. Specific information on food habits is lacking; presumably the species eats small invertebrates.

Reproduction. Sever (1975) reported that in Louisiana sperm production begins in August, strong development of cirri occurs abruptly in September, and although sperm may be present in the vasa deferentia until February, sperm transfer occurs in September. The Tulane collection contains eggs collected on 30 October that hatched 3–6 December, and Viosca (notes) found eggs on 6 January. Gravid females have been found in Alabama until February (Trauth 1983). The eggs usually number from 13 to 36, averaging 22 (Harrison 1973), but as many as 48 eggs have been deposited by a single female (Brimley 1923). The creamy white, unpigmented eggs are laid singly or in small groups and are attached to leaves and twigs.

The larvae, which early in their development resemble the transformed animals, are unusual for plethodontid larvae in that the tail fin extends onto the body, a feature exhibited otherwise only by *Hemidactylium* among Louisiana plethodontids (see *Hemidactylium* account for comparisons). Such a structure is indicative of the still waters usually utilized by this species. The gills are very bushy, also a feature correlated with quiet waters. Newly hatched larvae are available at dates ranging from early December in southeastern Louisiana to as late as 28 March near Minden in the northwestern portion of the state. Hatchlings are 11.5–12 mm in total length. Newly transformed specimens as small as 24 mm total length (14 mm snout-vent length) have been taken on 2 July in Union Parish, but transformation usually takes place from mid-April to late summer. The presence of transformed individuals as short as 24 mm snout-vent length in a 5 February collection suggests that even earlier metamorphosis may occur. The largest larva examined measures 48 mm total length and was taken 26 March. Larvae measuring only 22–28 mm total length were secured near Plain Dealing, Bossier Parish, on 27 July.

Hemidactylium scutatum Tschudi
Four-toed Salamander
Plate III

Recognition. A small salamander not exceeding 4 in. (102 mm) in total length; a conspic-

uous constriction at the base of the tail; four toes on each hind foot; belly white, spotted with black.

Distribution. Known only from Indian Mound, East Baton Rouge Parish, and from near Hickory, St. Tammany Parish (Map 12). The overall distribution includes many disjunct populations on the western and southern flanks of the range. Thus new discoveries from virtually anywhere outside the coastal marshes can be expected. The disjunct populations apparently are relics of a formerly more widespread distribution.

Map 12. Distribution of *Hemidactylium scutatum*. Solid circles represent specimens examined; hollow circles represent museum specimens not examined or literature records.

Taxonomic comments. No subspecies have been proposed, and no taxonomic study has been published. The most recent summary of literature on the species is that by Neill (1963).

Habitat and habits. The most frequent habitat in the South is hilly hardwood-conifer forest with still or slowly moving water or swampy ground nearby (see Dundee [1968] for further discussion). Our Louisiana specimens were found in wet pine-hardwood forests near acidic, temporary pools of water. *Hemidactylium scutatum* is a sluggish salamander that often lies in a curled position or curls up when disturbed. Individuals exhibit a weak territorial behavior, intimidating by confrontation any intruding *Hemidactylium* that comes to the shelter site. The most remarkable habit is that of voluntarily dropping off the tail at the constricted point when the animal is effecting an escape.

The food habits are poorly known—this species eats arthropods, but nesting females apparently refrain from feeding.

Reproduction. In Michigan mating takes place in the fall, and egg laying begins in mid-April, but in coastal Virginia the egg laying begins 24 February (Wood 1955). A single report from central Alabama (Mount 1975) mentions 23 February. Obviously some strikingly different dates might be expected whenever breeding activities are detected in Louisiana.

The females are known to swim to locate nesting sites, which usually are in sphagnum moss atop logs or hummocks, or in cavities in logs. The female deposits the eggs, numbering approximately 30, from an upside down or head-standing posture and then attends them for the 38 to 60+ days of incubation. Communal nests are common. Nests are above the water, and the larvae, on hatching, drop into the water.

The larvae hatch at a total length of approximately 12–13 mm. The pond-type larva requires over six weeks to reach the transformation size of 18–25 mm.

We have not examined larvae to determine how they may be distinguished from those of *Eurycea quadridigitata*, the dwarf four-toed salamander. Bishop's (1941, 1943) descriptions of larvae suggest that *Hemidactylium* is chunkier and has larger gills, a more reticulate pattern on the tail, and a higher dorsal fin that passes farther forward onto the back. The mature larvae of *E. quadridigitata* possess a fairly well-defined lateral black band apparently lacking or indefinite in *Hemidactylium*.

Plethodon glutinosus (Green) Slimy Salamander

Plate III

Recognition. A moderate-sized, strictly terrestrial, plethodontid salamander reaching 8⅛ in. (206 mm), but in Louisiana, as elsewhere in the South, generally much smaller, averaging 4¾–5 in. (120–140 mm); specimens from the Florida Parishes noticeably shorter on the average than those from the central Louisiana populations; tail circular in cross section, tapering to a sharp point; body black, usually with numerous white, silvery-, or brassy-colored flecks (especially in juveniles) on the back, and often with a profusion of such flecks on the lower sides giving the appearance of white, longitudinal bands; venter dark slate; costal grooves 16 or 17, usually 16, with 1 to 4 intercostal folds between the adpressed limbs.

Distribution. Widespread throughout uplands and bottomlands in the Florida Parishes and in the hill parishes of north-central Louisiana (Map 13).

Taxonomic comments. The Louisiana representatives belong to the widespread nominate subspecies, *Plethodon g. glutinosus* (Green), the slimy salamander. The most recent taxonomic study is that of Highton (1962). Biochemical studies by Highton and others may ultimately reveal that *P. glutinosus* is a complex of cryptic species.

Habitat and habits. This species' preferred habitat seems to be areas where hardwoods are common; most specimens are found under hardwood logs, even if pine logs are common in the vicinity. The habitats occupied may be surprisingly dry (e.g., the upper slopes of hills), but if some moisture is present beneath logs, the slimy salamander can survive without retreating to subterranean sites.

Plethodon glutinosus is secretive but

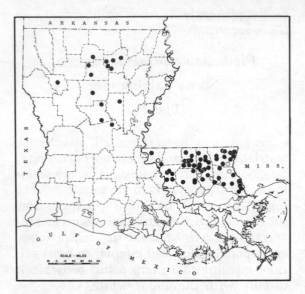

Map 13. Distribution of *Plethodon glutinosus.* Solid circles represent specimens examined; hollow circles represent museum specimens not examined or literature records.

emerges on cool, humid nights to forage for its food, reported to be the usual worms, snails, and arthropods eaten by many salamanders. Although this species is most commonly encountered in or under logs, it frequently makes its escape into the dense leaf litter that usually covers the forest floor or into mammal burrows beneath the logs; these animals are probably scattered throughout the forest under leaf litter or in burrows and holes in the forest floor. At night the slimy salamander can be found on damp road-cut banks, apparently having emerged from crevices and holes in the banks. The body and tail exude a viscous whitish secretion that feels slippery, but which quickly coagulates to form a strong "glue" that adheres firmly to anything it touches. One does not easily forget the slimy salamander after handling it—the coagulated skin secretion cannot be washed off, but must literally "wear off" the hands.

Reproduction. Although this is one of the most abundant salamanders in the eastern

United States, remarkably little is known about its reproductive habits. Fewer than a dozen clutches of eggs have been found. Highton (1956) conducted a study in northern peninsular Florida that provides data probably applicable to Louisiana. Highton found that the eggs are laid in late August and early September after a presumed late July or August courtship. The 7 to 11 eggs measuring 3.5–4.5 mm in diameter are guarded by the female in cavities in or under logs. Highton estimated incubation to be two months; hatching occurred as late as 1 November in the laboratory, although newly hatched young were not seen in the field until late December. Newly hatched young from the laboratory clutch measured 12–15 mm in snout-vent length and 20–26 mm in total length; the field-collected juveniles measured at least 15 mm in snout-vent length and 28 mm in total length. A specimen in the Tulane collections taken 14 November 1948 measures 15 mm snout-vent length and 28 mm total length, which confirms a probable mid-fall hatching period.

Plethodon serratus Grobman
Southern Red-backed Salamander
Plate III

Recognition. A small, wholly terrestrial salamander attaining a maximum length of approximately 4 in. (102 mm); dorsum with a reddish orange, saw-toothed middorsal stripe; sides dark gray; belly with dark and light mottling; costal grooves 18 or 19, with 6 to 9 intercostal folds between the adpressed limbs.

Distribution. Known only from two localities about 20 miles apart in west-central Louisiana—an area about 175 air-miles south of the nearest reported Arkansas locality for the species—and from another location about 75 miles east-northeast of these two sites (Map 14). These areas are part of the

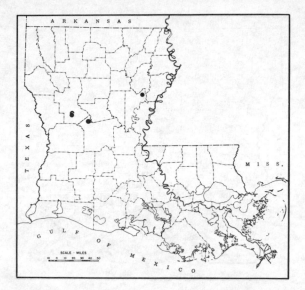

Map 14. Distribution of *Plethodon serratus.* Solid circles represent specimens examined; hollow circles represent museum specimens not examined or literature records.

Kisatchie Wold and consist of pine- and hardwood-forested hills with sandstone outcroppings of the Catahoula Formation. *Plethodon serratus* occurs in four other isolated unglaciated regions from Oklahoma and Missouri to North Carolina and Georgia (Highton and Webster 1976). We believe that additional populations will be discovered elsewhere in Louisiana where longleaf pine hills have stone outcroppings.

Taxonomic comments. This species was long recognized as a subspecies of *P. cinereus* until Highton and Webster (1976) established the present allocation on the basis of protein chemistry.

Habitat and habits. Relatively little is known about this species in Louisiana. The original report of its presence by Keiser and Conzelman (1969) indicated that heavy rainfall had saturated the area just prior to their early March collection. Most of the specimens were under stones on exposed slopes. Although these salamanders are much more tolerant of dry conditions than most Loui-

siana salamanders, they probably would not be encountered on the surface during late spring and summer months. The species has been found in Louisiana from mid-December to 28 April. The species is protected by state law, and studies can be conducted only with proper authorization from the Louisiana Department of Wildlife and Fisheries.

Elsewhere, this salamander is encountered under objects or in logs in moist forest regions. At night it crawls over the surface of the ground if the soil is moist and temperatures are moderate. Virtually any terrestrial invertebrate found in its habitat seems to be included in the diet.

Reproduction. Elsewhere, the mating season occurs in the fall, and eggs are deposited in the first half of summer. The mass of a dozen or so eggs resembles a cluster of grapes, hanging from a single gelatinous strand in a cavity within a rotted log or under a stone. The female attends the nest. The newly hatched animals probably are comparable to those of the closely related species *P. cinereus,* presumably 19–20 mm long and similar to the adult in appearance.

Plethodon websteri Highton
Webster's Salamander
Plate III

Recognition. A small, wholly terrestrial salamander reaching 1⅜ in. (35 mm) in snout-vent length and 2½ in. (63 mm) in total length in Louisiana, but elsewhere attaining 1⅔ in. (43 mm) in snout-vent length and 3 1/16 in. (78 mm) in total length; dorsum with a red, orange, or yellow, wavy-edged middorsal stripe; sides dark gray to brown; venter mottled and with some orange or red pigment; outside of Louisiana known to occur in a dark phase, lacking the middorsal stripe and having a gray to brown dorsum but retaining red in the ventral color; intermediates between striped and unstriped forms also occur; costal grooves usually 18, with 6 or 7 intercostal folds between adpressed limbs.

Similar species. Webster's salamander looks much like the southern red-backed salamander (*Plethodon serratus*), from which it differs in having the edges of the middorsal stripe wavy or lobed rather than saw-toothed. Most of the stripe lobes of Webster's salamander do not correspond to the costal grooves, whereas in the Ouachita red-backed salamander each "tooth" of the middorsal stripe generally points to a costal groove. Webster's salamander appears to be morphologically similar to *P. dorsalis* (see "Taxonomic comments").

Distribution. Known only from the Tunica Hills Nature Preserve west of Weyanoke, West Feliciana Parish (Map 15). Webster's salamander presumably may occur throughout the Blufflands area of the Florida Parishes and perhaps, like the toad *Bufo americanus*, it may even penetrate eastward into the pine-hardwoods uplands.

Taxonomic comments. We refer Louisiana animals to *P. websteri* rather than to the morphologically identical *P. dorsalis* Cope, a species from which *websteri* may be distinguished only by electrophoretic analysis. The original report from Louisiana (Rossman and Meier 1979) gave *P. dorsalis* as the identity, but at that time *P. websteri* was undescribed. *Plethodon websteri* has a disjunct distribution from South Carolina to east-central Mississippi and southwestern Alabama. *Plethodon dorsalis* occurs predominantly from northern Alabama, northward, and in a disjunct area of the western Ozark Plateau of Arkansas, Oklahoma, and Missouri. Southeastern Louisiana has geographic and ecological affinities with *P. websteri* distribution, hence our systematic allocation. There could be, however, a zoogeographic similarity in the disjunct occurrence of the Louisiana salamanders and that of the toad, *Bufo americanus*. A narrow hardwood corridor that extends from western Tennessee through west-

Map 15. Distribution of *Plethodon websteri.* Solid circles represent specimens examined; hollow circles represent museum specimens not examined or literature records.

central Mississippi into the Tunica Hills of Louisiana may have provided *P. dorsalis* a route into Louisiana. Dr. Richard Highton of the University of Maryland kindly examined some Louisiana specimens sent to him. Although they arrived dead, he was able to determine that nine critical proteins detected by electrophoresis did resemble those of *P. websteri.*

Habitat and habits. Webster's salamander inhabits woodlands, hiding by day beneath ground cover; the few Louisiana specimens were found under logs. Specimens collected in Louisiana were taken between 17 December and 11 March. Others were seen in the Tunica Hills Nature Preserve but left undisturbed as a conservation measure. In South Carolina, Semlitsch and West (1983) reported that the salamanders apparently remain underground from June to September, but are active in forest litter from October to May, particularly at night. Camp and Bozeman (1981) reported that smaller specimens in Georgia and Alabama ate mostly acarines and Collembola, but larger ones ate ants.

Reproduction. Semlitsch and West (1983) studied two populations of Webster's salamander in South Carolina and suggested that courtship and insemination probably occur between January and March, egg deposition occurs during June or July, and the eggs hatch during August or September. Gravid females contained an average of 5.8 (3 to 8) enlarged ovarian follicles. The hatchlings emerged in October and November and averaged 13 mm snout-vent length. Sexual maturity is reached at an age of 21 to 26 months and first reproductive activity occurs at 29 to 31 months.

One of the Louisiana specimens, 35 mm in snout-vent and 63 mm in total length, was a gravid female. The smallest Louisiana specimen, measuring 28 mm in total length and taken 17 December 1986, is a size that would be expected in South Carolina during November and December (see Semlitsch and West [1983], but our calculation is extrapolated from the few published data on snout-vent and total lengths—which may not be valid because these lengths are for adults, not juveniles, whose ratios probably are different).

A male (LSUMZ 46606) with a snout-vent length of 32.2 mm (preserved), taken 17 December 1986 in West Feliciana Parish, Louisiana, and another male (TU 19831), with a snout-vent length of 35.5 mm (freshly killed), taken 14 January 1987 in Hinds County, Mississippi, have swelling at the ventral ends of the nasolabial grooves that suggests rudimentary cirri. Cirri may become prominent in some male plethodontid salamanders during courtship periods, but cirri have not been mentioned in other reports on *P. websteri*. Also, the testes and vasa deferentia of the Hinds County specimen were darkly pigmented—features usually associated with courtship time in salamanders and stressed by Semlitsch and West (1983).

Pseudotriton montanus Baird
Mud Salamander
Plate III

Recognition. A moderately stocky salamander, adults averaging 3½–4 in. (90–102 mm) in total length, but reaching 4⅔ in. (119 mm); snout short, 1¼ to 1½ times the horizontal diameter of the eye, and strongly convex above; tail short, usually about 40 percent of total length; dorsum brownish salmon, covered with a number of small, well-separated black dots; venter salmon pink, unspotted; iris brown; costal grooves 16 or 17, with 6 to 7½ intercostal folds between the adpressed limbs.

Similar species. The eye color, snout shape and length, and the plain venter distinguish *Pseudotriton montanus* from the red salamander (*P. ruber*).

Distribution. Known only from the longleaf pine hills of Washington and St. Tammany parishes and just within the Pearl River bottomlands near Bogalusa (Map 16).

Taxonomic comments. Bruce (1968) suggested that this species has no clear-cut races, but most herpetologists recognize several subspecies. Louisiana specimens are assignable to *P. montanus flavissimus* Hallowell, the Gulf Coast mud salamander. No comprehensive taxonomic study has been undertaken, but Martof (1975a) listed literature pertinent to the systematics.

Habitat and habits. The usual habitat is swampy spring seepages or swampy ground adjacent to sluggish valley streams; such areas are often recognized by the presence of sphagnum moss. *Pseudotriton montanus* will probably be discovered throughout the northern Florida Parishes in suitable habitats.

Bruce (1975) indicated that these salamanders construct their own burrows in the muddy ground adjacent to water. The burrows usually are vertical, and the salamander

Map 16. Distribution of *Pseudotriton montanus*. Solid circles represent specimens examined; hollow circles represent museum specimens not examined or literature records.

tends to rest with the head at or near the opening. The burrows lead to subterranean channels and water. Occasionally individuals are found under logs and leaf piles. Larvae are more often encountered in Louisiana than are the adults; this suggests that special collecting techniques must be used to capture the animals in their burrows. We have seen no mention of the food habits.

Reproduction. Bruce (1968, 1974, 1975) studied mud salamanders in western South Carolina and suggested that this species deposits eggs in late autumn (approximately 1 December), hatches January to March (approximately 1 February), and requires about 19½ months of larval life before transformation. The earliest larvae seen were reported by Goin (1947a), who found a female with 27 eggs, many of which hatched just after their discovery on 14 January. The hatchlings ranged from 7.5 to 9.0 mm snout-vent and from 12.0 to 13.5 mm total length. Larvae metamorphose when the snout-vent length is about 37 mm, but they may attain much

larger sizes before transformation. Bruce (1968, 1974, 1975) also suggested that reproduction may be biennial. Larvae are light brown dorsally with scattered dark, irregular flecks. The brook-type larval form and high costal groove count of this species distinguish its larva from all other species except *P. ruber*, which utilizes the same habitat. (See *P. ruber* for statement of differences.)

Pseudotriton ruber (Sonnini)
Red Salamander
Plate III

Recognition. A robust salamander reaching 6¾ in. (162 mm) in total length but usually 4–5 in. (102–127 mm); snout length 1½ to 2 times the horizontal diameter of the eye and almost flat above; tail short, usually about 40 percent of the total length; dorsum salmon red to purplish brown, having numerous blue-black blotches often forming a "herringbone" pattern; venter spotted and distinctly lighter colored than the dorsum; snout and sides of the head peppered with white flecks; iris yellow; costal grooves usually 16, with 5 to 6½ intercostal folds between the adpressed limbs.

Similar species. The eye color, snout shape and length, and the spotted venter distinguish *Pseudotriton ruber* from the mud salamander, *P. montanus*.

Distribution. All verifiable records are from the longleaf pine hills and the edges of small streams in the bottomland hardwood forests in Washington Parish (Map 17). M. E. Palmer (1939) reported this species' occurrence in West Feliciana Parish; no specimen is extant, but he did include a photograph of the species.

Taxonomic comments. The subspecies occurring in Louisiana is the southern red salamander, *P. ruber vioscai* Bishop. Bruce (1968) suggested that this species has no clear-cut races, but we note that the southern red sala-

Map 17. Distribution of *Pseudotriton ruber*. Solid circles represent specimens examined; hollow circles represent museum specimens not examined or literature records.

mander is distinct in appearance from upland specimens. No comprehensive taxonomic study exists, but a list of papers pertinent to the systematics appeared in Martof (1975b).

Habitat and habits. The habitat is mainly along spring-fed streams in ravines or in bottomlands of small streams. Although this species might be found in the same area as the mud salamander, *P. montanus*, it selects drier, less swampy terrain. The animals are usually found under logs, debris, or leaves.

Very little is known of this race. Carr (1940) reported that in Florida specimens the stomach contents include beetles, beetle larvae, fly larvae, and hellgrammite larvae.

Reproduction. Very few data are available on this lowland race. Bishop (1943) found large ovarian eggs in a Florida female taken 31 August and reported some apparently recently hatched larvae (25 mm in total length and retaining considerable yolk) collected near Bogalusa, Washington Parish, 19 March. Bruce (1968, 1972, 1974) studied upland populations of *P. ruber* in South Carolina and

indicated that eggs are deposited about 1 October and hatch 1 December to begin a 33-month larval period. Bruce also suggested an annual breeding cycle for this species. The contrast in cited hatching dates indicates that much remains to be learned about the lowland *P. ruber* populations.

The larvae of *P. ruber* are darker than those of *P. montanus* and distinctly mottled or streaked. Large larvae may resemble the adult in terms of dorsal markings. The Tulane collections include a larva 57 mm in snout-vent length and 101 mm total length.

The brook-type larval form and high costal groove count separate *Pseudotriton* larvae from any other larvae found in their habitats.

FAMILY PROTEIDAE
MUDPUPPIES AND WATERDOGS

Living representatives of the family Proteidae include two genera and six species. Five species (*Necturus*) occur in the eastern United States and southeastern Canada, and the sixth species (*Proteus*) in southeastern Europe. Some authors place the European species, a blind, unpigmented cave dweller, in Proteidae and reclassify the North American species in the family Necturidae. All species are moderately large to large forms that dwell in streams and lakes and retain the gilled larval appearance throughout life. They are totally resistant to any attempts to force metamorphosis with hormonal stimulation.

Necturus beyeri Viosca
Gulf Coast Waterdog
Plate I

Recognition. A large (to 8¾ in., 222 mm, in total length) neotenic salamander with four toes on each hind foot, a brown back with numerous small dark spots, and a spotted belly in adults.

Similar species. The large size, the four toes, spotted belly, and the restriction of the dorsal fin to the tail readily distinguish this species from the larvae of the other four-toed salamanders of the state. The dorsal fin alone will distinguish the small larvae from those of *Eurycea quadridigitata* and *Hemidactylium scutatum*, whose dorsal fins extend onto the body. The spotted larvae separate this species from *Necturus maculosus*, whose larvae are striped. The spotted median area of the belly distinguishes adults from adult *N. maculosus*.

Distribution. Two disjunct areas are occupied: one, the streams of the Florida Parishes in the Mississippi River, Pearl River, and Lake Pontchartrain drainages, and the other in western Louisiana in drainages of the Sabine and Calcasieu rivers (Map 18).

Taxonomic comments. Several subspecies of *N. beyeri* may be recognized, but the systematics are complex (see Mount 1975).

Habitat and habits. Within its range this species is most abundant in the larger streams, yet it enters tributaries that may be only 10–13 ft wide. Within a stream the preferred habitats are those offering suitable cover, such as logs, stones, vegetation, and burrows. Juveniles are most frequently encountered in debris and leaves. Shoop and Gunning (1967) demonstrated that this species is active year-round, as evidenced by the stomach contents, which included principally crawfish plus some other invertebrates and small fishes. An electrical fish shocker was the most effective collecting tool used in their study, but they noted that baited hooks are also effective for catching adults, principally during the winter months when predatory fishes are not a deterrent to the salamanders' foraging away from cover. Waterdogs are nocturnal and may be seen walking over stream bottoms at night. Larvae can be easily collected from leaf accumulations by dip netting.

Shoop and Gunning (1967) found that waterdogs probably remain in a specific part of a

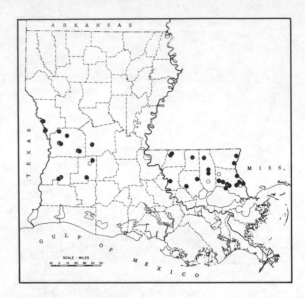

Map 18. Distribution of *Necturus beyeri*. Solid circles represent specimens examined; hollow circles represent museum specimens not examined or literature records.

stream for extended periods, and displaced animals often return to the site of original capture.

The large, blood-red gills of waterdogs are a gaudy sight. Captive specimens feed well on items such as earthworms, insects, and liver.

Reproduction. An excellent coverage of this subject appears in Shoop (1965). Males are sexually mature at a snout-vent length of 112–123 mm, and females at 115–135 mm. In southeastern Louisiana, males apparently produce spermatophores in December, and females deposit eggs in late April when water temperatures reach 18°–19°C (in nests found on 4 May there was some development of the eggs). The yellowish eggs, numbering up to 67, are slightly more than 6 mm in diameter and enclosed in an elastic gelatinous capsule that stretches downward into the nest cavity. The nests Shoop (1965) reported consisted of depressions scooped from the stream bottom under the edges of embedded projecting logs or under old boards embedded in the bottom.

The larvae hatched in 61 to 65 days after collection and had snout-vent lengths of 13–16 mm (21–26 mm total length).

Shoop (1962) presented data, unfortunately not included in his formally published version of 1965, revealing that *N. beyeri* has a growth pattern quite similar to that of *N. maculosus* in Louisiana. Both had growth patterns comparable to that Bishop (1941) showed for *N. maculosus* in New York. Some animals reach sexual maturity in their fifth or sixth year of life. Shoop also indicated that size groups for the individual years of birth are not as well discerned in Louisiana *Necturus*, a situation probably reflecting the more equitable temperatures of our more southern latitude.

Necturus maculosus Rafinesque
Mudpuppy
Plate I

Recognition. A large (to 11 in., 280 mm, total length) neotenic salamander having four toes on each hind foot; a tan or pale brownish ground color, darkest in the middorsal region, with a fairly distinct broad dorsolateral stripe on each side, and with numerous dorsal dark spots arranged in somewhat irregular rows; belly immaculate in larvae but in adults the lateral areas spotted and the median area immaculate; larvae with a yellowish ground color, a broad dark median stripe, and a dark stripe on either side, making the animal appear distinctly striped.

Similar species. Larvae are distinguishable from those of *Necturus beyeri* by virtue of being striped and from the other four-toed Louisiana salamanders by the dorsal fin being limited to the tail rather than extending onto the back. Adults lack the spotting in the median part of the belly seen in *N. beyeri*.

Distribution. Occurs only in the Red River drainage system of northern Louisiana (Map 19).

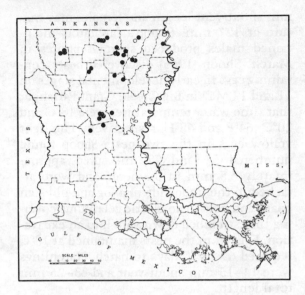

Map 19. Distribution of *Necturus maculosus.* Solid circles represent specimens examined; hollow circles represent museum specimens not examined or literature records.

Taxonomic comments. Several subspecies have been recognized, some of which various authors have allocated to either *N. beyeri* or *N. maculosus.* Fortunately the race found in Louisiana has not been involved in this controversy and is readily assigned to *N. maculosus louisianensis* Viosca, the Red River mudpuppy.

Mount (1975) gave an account of the various attempts to interpret *Necturus* systematics, as well as some of his own observations on this species in Alabama, the most critical area for the complex relationships.

Habitat and habits. This species is normally a stream dweller, but it thrives in impoundments such as Horseshoe Lake in Caldwell Parish and Lake D'Arbonne in Union Parish. It is most prevalent where submerged cover objects and burrows are available. The habits, as revealed by Shoop and Gunning (1967), are similar to those of *N. beyeri.*

Reproduction. Shoop (1965) reported that males may become sexually mature at 130 mm snout-vent length and females may mature at 127 mm. Shoop's laboratory-maintained males produced spermatophores in March. Shoop (1965) discovered nests containing eggs in early developmental stages on 11 and 17 May in Big Creek, Grant Parish; at that time water temperatures were 18°C and 20°C (64°F and 68°F), respectively. The light yellow eggs in the two nests Shoop found numbered 51 and 22, measured approximately 6.5 mm in diameter, and were attached to the underside of a log and old sign board and held in an elastic gelatinous covering that stretched downward into an excavation. Eggs from the nests maintained at 18°C required 69 to 70 days to hatch. Hatchlings were 14–15 mm snout-vent and 23–25 mm total length.

FAMILY SALAMANDRIDAE
NEWTS

The very successful family Salamandridae comprises 16 living genera having 53 species, of which 2 genera and 6 species occur in the United States. The others range throughout Europe and Asia and reach extreme northern Africa. The group exhibits a wide variety of life histories; some species reenter water after a postmetamorphic land phase, others never become secondarily aquatic, and still others may be neotenic. Some European species exhibit ovoviviparity. Aquatic adult phases are called newts; immature land phases are called efts.

Notophthalmus viridescens Rafinesque
Eastern Newt
Plate II

Recognition. Two phases of the post-larval animal must be considered: the eft, an immature phase found in terrestrial situations, and the adult newt, a secondarily aquatic form that develops after the eft stage or that may develop directly from larvae without entering the eft stage. Eft: total length 1¾–3 in. (43–77 mm); skin granular; costal grooves not evident or poorly developed; longitudinal cranial ridges present on the head; tail circular in cross section; dorsal color dull olive to red, with scattered black specks; venter yellowish orange with scattered black flecks. Newt: total length to 4¾ in. (122 mm); skin smoother than in eft; costal grooves not evident or poorly developed; tail compressed and with fins; breeding males with a strongly developed fin and with enlarged hind limbs bearing blackish excrescence; occasional adults with gill vestiges; color brown to olive with a black speckled yellow belly.

Distribution. Statewide except for the coastal salt marshes (Map 20).

Taxonomic comments. Only a single subspecies, *Notophthalmus viridescens louisianensis* (Wolterstorff), the central newt, occurs in Louisiana. No single study treats the taxonomy of this species, but Mecham (1967) summarized the current systematic allocations.

Habitat and habits. Efts are found most commonly in woodlands under logs, boards, and debris or well within the interior of decaying logs. The aquatic phases are commonly encountered in ditches, woodland ponds, swamps, and sluggish streams.

Although the skin of the efts has a dry appearance and they are relatively resistant to dehydration, they usually remain near a source of moisture. Animals found under boards and logs in dry pond beds may even appear to be emaciated.

The food is reported to be all sorts of invertebrates, especially arthropods and snails, and on occasion newts feed on the eggs of other species of salamanders. Cagle (notes) observed that some adults taken in June from St. Tammany Parish would feign death by rolling over on their backs, closing their eyes, and lying quiet for several seconds; the performance was repeated regularly when they were disturbed.

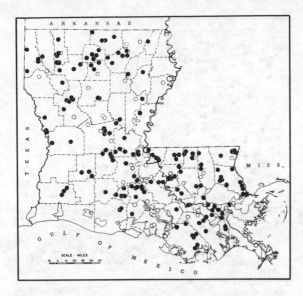

Map 20. Distribution of *Notophthalmus viridescens*. Solid circles represent specimens examined; hollow circles represent museum specimens not examined or literature records.

Reproduction. Viosca (according to Bishop 1943) reported collecting breeding pairs on 22 February 1938 in Grant Parish. Bishop (1943) indicated that he collected animals in breeding condition on 19 March 1936 in Livingston Parish. Eggs are surely laid much earlier than Viosca's observation would suggest; the newly hatched larvae are reported to measure 7.5 mm in total length, and the Tulane collection contains larvae measuring 19–33 mm collected on 14 March. Bishop (1943) stated that in New York, egg incubation required 20 to 35 days and the larval period might be 84 days. Allowing for latitudinal differences and growth rates, eggs could be laid in mid-January in southern Louisiana. The fact that ripe-appearing females have been taken on 8 June suggests that the breeding season is greatly prolonged, as was confirmed when Dundee collected larvae up to 33 mm long on 25 September in the Rigolets area of St. Tammany Parish and found 60 newly transformed young under a board in St. Charles Parish on 25 January 1973. Liner (1954) reported

courtship behavior in animals collected 2 March 1952.

The egg-laying habits probably are comparable to those of the nominate race, *N. v. viridescens*, whose reproductive activities Bishop (1941) detailed. Several hundred eggs are produced over a period of days and attached singly to vegetation.

The smallest larva seen in Louisiana was taken on 5 May and measures 9 mm total length; the largest measures 43 mm and was taken 15 April. Newly transformed individuals have been secured as early as 22 May. The larvae are of the pond type and are readily recognized by the black stripe that passes from the snout through the eye and onto the side of the head.

FAMILY SIRENIDAE
SIRENS

The family Sirenidae is an unusual assemblage of two living genera comprising three species. Members of this family have a number of features that differ from those of conventional salamanders, thus leading some systematists to place them in a separate order of amphibians. Externally, at least, they appear to be eel-like, aquatic, neotenic salamanders that have no hind limbs. The coastal plain of the southeastern United States is the primary area of distribution, but the range of one species extends northward through the Mississippi River drainage to central Illinois and northern Indiana, and southward to Mexico adjacent to the lower Rio Grande valley of Texas.

Siren intermedia Le Conte
Lesser Siren
Plate I

Recognition. An unusual neotenic salamander rarely exceeding 11 in. (280 mm) in total length in Louisiana (largest Louisiana specimen measures 16⁹⁄₁₀ in., 430 mm), but elsewhere averaging almost 20 in. (502 mm) and attaining a maximum of 27 in. (686 mm); body eel-like; no hind limbs; each foreleg with four toes; gills bushy but becoming considerably reduced under drought conditions; adult coloration grayish blue to olive, brown, or black, with scattered dark dots; juveniles proportioned like conventional salamanders, but a high costal groove count (36 to 40) to the vent is distinctive (newly hatched salamanders of other species sometimes not having all of the limbs or toes developed).

Distribution. Statewide in freshwater habitats (Map 21). Although no records are available from the northern Mississippi River floodplain, *Siren* probably occurs there.

Taxonomic comments. One subspecies, *S. intermedia nettingi* Goin, the western lesser siren, occurs in Louisiana. No comprehensive treatment of the taxonomy of this species exists, but Goin (1957) provided useful taxonomic criteria.

Habitat and habits. This species' major habitat is ditches and ponds, but it also utilizes small streams, swamps, woodland pools, and sloughs. Large numbers of lesser sirens are sometimes found in borrow pits along the Mississippi River batture near New Orleans; thus, they must inhabit large streams as well. Neill (1958a) cited a personal report by J. R. Dixon of a specimen in a brackish-water setting in Cameron Parish.

Sirens are secretive and usually burrow into the mud or debris of the bottom. The best time to capture lesser sirens is at night when they emerge, but by day electric fish shockers have proved quite effective in routing them from their hiding places. Cloth-covered wire funnel traps can also be used to capture sirens. If the habitat dries, this salamander may burrow into the bottom and can secrete a "cocoon" from the skin glands that will protect it from desiccation.

This species is named "siren" because it may give a yelping or whistling sound, or clicks.

The food habits have been debated because

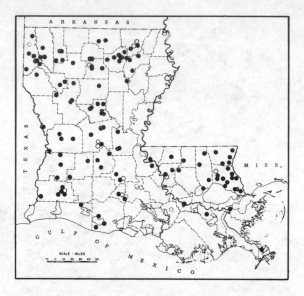

Map 21. Distribution of *Siren intermedia*. Solid circles represent specimens examined; hollow circles represent museum specimens not examined or literature records.

of the amount of vegetation found in the stomach contents. Scroggin and Davis (1956) have offered the plausible explanation that in many *Siren* habitats prey items, such as snails, crustaceans, and insects, hide in vegetation, and *Siren* ingests the vegetation along with the prey.

Reproduction. Virtually nothing is known about the reproductive behavior of this species; in fact, biologists are not certain if the Sirenidae have internal or external fertilization. The lack of cloacal glands in males and spermathecae in females suggests that fertilization may be external, but the distribution of some sirenid eggs (genus *Pseudobranchus*) is scattered, and such a distribution could be successfully carried out only if fertilization is internal. The few nests of *S. intermedia* that have been found, however, contained clusters of eggs, so the mystery remains. Nests discovered in Arkansas consisted of a small pocket in the bottom of a pond. The eggs, each about 3 mm in diameter and 6.0–6.5 mm including the gelatinous envelopes, numbered about 200. The eggs have pigment distributed on the surface. A specimen from near Blanchard, Caddo Parish, laid eight eggs in the laboratory on 30 January 1980. The eggs were somewhat clustered and attached to a leaf.

The probable time of hatching in Louisiana is midwinter. Newly hatched larvae have been reported to be about 11 mm in total length; near Slidell, larvae of 16 mm have been collected from 18 February to 12 March.

The coloration of the larvae is distinctively different from that of the adults. There is a middorsal light stripe, ventrolateral light stripes, and the snout and top of the head are marked with orange or red. The light band on the snout is persistent and makes a good identification feature of larvae.

ORDER ANURA: *Frogs and Toads*

The order Anura comprises more than 3,400 living species, constituting perhaps 20 to 21 families, and is cosmopolitan except that none occur in polar regions and only a few species reach the Arctic Circle. All of the species have abbreviated, chunky bodies, no tail (but a few primitive species have very short, fleshy, tail-like appendages), and elongated hind limbs used by most for leaping. The distinction between the terms "frog" and "toad" is poor, but the term "toad" is best applied to the members of the family Bufonidae, who have rather dry skins and prefer rather dry habitats. Most anurans live near the edge of a body of water, on a moist forest floor, or in the trees, but some are secretive and hide beneath objects. A few tropical species are wholly aquatic. All adult anurans are carnivores and may eat any animal small enough to swallow.

Reproduction and developmental processes of the Anura constitute an exciting field for study because of the many remarkable phenomena involved. In virtually every species of anuran the males have voices whose sounds can be modified and magnified by vocal sacs located beneath the throat or at its sides. Males go to breeding sites where they commence singing. Each species has a unique call that ordinarily attracts only females of that species. The females, at most, can utter only a few ill-defined peeps. Anurans have no copulatory organ except for a few primitive forms whose fleshy tail-like appendages guide sperm into the female cloaca. Thus, fertilization is external in virtually all anurans. When the female has been attracted to the male, he grasps her from behind between the fore and hind limbs, a process called amplexus. The male releases his sperm over the eggs as they emerge from the female. Five exotic species of anurans are known to be ovoviviparous, but their means of sperm transfer is unknown.

Typical anurans lay gelatinous eggs in water, but several hundred species lay eggs in damp places on land; still other species lay eggs in leaf envelopes above the water, or carry the eggs on the body, or within special pouches in the skin, or even within the mouth or the digestive tract. When eggs are laid somewhere other than in water, the developing young may undergo direct development (they have a tail but no gills) and emerge from the eggs as miniatures of the adults. In the typical development in water, the tadpole, a larval stage, emerges when the eggs hatch. For a few days the tadpole exhibits external gills, but they are soon concealed by a flap of flesh, the operculum, that forms a chamber by which usually a single small opening, the spiracle, connects to the exterior. The tadpole has a fleshy, finned tail; lidless eyes; and specialized larval teeth (made of keratin, a horny substance, hence not true teeth). Except for a few tropical species, the tadpoles are vegetarians or scavengers. The gut, a long coil resembling a watch spring, is an adaptation for digesting vegetable matter. As the tadpole ages, the limbs begin to appear, and during metamorphosis the tail and fins are resorbed, the skin becomes glandular, the eyes develop lids, the skull is restructured, true teeth form, and the gut becomes shorter as it becomes adapted for digesting flesh. The newly transformed froglet then undergoes a period of growth to reach its adult size.

KEY TO THE TRANSFORMED FROGS AND TOADS OF LOUISIANA

1. Snout distinctly pointed; tympanum absent; a transverse fold of skin across head in back of eyes (indistinct in many preserved specimens); toes unwebbed

    Gastrophryne carolinensis (p. 104)

    Snout rounded or only somewhat pointed; tympanum present; no fold of skin on head; toes webbed or not   2

2. Pupil of eye vertically elliptical; underside of heel with a single spadelike metatarsal tubercle; parotoid glands present

    Scaphiopus holbrookii (p. 105)

    Pupil rounded or horizontally elliptical; heel with two metatarsal spades or none; parotoid glands prominent or lacking   3

3. Distinct parotoid glands, cranial crests, and metatarsal spades present; skin dry and warty   4*

    No parotoid glands, cranial crests, or spades; skin moist and smooth or with small granular bumps   8

4. Adult size less than 35 mm snout-vent length; dorsum with 4 to 5 pairs of dark spots separated by a distinct middorsal light line

    Bufo quercicus (p. 80)

    Adult size more than 35 mm snout-vent length; if under 35 mm snout-vent length then parotoid glands not well developed; middorsal light line absent or present; no prominent paired blotches on dorsum, but spots of various form and size may be present   5

5. Parotoid glands short, usually triangular or somewhat circular in shape; strongly

developed, ridged, black-topped cranial crests on head; a broad, dark lateral stripe bordered above by a yellowish stripe

    Bufo valliceps (p. 82)

    Parotoids elongated, with straight edges, or elongated and kidney-bean shaped; cranial crests low, unpigmented, and rounded on top   6

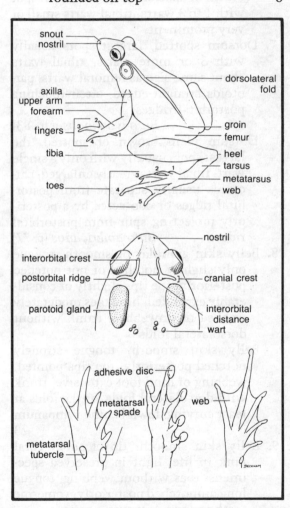

Figure 4.   Structural features of adult anurans: dorsolateral view of a ranid frog (upper); dorsal view of the head of a bufonid toad (middle); and ventral view of the hind foot of a toad, a treefrog, and a semiaquatic frog (lower, from left to right).

*Couplet 4 leads to members of the genus *Bufo*, the true toads. Extensive hybridization makes these animals difficult to identify by key. In southeastern Louisiana, known hybrids include *B. valliceps* × *B. woodhousei*, *B. valliceps* × *B. terrestris*, *B. valliceps* × *B. woodhousei* × *B. terrestris*, *B. terrestris* × *B. woodhousei*, and quite possibly hybrids of *B. americanus* with *B. valliceps*, *B. woodhousei*, and *B. terrestris* exist. In hybrids, morphological characters and voices are modified.

6. Posterior end of cranial crests with knoblike enlargements in adults; dorsal skin usually rough and spiny, strongly patterned with dark spots containing 1 to 3 warts each; tibial warts moderately large
Bufo terrestris (p. 80)

Posterior ends of cranial crests without knoblike enlargements; dorsal skin rugose, spiny or not; dorsum plain brown or spotted; if spotted, each spot with 1 to 3 warts; tibial warts small or very prominent   7

7. Dorsum spotted, largest spots usually with 3 or more warts; tibial warts about same size as femoral warts; parotoids straight-edged, often touching postorbital ridges
Bufo woodhousei (p. 83)

Dorsum plain brown or spotted, the largest spots usually with only a single wart; tibial warts greatly enlarged; parotoids usually separate from postorbital ridges or contacted by a posteriorly projecting spur from postorbital ridges   *Bufo americanus* (p. 77)

8. Belly skin granular or smooth; tongue only slightly notched or not notched posteriorly; toe tips slightly or considerably expanded; hind toes moderately webbed or unwebbed; trunk without dorsolateral folds   9

Belly skin smooth; tongue strongly notched posteriorly; toe tips pointed; webbing of hind foot extensive; trunk with dorsolateral folds, or the folds at least curving down behind tympanum   23

9. Belly skin smooth; tip of snout coral pink in life, light in preserved specimens; toes without webbing; tongue long, unnotched posteriorly; vomerine teeth in long, transverse series
Eleutherodactylus planirostris (p. 102)

Belly skin granular; tip of snout dark and dull colored, gray to green or brown; webbing of hind toes slight or moderate; tongue rounded and slightly notched or unnotched behind; vomerine teeth in compact, short, rounded patches   10

10. Toe tips only slightly broadened; rear of thigh with dark stripe or elongated, ragged band; snout with vertical light lines   11

Toe tips slightly or conspicuously broadened into adhesive discs; rear of thigh without dark, longitudinal stripes; snout lacking vertical light lines   12

11. Only 1½ to 2 joints of fourth toe free of webbing; rear of thigh with ragged-edged dark band; snout rounded
Acris crepitans (p. 85)

Three or more joints of fourth toe free of webbing, thus giving toe long, free-projecting appearance; rear of thigh with a smooth-edged dark stripe; snout pointed   *Acris gryllus* (p. 87)

12. Toe tips only slightly expanded (less than one-half the diameter of tympanum)   13

Toe tips broadened, at least one-half or more the diameter of tympanum   16

13. Dorsal pattern with three or more stripes, sometimes broken into linearly arranged spots; body form relatively slender   14

Dorsal pattern with a few large spots or two elongated bands; body stout   15

14. A dark, triangular blotch or expanded spot between the eyes; stripes dark, continuous, or broken into a series of spots, the middle one usually remaining as a single line; snout rounded
Pseudacris triseriata (p. 100)

Stripe between eyes not expanded laterally; stripes usually broken into spots and black in color; middle stripe tending to fork at posterior end; snout more pointed   *Pseudacris nigrita* (p. 100)
(Questionable in Louisiana. If occurring in the state it would be along the Pearl River in Washington and St. Tammany parishes. One report [Gartside 1980]

indicates that this species hybridizes with *P. triseriata* along the Pearl River boundary.)

15. Forearm stout, toadlike; a dark suborbital spot present; dorsal pattern spotted; sides often with several dark spots
Pseudacris streckeri (p. 99)
Forearm not so stout; no suborbital dark spot; dorsum plain or with two broad, dark, elongated bands; sides often with single dark spot
Pseudacris ornata (p. 98)

16. A light spot below each eye   17
No light spot   19

17. Rear of thigh partly green in life; skin relatively smooth   *Hyla avivoca* (p. 87)
Rear of thigh with yellow or orange in life; skin somewhat granular   18

18. Fresh erythrocytes (samples of 10) 17.9–23.8 μ long, average 20.56; each cell of nictitating membrane with 3 to 4 nucleoli; voice a slow trill
Hyla versicolor (p. 89)
Fresh erythrocytes 14.9–17.9 μ long, average 16.37; each cell of nictitating membrane with 1 to 2 nucleoli; voice a fast trill
Hyla chrysoscelis (p. 89)

19. Dorsum with a dark x-shaped mark or variation thereof; no light spots on rear of thigh
Hyla crucifer (p. 93)
Dorsum plain, spotted, or streaked, but never with suggestion of x-shaped pattern; light spots on rear of thigh present or absent   20

20. Yellow-orange light spots on rear of thigh in life; no light stripe on upper jaw or side of body
Hyla femoralis (p. 94)
Rear of thigh without light spots; upper jaw and/or body with light stripe   21

21. Dorsum granular and with numerous rounded or ovate, dark-bordered spots, but can become almost uniformly green; upper jaw with light pigment continuing on side of body as ragged

light stripe; snout-vent length to 70 mm   *Hyla gratiosa* (p. 95)
Dorsum smooth and usually uniformly green, or if spotted then spots irregular and not dark-bordered; upper jaw and side of body with sharply defined or ragged white line; snout-vent length to 65 mm, usually less than 60 mm   22

22. Dorsal color typically green with a few golden spots present; a sharply defined white lateral stripe; snout-vent length to 65 mm   *Hyla cinerea* (p. 91)
Dorsal color highly variable, plain green or olive to brown, with or without dark spots; lateral light stripe with poorly defined borders; maximum snout-vent length 43 mm   *Hyla squirella* (p. 97)

23. Dorsolateral folds on trunk   24
No dorsolateral folds on trunk; folds ending just behind tympanum   27

24. Dorsal pattern of large, dark spots; dorsolateral folds extending to groin   25
Dorsal pattern of small, dark spots or no spots; dorsolateral folds extending only about two-thirds the length of trunk   *Rana clamitans* (p. 111)

25. Dorsal spots invading dorsolateral folds; dorsal skin smooth or warty; body chunky; venter immaculate or heavily spotted; upper jaw without light line
Rana areolata (p. 107)
Dorsal spots not invading dorsolateral folds; dorsal skin smooth or with elongated narrow ridges; body more slender; venter immaculate; light line on upper jaw   26

26. Dorsal spots between dorsolateral folds squarish, arranged into 2 longitudinal rows and larger than interspaces; groin and underside of legs yellow to orange in life   *Rana palustris* (p. 114)
Dorsal spots more rounded or oval, usually irregularly arranged or in somewhat longitudinal rows; interspaces larger than spots; groin and underside of legs without yellow or orange
Rana sphenocephala (p. 115)

27. Fifth toe, when adpressed to 4th toe, reaching to or beyond base of next to last joint of 4th toe; head more pointed, the T/E ratio (the distance between the eyes when divided into the distance between midpoints of tympana) usually (75 percent) exceeding 8.8, never less than 7.0; young, and occasionally adults, with a pair of broad tan dorsolateral bands   *Rana grylio* (p. 113)

Fifth toe, when adpressed to 4th toe, short of base of next to last joint of 4th toe; head more rounded, the T/E ratio less than 8.8 (less than 7.0 in 33 percent of specimens); young and adults often mottled or with pinhead-sized dark spots but never with tan dorsolateral bands

Rana catesbeiana (p. 109)

KEY TO THE TADPOLES OF LOUISIANA

1. No free-living tadpoles; eggs laid on land
Eleutherodactylus planirostris (p. 102)
Tadpoles free in water   2
2. Mouthparts simple; no oral disc, labial teeth, beak, or labial papillae
Gastrophryne carolinensis (p. 104)
Mouthparts complex; oral disc, labial teeth, beak, and labial papillae present
3
3. Anus median; eyes dorsal; no submarginal papillae on lower lip; total length less than 40 mm   4
Anus opens on right side of tail fin; eyes dorsal or lateral; submarginal papillae on lower lip; total length often exceeding 40 mm (as much as 170 mm)   9
4. Lips not infolded; marginal papillae along full length of lower lip; nostrils small   *Scaphiopus holbrookii* (p. 105)
Lips infolded laterally; marginal papillae confined to sides of lips, leaving dorsal and ventral gaps; nostrils often large   5*

5. Dorsal fin dark, with complex reticulation; lower labial tooth rows about equal in length or P–3 subequal to P–1; dorsal tail musculature dark with light spots along margin; younger larvae with bicolored musculature
Bufo valliceps (p. 82)
Dorsal fin dark, without complex reticu-

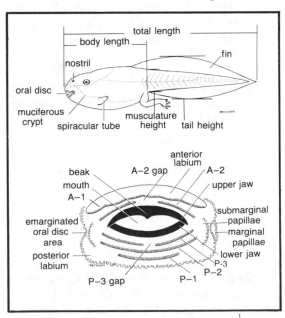

Figure 5.   Structural features of larval anurans: lateral view of a tadpole (upper) and front view of an oral disc (lower).

NOTE: Adapted in part from Altig, R. 1970. A key to the tadpoles of the United States and Canada. *Herpetologica* 26:180–207.
    *Hybridization is common among the four large species of toads in Louisiana (*Bufo valliceps, B. americanus, B. terrestris, B. woodhousei*), and tadpoles resulting from hybrid crosses may not separate successfully in this key—or any key.

lation; P–3 shorter than P–1; tail musculature usually bicolored, with or without lighter areas in dorsal margin 6

6. Dorsal tail musculature with light saddles in dorsal margin
    Bufo quercicus (p. 80)
    Dorsal tail musculature rather uniformly pigmented and with regular melanophore border 7

7. Dorsal fin often higher than ventral fin; dorsum dark brown or black with light, oblique mark behind each eye in life *Bufo terrestris* (p. 80)
    Dorsal and ventral fins approximately equal in height; dorsum dark or mottled; no light mark behind eye in life 8

8. Dorsum unicolored, dark; throat largely pigmented; dorsal tail musculature usually dark; eye small; snout sloping in lateral view; tail height/musculature height 2.0 or less
    Bufo americanus (p. 77)
    Dorsum with light mottlings in life; throat usually light or with clear patch; dorsal tail musculature often with unpigmented patches; snout rounded; eye large; tail height/musculature height 2.0 or more
    Bufo woodhousei (p. 83)

9. Eyes dorsal; lips infolded laterally; papillary border not or barely reaching above lateral tips of A–1; total length to 170 mm 10
    Eyes lateral or dorsal; lips not infolded laterally; papillary border reaching well above lateral tips of A–1; total length usually less than 55 mm but may reach 71 mm 15

10. Body and tail green, unicolored or usually with numerous distinct black dots; fins also with dots, more so in dorsal fin; venter cream or yellow, often with contrasting pattern; nostrils small, indistinct; beak with nar-

row, black edges; length often exceeding 100 mm
    Rana catesbeiana (p. 109)
    Body and tail green or not, seldom with black dots; fins variously patterned; venter white or dark, with or without contrasting pattern; nostrils small or moderately large; beak with narrow, moderate, or wide black edges; size to 100 mm 11

11. Beak and lower jaw with narrow, black edges; nostrils small; skin thick or not, but gut usually not visible 12
    Beak and lower jaw with wide, black edges; nostrils medium-sized; skin thin, usually rendering gut visible 13

12. Dorsal fin with a stripe or row of dots; tail musculature with less prominent stripe; edges of fins with light spots surrounded by dark pigment; tooth rows 1/3 or 3/3; tail crest high, tapering steeply to the sharply pointed tip
    Rana grylio (p. 113)
    Dorsal fin and tail musculature without stripe; edges of fins without light spots surrounded by dark pigment, or spots indistinct; tooth rows 1/3, 2/3, or 3/3; tail crest lower; tail tip acute
    Rana clamitans (p. 111)

13. A–2 gap ratio 2.0 or more; marginal papillae below P–3 large, 10 or fewer present; fins usually heavily marked, often with dark suffusion; P–1/P–3 1.3 or more; tooth rows 1/3 or 2/3
    Rana palustris (p. 114)
    A–2 gap ratio less than 2.0; marginal papillae below P–3 small, more than 10 present; fins clear to heavily mottled, speckled, or spotted; P–1/P–3 1.5 or less; tooth rows 1/3, 2/3, or 3/3 14

14. Gut usually visible; throat, if pigmented, usually with an unpigmented patch; tail, if marked, usually without large spots; dorsum not stippled; dorsal fin rounded; keratinized areas at medial tips of P–1 absent; body not conspic-

uously marked with yellow; muciferous crypts not conspicuous

> *Rana sphenocephala* (p. 115)

Gut visible or not; throat unpigmented or evenly pigmented; tail, if marked, usually with large spots; dorsum often stippled; dorsal fin frequently triangular; keratinized areas present at medial tips of P–1 in large specimens; body in southeastern Louisiana conspicuously marked with yellow; muciferous crypts conspicuous

> *Rana areolata* (p. 107)

15. Posterior labium with two rows of teeth 16

Posterior labium with three rows of teeth 19

16. A–2 gap wide; spiracular tube at least partially free from body wall; tail tip frequently black; eyes dorsolateral; nostrils large; body slightly depressed; fins without bold markings 17

A–2 gap narrow; spiracular tube almost fully attached to body wall; tail tip never black; eyes lateral; nostrils small or large; body globular; fins with or without bold markings 18

17. Spiracular tube mostly free from body wall; throat dark; body dark and without pattern; tail musculature finely flecked *Acris gryllus* (p. 87)

Spiracular tube free for one-half or less its length; throat light; body pale, with contrasting dark saddles; dorsal tail musculature usually banded

> *Acris crepitans* (p. 85)

18. Tail musculature unicolored or bicolored; one row of marginal papillae; tail fins weakly pigmented; A–2 nearly equal to A–1

> *Pseudacris triseriata* (part) (p. 100)

Tail musculature heavily mottled; two rows of marginal papillae; tail fins heavily mottled; A–2 longer than A–1
Hyla crucifer (part) (p. 93)

19. Papillary border with a posterior gap
Hyla crucifer (part) (p. 93)

Papillary border without a posterior gap 20

20. Tail musculature dark with light (coppery red in life) dorsal saddles; fins dark with at most only fine markings; light orbitonasal and interorbital bands present in life; gut not visible; total length to 32 mm

> *Hyla avivoca* (p. 87)

Tail musculature dark or light without dorsal saddles; tail fin clear or variously patterned; no interorbital light band, orbitonasal light band present or not; gut visible or not; total length to 71 mm 21

21. P–3 long, 0.65 or more times as long as P–2 and longer than upper jaw; submarginal papillae well developed 22

P–3 short, less than 0.65 times as long as P–2 and equal to or shorter than upper jaw; submarginal papillae poorly developed or absent 24

22. Tail musculature striped; fins flecked or blotched, with clear areas near musculature; clear part of fin red in large, living specimens; flagellum well developed and unpigmented; total length to 36 mm *Hyla femoralis* (p. 94)

Tail musculature not distinctly striped; fins blotched or not, with or without clear area near musculature; clear part of fin red or not; flagellum moderately developed; total length to 50 mm 23

23. Tail height/body height in lateral view 1.5 or less; dorsal fin equal to or greater than musculature height; greatest body width/basal width of tail musculature 2.7 or more; throat usually unpigmented; large specimens with red fins; total length to 50 mm

> *Hyla chrysoscelis–Hyla versicolor*
> complex (p. 89)

Tail height/body height in lateral view 1.5 or more; dorsal fin less than musculature height; greatest body width/basal width of tail musculature 2.7 or less; throat usually pigmented; large specimens without red fins; total length to 38 mm

Hyla squirella (p. 97)

24. Jaw wide; upper jaw angulate; dorsal fin high, terminating anterior to spiracle; tail clear, black, or mottled; dorsal tail musculature of specimens less than 30 mm total length with a conspicuous black saddle; total length to 71 mm

Hyla gratiosa (p. 95)

Jaw narrow to moderately wide; upper jaw not angulate; dorsal fin high or not; tail clear or blotched; no black saddle in tail fin; length to 43 mm   25

25. Fins and tail musculature usually mottled or reticulated, with no clear area near musculature; A–2 gap ratio 3.0 or more; light orbitonasal stripe present in life; small specimens with an incomplete transverse body band formed from two light blotches

Hyla cinerea (p. 91)

Fins not mottled or reticulated but sometimes blotched; if blotched, a clear area present near musculature; A–2

gap ratio 3.0 or less; no orbitonasal light stripe or light body blotches   26

26. Fins blotched; tail musculature mottled; P–3 very short

Hyla crucifer (part) (p. 93)

Fins clear or with a few melanophores; tail musculature mottled, unicolored, bicolored, or striped   27

27. Tail height usually 2.8 times or less the musculature height; dorsal fin low, terminating posterior to spiracle; tail musculature unicolored or indistinctly bicolored; P–1 without median gap; fins often pigmented

Pseudacris triseriata (part) (p. 100)

Tail height usually 3.5 times the musculature height; dorsal fin high, terminating anterior to spiracle; tail musculature distinctly bicolored; P–1 with or without median gap, or at least indented; fins clear or only slightly pigmented   28

28. P–3 almost as long as either half of A–2

Pseudacris ornata (p. 98)

P–3 much shorter than either half of A–2

Pseudacris streckeri (p. 99)

During much of the year the vocalizations of male frogs and toads are a conspicuous part of the nighttime environment in rural and urban Louisiana. As long as temperatures remain several degrees above freezing, some species of anuran is likely to be singing, at least at night. Some of the sounds are a pleasure to hear, but others, particularly in large choruses, may be annoying. Experienced biologists soon learn to recognize and even imitate the characteristic sounds of the various species and thus can locate their desired quarry or plot its distribution without ever seeing an anuran. Differences in the vocalizations, habitats where breeding pools are located, time of year of breeding, and temperature requirements for breeding all help reduce competition between breeding anurans and provide for reproductive isolation that will ensure retention of species identity. Each species may have a particular kind of water requirement—temporary, permanent, shallow, deep, clear, murky, open, weedy, etc.—and if the same pool is utilized it may be at a different season or in a part of the pool offering the correct conditions.

Figure 6 depicts the seasons when Louisiana anurans sing, and Figure 7, the temperature range for known vocalization of each species. Figure 7, however, gives only air temperatures; the critical temperature actually is the body temperature of the singing animal, not of the air. Some time may elapse before body temperatures equilibrate with air or water temperatures.

The following summary of sounds anurans emit will assist the novice in identifying species by call. The ultimate proof of identification, of course, is seeing the actual animal in song. By combining the data presented in Figures 6 and 7 with this summary, the observer can achieve a high degree of accuracy of identification.

Deep hum or drone, "brrr woom," "ooohoo-oom," or "ooowoom"
> *Rana catesbeiana*

Piglike grunt *Rana grylio*

Snorelike quality
> Low snore of 1–2 seconds duration
> > *Rana palustris*
> Deep snore *Rana areolata*

Sheeplike "waaah" with nasal quality and of about 2 seconds duration
> *Bufo woodhousei*

Deep, explosive, nasal "waank" or "waagh"
> *Scaphiopus holbrookii*

Low buzz, "b-zzzzz"
> *Gastrophryne carolinensis*

Banjolike quality, explosive single note or series of plunks descending in scale; sometimes a faint banjolike plunk
> *Rana clamitans*

Clicking or rattling sound like pebbles being struck together in rapid sequence, "gick, gick, gick . . ." *Acris crepitans*

As above, but somewhat nasal
> *Acris gryllus*

Whistle, peep, or chirp
> Whistle, such as might be emitted from pursed lips as short pipings *Hyla avivoca*
> Whistlelike high peep, somewhat slurred and higher pitched at end and given in 1-second intervals *Hyla crucifer*
> Faint peep, like a chick's (but in large chorus, the noise is loud), slurred downward at end *Bufo quercicus*
> Clear peep resembling sound of hammer striking a chisel and given at 1–1½-second intervals *Pseudacris ornata*
> "Ka week" like a turning, ungreased wooden wheel *Pseudacris streckeri*

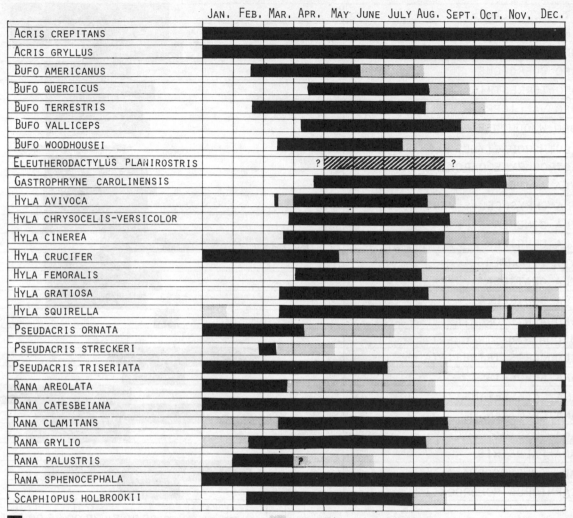

	Jan.	Feb.	Mar.	Apr.	May	June	July	Aug.	Sept.	Oct.	Nov.	Dec.
Acris crepitans												
Acris gryllus												
Bufo americanus												
Bufo quercicus												
Bufo terrestris												
Bufo valliceps												
Bufo woodhousei												
Eleutherodactylus planirostris												
Gastrophryne carolinensis												
Hyla avivoca												
Hyla chrysocelis-versicolor												
Hyla cinerea												
Hyla crucifer												
Hyla femoralis												
Hyla gratiosa												
Hyla squirella												
Pseudacris ornata												
Pseudacris streckeri												
Pseudacris triseriata												
Rana areolata												
Rana catesbeiana												
Rana clamitans												
Rana grylio												
Rana palustris												
Rana sphenocephala												
Scaphiopus holbrookii												

■ SINGING. EGGS AND/OR LARVAE MAY BE PRESENT.   ▨ EGGS AND/OR LARVAE TO BE EXPECTED.

▨ SPECULATIVE...NO DATA AVAILABLE.

Figure 6. Seasonal reproductive aspects of Louisiana frogs and toads. Where the stippled area extends beyond the black bar, eggs can be expected for only a brief period (the length of the incubation period is highly variable, depending on temperature, or is not known for this area). The end of the stippled line depicts the expected latest date, assuming that eggs were deposited at the last known date for singing and that development to transformation takes the maximum known (or estimated) time.

Faint, cricketlike chirp
     Eleutherodactylus planirostris
Rasping chirp, "waaaak," 1–2 seconds long
  and in series   *Hyla squirella*
Rasping, grating chirp such as made by fin-

ger running over a coarse-toothed comb
     Pseudacris triseriata
Rapid clicking like a telegraph key or riveting
machine, only more throaty
     Hyla femoralis

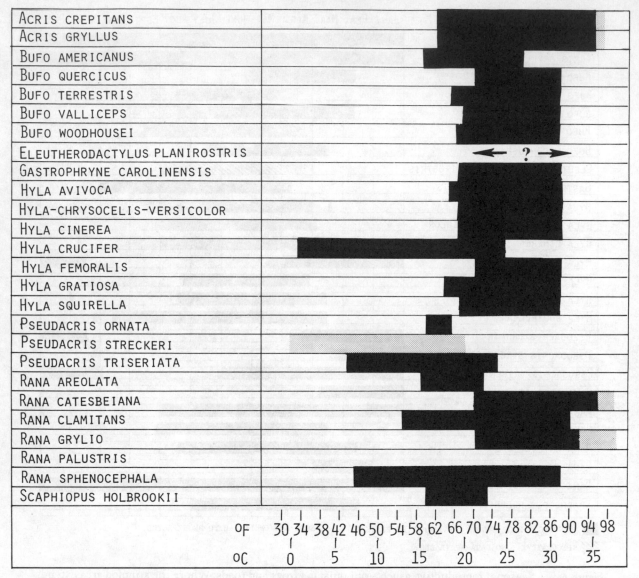

Figure 7. Singing temperatures for Louisiana frogs and toads. Values given are air temperatures, not actual animal body temperatures or water temperatures if the animals were in water. Blackened spaces represent temperatures at which animals were observed singing in Louisiana, except the temperatures shown for *Pseudacris streckeri*, which represent values observed in other states. Stippled areas indicate summer daytime singing, but animals may have been in water and perhaps were singing at temperatures lower than the air temperature. Temperatures reported from elsewhere may exceed those actually known for Louisiana.

Trill
  Brief, hoarse, 2–6 seconds long, and somewhat explosive
       Hyla chrysoscelis–Hyla versicolor

Musical, prolonged 5–30 seconds and high-pitched   *Bufo americanus*
Musical, prolonged 2–8 seconds, and an octave higher than *Bufo americanus*
       Bufo terrestris

Prolonged, hoarse, 2–6 seconds
Bufo valliceps
Dull, bell-like
Cowbell sound, a monotonous "quonk" at
one or more per second   *Hyla cinerea*
Deeper, explosive cowbell "tonk, toonk,"
or "tunk," 1–2 seconds apart
Hyla gratiosa
Low chuckling "chuck, chuck," often ending
with raspy sound like that produced by
rubbing finger over a balloon
Rana sphenocephala

FAMILY BUFONIDAE
TOADS

In the jumble of anuran systematics, the
family Bufonidae is variously interpreted;
one version assigns it 25 living genera and
335 species. The family's distribution is
worldwide, except that its natural distribution does not include Australia, New
Guinea, New Zealand, Greenland, Madagascar, or the Pacific islands, and toads are absent from much of arid North Africa and the
Arabian Peninsula. One large tropical form
has been deliberately introduced into Australia and many islands, as well as elsewhere, for insect control. Most bufonids lay
long strings of eggs in water, but some species lay eggs on land, and the African genus
Nectophrynoides has internal fertilization
and is ovoviviparous.

Bufo americanus Holbrook
American Toad
Plate IV

Recognition. A small toad attaining a maximum length of only 1¾–2¾ in. (44–70 mm)
in Louisiana; parotoid glands often having
curved lateral margins, giving a "kidney
shape" appearance; parotoid glands usually
separated from the postorbital cranial ridges,
or at most each connected to a ridge by
a short, posteriorly projecting spur from

the lateral end of the ridge; large warts on
the tibiae; dorsum relatively unpatterned
brownish, red, or gray, with a very narrow, not
strikingly evident middorsal stripe; dorsal
spots, when present, few and rarely more
than a single wart per spot; venter immaculate or only slightly spotted.

Distribution. The northwestern Florida Parishes in an area apparently disjunct from the
overall distribution of the species, and possibly from De Soto Parish in northwestern
Louisiana, which is disjunct from records in
adjacent states (Map 22). Seifert (1978) reported the De Soto specimen, which we have
been unable to examine because of the lack of
response to our loan request by the Dallas
Museum of Natural History where it was deposited, and he described this specimen as
showing some "intergradation" with *Bufo
valliceps* (see further remarks under "Taxonomic comments"). A record from Webster
Parish is based on uncertain determination of
some tadpoles; no adult toad, particularly
one with the vocalization of *B. americanus*,

Map 22. Distribution of *Bufo americanus*.
Solid circles represent specimens examined; hollow circles represent museum specimens not examined or literature records.

has been found in northern Louisiana areas often included in distribution maps for this species. Robert A. Thomas has told us of hearing *B. americanus* in Caddo and Rapides parishes, but no specimens are available for substantiation.

Taxonomic comments. The Louisiana populations presumably represent the race *B. americanus charlesmithi* Bragg, the dwarf American toad. Toads pose special problems because of their tendency to hybridize. No hybrids of *B. americanus* with other toads are known from Louisiana, but to the inexperienced observer this species could be confused with *B. woodhousei* or *B. terrestris*, with which it may hybridize. The lack of enlarged knobs on the cranial ridges separates *B. americanus* from *B. terrestris*; also, the skin of *B. americanus* is less spiny, and usually no conspicuous pattern of spots is present, as in *B. terrestris*. The American toad can be distinguished from *B. woodhousei* by the lack of pattern, or if patterned, by the presence of only one or two warts per spot rather than three or more warts per spot, by the presence of large tibial warts, by the absence of a distinct middorsal white line and lateral whitish stripes, and by the more immaculate venter. Additionally, *B. woodhousei* individuals, particularly those from west of the Mississippi River, tend to be spinier, and the cranial ridges are narrower and more sharply ridged. Contrary to popular field guide descriptions, the parotoid glands do not touch the postorbital cranial ridge, at least not in typical Louisiana *B. woodhousei*; hence this is not a reliable character to seek in Louisiana toads. The vocalizations of male toads are the best field criterion for identification. The musical trill of *B. americanus* readily separates it from *B. woodhousei*'s nasal "whaaah." For *B. terrestris*, however, analyzing trill difference requires an acute ear that can detect the slower trill rate and somewhat lower pitch of *B. americanus*; otherwise one must rely on special recording

analysis (sonographs) based on songs of toads with known body temperatures.

Our doubts about the specimen reported by Seifert (1978) (see "Distribution") are bolstered by Sanders' (1986) indications that in northeastern Texas *B. americanus*, *B. woodhousei*, *B. velatus* (*B. w. velatus* in our interpretation), and *B. valliceps* may hybridize, thus creating a complex systematic situation. Some Louisiana toads that we call *B. woodhousei velatus* have been identified by various persons as *B. americanus*, but none has confirmed that by voice identification.

There is no single taxonomic study of this species, but there is a vast literature on its relationships to other species.

Habitat and habits. Within the western Florida Parishes, habitats occupied by *B. americanus* include sharply dissected uplands with few situations for breeding sites, stream bottomlands, and upland, replanted pine forests. The very narrow hardwood corridor that extends from western Tennessee through Mississippi into the western Florida Parishes (Delcourt and Delcourt 1975) probably represents the route by which the American toad spread into Louisiana. Subsequent dispersal appears to be confined to the shortleaf pine-hardwood uplands immediately east of the Blufflands.

Breeding sites utilized by the American toad in Louisiana include temporary pools, roadside ditches, shallow-flowing streams, and at least one permanent-water farm pond. Like all other species of toads, *B. americanus* is primarily a nocturnal animal, emerging by night, especially when humidity is high or rains have occurred, to feed on insects and other invertebrates. Feeding is indiscriminate—if it moves and is small enough, this toad will eat it—but does not seem to include cannibalism. Toads are rarely found abroad when air temperatures are below 50°F (10°C). They hide beneath logs and debris or in burrows. These toads have small, spadelike tubercles on the tarsus that they use to loosen sandy soils so that they can literally wriggle their way backward into the ground.

When handled roughly this toad, like all toads, may exude a milky secretion from the parotoid glands and warts. This secretion can be irritating to the mucous membranes that line the mouth and nose, and can cause eye inflammation as well. Thus, these animals have a certain amount of protection from the mammals that prey on them. Unfortunately for the toads, the secretions do not deter hog-nosed snakes or garter snakes, the former of which are especially fond of eating toads.

Reproduction. This species usually is our earliest singer among the toads, commencing in late February; the latest date is 6 June. The temperatures at which singing occurs are the lowest for any Louisiana toad: air temperatures of 57.5°–68°F (14°–20°C) have been noted at night (toad body temperatures as low as 58°F), and Rossman heard them singing in the afternoon when air temperatures were near 80°F (27°C). The voice is a pleasant musical trill sustained for half a minute or more. The voice can be imitated by placing one's tongue tip against the upper teeth, parting the lips widely, and then exhaling steadily to cause the tongue to vibrate.

The eggs are laid in long, tubular, gelatinous strings released free on the pool bottom or entwined into vegetation. A set of eggs produced in the laboratory on 19 March 1987 by an amplexing pair captured in St. Helena Parish the previous day offers some interesting comparisons to other data reported for *B. americanus.*

Wright and Wright (1949) stated that the egg complements of *B. a. americanus* ranged from 4,000 to 8,000, whereas Livezey and Wright (1947) listed the number as 4,000–12,000. An extrapolation based on volumetric samples for our set is 3,341. Wright and Wright (1949) gave the outer envelope diameter as 3.4–4.0 mm, Livezey and Wright (1947) gave 2.86–4.0 mm, and our eggs were 2.9–3.1 mm. Inner-envelope diameter, ac-

cording to both Wright and Wright and Livezey and Wright, is 1.6–2.2 mm; ours had a diameter of 2.1 mm. The vitellus diameter is given by Wright and Wright and Livezey and Wright as 1.0–1.4 mm; ours are larger—1.3–1.7 mm, mostly 1.7 mm. P. W. Smith (1961) reported vitelli of 1.2–1.4 mm for *B. a. americanus* and 1.5–2.0 mm for *B. a. charlesmithi* in Illinois. Thus not only are the vitelli of *B. a. charlesmithi* larger, but there is also substantial contrast in the number of eggs per string unit—15–17 per inch according to Livezey and Wright (1947), but only 7.47 per inch in our set. The wide spacing is evident to the eye when our eggs are compared to illustrations in Livezey and Wright's report. Bragg (1954) found no partitions between the individual eggs of Oklahoma *charlesmithi,* but Livezey and Wright found partitions in *americanus,* and they are present in our set, although we did not see them at first in the freshly laid eggs.

The tadpoles, reported to reach 27 mm in length (Wright and Wright 1949), are black and usually have distinctly bicolored tail musculature. Transformation in Louisiana should be rapid, presumably within two months of egg deposition. Rossman saw many newly transformed individuals on 16 May 1983. Newly transformed young are barely 6–8 mm long.

To date, we have found no sympatric singing populations of *B. americanus* and *B. terrestris.* Not only does the possibility of hybridization of the two species offer an interesting study, but the basis for ecological segregation of the species warrants special attention. Examination of field data suggests that *B. terrestris* selects higher temperatures for breeding activity (usually 70°F or higher, compared to 68°F or lower for *B. americanus*) and that, probably because of these preferred temperature factors, *B. terrestris* generally begins its breeding activities later, usually after *B. americanus* has concluded its reproductive efforts.

Bufo quercicus Holbrook
Oak Toad
Plate IV

Recognition. A tiny toad rarely exceeding 1¼ in. (32 mm) in length (record size, 33 mm), representing the only adult Louisiana toad under 1¾ in. (45 mm) and the only toad species 33 mm long or less having conspicuous parotoid glands; a distinct white middorsal stripe, bordered on either side by several pairs of dark brown or black blotches.

Distribution. The name is a misnomer. The oak toad is primarily an inhabitant of pine woods, which may or may not include oak trees. The distribution in the Florida Parishes includes both uplands and pine flats, but the areas of greatest abundance are wet pine flats where large areas of grass and grass clumps are present (Map 23). The species appears to be absent from the hardwood areas of the Blufflands.

Taxonomic comments. No systematic study has been attempted. The most recent coverage of literature on this species is that by Ashton and Franz (1979).

Habitat and habits. Similar to those of other toads (see under *Bufo americanus*).

Reproduction. Breeding choruses have been heard from 11 April to 11 August when air temperatures have exceeded 70°F (21°C). Warm rains seem to be essential for much vocalization, which may occur by day as well as at night. The voice, as one might suspect from the small size of this toad, is a feeble sound, much like the peeping of young chicks. The singing males usually hide in clumps of grass. The eggs, as described by Volpe and Dobie (1959), are "laid in small groups, each consisting of a short strand or 'bar' of three to six eggs . . . the jelly tube was drawn out and pinched between individual bars of eggs." Wright (1932) suggested that the larval period is 39–44 days long. Volpe and Dobie (1959) estimated that 500 eggs are deposited by the female.

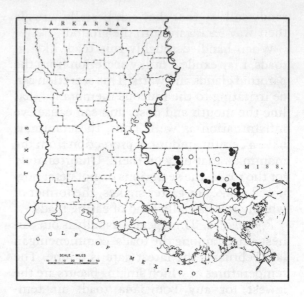

Map 23. Distribution of *Bufo quercicus*. Solid circles represent specimens examined; hollow circles represent museum specimens not examined or literature records.

The tadpoles reared by Volpe and Dobie (1959) reached a maximum length of 19.4 mm and transformed into toadlets averaging 8.2 mm (7.2–8.9 mm). The most conspicuous feature of the tadpoles is a marking on the tail musculature resembling six or seven black saddles separated by yellowish light areas.

Bufo terrestris (Bonnaterre)
Southern Toad
Plate IV

Recognition. A highly variable species 1¾–2½ in. (44–64 mm) long in Louisiana and reaching almost 4½ in. (113 mm) elsewhere; best recognized by the presence of relatively high cranial crests having knoblike enlargements at the posterior ends of the interorbital crests; middorsal light line poorly developed; venter at most lightly marked except for spotting in pectoral region.

Similar species. Bufo terrestris often hybridizes with *B. woodhousei*, usually the only species with which it is confused; the hybrids may have intermediate patterns, interorbital crest knob conditions, and voices. Within the area where both *terrestris* and *woodhousei* occur, *terrestris* is a spinier toad than *woodhousei* with more prominent warts and with fewer warts per spot (usually two or fewer, but occasionally more).

Distribution. The Florida Parishes, where this species tends to occupy higher, better-drained ground than *B. woodhousei* (Map 24). A student collected a specimen in the LSUMZ collections from the Bonnet Carre Spillway in St. Charles Parish. However, despite many years of collecting by Tulane University students and staff, we are unable to confirm this locality with additional material. West Feliciana Parish records attributed to *B. terrestris* are based on larvae and a somewhat dehydrated animal and thus may be questionable. Many literature records for areas outside the Florida Parishes are in error.

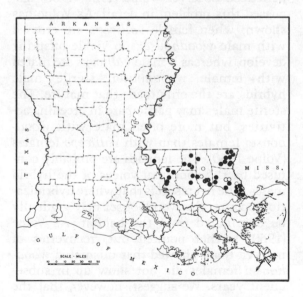

Map 24. Distribution of *Bufo terrestris*. Solid circles represent specimens examined; hollow circles represent museum specimens not examined or literature records.

Taxonomic comments. No subspecies are currently recognized, and no taxonomic study has been published. Blem (1979) summarized the nomenclatural history.

Male toads are notoriously indiscriminate in their selection of mating partners, seizing any anuran (or small moving thing, fingers included) that may pass their way. The net result is that many interspecific matings may occur in the field; the resultant hybrids complicate an already difficult situation of limited taxonomic features, and herpetologists are hampered in their attempts to identify animals at hand. In the field, at least, recourse to identification by voice characteristics can reduce, but not fully resolve, the confusion. Thus, in reference to the remarks under "Similar species," we would have little difficulty distinguishing between the musical trill of *B. terrestris* and the hoarse, sheeplike "waah" of *B. woodhousei*. Hybrids, of course, would have intermediate voices. Volpe (1959) and W. F. Blair (1972) discussed the problems due to hybridization in toads. Volpe (1959) summarized morphological characters of hybrids between *B. terrestris* and *B. woodhousei*. Further complications may exist now that we know *B. americanus* also occurs in Louisiana (see under *B. americanus*).

Habitat and habits. See under *B. americanus*. Geographic relations to *B. americanus* need to be determined; to date we have no evidence that *B. terrestris* and *B. americanus* occur at the same site, but they are known to occur within 5–10 miles of each other in St. Helena Parish.

Reproduction. Singing males have been found from 18 February to 11 August on nights when air temperatures exceeded 65°F (18.3°C); they usually do not sing at temperatures below 70°F (21°C), and hence are rarely heard before late March. These toads utilize farm ponds, ditches, flooded fields, wheel ruts, or almost any water-filled depression as breeding sites. The voice is a lovely musical trill (see *B. americanus* for

81

comments). The egg masses are the gelatinous strings usually produced by toads. The black or dark brown tadpoles have a light oblique mark behind each eye. Tadpoles reach a length of approximately 25 mm and transform after one or two months. Tadpoles taken at St. Francisville, West Feliciana Parish, on 28 February are sufficiently large to suggest that breeding may have occurred earlier than our earliest singing date of 18 February.

Bufo valliceps Wiegmann
Gulf Coast Toad
Plate IV

Recognition. An easily recognized large toad attaining a maximum length of nearly 5 in. (125 mm) in Louisiana, although adults typically are about 3 in. (76 mm) long; parotoid glands often triangular, characteristically diverging; cranial crests well developed, sharply ridged; top of the head between the cranial crests with a broad, deep depression; each cranial crest with diverging ends forming a prominent "Y" shape with the crests; a conspicuous yellowish cream middorsal stripe and a broad yellowish cream dorsolateral stripe on each side.

Distribution. Throughout Louisiana south of the Red River and east of the Mississippi River (Map 25). Several records in northern Louisiana and in Washington Parish suggest migrations via river valleys.

Taxonomic comments. Louisiana representatives of this species are referable to *Bufo v. valliceps* Wiegmann, the Gulf Coast toad. Porter (1970) commented that although several races of *B. valliceps* have been proposed, lack of a thorough study of geographic variation makes a subspecific evaluation impossible.

Because this species hybridizes with *B. woodhousei,* intermediate animals may

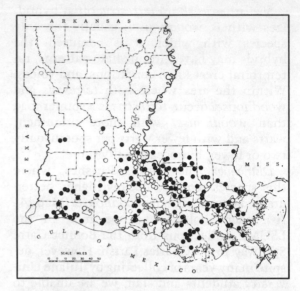

Map 25. Distribution of *Bufo valliceps.* Solid circles represent specimens examined; hollow circles represent museum specimens not examined or literature records.

make identification difficult for the inexperienced observer. Volpe (1956, 1960) discussed this problem in detail. As Volpe has shown, when female *valliceps* are crossed with male *woodhousei,* no viable offspring develop, whereas if male *valliceps* are mated with female *woodhousei,* sterile male hybrids are the only toads that mature. The sterile males may participate in breeding activities, but more often mate with *woodhousei* females than with *valliceps* females (Volpe 1960). The females are probably confused by the abnormal voices of the hybrid males. The net result is that where hybridization occurs, the *woodhousei* may gradually be eliminated from the habitat. As Volpe (1960) further pointed out, recoveries of marked toads showed that mismated *woodhousei* females did not show up in subsequent years. We suggest, however, that the integrity of *woodhousei* is perhaps maintained because it commences breeding almost a month earlier than *valliceps.*

Habitat and habits. Habits are described under *B. americanus.* The Gulf Coast toad is uncommon in pinelands; it appears to predominate in agricultural and wet hardwood areas. It is quite successful in urban settings and breeds throughout the city of New Orleans. It is abundant during the winter under logs in hardwood forests.

As noted under "Taxonomic Comments," hybridization takes place with *B. woodhousei. Bufo valliceps* and *B. woodhousei* still occur together in woodlands in the Mississippi River floodplain upriver from New Orleans. Studies on both species are sorely needed to determine the type of ecological alteration that may force the two toads into sharing breeding sites, resulting in subsequent hybridization. For instance, on the night of 11 June 1984, abundant *B. valliceps* were singing along deep canals at the margins of woods in the Bonnet Carre Spillway in St. Charles Parish, but in a cleared area *woodhousei* males outnumbered *valliceps* by perhaps two to one. All animals seen appeared to be pure stock, none showing hybrid features.

Reproduction. Vocalization has been heard from 5 April to 15 September. The lowest air temperature noted when singing males were heard was 68°F (20°C). The voice is a low trill similar to that of *B. americanus* and *B. terrestris,* but more guttural and hence less musical.

The eggs, laid in the usual long gelatinous string characteristic of toads, often are arranged in double rows within the tube. The dark tadpoles have dark tail musculature with light dorsal saddles. The shallow pools often selected for breeding necessitate rapid larval development because of the high temperature, hence high evaporation rates, within the species' geographic range. Volpe (1957) showed embryonic tolerance to encompass a range of 64°–95°F (18°–35°C). Larval development thus takes place in 20 to 30 days, and the tadpoles may reach a length of 25 mm.

J. R. Dixon (according to Neill 1958a) found Gulf Coast toads in a salt marsh 10 miles south of Hackberry, Cameron Parish, but did not indicate if they bred in brackish water. Burger, Smith, and Smith (1949) reported that *B. valliceps* bred immediately west of the Louisiana border in pools in the coastal marsh near Sabine Pass, Jefferson County, Texas. They stated that blennies (small marine fishes) were common in the water; thus we must assume that the water was brackish. Viosca (1926) stated that *B. valliceps* often occupies lowlands of brackish water marshes. From all of the foregoing data, we would surmise that *B. valliceps* probably breeds in brackish waters in Louisiana.

Bufo woodhousei Girard
Woodhouse's Toad
Plate IV

Recognition. A moderate-sized toad 2–3 in. (51–76 mm) long with elongate parotoid glands often touching the postorbital ridges; cranial crests narrow, low, and usually sharply ridged; a light middorsal stripe; ground color yellowish to gray with dark brown or black dorsal spots, each with three or more warts; venter immaculate to heavily spotted.

Distribution. Throughout Louisiana except for the coastal marshes (Map 26). The records for Cameron Parish that seemed to be from the Marsh have proved to be from the cheniers.

Taxonomic comments. This is a highly variable toad in Lousiana, in part due to complications caused by hybridization with *Bufo terrestris* and *B. valliceps,* and perhaps because of genetic traits received from other, earlier hybridizations with members of the *B. americanus* group; otherwise it is a blend of two or more races in Louisiana. East of the Mississippi River in the Florida Parishes, the toad may be referred to as *B. woodhousei*

83

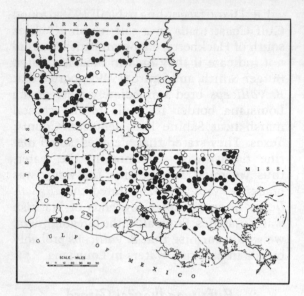

Map 26. Distribution of *Bufo woodhousei*. Solid circles represent specimens examined; hollow circles represent museum specimens not examined or literature records.

fowleri Hinckley, Fowler's toad, a fairly light-colored race with an immaculate venter or a single dark breast spot, but over most of the state the animals probably are intergrades with *B. w. woodhousei* Girard, Woodhouse's toad. Some writers (e.g., Keiser and Wilson 1979) have referred to Louisiana specimens from west of the Mississippi River as *B. w. velatus* Bragg and Sanders, the East Texas toad, which is much darker than *B. w. woodhousei*, has a heavily spotted breast, and a rather spiny body. Conant (1975) referred to the latter animals as intergrades influenced by hybrids from other species. Hybridization with *B. valliceps* is common near New Orleans (see *valliceps* account), and *B. woodhousei* frequently hybridizes with *B. terrestris* throughout the Florida Parishes. Volpe (1956, 1959, 1960) discussed in detail the results of hybridization.

Sanders (1986) regarded *B. w. velatus* as a distinct species, *B. velatus*, and thus regarded *B. w. fowleri* as *B. fowleri*. He based his conclusion primarily on the dark pectoral coloration and presence of a supratympanic ridge between the parotoid gland and the postorbital crest in *velatus*. He further remarked that *B. woodhousei* and *B. velatus* chiefly occupy separate ecological areas in Texas and that there are no *fowleri* in Texas. But Sanders did acknowledge various hybrid combinations in eastern Texas toads and the occurrence of pectoral spots and supratympanic ridges in some *B. woodhousei* where the two "species" overlap. Sanders did not explore the eastern boundaries of *velatus*, nor did he give consideration to breeding songs, nor did he explore areas to the north where *woodhousei* and *fowleri* meet. In view of these latter discrepancies, we are inclined to regard *velatus* as a racial variant of *woodhousei* produced from various gene introgressions from other species of toads. We are cognizant, however, that Conant (1975) showed intergradation of *fowleri* and *woodhousei* has not been demonstrated for Missouri, Kansas, or northeastern Oklahoma.

No formal taxonomic revision has been made, but the literature on the systematics of *B. woodhousei* and other members of the *B. americanus* group is vast.

Habitat and habits. In the Florida Parishes, Woodhouse's toad (as the race *B. w. fowleri*) occurs most frequently in the bottomlands, where *B. terrestris* occupies the higher ground. Elsewhere in its range, *B. woodhousei* is fairly ubiquitous. In most other respects this toad's habits are much like those of *B. americanus*.

Reproduction. Bufo woodhousei sings from at least 11 March to early July. As a rule it is rarely heard before April and then only if air temperatures exceed 67°F (19.5°C). The voice, a nasal "waaah," is easily recognized, but hybrids may have modified voices—trills, reduced volume, etc.

The eggs usually are arranged in single lines in the tube, sometimes double. The dark tadpoles, which may reach 20–21 mm in total length before transforming, often have a darkly pigmented throat patch. Wright and

Wright (1949) suggested that the larval period may last as long as 60 days.

Bufo woodhousei normally breeds in temporary pools, but it may also use quiet pools in streams. J. R. Dixon (according to Neill 1958a) found specimens in a salt marsh 10 miles south of Hackberry, Cameron Parish; however, he did not indicate where breeding might take place.

FAMILY HYLIDAE
TREEFROGS AND OTHER HYLIDS

The large family Hylidae contains approximately 37 living genera comprising 630 species (if we do not remove New Guinean and Australian forms to a different family) distributed throughout much of North and South America, southern Europe, and Asia, a small part of northwestern Africa, and the Australia–New Guinea land masses. Three species were successfully introduced into New Zealand more than a century ago. Although the hylids are called treefrogs, the family has no monopoly on arboreal habits, and some of its species are ground dwellers. Development usually is via eggs deposited in water, but direct development occurs in some species that carry the eggs in various ways on or in the body. Size ranges from tiny species that never exceed 17 mm in body length to an Australian species that reaches 135 mm. A prominent characteristic of most hylids is the presence of expanded adhesive discs on the toes.

Acris crepitans Baird
Northern Cricket Frog
Plate V

Recognition. A small, agile, ground-dwelling member of the treefrog family reaching 1⅜ in. (35 mm) snout-vent length; skin warty; two light-colored anal warts; toe discs scarcely wider than the toes; toes extensively webbed, the webs reaching to at least the last 1½ to 2 joints of the longest toe; hind legs, when rotated forward, with heel just reaching the end of the snout; dorsum with elongate dark spots on a gray to green or rust background, sometimes with a prominent green, yellow, or rusty orange middorsal stripe; snout with numerous vertical dark and light bars; dark triangle present between the eyes; belly white; back of the thigh with an irregularly edged dark stripe.

Similar species. This species is easily confused with the southern cricket frog, *Acris gryllus.* In the southern cricket frog, the middle toe of the hind foot appears much longer than in the northern cricket frog because the webbing reaches no farther than the base of the last three joints. Also, the southern cricket frog has a smooth-edged postfemoral stripe on the thigh. An experienced observer will also detect the more pointed snout of *A. gryllus,* as well as the more nasal sound of the male's song. Tadpoles are readily distinguishable; the long spiracular tube of *A. gryllus* sets it apart from any other tadpole in Louisiana. All cricket frogs from west of the Mississippi River are *A. crepitans;* careful identification is needed only in the Florida Parishes.

Distribution. Literally ubiquitous in Louisiana but most frequently found at the margins of permanent freshwater lakes and along streams (Map 27).

Taxonomic comments. Only the nominate subspecies, *Acris c. crepitans* Baird, the northern cricket frog, occurs in Louisiana. For many years the two species of cricket frog were confused, and all were listed as races of *A. gryllus.* The most recent systematic studies of *A. crepitans* are those by Neill (1950) and Burger, Smith, and Smith (1949), but no comprehensive taxonomic study has been published.

Habitat and habits. These treefrogs always remain on the ground and rarely stray from water except during rains. When disturbed,

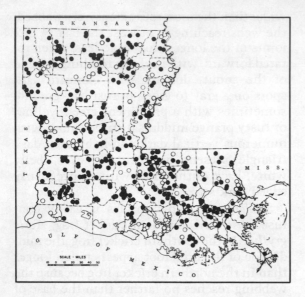

Map 27. Distribution of *Acris crepitans*. Solid circles represent specimens examined; hollow circles represent museum specimens not examined or literature records.

they make tremendous leaps, perhaps up to a yard, plunging into the water and hiding submerged among vegetation. They remain active throughout the year as long as the weather is mild.

In the Florida Parishes, *A. crepitans* is less common than *A. gryllus* and tends to occupy somewhat lower ground than the latter, being primarily an inhabitant of the river bottoms. Occasionally the two species occur together. Bayless (1966) studied the two species at a pond in St. Tammany Parish, where he found that males selected somewhat different singing sites: *crepitans* preferred shaded spots and *gryllus* the more open places along the pond perimeter. He also indicated that *gryllus* was far more abundant at meadow pools and drainage ditches, whereas *crepitans* predominated at the pond.

A clear definition of the distribution of the species in the Florida Parishes is needed. This should clarify the ecological relationships of the two species of cricket frogs.

This species eats tiny arthropods, especially insects and spiders, as well as some snails, worms, crustaceans, and other invertebrates. In Bayless' (1966) study, Collembola (springtails), Hymenoptera (bees, ants, etc.), Diptera (flies), and Arachnida (spiders) were the most numerous items eaten and in that order.

Reproduction. The northern cricket frog may sing in any month of the year, but its major breeding activity occurs from March through September. This species is more prone to sing by day than any other Louisiana frog, but choruses are greatest at night. Singing has been recorded in Louisiana when air temperatures were as low as 62°F (16.6°C) and as high as 95°F (35°C). The frogs are wary and hard to spot on a grassy bank or amid vegetation in the water.

The voice is a rapidly repeated "gick," sounding much like the striking together of two pebbles. A single animal may be heard to utter the sounds slowly at spaced intervals, "gick-gick-gick, gick gick"; the total song consists of 20 to 30 rapid beats. The choruses sound like a high-pitched rattling.

The eggs measure about 1 mm in diameter at the vitellus and 2.3–3.5 mm in envelope diameter and are laid singly or in small masses. They are dropped into water and fall to the bottom or occasionally adhere to grasses. A single female may produce as many as 250 eggs.

The developmental period is 40 to 90 days; newly transformed young are usually found only in the warmer months because little development takes place during the winter. The tadpoles attain a length of 30–46 mm and are characterized by a black-tipped tail. Growth is rapid, and adult size may be reached two months after metamorphosis.

Although the chosen breeding sites are in fresh water, Burger, Smith, and Smith (1949) described a new race, *A. gryllus* (= *crepitans*) *pallidicola*, from Jefferson County, Texas, just west of Sabine Pass, which separates

Texas and Louisiana, indicating that the frogs were singing in shallow pools of the coastal marsh very near the ocean. They reported that blennies, brackish- and saline-water fishes, were in the breeding pools, but they did not indicate whether the pools were actually saline.

Acris gryllus (Le Conte)
Southern Cricket Frog
Plate V

Recognition. A small frog reaching a snout-vent length of 1¼ in. (32 mm); skin warty; head pointed; toe discs scarcely wider than the toes; toes webbed but longest toe with the last three joints free of web; hind legs, when rotated forward, with heel reaching beyond the tip of the snout; dorsum with elongate dark spots on a gray to green or rust background, usually with a bright green, yellow, or red middorsal stripe; snout with numerous vertical dark and light bars; a dark triangle between the eyes; belly white; back of the thigh with a sharply defined postfemoral stripe.

Similar species. Acris gryllus is often confused with the northern cricket frog, *A. crepitans* (see that account for distinguishing details).

Distribution. Confined to the Florida Parishes (Map 28). Two specimens in the Tulane collection recorded as being from Plaquemines Parish presumably have erroneous field data.

Taxonomic comments. The Louisiana subspecies is *A. g. gryllus* (Le Conte), the southern cricket frog. A number of literature records from various localities in the state were published during a time when *A. gryllus* and *A. crepitans* were not recognized as distinct species.

Some specimens in the LSUMZ collection from Beauregard Parish have sharply defined postfemoral stripes, but the webbing and

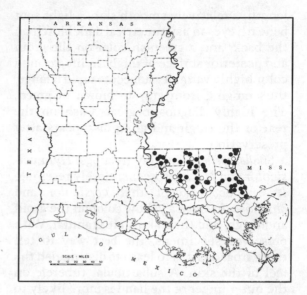

Map 28. Distribution of *Acris gryllus*. Solid circles represent specimens examined; hollow circles represent museum specimens not examined or literature records.

snout are typical of *A. crepitans*. The "gryllus-like" specimens are small; larger individuals from the same site had irregular postfemoral stripes. The tadpoles are characterized by a long, free-projecting spiracular tube.

The most recent systematic study is that by Neill (1950), but no comprehensive taxonomic study has been published.

Habitat and habits. These frogs are abundant along roadside ditches, woodland and meadow pools, and artesian-fed ponds.

See the account of the northern cricket frog (*A. crepitans*) for details of habits and reproduction.

The voice is much like that of *A. crepitans*, but has a more nasal quality.

Hyla avivoca Viosca
Bird-voiced Treefrog
Plate VI

Recognition. A medium-sized treefrog reaching almost 2 in. (49 mm) in snout-vent length; a relatively smooth skin; a light spot beneath eye, an asymmetrical dark blotch on the back, and a greenish color on the groin and posterior surface of thighs in life; ground color highly variable, subject to rapid change, thus ranging from gray to brown or green. The highly diagnostic green wash on the rear of the thigh and groin disappears after preservation.

Similar species. The gray treefrogs, *Hyla versicolor* and *H. chrysoscelis,* closely resemble *H. avivoca,* except that *versicolor* and *chrysoscelis* have a yellow color on the groin and thigh, and their skins are granular. With preserved specimens, the best way to tell these frogs apart is to learn to distinguish the feel of the skin. A subarticular tubercle on the outer finger of the hand is more likely to be divided by a longitudinal furrow in *H. avivoca,* rather than to be predominantly simple as in the gray treefrogs. In life the voices are absolutely distinctive.

Distribution. The Florida Parishes and swampy areas just to the south of Lake Pontchartrain and in Rapides, Grant, and Evangeline parishes in central Louisiana (Map 29). The first report of *H. avivoca* west of the Mississippi River came from A. P. Blair and Lindsay (1961), who found specimens in extreme southeastern Oklahoma. Fouquette and Delahoussaye (1966) provided the records from Rapides and Evangeline parishes. The Grant Parish site, Lake Iatt, is represented by six specimens (TU 1706) collected in 1947.

Taxonomic comments. Only the western subspecies, *H. a. avivoca* Viosca, the western bird-voiced treefrog, occurs in Louisiana. The most recent taxonomic study is that by P. W. Smith (1953).

Habitat and habits. The bird-voiced treefrog primarily inhabits the forested and swampy floodplains of larger rivers. Fouquette and Delahoussaye (1966) suggested that the species probably would be discovered in additional cypress-tupelo gum swamps along the Red River valley.

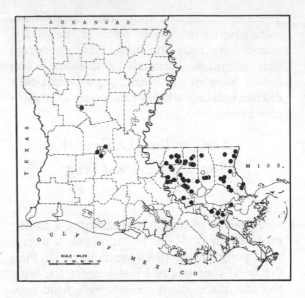

Map 29. Distribution of *Hyla avivoca.* Solid circles represent specimens examined; hollow circles represent museum specimens not examined or literature records.

Most *H. avivoca* breeding sites are in more or less permanent swamp pools in which shrubs such as buttonbush (*Cephalanthus*) provide perching places for the singing males. Unless such habitats are readily accessible by road, the presence of *H. avivoca* might indeed remain unsuspected.

Outside the breeding season, this frog may be encountered under logs, in rotting stumps, clinging to palmettos, or hiding within crevices in trees. Otherwise little is known of this species.

Reproduction. Singing males at breeding sites have been noted from 1 April to 11 August in Louisiana, and Dundee has heard them as early as 22 March in the Florida Panhandle. Males may "talk" from trees for several weeks before going to the breeding pools. On 12 March 1976, Dundee heard a single male in the daytime in a forest in St. Charles Parish, but does not know if that animal was at a breeding pool or simply somewhere in the trees. Other than season, a primary factor in when this species commences singing is air temperature, which must reach 65°F (18.4°C) or higher; chorus activity decreases markedly as temperatures decline toward this apparent minimum. Most singing is at night. Almost without fail, the males sing from perches several feet above the water, and the pools chosen are basically permanent, only rarely becoming dry.

The song is one of the loveliest produced by a Louisiana frog. It consists of a series of rapidly repeated clear whistles. The sound is easily imitated by pursing the lips and exhaling as quickly as possible in successive pipings.

The eggs, numbering about 600, are laid in small packets of 6 to 15 each and tend to adhere to the pool bottom or to vegetation in the water. Volpe, Wilkens, and Dobie (1961) presented detailed descriptions of the eggs and development and established that at laboratory temperatures of 83–89°F (28.5°–35.5°C), hatching occurs at 40 hours and transformation is completed in 29 days.

The larvae attain a length of approximately 32 mm, and the transformed froglets are about 9 mm long. The mature larvae exhibit a light preorbital stripe, a butterfly-shaped mark between the eyes, and a series of vivid red saddles on the tail musculature.

Hyla chrysoscelis-versicolor Complex
Hyla chrysoscelis Cope
Cope's Gray Treefrog
Hyla versicolor Le Conte
Gray Treefrog
Plate VI

Recognition. Moderately large treefrogs reaching 2⅜ in. (60 mm) in snout-vent length; skin granular or warty; dorsum various shades of gray to brown or green and with a large irregular dark blotch or blotches forming elongate armlike projections; rear of thighs yellow or yellowish orange with dark markings; a light spot under eye. Further description under "Taxonomic comments."

Similar species. See comments under *Hyla avivoca.*

Distribution. Under the original concept of a single species, *H. versicolor,* the distribution was statewide, but current recognition of two sibling species leaves our knowledge of distribution in a state of limbo. The current interpretation is that *H. chrysoscelis* occurs statewide and *H. versicolor* occurs primarily in the longleaf pine forests of west-central Louisiana (Maps 30, 31). James P. Bogart's (pers. com.) histological examination of preserved specimens, however, revealed that *H. versicolor* also occurs in the bottomland forests of Iberville and Lafourche parishes. *Hyla chrysoscelis* also occurs at all localities where *H. versicolor* is known. Dundee discovered *H. versicolor* near Vicksburg, Mississippi, in 1987; thus we suspect that this species may occur in northeastern Louisiana and the western Florida Parishes.

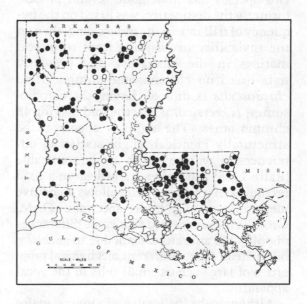

Map 30. Distribution of *Hyla chrysoscelis-versicolor.* Solid circles represent specimens examined; hollow circles represent museum specimens not examined or literature records.

Map 31. Distribution of *Hyla versicolor*. Solid circles represent specimens examined; hollow circles represent museum specimens not examined or literature records.

Taxonomic comments. The separation of these two species has undergone several phases: formerly the distinction was based on the frequency of trill rate in the male's song, then on the inviability of offspring from reciprocal matings in the laboratory, and presently it is based on chromosome number. *Hyla chrysoscelis* is diploid, having 24 chromosomes; *H. versicolor* is tetraploid, having 48 chromosomes. The animals appear to be structurally identical; slight statistical differences in average length are demonstrable (Ralin 1968), but only a trained ear or a good recording of a singing male allows a positive identification of a living specimen. D. M. Green (1982) suggested that voice differences of polyploid anurans are not due to genetics, but instead reflect different mechanical properties of large versus small cells in the vocal apparatus.

Although the trill rates of singing males vary with temperature, at the same body temperature the song of *H. versicolor* is ut-

tered at a much slower rate than that of *H. chrysoscelis*. The data thus far reported show that *H. versicolor* trills range from about 16 to 35 notes per second, whereas those of *H. chrysoscelis* range from 29 to 64 notes per second. The problem of identifying nonsinging males, living females, or preserved animals can be facilitated by examination of cell size or cell nucleus counts, or both. The tetraploid *H. versicolor* should have half as many and larger cells than the diploid *H. chrysoscelis*, and each cell should contain more DNA. Cash and Bogart (1978) showed that the cells of *versicolor* are larger (mean nuclear diameter 6.0 units versus 4.6 units for *chrysoscelis*), and the mean number of nucleoli per cell is 2.6 for *versicolor* and 1.9 for *chrysoscelis*. Additionally, as Dundee has found, the lengths of the fresh red blood cells of the two species differ when averages of 10 cells are calculated (*versicolor* cells are 1.26 times longer than those of *chrysoscelis*). The latter finding, however, requires more substantiation based on adequate numbers of animals of different sizes from more localities. Until such a time as useful techniques for cell study are worked out, the identity of the majority of museum specimens must remain unresolved. Accurate determination of the geographic ranges of the species may allow identification of many animals on the basis of locality alone.

Habitat and habits. The gray treefrogs are forest dwellers, but they are frequently encountered in pastures and open areas when they come there to breed. Like most treefrogs, they can be found on vegetation or, especially in the winter, under cover objects. They are extremely arboreal, and males can be heard "talking" high in trees. Fitch (1956a) reported that they tolerate unusually high body temperatures (92.7°F, 33.7°C).

Ralin (1968) did a comparative study of the gray treefrogs in southeastern Texas and found *H. chrysoscelis* to be more arboreal than *H. versicolor*, tending to sing from bushes or trees, whereas *H. versicolor* sang more frequently from the ground. He suggested that *H. chrysoscelis* could tolerate or perhaps preferred lower relative humidity and thus was better able to develop arboreal habits. He found both species to eat insects, but found a higher percentage of arboreal insects in the diet of *H. chrysoscelis*, which reflects this habitat difference.

Reproduction. Singing males have been heard from 25 March to 5 September; eggs have been found as late as 5 September. The "talking" of males in the trees has been heard as early as 15 March. Frogs definitely identified as *H. versicolor* have been heard from late May to 14 June. The song, either a harsh or a somewhat melodious trill, can be imitated by placing the tip of the tongue just at the junction of the upper teeth and palate and exhaling to vibrate the tongue. A short, harsh burst approximates the call of *H. chrysoscelis* and a slow, softened burst resembles the song of *H. versicolor*. Neither song has the musical quality of the dwarf American toad, whose voice can be imitated in much the same way. Air temperatures during the singing periods in Louisiana ranged from 67°–86°F (19.5°–30°C).

The breeding sites include semipermanent farm ponds, woodland pools, and especially ditches, even muddy ones. Males may sing from perches or from the ground, and their activity is notably intensified by warm rains.

The eggs, numbering up to 2,000, are laid in shallow water in small packets of 6 to 45, either free-floating or loosely attached to vegetation. Tadpoles reach 50 mm in length and have large, dark blotches on the long, red-finned tails. Newly transformed frogs are 13–20 mm in snout-vent length. Wright and Wright (1949) found the larval period to be 45 to 65 days; we have transforming tadpoles collected on 12 June in Catahoula Parish and also have large (41 mm) tadpoles collected as late as 30 September. That tadpoles 45 mm long were collected 16 May in

Neshoba County, Mississippi, indicates that the breeding season may begin earlier than we have observed or that larval development is more rapid than reported.

Hyla cinerea (Schneider)
Green Treefrog
Plate VI

Recognition. A medium-sized treefrog attaining a maximum snout-vent length of 2½ in. (65 mm) based on a preserved specimen from Lawrence County, Arkansas, in the Tulane collections; usually light to dark green and with a well-defined, sharp-edged white or yellow stripe extending from the upper lip almost to the groin; back usually with some scattered golden flecks; posterior edge of the lower hind limb and foot marked with a light stripe; cool or concealed specimens gray in color.

Similar species. Several kinds of treefrogs may show green color phases. The squirrel treefrog (*Hyla squirella*) is smaller (under 41 mm) than the green treefrog, and the lateral stripe is poorly defined with a ragged edge and usually ends on the anterior part of trunk. Otherwise, the squirrel treefrog is often a brownish color and may have a number of dark dorsal spots, but no golden flecks; the striping on the hind leg is at most a dull, ill-defined light area. The larger barking treefrog (*H. gratiosa*) occasionally has an irregular light lateral stripe, but has a granular skin and conspicuous or indistinct round, light-edged dark spots.

Distribution. Statewide wherever freshwater breeding sites are available (Map 32). The National Museum of Natural History has a specimen that was collected in a trawl in the Gulf of Mexico off Timbalier Island, Terrebonne Parish. This animal probably fell from a boat rather than swam out to sea.

Taxonomic comments. No taxonomic study of the species has been published. The most re-

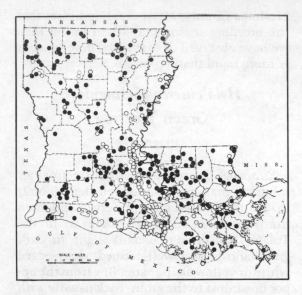

Map 32. Distribution of *Hyla cinerea*. Solid circles represent specimens examined; hollow circles represent museum specimens not examined or literature records.

cent study relating to systematics of the species is that of Reed (1956).

A subadult specimen Dundee found near Slidell, St. Tammany Parish, looked like *H. cinerea* but had dark spots on the anterior part of the dorsum. E. P. Volpe (pers. com.) believed it to be a hybrid of *H. cinerea* and *H. gratiosa*. Mecham (1960) reported that considerable hybridization takes place between the two species at Auburn, Alabama, and that the natural hybrids form a breeding population that is partially isolated reproductively from either parent species. Fortman and Altig (1974) gave numerous details of the characteristics of hybrids.

Habitat and habits. Green treefrogs are most abundant in forested areas or around water courses, ponds, and lake margins. In cool weather they hide under bark and in or under logs, but during most of the year they sit on leaves, in crevices, under the eaves of buildings, or on almost any vertical surface.

The food consists primarily of arthropods. Cagle (notes) examined several Louisiana specimens and found snails, beetles, and spiders in the stomachs.

Because they live and mate near water, these frogs not surprisingly are often eaten by large aquatic birds, ribbon snakes, garter snakes, water snakes, raccoons, and fishes.

Great numbers of these frogs, often exceeding one per square meter, may be killed on the road after heavy spring rains.

Reproduction. The spontaneous singing of males has been heard from 1 April to 1 September (M. E. Palmer [1939] reported the latter part of March) and consists of a monotonous "quonk, quonk, quonk" sound that resembles a dull ringing of a cowbell. Most singing is nocturnal, and 67°F (19.5°C) is the lowest recorded air temperature at which singing has been heard in Louisiana.

The males usually sing from perches above the water, and the breeding sites selected range from temporary ditches to lake, slough, and lagoon margins. William Brode (according to Neill 1958a) reported *H. cinerea* breeding in brackish marshes near Bay St. Louis, Mississippi, not far from the Louisiana border, and Burger, Smith, and Smith (1949) reported this species using shallow pools in the coastal marsh of Texas just across from Louisiana.

The eggs, as described by Livezey and Wright (1947), number 340 to 500 and are laid in indistinct surface masses of 5 to 40 that are attached to floating vegetation. Freshly deposited eggs have been observed as late as 11 August in Louisiana (Dundee notes).

Tadpoles reach at least 49 mm (Siekmann 1949) and have mottled or reticulated tail fins and musculature, a light stripe from eye to snout, and sometimes two light body blotches. Wright and Wright (1949) found the larval period to be 55 to 63 days long. Transformation has been noted as early as 2 July and as late as 22 October.

Hyla crucifer Wied
Spring Peeper
Plate VI

Recognition. A small treefrog (maximum length 1⅜ in., 35 mm); brown to brownish olive with a dark transverse mark between the eyes and a large, more or less X-shaped mark on the back (X-shaped mark sometimes reduced or missing).

Similar species. The pine woods treefrog (*Hyla femoralis*) is of comparable size and may have dark angled markings on the back, but the orange or yellow spots on the back of its thigh distinguish it from the spring peeper.

Distribution. Statewide except for the coastal marshes (Map 33).

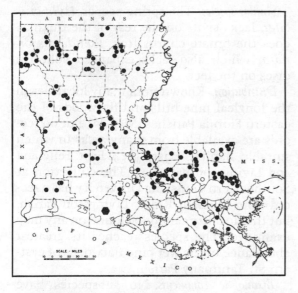

Map 33. Distribution of *Hyla crucifer*. Solid circles represent specimens examined; hollow circles represent museum specimens not examined or literature records.

Taxonomic comments. Two subspecies are recognized; in Louisiana the representative is *H. c. crucifer* Wied, the northern spring peeper. The most recent systematic study is that of

Harper (1939), but the generic designation is currently in question. Hedges (1986), using an electrophoretic analysis, assigned *H. crucifer* to the genus *Pseudacris*. He pointed out that *H. crucifer* and *Pseudacris* both are cold-weather breeders that dwell on the ground or in low vegetation and have small digital pads and dark, spherical or ovoid testes. Holarctic *Hyla*, in contrast, breed during warm weather, are arboreal, have larger digital pads, and have elongate white or yellowish testes.

Hardy and Borroughs (1986) recommended that *H. crucifer* be placed in a newly proposed genus, *Parapseudacris*. These authors reviewed many morphological and behavioral features of *H. crucifer* and examined leg muscle proteins with electrophoresis. They listed ten characters associated with *Hyla*, eight associated with *Pseudacris*, two shared by *Hyla* and *Pseudacris* (in part or whole), and one minor osteological feature exclusive to *H. crucifer*. Hardy and Borroughs' (1986) interpretations contrast with those of Hedges (1986) in that the former considered the digital pads to be expanded like those of *Hyla* and regarded the leg muscle proteins also to be like those of *Hyla*.

We are not prepared to judge which interpretation is most accurate, but we do agree that *H. crucifer*, as noted by Hedges (1986) and Hardy and Borroughs (1986), is less *Hyla*-like than the other representatives of that genus. A more convincing argument for assigning *H. crucifer* to a new genus would be the presence of some distinctive unique feature(s). Otherwise a strongly intermediate position is what we might expect in evolutionary change, and assignment to the parental stock or a derived genus becomes a matter of the individual systematist's judgment.

Habitat and habits. The spring peeper is a woodland species, abundant when singing but not often encountered away from the breeding sites. Little is known of this species in the southern states, but Oplinger (1963) has studied the life history in New York. Apparently the spring peepers have typical treefrog habits, except that they do not ascend, as a rule, into vegetation much higher than low shrubs. In summer in Louisiana they have been found in the axils of spider lilies (*Hymenocallis*), which are wet-ground plants.

Oplinger (1967) indicated that the young frogs were most often found in the early, dewy mornings in the summer, and both young and adults could be found on roads during late afternoon and early evening showers, but few could be found in nocturnal earches.

The food consists mostly of arthropods and cast skins (Oplinger 1967). Carr (1940) observed groups of peepers gathered around fresh cattle dung, where they fed on coprophagous insects; he also saw them feeding on emerging midges at woodland ponds.

Reproduction. The name "spring peeper" does not reflect the behavior of this animal in the South. In Louisiana spring peepers sing regularly from as early as 12 November through the cool months to as late as 12 May in St. Tammany Parish. The eggs have been observed from 26 January to 16 April. Most of the singing is nocturnal and may occur until air temperatures drop to the mid 30s F (2°C). These frogs have been heard at air temperatures as high as 78°F (25.5°C).

The voice is one of the truly pleasant sounds of night. It is a clear, single-note whistle repeated at approximately 1-second intervals. It may be imitated by pursing the lips tightly and exhaling to produce as high a pitch as possible. There is a characteristic structure to the sound of peeper choruses; Goin (1949) analyzed it, showing that the frogs sing in trios (the note sequence being A, G♯, B), each individual giving but one note.

The 250 to 1,000 eggs are deposited singly and attached to vegetation in temporary or semipermanent pools. The eggs are small; the single jelly envelope is less than 2 mm in diameter.

The tadpoles, which are variable in oral structure and not easily characterized, reach a total length of 35 mm and metamorphose into tiny frogs 9–14 mm long. The developmental period in the North is 90 to 100 days. Investigation is needed to establish the length of the larval period in southern latitudes, but Gosner and Rossman (1960) indicated that at least 45 days were required for lab-reared Florida larvae to transform.

Hyla femoralis Bosc
Pine Woods Treefrog
Plate VI

Recognition. A small treefrog (maximum length 1¾ in., 44 mm); the back ranging from green or greenish gray to reddish brown with dark, elongate, often fused blotches, and with small yellow, orange, or whitish spots on the back of each thigh.

Similar species. The spring peeper, *Hyla crucifer*, lacks spots on the rear of the thigh as does the ornate chorus frog, *Pseudacris ornata*, which also lacks expanded adhesive discs on the feet.

Distribution. Known from many localities in the longleaf pine hills and flatwoods of the eastern Florida Parishes (Map 34), but no records are available from many areas in which suitable habitat exists (i.e., East Feliciana and Livingston parishes). The collection at Southeastern Louisiana University has a record from Pleasant Ridge, Livingston Parish, but that locality cannot be found on any map examined. The species reaches its greatest abundance in the wet pine flatwoods of eastern St. Tammany Parish.

Taxonomic comments. No subspecies have been proposed, and no taxonomic study has been published.

Habitat and habits. Abundant when at breeding sites but otherwise widely scattered throughout the forests, where this species is said to go to the tops of the highest pine trees. Specimens occasionally are taken under logs or bark in cool seasons.

Map 34. Distribution of *Hyla femoralis*. Solid circles represent specimens examined; hollow circles represent museum specimens not examined or literature records.

The food is the usual array of small arthropods. Carr (1940) told of *H. femoralis* sitting atop fresh cow dung waiting for insects.

Reproduction. Breeding sites are always temporary pools such as flooded ditches and depressions. At Bay St. Louis, Mississippi, near the Louisiana border, they breed in brackish marshes (William Brode, according to Neill 1958a). The earliest and latest known breeding dates in Louisiana are 2 April and 11 August; the air temperatures noted were 70°–84°F (21°–29°C). *Hyla femoralis* sings chiefly at night.

The choruses may be very large, and the singing males will almost inevitably be found perched on emergent vegetation or logs above the water and in clear, shallow water. The voice has been likened to the rapid, amateurish use of a telegraph key, or to a riveting machine. The voice can be imitated by opening the mouth, compressing the lower pharynx, holding the nose, and emitting a series of quick, consecutive exhalations. The actual voice has a ventriloquistic effect, and looking for a singing male in a bush does recall the cliche of "looking for a needle in a haystack."

The yellow-and-brown eggs, as described by Wright (1932), number up to 800 and are laid in packets of about 100 each, either as a surface film or attached to vegetation near the surface. Hatching and development are rapid, as would be expected from the transient nature of the breeding sites. Wright (1932) said that about 50 to 75 days are required for transformation. At transformation the tadpoles are 33–36 mm in length and the newly transformed froglets measure about 13 mm. Transforming animals of those sizes have been taken on 21 August in St. Tammany Parish.

The tadpoles have striped tail musculature and heavily blotched fins that are reddish in the clear parts.

Hyla gratiosa Le Conte
Barking Treefrog
Plate VI

Recognition. The largest and stockiest of the Louisiana treefrogs, adults typically 2 in. (51 mm) or more in length (maximum of 2¾ in., 70 mm); dorsal skin distinctly granular; dorsum green or brown with a number of more or less rounded, light-edged dark spots, each side occasionally having an irregularly formed light stripe and some reddish brown or purple spots. Like most treefrogs, this one can change to an almost uniform color—gray to green or brown—but some spots will be faintly evident, regardless of ground color.

Distribution. Found only in the Florida Parishes, where it is principally a resident of the pine and pine-hardwood uplands (Map 35).

Taxonomic comments. No taxonomic study has been published, and no subspecies have been described. Hybridization between *Hyla gratiosa* and *H. cinerea* has been reported nu-

Map 35. Distribution of *Hyla gratiosa*. Solid circles represent specimens examined; hollow circles represent museum specimens not examined or literature records.

merous times (Caldwell 1982); see also "Taxonomic comments" under *H. cinerea*.

Habitat and habits. The barking treefrog is less arboreal than any other Louisiana *Hyla* except *H. crucifer*. There is some evidence from Florida that *H. gratiosa* burrows into loose sand, perhaps partly for winter hibernation, but also for moisture retention and coolness during the warm season. Neill (1958b) has described the barking call as "uk-oh-oh-oh-oh-oh-oh-ohk-ohk-ohk" and suggested that it is given only from trees, principally during the day and dusk, and serves to keep individual males aware of each other and oriented to the breeding pond to which they move at night and where a different sound, the breeding song, is uttered.

Reproduction. The limited observations available for Louisiana show that this frog sings from 14 March to 11 August, but the barking call has been heard from 1 March until 23 October. Dundee has recorded the song at air temperatures of 75°F (24°C) in Louisiana, but in the Florida Panhandle he

heard the song at a temperature of 64°F (17.8°C). The song is a hollow "toonk," "tonk," or "tunk," somewhat reminiscent of *H. cinerea* but more infrequent and more explosive, given while the male floats in the water. Neill (1958b) reported that males will form trios, each singing one of the notes described above. The breeding sites are usually semipermanent or permanent ponds, but William Brode (according to Neill 1958a) found this species breeding in brackish marshes near Bay St. Louis, Mississippi, close to the Louisiana border. A breeding congress rarely consists of more than 20 males.

As many as 1,084 eggs, each having a single jelly envelope, are deposited singly on the bottom of the pond.

The tadpoles are the largest of eastern U.S. hylids. Altig (1970) gave the maximum length for the larvae as 55 mm, but at Tulane a graded series reared in the laboratory reached 71 mm (preserved measurements) after 131 days at 71.6°F (22°C). Wright (1932) estimated the larval period to be 41 to 65 days, but his estimates were based on presumed breeding dates as interpreted from April and May rains. He ignored the possibility of a March breeding period, which probably accounts for the period he calculated being shorter than the 131-day period for the laboratory-reared series described above. Additionally, of course, the higher temperatures of ponds that Wright studied during 1921–1922 at dates of 21 April and later represented an accelerating factor. A detailed analysis of *H. gratiosa*'s developmental rates at varying temperatures is sorely needed to clarify our understanding of the life history.

The smallest larvae have four dark stripes on the dorsum; somewhat larger larvae lack the stripes but have a dark saddle near the midpoint of the tail musculature. The saddles are absent in larger larvae. The dorsal fin is very high in this species. The newly transformed young are 18–23 mm long.

Hyla squirella Bosc
Squirrel Treefrog
Plate VI

Recognition. A small treefrog (maximum length 1$\frac{11}{16}$ in., 43 mm), varying from green to brown, often with irregularly distributed small, dark spots on the back; a poorly defined wavy or ragged-edged light stripe from the upper lip to the anterior part of the side; frog nondescript, often easiest to identify by a process of elimination or by recognizing the basic appearance of the light stripe.

Similar species. Most likely to be confused with small *Hyla cinerea;* see the description of that species for comparison.

Distribution. Abundant in southern Louisiana lowlands and flatlands where suitable temporary freshwater pools may form (Map 36). This species also occurs in scattered localities in central and northern Louisiana in hardwood stream valleys.

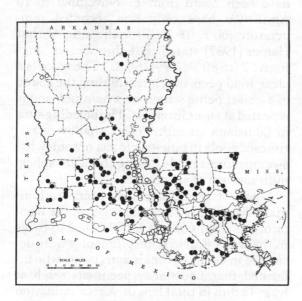

Map 36. Distribution of *Hyla squirella.* Solid circles represent specimens examined; hollow circles represent museum specimens not examined or literature records.

Taxonomic comments. No significant studies have been done. The most recent review of literature is that of Martof (1975c).

Habitat and habits. Squirrel treefrogs are abundant and thrive in many urban areas so long as suitable breeding pools can form. These frogs prefer shallow, weedy, temporary pools for breeding sites; the males are markedly responsive to rain, which will stimulate them to sing. William Brode (according to Neill 1958a) reported them breeding in brackish marshes near Bay St. Louis, Mississippi, not far from the Louisiana border. Viosca (1923) said that this species' distribution extends to the very edge of the Gulf. Squirrel treefrogs gather around lights and lighted windowpanes, where they feed voraciously on insects. Males frequently "talk" in the daytime from arboreal perches, especially just before rains. In the cool months they are often discovered under ground litter, logs, bark, and so forth.

Reproduction. Breeding choruses have been observed from 16 March to 4 November; several males were heard 3 December 1983 in Metairie, Jefferson Parish, after a heavy rain. In this species, chorusing normally follows warm rains; the lowest air temperature noted for the breeding song was 67°F (19.5°C) and the highest 84°F (29°C). The song is a raucous "waaak," "waaak," rapidly repeated, and usually uttered from a low perch or from the bank wherever there is emergent vegetation at the breeding pool.

The eggs, numbering close to 1,000, are enclosed in two jelly envelopes and deposited singly on the bottom of the breeding pool. The greenish tadpoles, which possess a pigmented throat and mottled fins, reach a length of 32–38 mm. Wright (1932) indirectly estimated that the larval period lasts 40 to 50 days; quite probably the larval period may be much longer. Newly transformed individuals measure 11–13 mm in snout-vent length. Our only date for newly transformed animals is 25 September; large larvae have been collected as late as 30 September.

Pseudacris ornata (Holbrook)
Ornate Chorus Frog

Plate V

Recognition. A small, stout frog, reaching a maximum length of $1\frac{7}{16}$ in. (37 mm); adhesive discs small, scarcely wider than the toes; ground color usually reddish brown but varying to green or silvery gray; a dark triangular spot often present between the eyes; a dark mask through the eye, and a dark suborbital spot; body usually with irregularly placed dark dorsal and lateral spots; groin yellow.

Distribution. Known only from the longleaf pine forest and the pine flatwoods of extreme eastern Washington and St. Tammany parishes (Map 37). It presumably should occur throughout suitable habitat in the Florida Parishes. The known localities in Louisiana are being rapidly eliminated by urbanization.

Taxonomic comments. No subspecies have been described, and no detailed study has been made.

Habitat and habits. Pseudacris ornata is a poorly known species, rarely encountered except when it is breeding. It is a resident of the sandy-soil pine forests although it may resort to cypress ponds for breeding. Carr (1940) suggested that it might be fossorial. Harper (1937) mentioned that ornate chorus frogs have only a slight reflection from the eyes (eye-shine), and also reported considerable daytime singing; from this we would guess that *P. ornata* is either fossorial or substantially more diurnal than most hylid frogs. Carr (1940) also found captive adults to eat insects and worms, and the newly emerged young to feed on nymphal orthopterans around the breeding ponds.

Reproduction. This is a winter-breeding species, and most singing occurs from December to early February; in Louisiana male *P. ornata*

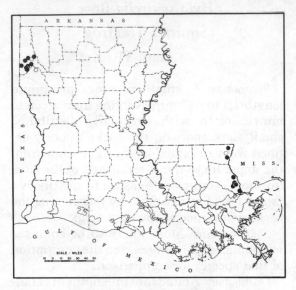

Map 37. Distribution of *Pseudacris ornata* and *Pseudacris streckeri*. Solid circles represent specimens examined; hollow circles represent museum specimens not examined or literature records.

have been heard from 11 November to 10 April. We have only one recorded temperature (60°F, 15.5°C) for the singing, but Harper (1937) stated that this species sings from 27° to 80°F (2.8°–26.7°C). The voice is a clear, loud peep, much resembling the sound of a chisel being struck by a hammer, and is repeated at short intervals. The breeding sites in Louisiana are either clear, shallow, grass-rimmed pools in pine-oak forest or somewhat swampy forest pools having abundant sphagnum moss at their margins.

A pair of amplexing frogs from St. Tammany Parish laid numerous eggs in the laboratory in groups of 6 to 100 attached to twigs in the water (Cagle notes). Tadpoles were described in detail by Siekmann (1949), who indicated that Louisiana specimens reach at least 42 mm in total length. A reexamination of the Tulane larvae Siekmann studied revealed that even though preserved, some of the larvae actually measure 43 mm. Other than a bicolored tail musculature and a high fin, the tadpole has no distinctive appearance.

Tulane field parties collected a large number of breeding *P. ornata* at a pond near Hickory, St. Tammany Parish, 17–19 December 1948. From this same pond, larvae measuring 15–26 mm were secured on 2 January 1949. By 18 February some larvae had reached a length of 41 mm, and on 12 March most larvae were 35–41 mm long and beginning to transform, some completing the process on 18 March at a body length of 14–15 mm. These data indicate that the larval period for *P. ornata* is approximately 90 days.

Pseudacris streckeri Wright and Wright
Strecker's Chorus Frog
Plate V

Recognition. A stocky little frog attaining a maximum length of $1\frac{7}{8}$ in. (48 mm); adhesive discs small, scarcely wider than the toes; forearms stout and toadlike; ground color gray to brown or green; a dark triangular spot present between the eyes; a dark mask through the eye, and a dark suborbital spot; body usually with irregularly placed dark dorsal and lateral spots; groin yellowish.

Distribution. Known in Louisiana only from the vicinity of Shreveport southward into extreme northern De Soto Parish (Map 37).

Taxonomic comments. No extensive study has been undertaken. P. W. Smith (1951) named an isolated northern subspecies; thus the Louisiana population is assignable to the nominate subspecies, *Pseudacris s. streckeri* Wright and Wright, Strecker's chorus frog.

Habitat and habits. The only known Louisiana records are from pasture lands along Cross Lake at Shreveport, just above the Red River floodplain, and from the banks of Wallace Bayou, a tributary of the Red River. This frog species occurs in other states in a variety of habitats, from bottomlands to uplands, but the Louisiana records, which represent an eastern extreme of the range of *P. s. streckeri*, suggest that the species has dispersed eastward via the corridor created by the Red River. Morizot and Douglas (1967, 1970) believed their Caddo Parish records to represent the first report from Louisiana, but Strecker and Frierson (1935) had previously presented the Wallace Bayou records under the name *P. occidentalis* (Baird and Girard). A footnote by the editor of the collection of papers in which the Strecker-Frierson paper appeared indicated that the name referred to *P. streckeri*. Dr. Bryce Brown (pers. com.) of the Strecker Museum at Baylor University says that the De Soto Parish specimens cannot be found now, but that they perhaps reside elsewhere as a result of earlier loans made by Strecker.

In other states *P. streckeri* is encountered feeding on insects along and on roadways after rains from March to October; it is known to burrow headfirst by digging with the forelimbs.

Reproduction. In Louisiana, singing males have been found from 26 January to 12 March (Morizot and Douglas 1970), but elsewhere the breeding season is reported to be from December to 23 May, with most singing occurring in the winter and especially at lower temperatures—even when air temperatures are at the freezing level. The song, a distinctive "ka weeek," much resembling the sound of an ungreased wooden wheel, is sung from the bank or while the male clings to vegetation in the water. Breeding sites are temporary to semipermanent flooded ditches, cattle ponds, sloughs, and the like.

The 400 to 700 eggs are usually deposited in clusters of 20 to 50 below the water surface and are attached to vegetation. The indistinctly marked and skittish tadpoles have sloped snouts in profile and reach a length of at least 35 mm in *P. s. streckeri* before transforming after about 60 days into froglets of 12–16 mm in snout-vent length.

Pseudacris triseriata (Wied)
Striped Chorus Frog
Plate V

Recognition. A small, slender frog (maximum length of 1⅜ in., 35 mm); dorsal pattern variable, usually consisting of three longitudinal dark stripes or linearly arranged streaks and/or spots on a gray to brown ground color; a dark triangular mark usually present between eyes; upper lip with a light stripe; a dark stripe passing from the snout, through the eye, and along the side to the groin; individuals occasionally lacking dorsal pattern, but with the lip stripe and lateral stripe present.

Similar species. At the Pearl River, the eastern boundary of the Florida Parishes, the southern chorus frog, *Pseudacris nigrita*, may enter Louisiana, and distinguishing it from the striped chorus frog may be difficult. Gartside (1980) demonstrated that both morphological and electrophoretic data provide evidence that *P. triseriata* and *P. nigrita* hybridize in a narrow zone, between 4 and 12 miles wide, between Picayune, Mississippi, and Slidell and Hickory, St. Tammany Parish, Louisiana (i.e., an area near the Pearl River). The southern chorus frog tends to have black rather than dark dorsal spots; its dorsal marks tend to break into rows of large spots; its interorbital mark is not expanded into a triangle; and the middorsal stripe has a tendency to fork into two rows posteriorly. The snout of the southern chorus frog is more pointed than that of *P. triseriata*. A trained ear can distinguish the songs of the two chorus frogs.

Distribution. Statewide except for the Marsh (Map 38). Several records seemingly from the Marsh are actually from cheniers or cypress forest–bottomland hardwood habitats.

Taxonomic comments. Several subspecies have been described; Louisiana frogs are referable to *P. triseriata feriarum* (Baird), the upland chorus frog, according to P. W. Smith and

D. M. Smith (1952). A number of recent studies based on reciprocal matings and voice analysis have resulted in the present taxonomic interpretation. M. J. Fouquette (according to Gartside 1980) indicated that mating calls of Louisiana *P. triseriata* and members of the *P. nigrita* complex from the Pearl River and southern Mississippi are essentially similar. Thus the presumed inability of the females in the Pearl River hybrid zone to discriminate between males would facilitate hybridization.

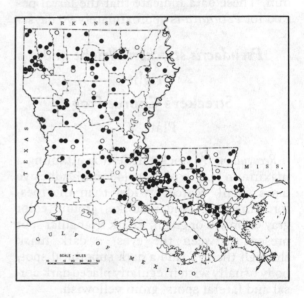

Map 38. Distribution of *Pseudacris triseriata*. Solid circles represent specimens examined; hollow circles represent museum specimens not examined or literature records.

Some authors have suggested that *P. t. feriarum* is a distinct species, *P. feriarum*. Ralin (1970) suggested this allocation on the basis of electrophoresis and because he found *P. t. feriarum* and *P. t. triseriata* individuals side by side but with different morphologies and different voices. Hedges (1986) supported this conclusion with studies based on an electrophoretic analysis of four *feriarum* from eastern Tennessee and two *triseriata* from central Illinois. But, in contrast to those studies, Smith and Smith (1952), using morphological data, claimed that intergradation of the two races occurs in a narrow band from southwestern Ohio, southern Indiana, and southern Illinois, through far northern Kentucky and far northern Arkansas, into northeastern Oklahoma. Conant (1975) did not include the Arkansas and Oklahoma area, but both the Smith and Smith and the Conant maps show an area in Oklahoma as a contact zone with no intergradation. Rossman (1959) and P. W. Smith (1961), using morphological data, demonstrated intergradation in southern Illinois. Further complicating judgments concerning the validity of the opposing assignments are Harper's (1955) and Conant's (1975) statements that intergrades between *P. t. kalmi* and *P. t. triseriata* exist in New Jersey and Pennsylvania, and Hedges' (1986) opinion, based on electrophoretic analysis of four specimens of *kalmi* from Maryland, that *kalmi* warrants recognition as a full species. A final solution to these controversial views must await more extensive studies on samples of specimens from more parts of the range of *P. triseriata*; this wide-ranging species clearly poses problems for modern systematics.

Habitat and habits. This ground-dwelling frog occurs in all kinds of habitats from cultivated fields to forestlands but is especially abundant in forested areas. Like so many of our temporary water breeders, this frog is seldom discovered outside of the reproductive season, but it is seen occasionally hopping through weedy fields or over the forest floor. This species also is sometimes found amidst low, weedy vegetation or under some piece of ground cover. Scattered reports indicate that *P. triseriata* consumes the usual array of small insects and invertebrates. Striped chorus frogs are preyed upon by various vertebrates; a western ribbon snake, *Thamnophis proximus*, from St. Charles Parish regurgitated one of these frogs.

Reproduction. Pseudacris triseriata, principally a winter breeder, commences singing as early as 28 October and is rarely heard after early April. Viosca (notes) heard a few of these frogs at Port Allen, West Baton Rouge Parish, on 3 July 1940. The voice is a grating chirp that can be simulated by running the thumb along the teeth of a stiff comb; the trills are repeated fairly continuously. Vocalization is greatly stimulated by rainfall and is frequently heard in the daytime, though it is primarily nocturnal. The recorded air temperatures for singing in Louisiana are 44°–75°F (6.5°–24°C).

The breeding sites are invariably shallow temporary pools, ditches, and flooded fields where emergent vegetation or a grassy margin is present. The males usually sit concealed among grasses in the water. A quiet approach can bring the observer directly to the frog—but be cautious, the frog may be closer than it seems because the sound volume of a single individual can be very loud from 2 to 3 ft away.

Females lay 500 to 1,500 eggs in the form of rather soft jellied clusters of 7 to 176, which are attached to vegetation. Livezey (1952) reported that tadpoles in eastern Texas reach 40 mm in total length and require 48 to 80+ days to metamorphose. The Tulane collections have larvae that measure as long as 43 mm. The tadpoles usually have dark dots on the dorsum, a bicolored tail musculature with a dark stripe on each side of the pigmented area, and freckled tail fins.

Newly transformed frogs in Louisiana measure 8.5–13.5 mm in snout-vent length. Fifteen juveniles taken 20 April in St. Charles Parish range from 12 to 19 mm. Whitaker (1971) stated the approximate age of 19-mm young to be three months past transformation. Extrapolation of these figures, correlated with the known breeding dates for Louisiana, suggests that Livezey's (1952) Texas data may be applicable here for the maximum larval period.

FAMILY LEPTODACTYLIDAE
SOUTHERN FROGS

The huge and complex family Leptodactylidae includes perhaps 51 living genera comprising 710 species, yet the natural range is only from southern Arizona, southern New Mexico, and south-central Texas southward through most of South America and the West Indies. One introduced species is widespread in peninsular Florida and more recently has appeared in Louisiana. The group includes the smallest species of frog known as well as perhaps the second largest species. All modes of life history occur in the family: oviparous in water, oviparous on land, and even one that is ovoviviparous. Some are entirely aquatic and others are arboreal. The United States is home to three native genera comprising five species and an introduced genus consisting of a single species.

Eleutherodactylus planirostris (Cope)
Greenhouse Frog
Plate V

Recognition. A small, totally terrestrial frog attaining a length of 1¼ in. (32 mm); toes long, slender, unwebbed, with strongly developed tubercles at the joints, the tips ending in adhesive discs; vomerine teeth in transverse series behind internal nares; dorsal pattern either with irregularly distributed dark spots on a brownish olive ground color or striped, with a light dorsolateral stripe on either side; usually a black interorbital blotch; tip of snout red.

Similar species. This species strongly resembles the cricket frog (*Acris*) at first sight, but lacks webbing on the toes. It also may be confused with a small *Hyla* or *Pseudacris triseriata*; however, it has less conspicuous toe discs than *Hyla* and lacks the dark line through the eye that *P. triseriata* has. If in

doubt, open the frog's mouth and examine the vomerine tooth arrangement.

Distribution. Known from Audubon Park in New Orleans where a thriving colony has been established since at least 1975 (Plotkin and Atkinson 1979) in an area no more than 150 ft in diameter (Map 39). Several animals were released at Dundee's home in 1977, and in 1979 a subadult was found. Apparently New Orleans is a suitable locality for this species to spread. In July 1980 many young, recently hatched individuals were discovered in a garden one-half mile from the Audubon Park location. In mid-June 1981 eggs with developed froglets were found at a location 7 miles northeast of Audubon Park, and in early August 1981 numerous juveniles were found close to that location.

Map 39. Distribution of *Eleutherodactylus planirostris.* Solid circles represent specimens examined; hollow circles represent museum specimens not examined or literature records.

The 1981 locations are not far from a large nursery that handles plantings for the New Orleans park system. We suspect that the nursery may have been the source for the original introduction of greenhouse frogs in

New Orleans because it acquires many plants from Florida. Although these frogs probably came from Florida, where they are widespread, the original distribution of the species was Cuba, the Cayman Islands, and the Bahama Islands. This species probably entered the United States on imported plants.

Taxonomic comments. Four races are known, of which only *Eleutherodactylus p. planirostris* (Cope), the greenhouse frog, is known from the United States. The striped phase represents a dominant inherited pattern. Floridian populations may contain all striped, all mottled, or both striped and mottled phases in varying percentages. The Audubon Park population apparently descended from an introduction of mottled parents of pure recessive stock, but in October 1981 a striped specimen was found in a population close to Audubon Park, suggesting, therefore, that a low genetic frequency for striping may exist in the Audubon area animals. Striped specimens characterize the animals from near the nursery 7 miles to the northeast. As the frogs continue to spread in the New Orleans area, we will probably encounter mixed-pattern populations.

Habitat and habits. Because the entire life cycle of this frog occurs on land, it is a highly mobile species, requiring only moist areas in which to hide or lay the eggs. The frogs are common in city gardens as well as in the countryside in Florida and may also form colonies indoors in greenhouses. Since 1875 they have spread from southern to northern Florida and may well expand their range similarly in southern Louisiana. In wet weather and at night, they may be found hopping in the open; otherwise they are readily found under stones, leaves, boards, logs, and debris that provide moist shelter. Their presence often is revealed by the series of four to six faint, whistling chirps uttered at night or in rainy weather. The voice is decidedly insectlike.

In an intensive study in Florida, Goin (1947b) noted that the diet included a large variety of insects, some miscellaneous arthropods, and rarely an earthworm.

Reproduction. Goin (1947b) noted that actual breeding occurred from late May to September in northern Florida. Egg clutches that he observed contained 3 to 26 eggs, the monthly averages ranging from 7.0 to 17.5, with the largest clutches being laid in midsummer. The eggs measured 3–4 mm in overall diameter, and females often kicked dirt over the eggs. Deposition usually was under objects where 100 percent humidity could be maintained. In 13 to 20 days the eggs hatched, releasing tiny frogs only 4.3–5.7 mm long. Development is direct—there is no tadpole stage.

As noted under "Distribution," eggs and young have been discovered in New Orleans from mid-June to July.

FAMILY MICROHYLIDAE
NARROW-MOUTHED TOADS

The diverse family Microhylidae contains about 60 genera comprising 280 species distributed from the southeastern and south-central United States and extreme southern Arizona southward through much of South America; the family also occurs in southern Africa, Madagascar, southeastern Asia, and the Indo-Australian Archipelago throughout New Guinea, and just barely enters northwestern Australia. Two genera occur in the United States, one in Louisiana. Although termed narrow-mouthed toads because most species have small, pointed heads, some have normally shaped heads. Most are terrestrial, semifossorial, ant- and termite-eating creatures, but at least one Madagascan species is arboreal and has expanded toe discs. Tadpoles lack beaks and "teeth." Most species have aquatic tadpoles, but in some there may be direct development of terrestrial eggs from which advanced tadpoles hatch to finish development in the nest. Several species lay eggs in bromeliads or in leaf axils of banana and similar plants.

Gastrophryne carolinensis (Holbrook)
Eastern Narrow-mouthed Toad

Plate IV

Recognition. A squat, short-limbed frog reaching an adult size of 1–1½ in. (25–38 mm); the head pointed with a transverse fold of skin across it just in back of the eyes; toes unwebbed; ground color gray, brown, or reddish tan; middorsal region usually with a wide, black-margined dark area that tapers toward the head; venter mottled gray and dirty white.

Distribution. Statewide (Map 40).

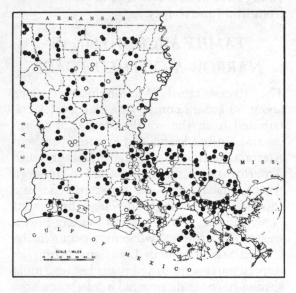

Map 40. Distribution of *Gastrophryne carolinensis.* Solid circles represent specimens examined; hollow circles represent museum specimens not examined or literature records.

Taxonomic comments. No subspecies are recognized, but Hecht and Matalas (1946) considered *Gastrophryne carolinensis* to be a race of *G. olivacea.* Current interpretations are that *olivacea* and *carolinensis* may

hybridize. The most recent taxonomic study is by Nelson (1972).

Habitat and habits. Forested areas are the best places to find *G. carolinensis,* especially in hardwood floodplain sites, but meadows also are utilized if suitable ground cover exists. Narrow-mouthed toads are common even in vacant city lots. Viosca (1923) found narrow-mouthed toads on sea beaches in southeastern Louisiana, and J. R. Dixon (according to Neill 1958a) found them under boards in a salt marsh in Cameron Parish. William Brode (according to Neill 1958a) said that they breed in water too salty to drink at Bay St. Louis, Mississippi, close to the Louisiana border. Breeding sites usually are permanent or temporary pools, though the latter are by far the preferred places. P. K. Anderson (1954) gave a substantial description of the habits in a study based mostly on Louisiana localities.

These small toads are secretive by day but move into the open after dark. When disturbed, they scramble away; if undisturbed they walk. Leaping in typical anuran fashion is only rarely observed.

These little toads are often gregarious, many being found under a single board, piece of cardboard, or log, or within the loose, pulpy wood of old stumps and logs. They often occupy rather wet ground and may dive into crawfish burrows that open beneath cover objects.

This species eats all sorts of arthropods and a few snails, but the major food items are ants and termites.

The skin secretions, irritating to the human eye and to mucous membranes of the mouth, protect the frog from the ants on which it often feeds.

One remarkable habit of a near relative, *G. olivacea,* needs to be checked in *G. carolinensis.* The former often lives under the same stone as tarantulas in Texas, Oklahoma, and Arkansas; the same tarantula (*Dugesiella hentzi*) occurs in western Louisiana (Rossman 1984), and *G. carolinensis* also enters the range of *G. olivacea.*

Reproduction. The voice of singing males has been heard from 21 March to 3 October, but most breeding activity appears to occur from late April to September and has been noted only when air temperatures have exceeded 67°F (19.5°C). Most singing occurs at night, but some may be heard by day. Based on our observations and those reported in the literature, the water temperatures can reach 36°C (97°F) and air temperatures 33°C (91.5°F) when singing occurs. Of the many kinds of breeding sites utilized, the major prerequisite appears to be some suitable plant growth or debris to which the singing male can cling. The preferred singing stations are amid clumps of grass in the water. The voice is a low "b-zzzzzz," prolonged for a second or so. P. K. Anderson (1954) suggested that the sequences of songs by individual males fall into a pattern that indicates a coordinated social relationship.

The eggs, numbering up to 1,059, are laid in masses of 10 to 150 that form a surface film. The eggs within the small film (maximum size 102 × 178 mm) are flat above and distinct so that the mass appears to be a mosaic composed of glass marbles. Hatching occurs quickly, usually within a few days, and the tadpoles transform at a length of about 10 mm from May to October. The tadpoles are distinctive, resembling wide, flat miniature frying pans, and lack any kind of horny mouthparts. Wright and Wright (1949) indicated that the larval period lasts from 20 to 70 days.

FAMILY PELOBATIDAE
SPADE-FOOTED TOADS

The family Pelobatidae is composed of 8 to 10 living genera comprising 80 to 85 species ranging from fossorial to terrestrial in habits; all lay eggs in water. The skin is rather smooth, the limbs are short, and these animals spend much time far from water, thus qualifying in part for the concept of "toad."

Although the group is generally called "spadefoots," only species living north of the tropics possess spadelike metatarsal tubercles. The family is distributed through much of southern North America, throughout continental Europe into Eurasia, and from western China into the large islands of the East Indies. One genus of five species inhabits the United States.

Scaphiopus holbrookii (Harlan)
Eastern Spadefoot
Plate IV

Recognition. A medium-sized toad attaining a length of 3¼ in. (83 mm); body moderately tuberculate; parotoid glands distinct but cranial ridges absent; pupil of the eye vertically elliptical in bright light; each hind foot webbed and with a single, black, horny spadelike tubercle on the inner surface; two distinct pectoral glands on the venter; ground color gray to brown or olive; dorsum with two broad yellow lines from eye to vent forming a roughly hourglass-shaped pattern.

Distribution. The Florida Parishes and the uplands and flatwoods of northern and west-central Louisiana (Map 41); absent from the Mississippi River alluvial plain, the Prairie, and the Marsh.

Taxonomic comments. Two subspecies occur in Louisiana: *Scaphiopus h. holbrookii* (Harlan), the eastern spadefoot, which has a level space between the orbits, and *S. h. hurterii* Strecker, Hurter's spadefoot, which has a raised area (boss) between the eyes. The Mississippi River alluvial plain completely isolates the eastern *S. h. holbrookii* populations from the western *S. h. hurterii* populations. *Scaphiopus h. holbrookii* is smaller than *S. h. hurterii*, reaching a maximum size of only 73 mm. The most recent review of this species is that by Wasserman (1968).

Habitat and habits. Scaphiopus holbrookii is an inhabitant of forested areas and savannas, both in river bottomlands and uplands.

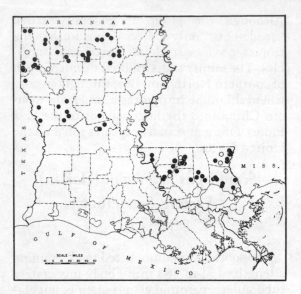

Map 41. Distribution of *Scaphiopus hol-brookii*. Solid circles represent specimens examined; hollow circles represent museum specimens not examined or literature records.

Spadefoots may be found hidden under surface objects, but they are adept at burrowing into loose, sandy soils to reach suitably moist levels. The burrow may be repeatedly used as a retreat, and the toad emerges from the burrow at night to range abroad for its food, which includes worms and all sorts of arthropods. Hurter's spadefoot is especially apt to come onto roadways at night to feed, sometimes even gathering beneath streetlights in small towns.

The skin secretions have an odd, musty smell and may irritate both eyes and nose of the unwary person who rubs his face after handling a spadefoot.

Reproduction. Spadefoot breeding is closely associated with torrential rains that can cause rapid formation of temporary pools. When the toads lying in their burrows are adequately stimulated by the rain, they move to pools where the first males have begun to sing. Farm ponds are sometimes used, but genuinely permanent water is shunned. The

chorus size after a heavy rain may be large, numbering in the hundreds, and the voice, a somewhat nasal, explosive "waaank" or "waagh" given at intervals of 3–4 seconds, may carry for long distances. Large diurnal choruses are not infrequent, but most singing is done at night.

The actual breeding season extends from at least 18 February to 27 July for *S. h. holbrookii* in Louisiana and from 10 February to 24 April for *S. h. hurterii*. The latter race surely breeds later than the known dates but field data are not available. Viosca (notes) collected 10 spadefoots on 18 September 1920 but did not state that they were singing. The lowest air temperature at which singing has been noted in Louisiana is 60.5°F (16°C), but because the males sing while floating in water, their body temperatures may be significantly different from the air temperature. In Connecticut, spadefoots may sing at temperatures below 50°F (10°C) (Ball 1936).

The 200+ eggs are laid in strings, sometimes with small clusters intervening, amid vegetation. Unlike typical true toad (*Bufo*) eggs, the spadefoot eggs are not encased in a tubular gelatinous covering.

Development of spadefoots is a rapid process, an evolutionary feature perhaps related to their apparent origin in dry environments where surface waters are very ephemeral. The larval period may be only a dozen days or as long as 40 days.

The tadpoles can be readily identified in Louisiana because spadefoots are the only species having a medial anus and the mouth not laterally infolded (i.e., not emarginate). The typical appearance is somewhat flattened, and the posterior part of the body is wider than the anterior part. The tadpole of the eastern spadefoot is uniformly bronze in color, whereas Hurter's spadefoot tadpoles are gray with numerous scattered silvery chromatophores arranged so that a light hourglass pattern, forerunner of the adult pattern, is apparent. The tadpoles reach 28 mm in total length, and at transformation the toadlets are 8.5–12 mm long.

FAMILY RANIDAE
TRUE FROGS

What most Americans have seen and recognize as a frog is most likely a member of the family Ranidae. This large cosmopolitan family is absent only from Antarctica, southern South America, most of Australia, Madagascar, New Zealand, a section of western Africa, and the coldest parts of Eurasia.

About 47 living genera comprising 667 species, ranging from semiarboreal to fossorial forms, are included in the group. Most are semiaquatic and have extensive webbing of the hind feet. The largest known anuran is an African ranid that reaches about a foot (305 mm) in body length and weighs in excess of 10 lb (4.5 kg). Virtually all species lay eggs in still water, where the tadpole stage may last as long as two years. A few species have direct development on land.

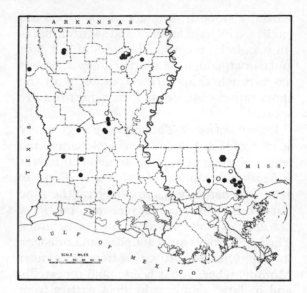

Map 42.   Distribution of *Rana areolata*. Solid circles represent specimens examined; hollow circles represent museum specimens not examined or literature records; a hexagon in the middle of a parish represents a literature record for the parish with no specific locality stated.

Rana areolata Baird and Girard
Crawfish Frog
Plate VII

Recognition. A large, stockily built frog (maximum snout-vent length 3⅞ in., 98 mm); skin smooth to wrinkled or warty; dorsolateral ridges present, distinct, dull colored, and considerably invaded by dorsal spots; dorsal and lateral pattern of prominent spots interspersed with numerous small dark markings on a gray to brown ground color, the upper lip heavily mottled; venter light and unpatterned; groin and concealed portions of the thighs yellow.

Distribution. Disjunct; one area in the eastern Florida Parishes, the other in western Louisiana (Map 42). Absent from the Marsh. Perhaps widespread throughout the wet forested areas, prairie, and floodplains of west-

ern Louisiana. A locality in Tangipahoa Parish was questioned by Goin and Netting (1940), who reported the animals to be of the wrong race and to have a questionable source and collection history.

Taxonomic comments. Two subspecies are recognized in Louisiana, *Rana a. areolata* Baird and Girard, the southern crawfish frog, which occurs west of the Mississippi River, and *R. a. sevosa* Goin and Netting, the dusky crawfish frog, a resident of the Florida Parishes. Actual contact between the two races is not known, but Neill (1957) indicated that intermediates between *R. sevosa*, as *R. a. sevosa* was then known, and *R. areolata* occurred in Mississippi, presumably reflecting contact between the two forms at some time in the past. Dundee feels that the similarity of the two forms justifies Neill's allocation of them to the single species, *R. areolata*.

Rana a. areolata is characterized by an essentially smooth skin, dorsal spots that are encircled by light borders, and a venter that is immaculate except for the sides of the chin and throat, which are spotted. *Rana a. sevosa* has a rough skin, dark coloration with the spots rather obscure, and the venter heavily spotted.

Habitat and habits. These are shy frogs, rarely seen except at the breeding sites, where the least disturbance will cause them to retreat beneath the surface of the water. *Rana a. sevosa* apparently occurs only in the pine flatwoods, where it is a rare frog, but *R. a. areolata* exhibits a wider range of habitats. The latter frog is most abundant in Louisiana in the Ouachita River bottomlands near Monroe, where it has been found repeatedly and in large numbers by field parties from Northeast Louisiana University. Reports from other states, especially that of Bragg (1953), indicate that the southern crawfish frog, *R. a. areolata*, may utilize pasture ponds or breeding pools in river floodplains, prairies, woodlands, etc. Our knowledge of *R. areolata* in Louisiana is limited primarily because of the secretive nature of this species and its winter breeding habits and brief breeding periods. If more effort is made to sample tadpoles around the state, we may be able to fill in many of the current distributional gaps.

Both races of *Rana areolata* may be called fossorial, the main difference being that *R. a. areolata* utilizes crawfish burrows in low ground for its hiding places, and *R. a. sevosa*, at least in Mississippi (M. J. Allen 1932), uses gopher tortoise burrows for its shelter. We suspect, however, that *R. a. sevosa* uses crawfish burrows in Louisiana because the gopher tortoise is scarce in the areas where crawfish frogs have been found repeatedly over the past 30 years. Percy Viosca and H. B. Chase (according to Wright and Wright 1949) reported finding *R. a. sevosa* in holes under stumps. Viosca (notes) collected 15 of these frogs at Slidell on 15 July 1927; there is no indication if they were breeding, newly trans-

formed, or adults discovered in hiding places. In mid-summer of 1945, Dundee found a crawfish frog hopping across his military gear as it lay on the ground in a dry, grassy, pine forest north of Alexandria.

We know nothing about the food habits of *R. a. sevosa*, but Goin and Netting (1940) made the interesting observation that *R. a. areolata* feeds on insects, spiders, and crawfish and has a relatively narrow head, whereas *R. a. aesopus*, a Florida form, preys on toads and frogs and has the largest mouth of any race of *R. areolata*. From these observations they deduced that *sevosa*, with a mouth almost as large as that of *aesopus*, probably feeds on anurans and insects.

Individuals of both races produce a somewhat offensive-smelling skin secretion.

Reproduction. *Rana a. areolata* sings in Louisiana from 14 January to 3 March, and we have records of *R. a. sevosa* singing from 29 December to 21 March; Viosca (notes) secured four (singing?) on 11 April. Both races apparently sing after heavy, warm winter rains, and each has a voice that resembles a guttural snore such as may be made by inhaling through the mouth and vibrating the soft palate. Francis Rose (pers. com.) said that he had heard some of them singing from beneath the water. Water and air temperatures during the breeding period of *R. a. sevosa* have been recorded from 59° to 72°F (15°–22°C).

Over many years Tulane field parties have sought the elusive dusky crawfish frog at a site near Pearl River, St. Tammany Parish. Study of both this site and another not too far distant, and the difficulty in finding breeding congresses, suggests that these frogs may breed only in alternate years. Choruses rarely consist of more than a dozen males, and the sound is not easily heard, but the sites are investigated whenever weather conditions seem suitable. The original site, a clear woodland pool, has been destroyed by urbanization; the newer site, a depressed grassy clearing in a pine forest, failed to fill up for several seasons, and in 1981 the land was cleared for tree planting. The future of this frog in the Florida Parishes seems bleak as more and more land is converted to agriculture, estates, and tree farms.

The 3,000 to 7,000 eggs are deposited as a large mass 12–15 cm in diameter and attached beneath the surface to vegetation.

The tadpoles have distinct lines of muciferous crypts of pits from head to tail, usually possess strong mottling on body and tail, and often (especially in *R. a. sevosa*) have considerable yellow pigmentation.

Tadpoles of *R. a. areolata* reach at least 63 mm in length and transform in about 63 days (Bragg 1953); *R. a. sevosa* reared in the laboratory reach 74 mm in length and transform in 141 to 155 days when kept at 20±3°C (Volpe 1957). Newly transformed specimens may be as long as 30 mm. Volpe succeeded in rearing some of the transformed frogs for more than 9½ months past transformation, at which time the body lengths were 48–50+ mm.

Rana catesbeiana Shaw
Bullfrog
Plate VII

Recognition. The largest frog in the United States (maximum length 8 in., 203 mm); skin usually with numerous small tubercles; dorsolateral ridges absent from trunk, instead turning downward just behind the large tympanum (eardrum); toes of hind feet extensively webbed, but longest toe projecting beyond end of web; dorsum green or brown, with scattered black dots, mottling (sometimes forming a reticulum), or a maze of broadly curving dark marks; venter white or yellow, often heavily mottled with dark areas.

Similar species. Rana catesbeiana is often confused with the pig frog, *R. grylio*, which differs in having (1) the web extending more nearly to the end of the toes; (2) the tip of the fifth toe, when the fourth and fifth are adpressed, extending to or beyond the base of the next to last joint of the fourth toe, whereas in *R. catesbeiana* the tip of the fifth falls short of the next to last joint; (3) a narrower head (ratio of width between midpoints of tympana to width between eyes exceeds 8.8:1, the maximum for *catesbeiana*, in 75 percent of *grylio*, and is never lower than 7:1, but lower values occur in at least 33 percent of *catesbeiana*); and (4) a pair of tan dorsolateral stripes in small- to medium-sized individuals (see Plate VII).

Distribution. Statewide wherever permanent freshwater habitats exist (Map 43).

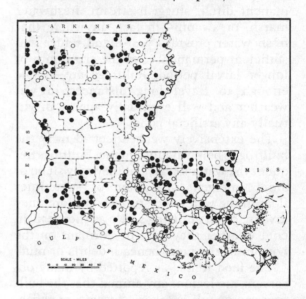

Map 43. Distribution of *Rana catesbeiana*. Solid circles represent specimens examined; hollow circles represent museum specimens not examined or literature records.

Taxonomic comments. No real systematic studies have been attempted, and in fact, they might be difficult because of the numerous accidental and deliberate introductions of bullfrogs into parts of the natural range and into many areas where the species does not occur naturally. Nonetheless, Dundee believes that there may either be justification for recognition of two or more subspecies of bullfrog, or that there may actually be two species of frog designated *Rana catesbeiana*. The latter view is suggested because northern bullfrogs and upland bullfrogs usually are unmottled dorsally, are olive green above, and have black punctate dots on the dorsum, whereas those from the swamplands, especially the Atchafalaya Basin of southern Louisiana, have a reticulum or maze pattern on the back and in general have rich green and reddish brown coloration in the dorsal pattern. Initial investigation is currently underway using karyotype and protein analysis data.

Habitat and habits. Bullfrogs can be found around almost any lake, pond, slough, permanent ditch, sluggish stream, freshwater marsh, or swamp—in fact, anywhere that fresh water provides year-round refuge and sufficient permanence for the six-month or longer larval period. Bullfrogs are mobile enough to travel long distances in wet weather and will eventually appear in virtually any artificial pond.

The extensively webbed feet identify the bullfrog as being highly aquatic. Bullfrogs frequent the water's edge, but they may sit on or amid emergent vegetation or sometimes float in the water. If disturbed on shore, they dive in, often emitting a yelp as they leap. In cold weather they may lie dormant on the bottom of the pond beneath debris or mud.

The food items, as reported by many observers, are legion: any animal that the bullfrog can engulf is taken—insects, crawfish, fishes, frogs, salamanders, snakes, birds, mice, bats, and so forth. Viosca (1934) considered insects the primary food of young bullfrogs in Louisiana and crawfish the major item for adults.

Reproduction. The voice of the bullfrog has been heard from 28 December through the summer months, but actual breeding in Louisiana appears to take place from 1 March through the summer, peaking in May and June. Bullfrogs rarely sing if the air temperature is below 70°F (21°C) and often sing in the daytime, almost invariably from a bank or atop floating vegetation. The voice is unmistakable and sounds like a resonant "brrr woooom"; it may be imitated by inflating the cheeks, puckering the lips, tightening the throat and then exhaling strongly while uttering the "brrr" with the lips flattening and widening as the exhalation occurs. Singing males are well separated along shorelines in a semblance of territorial spacing.

The egg mass, an enormous floating film sometimes 2–4 ft (500–1000+ mm) across, is deposited among water plants and shrubs in the water. Each of the 10,000 to 20,000 eggs is contained in a single gelatinous envelope.

The larval period is variable, depending on latitude. In Louisiana the larvae may require five to six months (never more than a year) for transformation, but farther north almost two years may be required. The tadpole is green and peppered dorsally with black dots; dots also are sprinkled throughout the fins. The belly of the tadpole is white or pale yellow and may be mottled with dark pigment. Wright (1929) found the tadpoles to reach 170 mm in length, but the largest we have noted in Louisiana measured only 125 mm. This large Louisiana tadpole, however, has no legs and thus had probably not reached its greatest size. Newly transformed young may measure 31–59 mm in length.

Remarks. Bullfrogs have long been Louisiana's most economically important frog because of the great demand for their flesh, especially as frog legs. The bullfrog and the pig frog have long been protected under Louisiana law, and a valid fishing license is required to take them during the limited season. Still, this once-great industry has been severely diminished, both by overcollecting and by the pollution and destruction of breeding sites. The bullfrog legs people eat today may come from frog farms in Japan, Bangladesh, and Indonesia rather than from Louisiana. India recently started to protect the frogs as a form of mosquito control.

Gowanloch (1935) provided some interesting data on the frog industry. He noted that the frogs are marketable in three sizes: jumbo, medium, and small. A 5½-in. (140 mm) frog weighing 8½ oz (241 g) provides 5½ oz (156 g) of dressed-out weight; a 7-in. (178 mm) frog weighing 17 oz (482 g) dresses out at 11 oz (312 g). In 1917, larger frogs, dressed out, brought a price of $3 per dozen. Gowanloch quoted a packer who stated that most Louisiana market frogs come from the area between the Atchafalaya Basin and the Sabine River, and from the Gulf northward to the 31st parallel (i.e., the northern border of the Florida Parishes). A dressed jumbo frog weighs up to 14 oz (397 g). Collectors received $1 to $3 per dozen, and in the winter up to $4.50 per dozen for larger frogs. The packer stated that his firm handled 400,000 frogs per season. Other statistics Gowanloch gave for Louisiana show that in 1926 (when data collection began in the state), 44,457 lb (20,208 kg) of frogs valued at $6,668 were marketed; in 1931 the catch was 1,856,354 lb (843,797 kg) valued at $464,089, and in 1933, 1,817,450 lb (826,114 kg) valued at $276,618. A vice president of a frog-shipping firm in Rayne, Bobby Hebert, spoke in the 1960s of shipping only 500 to 600 frogs during peak summer days, whereas in the 1940s his firm shipped 15,000 a day. In mid-1976, a New Orleans seafood market asked $3.48 per pound for frog legs, and those are imported legs priced lower than domestic supplies. The dealer remembers prices of 10¢ per pound.

Can we regain a valuable industry in frogs? Certainly it seems feasible, according to procedures for frog ranching described by Viosca (1934). Viosca's methodology suggests that rice, muskrats, and frogs can be produced from the same field, but he also tells of pond-culture methods. Asian countries use low-cost labor to do their artificial frog propagation, but at today's inflated prices, a domestic production may indeed be within reality. Culley et al. (1976) have developed successful

techniques for laboratory propagation of bullfrogs.

Rana clamitans Latreille
Green Frog
Plate VII

Recognition. A medium-sized frog attaining a maximum length of 3½ in. (86 mm); toes extensively webbed; dorsolateral ridges on the back; a plain brown to dull bronze back with indistinct, irregularly placed dark spots; venter usually white in adults, but subadults may have extensive dark wormlike markings, especially on the legs and throat.

Distribution. Statewide wherever suitable freshwater pools are available, but absent from brackish or salty areas of the Marsh (Map 44).

Taxonomic comments. In Louisiana, *Rana clamitans* is represented by the nominate subspecies, *R. c. clamitans* Latreille, the

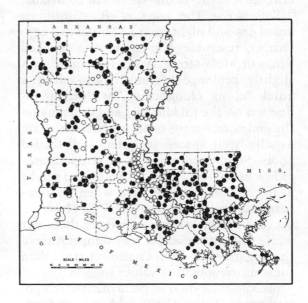

Map 44. Distribution of *Rana clamitans*. Solid circles represent specimens examined; hollow circles represent museum specimens not examined or literature records.

bronze frog. The most recent taxonomic study is by Mecham (1954). Stewart (1983) provided an updated summary of pertinent literature.

Habitat and habits. This species is the most frequently encountered Louisiana ranid frog. *Rana clamitans* is especially prevalent in swamps, marsh margins, and forested areas, where it prefers pools but also commonly occurs along streams. It is often taken under ground litter, logs, boards, etc., in cooler weather. When disturbed, this species often gives a shrill "squawk" as it leaps into the water. It will then swim a short distance under water and lie motionless, either exposed or usually just under loose leaf debris. On rainy or wet nights this species is found in quantity on roadways.

The diet, as noted by Carr (1940), regularly includes gastropods in addition to the usual array of arthropods taken by frogs. Predators of *R. clamitans* include water snakes and ribbon snakes, the stomachs of which often contain the remains of this species in Louisiana.

Reproduction. The song of *R. clamitans*, heard day and night from 12 March to 3 September, resembles the sound of a plucked banjo or viola string. A single "clung" or a slightly prolonged "clung" followed by a quick "clung, clung, clung," with rising inflection on the middle note and dropping on the end note, are the usual sounds. Males are usually well spaced in quiet, well-shaded pools. Singing commences at temperatures as low as 55°–60°F (12.5°–15.5°C) and can be heard on hot summer days when air temperatures may reach 90°F (32.5°C). However, because the male often sprawls in the water while singing, the actual body temperature of the frog may be within a narrower range than these air-temperature values suggest.

Breeding sites may be permanent or temporary pools. Tinkle (1959) told of large numbers of tadpoles dying as temporary pools in a Louisiana swamp dried up. The 1,000 to 3,000 eggs are deposited in a surface film, either in the open or attached to vegetation. A single mass may cover an area up to a foot square (300 × 300 mm). Each egg is enclosed in two gelatinous envelopes.

The tadpoles have an olive green dorsum with numerous dark spots. The tail is long and heavily mottled or even black; the fins are relatively low, emphasizing the elongate appearance of the tail. Martof (1956) dispelled an earlier belief that the larval period in this frog always requires overwintering. Larvae he observed in Michigan might transform in 70 to 85 days if they were from eggs laid early in the season; for those laid later, overwintering could stretch the developmental period to 360 days. We cannot confirm that his observations apply to the southern race, but, in view of the mild Louisiana climate, a larval period of 70 to 85 days would seem logical. However, because of late breeding activity, overwintering could be expected. A survey of southeastern Louisiana larvae in the Tulane University collections shows that groups of tadpoles 38–60 mm long have been taken 1 December; tadpoles 33–50 mm, on 16 January; larvae 53 mm, on 5 February; and animals without front leg appearance up to 86 mm on 22 March. These records certainly suggest that late-season tadpoles may grow rapidly during the winter months, but are unable to transform until warm weather sets in. The largest larvae always seem to be from spring collections, not summer and fall, as one would expect for the main crop from the spring or early summer breeders.

Wright (1929) gave the maximum size for larvae of *R. c. clamitans* as 84.8 mm. The Tulane collections include a tadpole 100 mm long from Jackson Parish that is close to metamorphosis, and several others from various localities reach 86–88 mm. Newly transformed *R. c. clamitans* in Louisiana measure 21–24 mm in length.

Rana grylio Stejneger
Pig Frog
Plate VII

Recognition. A large frog somewhat resembling the bullfrog but not reaching such an extreme size (maximum length 6⅜ in., 162 mm); dorsolateral ridges absent from trunk, turning downward just behind the large tympanum (eardrum); head more pointed than that of the bullfrog; toes of the hind feet extensively webbed, almost to the toe tips; dorsal coloration of adults metallic green to olive or blackish brown, often with obscure dark markings; venter white or yellowish white, usually with considerable dark mottling, especially posteriorly and on legs; juveniles and subadults with tan dorsolateral stripes giving animals superficial appearance of having dorsolateral ridges.

Similar species. See the bullfrog (*Rana catesbeiana*) account for methods of distinguishing the pig frog from the bullfrog.

Distribution. Lowlands of the southern third of the state in flatwoods, bottomlands, and freshwater sections of the Marsh; locally distributed in the Florida Parishes (Map 45). Viosca (1923) stated that pig frogs may tolerate moderate salinity in marshland waters.

Taxonomic comments. No special study has been undertaken, but Dundee (1974b) indicated that Florida specimens differ in coloration and spotting from those of Louisiana.

Habitat and habits. This species is the most aquatic of our native frogs, sometimes appearing on roadways in wet weather, but usually found in heavily vegetated, deeper waters. In the Florida Parishes it is not infrequent in permanent roadside ditches, but the most favored habitats are swamp pools, marsh pools, and clear freshwater lakes in the Marsh. Because of its habitat preferences and the limited number of known localities, this species should be sought by boat rather than by foot. Pig frogs are shy but can be secured at night by shining a flashlight in their eyes.

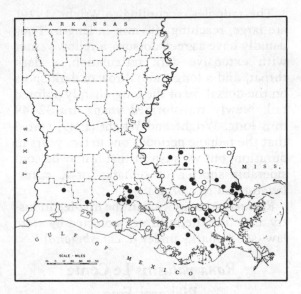

Map 45. Distribution of *Rana grylio*. Solid circles represent specimens examined; hollow circles represent museum specimens not examined or literature records.

The diet of pig frogs in southern Florida includes insects, crawfish, leeches, miscellaneous arthropods, small fishes, frogs, and snakes (Duellman and Schwartz 1958). Lamb (1984) found that arthropods constituted 95 percent of the prey in Georgia, and Carr (1940) reported crawfish to be the major prey in Florida.

Reproduction. The piglike grunting call of *R. grylio,* uttered by floating males, has been heard from 16 February to 11 August in Louisiana; in Florida it is heard year-round, but the actual breeding season extends from March to mid-September (Carr 1940). Despite the large size of this species, Mount (1975) reported two small singing males, 52 and 59 mm, one of which he determined to be sexually mature. Singing occurs night and day, rarely at temperatures below 70°F (21°C).

The 8,000 to 15,000 eggs are deposited in a large surface film measuring 1 × 1 to 1 × 2 ft (305 × 305 to 305 × 610 mm), which is usually attached to vegetation. Each egg is contained in two gelatinous envelopes.

The tadpoles, according to Wright (1929), are large, reaching 100 mm in length. They usually have a green dorsum, a yellow venter with extensive dark reticulation, a dark throat, and a longitudinal row of dark spots on the dorsal fin of the long, sharply pointed tail. Newly transformed young are 32–49 mm long. Wright and Wright (1949) stated that the tadpole period is one to two years in duration, but we suspect that it may be considerably shorter (cf. remarks for *R. catesbeiana* and *R. clamitans*).

Remarks. A major frog in the frog-leg industry and, like the bullfrog, protected by state law (see remarks under *R. catesbeiana*).

Rana palustris Le Conte
Pickerel Frog
Plate VII

Recognition. A medium-sized (maximum length $3\frac{7}{16}$ in., 87 mm), spotted frog; tympanum without a light spot; toes of hind feet webbed for more than half their length; dorsal spots more-or-less square, dark brown or black on a gray or tan ground color, and arranged in two parallel rows, each just medial to dorsolateral ridges; posterior part of venter and groin of adults yellow or orange in life.

Similar species. This species may be confused with the southern leopard frog, *Rana sphenocephala*, but the yellow groin and square dorsal spots of the pickerel frog assure its identification.

Distribution. Upland areas of northern Louisiana and the Florida Parishes; probably occurs in pine forests as far south as Lake Charles (Map 46). The species is absent from the Mississippi River alluvial plain.

Taxonomic comments. The recent study by Schaaf and Smith (1970) recognized no subspecies but indicated that the pickerel frog is variable within its range.

Habitat and habits. Field parties from Northeast Louisiana University and Louisiana

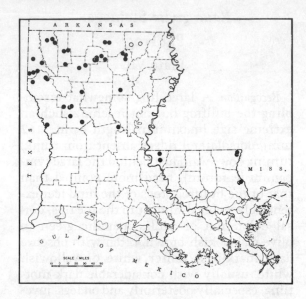

Map 46. Distribution of *Rana palustris*. Solid circles represent specimens examined; hollow circles represent museum specimens not examined or literature records.

Tech University have found this frog crossing the roads in large numbers on rainy nights from February to April; otherwise most collections represent single animals found hopping on roads or in woodlands. The mass movements on roads are said to be mostly unidirectional and apparently represent treks to breeding pools. We have little knowledge of the basic habitat of this species in Louisiana, but Schaaf and Smith (1970) indicated that eastern Texas records often bear notations of "wet floodplain" or "river forest." Our impression here is that the frogs may utilize woodland pools in flatter parts of the terrain for their breeding, but are otherwise nomadic, dispersing to streams that traverse the surrounding lands or remaining terrestrial in moist situations.

Specific information on the diet of the pickerel frog is scarce; the food habits are vaguely stated to be "voracious" (Pope 1947) and the diet probably to consist of arthropods and mollusks (P. W. Smith 1961), but actual studies of digestive tract contents have not been reported.

Pickerel frogs produce skin mucus that is irritating to the eyes, nose, and mouth, and for some people, even to the skin. The secretion is said to be unsavory to snakes and therefore to provide the frogs with protection against major predators. This concept was contradicted by Manion and Cory (1952). Many herpetologists recommend against placing pickerel frogs in collecting bags with other frogs, but Mulcare (1966) refuted the idea that pickerel frogs are toxic to other amphibians. Manion and Cory (1952) found that specimens of *R. palustris* confined with other species of *Rana* were the first to die.

Reproduction. No specific data are available for Louisiana except for remarks by Neil Douglas (pers. com.) that a few have been heard in northern Louisiana when large numbers have been found on the roads. This places the breeding season from early February to April. Winter breeding would seem more probable for more southerly regions of Louisiana. Breeding sites are said to be temporary and permanent woodland pools, quiet pools of small streams, sloughs, and the like (Mount 1975; P. W. Smith 1961; Wright and Wright 1949). The voice is a low, brief, snoring sound that may be emitted under water. The sound may be confused with some of the variations of leopard frog songs.

The eggs are laid in firm, globular clusters of 2,000 to 3,000, each contained in two envelopes. The egg mass is usually placed below the surface and attached to vegetation.

The olive-green tadpoles are marked dorsally with fine black and yellow spots; the tail may have grouped yellow spots or may be almost black; the belly is cream colored. Tadpoles reach lengths up to 76 mm and transform in 70 to 80 days into frogs 19–27 mm in snout-vent length.

Rana sphenocephala Harlan
Southern Leopard Frog
Plate VII

Recognition. A medium-sized (maximum length 5 in., 127 mm, but largest Louisiana specimen examined measuring 92 mm), spotted frog; tympanum usually with a light spot in center; toes of hind feet webbed for more than half their length; dorsal spots rounded and somewhat elongated, irregularly placed, dark brown or black on a gray, tan, or green ground color.

Similar species. This frog may be confused with the pickerel frog, *Rana palustris*, but the lack of yellow underparts, the rounded dorsal spots, and the tympanic light spot will identify the leopard frog. Rarely are the dorsal spots lacking.

Distribution. Ubiquitous in Louisiana near any temporary or permanent fresh water (Map 47).

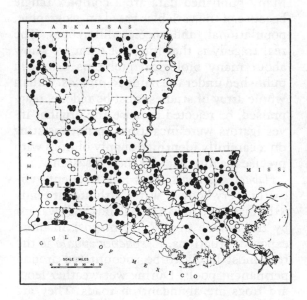

Map 47. Distribution of *Rana sphenocephala*. Solid circles represent specimens examined; hollow circles represent museum specimens not examined or literature records.

Taxonomic comments. Pace (1974), who examined a number of approaches to leopard frog relationships, indicated that an older name, *Rana utricularia*, should be applied to this species. A vast literature exists in which this species is referred to as *R. sphenocephala* or *R. pipiens sphenocephala*. A request for suppression of the name *R. utricularia* has been made to the International Commission on Zoological Nomenclature. The leopard frog complex, a number of species once lumped under the name *R. pipiens*, is distributed from middle latitudes in Canada southward and westward to California, Costa Rica, and the Florida Keys. The traditional morphological approach to classification has been hampered by behavioral, vocal, embryological, physiological, serological, geographical, and other variations, and the systematics are far from being resolved. Additional species probably remain to be recognized, and the comparative details of morphology, ecology, and life history are yet to be clarified. Many published data are a complex tangle because of the variables based on geographic, populational, and species differences. The real tragedy is that much of what we know about many biological problems has been published under the name *R. pipiens*. Thus a whole array of studies must be redone, reappraised, or rejected because the original investigators were incautious in not insisting on a carefully identified supply of frogs with precise locality data for their research.

Habitat and habits. This frog frequents virtually every body of water, although it tends to be displaced in wet woodlands and swamps by the bronze frog (*R. clamitans*). In more exposed situations, *R. sphenocephala* is the frog most likely to be encountered around permanent pools. During wet weather leopard frogs are abundant on roads. They are agile, powerful leapers and difficult to capture, even with the aid of a flashlight at night. In the marshes near New Orleans, leopard frogs are common enough to indicate that they probably can tolerate some degree of brackishness. Viosca (1923) and Liner (1954) reported leopard frogs from brackish-water situations, but we do not know for certain that the frogs actually breed in such waters. Pearse (1911) reported leopard frogs in water containing up to 2.14 percent salt in North Carolina.

Force (1925) found the food habits of southern leopard frogs in Oklahoma to consist mainly of insects. In Florida they are described as indiscriminate feeders (Carr 1940) or as having a varied diet of arthropods, snails, and anurans (Duellman and Schwartz 1958). In Florida, leopard frogs are much larger than in Louisiana and, as a result, a more varied diet would be expected. Predators such as birds, snakes, and raccoons feed extensively on leopard frogs, and a shrill scream heard in a marsh more often than not arises from a captured leopard frog.

Reproduction. Leopard frogs sing and lay eggs throughout the year, but the most intensive breeding period extends from December through February, at least in southern Louisiana. Males sing while sprawled out in the water, sometimes in the daytime but predominantly at night. The temperature range for singing is from 45°–80°+F (7°–26°+C), but water temperatures keep the frog's body in a more moderate range than the air temperatures suggest. The voice is varied; it may be a series of clucks, a low guttural trill, or a chuckling, all rather low pitched.

The egg mass is the plinth type (a somewhat flattened mass) and contains 1,000 to 1,500 eggs, each in a double envelope. It is either attached to vegetation or lies free on the bottom. Most egg masses are deposited in shallow water, and hundreds of egg masses, closely grouped, are sometimes found amid the weeds of flooded fields.

The tadpoles are olive to yellowish olive and often have dark spots on the sides and back; the tail fins and muscle may be marked with fine mottling and small flecks or with dark spots. In Louisiana the largest tadpole examined by Siekmann (1949) was 83 mm long, and the newly transformed young were 22–25 mm long. Wright (1932) estimated the larval period in the South to be 50 to 75 days.

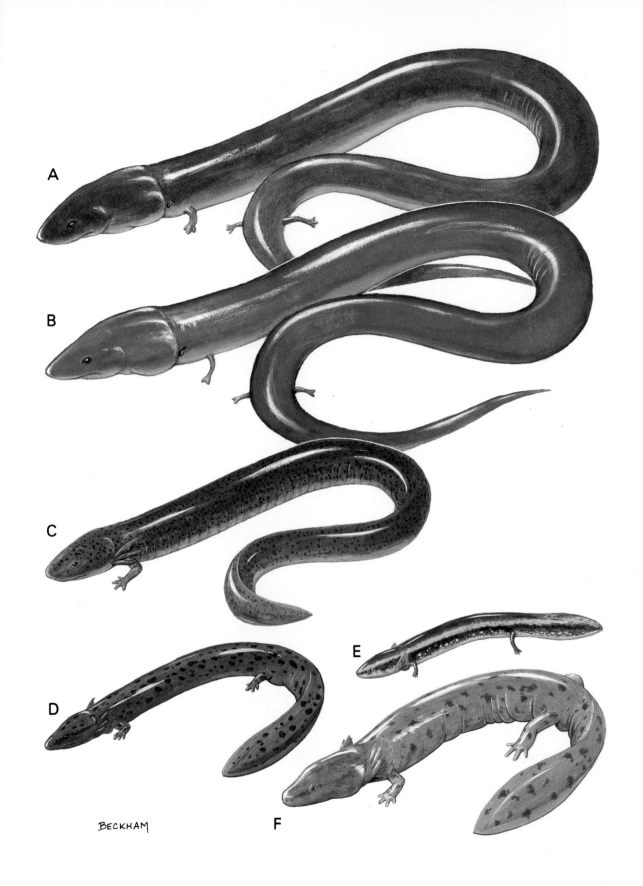

BECKHAM

Plate II.   Mole salamanders and newts
   A. Spotted salamander, *Ambystoma maculatum* (p. 35)
   B. Tiger salamander, *Ambystoma tigrinum* (p. 41)
   C. Mole salamander, *Ambystoma talpoideum* (p. 38)
   D. Marbled salamander, *Ambystoma opacum* (p. 37)
   E. Small-mouthed salamander, *Ambystoma texanum* (p. 39)
   F. Adult central newt, *Notophthalmus viridescens* (p. 62)
   G. Eft phase of the central newt, *Notophthalmus viridescens* (p. 62)

BECKHAM

Plate IV. Narrow-mouthed, spade-footed, and true toads

A. Eastern narrow-mouthed toad, *Gastrophryne carolinensis* (p. 104)
B. Eastern spadefoot, *Scaphiopus holbrookii* (p. 105)
C. Female American toad, *Bufo americanus* (p. 77)
D. Male American toad, *Bufo americanus* (p. 77)
E. Southern toad, *Bufo terrestris* (p. 80)
F. Oak toad, *Bufo quercicus* (p. 80)
G. Gulf Coast toad, *Bufo valliceps* (p. 82)
H. Woodhouse's toad, *Bufo woodhousei* (p. 83)

BECKHAM

Plate V. Chorus, greenhouse, and cricket frogs
  A. Striped phase of the striped chorus frog, *Pseudacris triseriata* (p. 100)
  B. Spotted phase of the striped chorus frog, *Pseudacris triseriata* (p. 100)
  C. Strecker's chorus frog, *Pseudacris streckeri* (p. 99)
  D. Striped phase of the greenhouse frog, *Eleutherodactylus planirostris* (p. 102)
  E. Mottled phase of the greenhouse frog, *Eleutherodactylus planirostris* (p. 102)
  F. Green phase of the ornate chorus frog, *Pseudacris ornata* (p. 98)
  G. Red phase of the ornate chorus frog, *Pseudacris ornata* (p. 98)
  H. Southern cricket frog, *Acris gryllus* (p. 87)
  I. Thigh pattern of the southern cricket frog, *Acris gryllus* (p. 87)
  J. Northern cricket frog, *Acris crepitans* (p. 85)
  K. Thigh pattern of the northern cricket frog, *Acris crepitans* (p. 85)

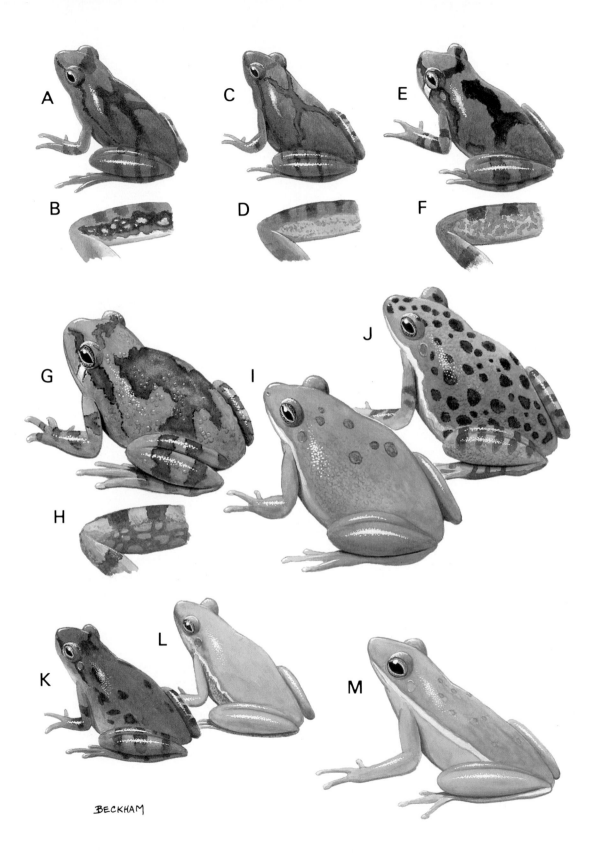

BECKHAM

Plate VII.   True frogs

A. Dusky crawfish frog, *Rana areolata sevosa* (p. 107)
B. Southern crawfish frog, *Rana areolata areolata* (p. 107)
C. Pickerel frog, *Rana palustris* (p. 114)
D. Southern leopard frog, *Rana sphenocephala* (p. 115)
E. Bronze frog, *Rana clamitans* (p. 111)
F. Unspotted phase of the bullfrog, *Rana catesbeiana* (p. 109)
G. Mottled phase of the bullfrog, *Rana catesbeiana* (p. 109)
H. Juvenile pig frog, *Rana grylio* (p. 113)
I. Adult pig frog, *Rana grylio* (p. 113)

BECKHAM

Plate VIII. Snapping, mud, and musk turtles
   A. Alligator snapping turtle, *Macroclemys temminckii* (p. 176)
   B. Snapping turtle, *Chelydra serpentina* (p. 174)
   C. Eastern mud turtle, *Kinosternon subrubrum* (p. 199)
   D. Stinkpot, *Sternotherus odoratus* (p. 203)
   E. Loggerhead musk turtle, *Sternotherus minor* (p. 202)
   F. Razor-backed musk turtle, *Sternotherus carinatus* (p. 201)

A

B

C

D

E

F

BECKHAM

Plate IX.   Cooters, painted turtle, slider, and chicken turtle
  A. Mobile cooter, *Pseudemys concinna mobilensis* (p. 189)
  B. Hieroglyphic river cooter, *Pseudemys concinna hieroglyphica* (p. 189)
  C. Cooter, *Pseudemys floridana* (p. 191)
  D. Painted turtle, *Chrysemys picta* (p. 180)
  E. Female slider, *Trachemys scripta* (p. 197)
  F. Male slider, *Trachemys scripta* (p. 197)
  G. Chicken turtle, *Deirochelys reticularia* (p. 181)

BECKHAM

Plate XI.   Gopher tortoise, diamond-backed terrapin, and box turtles

   A. Gopher tortoise, *Gopherus polyphemus* (p. 204)
   B. Diamond-backed terrapin, *Malaclemys terrapin* (p. 187)
   C. Gulf Coast box turtle, *Terrapene carolina major* (p. 192)
   D. Horn-colored phase of the three-toed box turtle, *Terrapene carolina triunguis* (p. 192)
   E. Dark phase of the three-toed box turtle, *Terrapene carolina triunguis* (p. 192)
   F. Western box turtle, *Terrapene ornata* (p. 196)

Plate XII.   Sea turtles and soft-shelled turtles
- A. Green turtle, *Chelonia mydas* (p. 171)
- B. Loggerhead, *Caretta caretta* (p. 170)
- C. Hawksbill, *Eretmochelys imbricata* (p. 172)
- D. Atlantic ridley, *Lepidochelys kempi* (p. 173)
- E. Leatherback, *Dermochelys coriacea* (p. 178)
- F. Smooth softshell, *Apalone mutica* (p. 205)
- G. Spiny softshell, *Apalone spinifera* (p. 207)

Plate XIII. Horned, collared, and fence lizards; Mediterranean gecko; green anole; and glass lizards

A. Texas horned lizard, *Phrynosoma cornutum* (p. 216)

B. Collared lizard, *Crotaphytus collaris* (p. 215)

C. Female eastern fence lizard, *Sceloporus undulatus* (p. 217)

D. Male eastern fence lizard, *Sceloporus undulatus* (p. 217)

E. Mediterranean gecko, *Hemidactylus turcicus* (p. 212)

F. Green phase of the green anole, *Anolis carolinensis* (p. 214)

G. Male green anole with the dewlap extended, *Anolis carolinensis* (p. 214)

H. Brown phase of the green anole, *Anolis carolinensis* (p. 214)

I. Adult eastern glass lizard, *Ophisaurus ventralis* (p. 212)

J. Juvenile eastern glass lizard, *Ophisaurus ventralis* (p. 212)

K. Adult slender glass lizard, *Ophisaurus attenuatus* (p. 210)

L. Juvenile slender glass lizard, *Ophisaurus attenuatus* (p. 210)

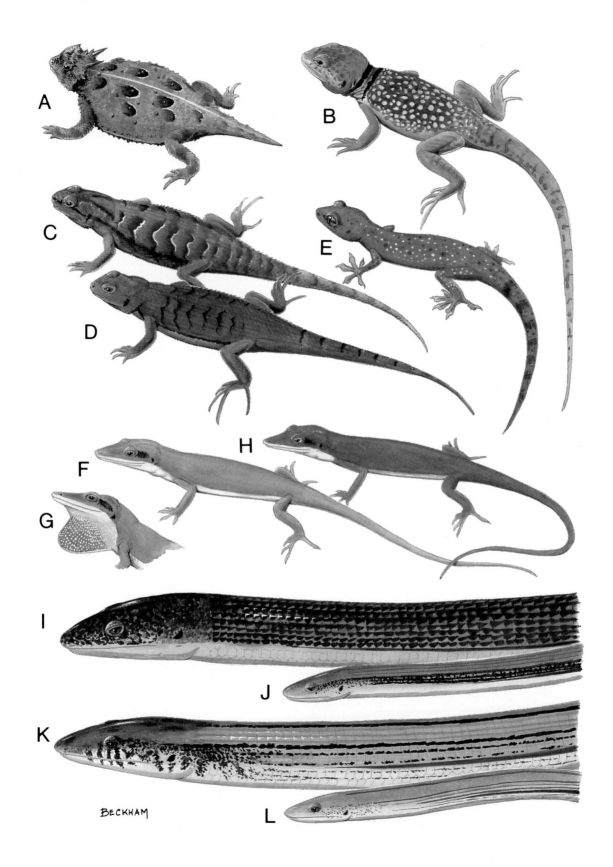

BECKHAM

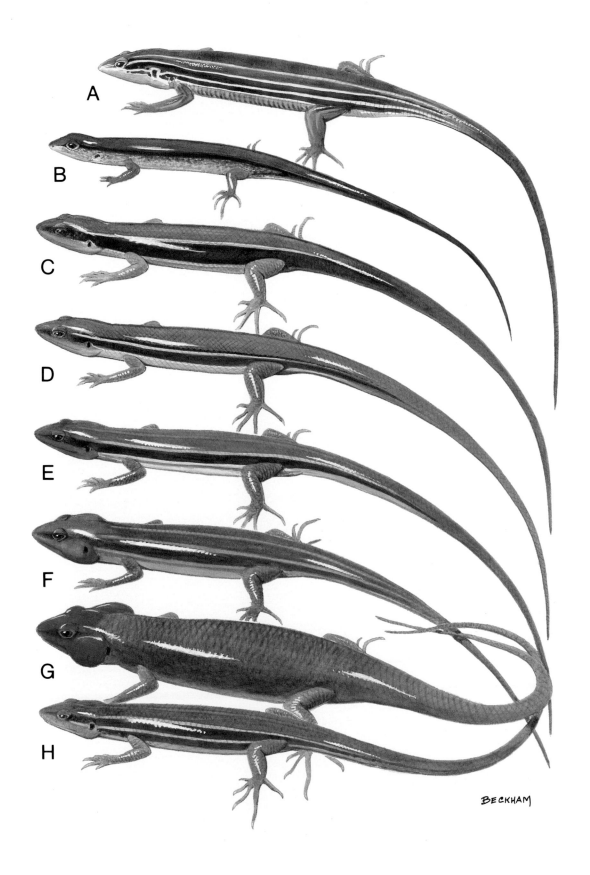

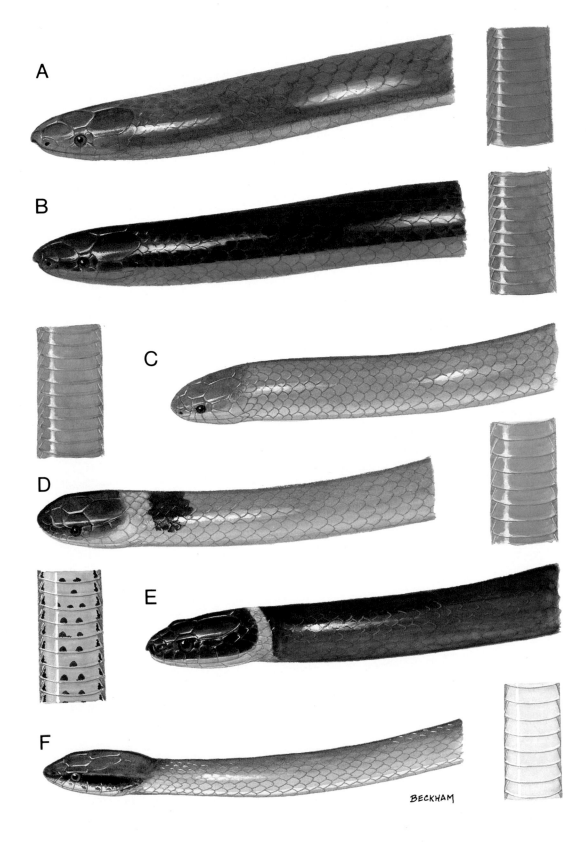

BECKHAM

Plate XVI. Rat and pine snakes

A. Corn snake, *Elaphe guttata guttata* (p. 231)
B. Great Plains rat snake, *Elaphe guttata emoryi* (p. 231)
C. Adult black rat snake, *Elaphe obsoleta obsoleta* (p. 232)
D. Juvenile black rat snake, *Elaphe obsoleta* (p. 232)
E. Adult Texas rat snake, *Elaphe obsoleta lindheimeri* (p. 232)
F. Louisiana pine snake, *Pituophis melanoleucus ruthveni* (p. 248)
G. Black pine snake, *Pituophis melanoleucus lodingi* (p. 248)
H. Full-body view of the black pine snake, *Pituophis melanoleucus lodingi* (p. 248)

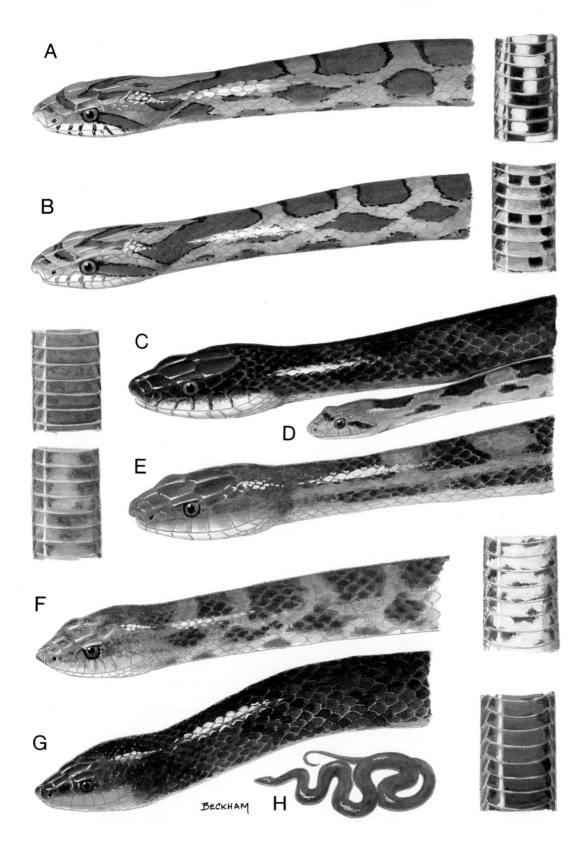

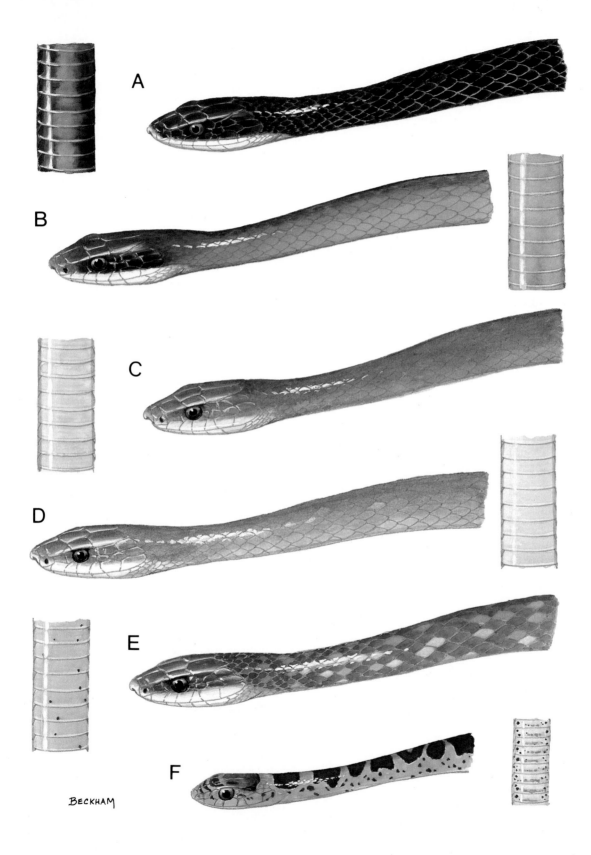

A

B

C

D

E

F

BECKHAM

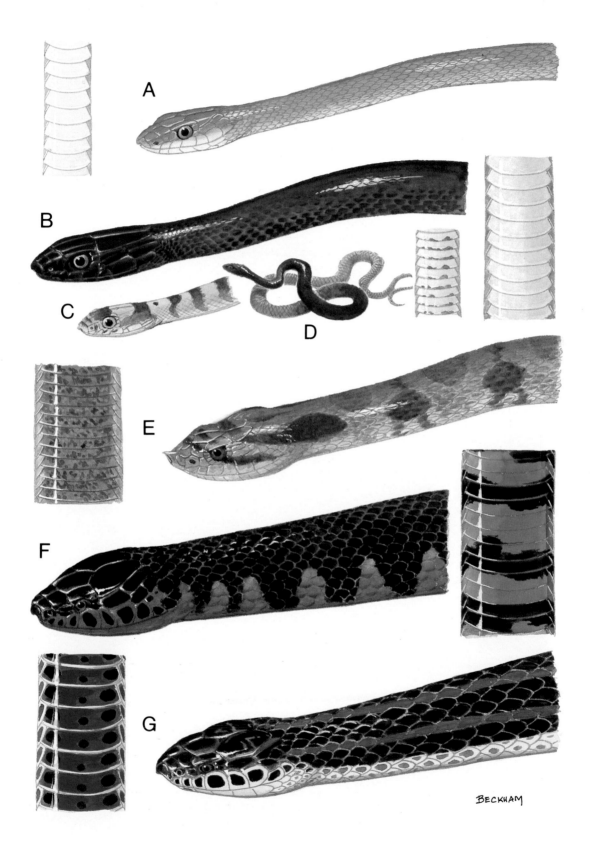

BECKHAM

Plate XIX. King, milk, and scarlet snakes

A. Common kingsnake, *Lampropeltis getulus* (p. 237)
B. Prairie kingsnake, *Lampropeltis calligaster calligaster* (p. 236)
C. Mole kingsnake, *Lampropeltis calligaster rhombomaculata* (p. 236)
D. Louisiana milk snake, *Lampropeltis triangulum amaura* (p. 238)
E. Scarlet kingsnake, *Lampropeltis triangulum elapsoides* (p. 238)
F. Scarlet snake, *Cemphora coccinea* (p. 228)

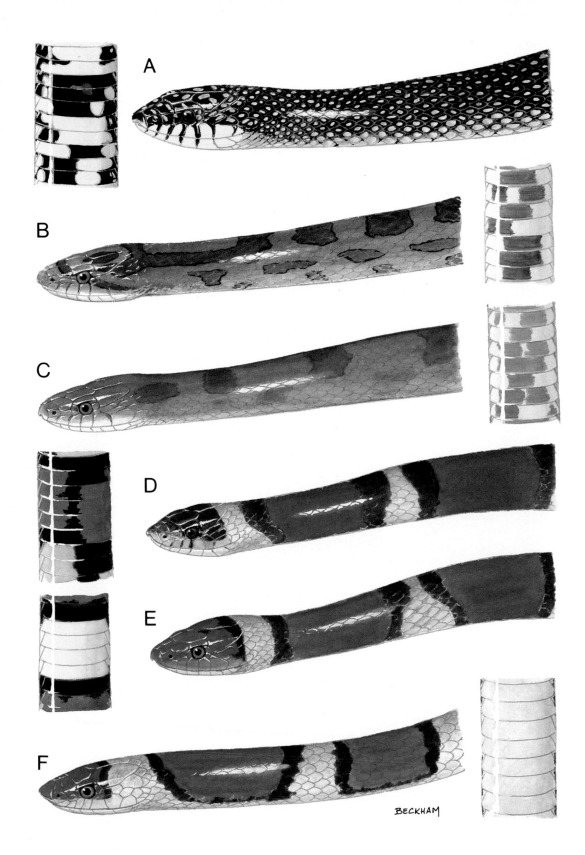

Plate XX.   Water snakes
  A. Diamond-backed water snake, *Nerodia rhombifera* (p. 245)
  B. Western green water snake, *Nerodia cyclopion* (p. 241)
  C. Yellow-bellied water snake, *Nerodia erythrogaster flavigaster* (p. 242)
  D. Blotched water snake, *Nerodia erythrogaster transversa* (p. 242)
  E. Dark phase of the southern water snake, *Nerodia fasciata* (p. 244)
  F. Light phase of the southern water snake, *Nerodia fasciata* (p. 244)
  G. Northern water snake, *Nerodia sipedon* (p. 246)
  H. Salt marsh snake, *Nerodia clarkii* (p. 240)

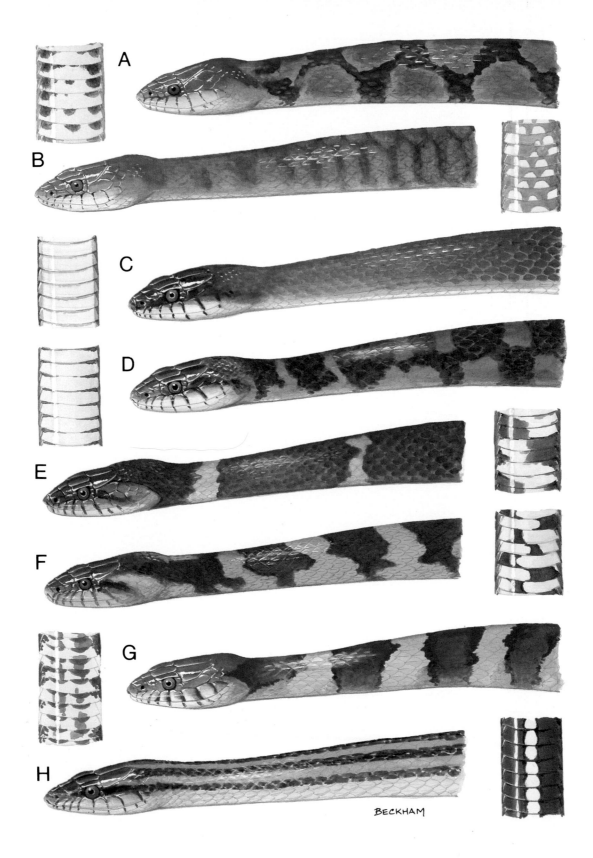

BECKHAM

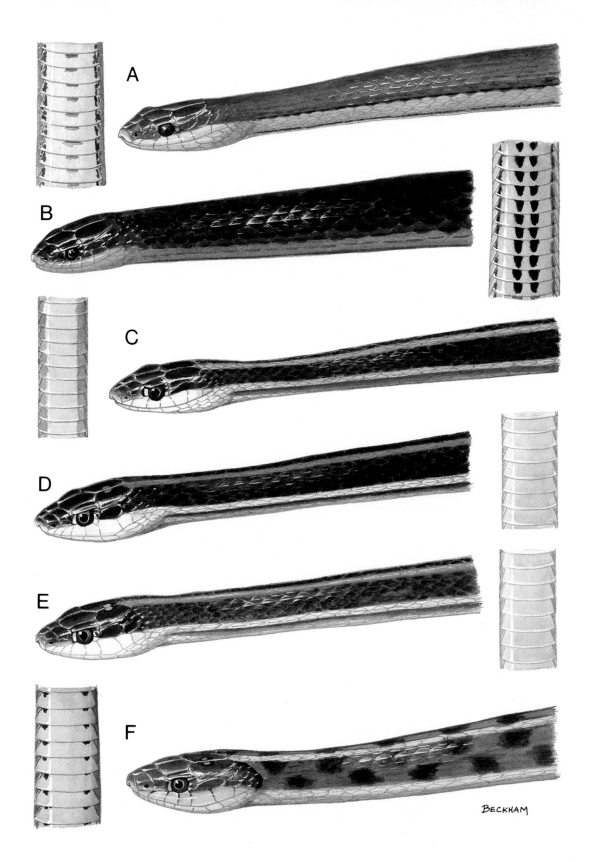

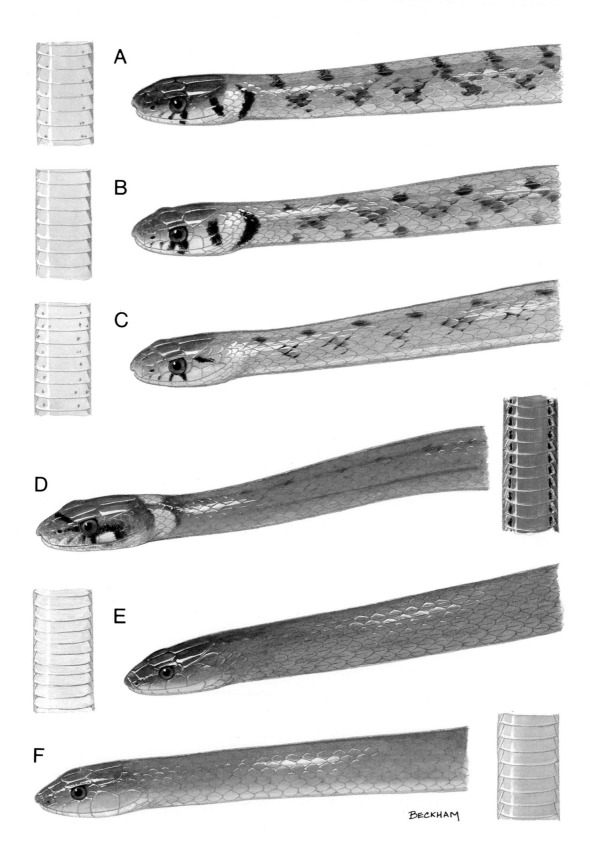

BECKHAM

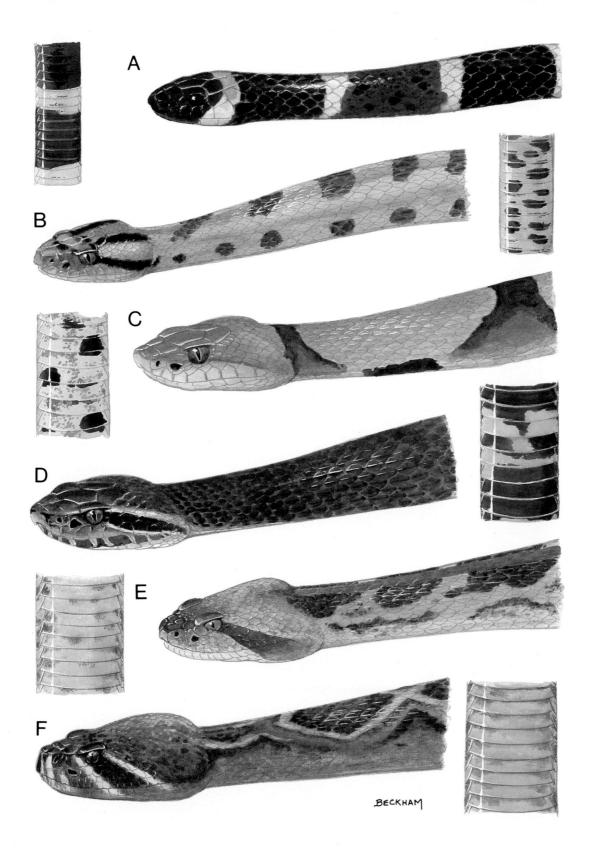

A

B

BECKHAM

Class Reptilia: Turtles, Lizards, Amphisbaenians, Snakes, Tuatara, and Crocodilians

Reptiles, derived from the amphibians about 350 million years ago, represent the first truly successful land vertebrates. They achieved success by developing rather impermeable skins, often covered with scales; by practicing internal fertilization via use of a copulatory organ that could place sperm within the female's body; by producing eggs that were either retained within the mother's body or, if laid outside her body, were equipped with a hard or leathery shell; and by conserving water through converting nitrogenous body wastes into a nontoxic solid substance, uric acid.

Reptiles are often characterized by the layman as "cold-blooded." In actuality, although reptiles are essentially unable to produce their own body heat, they tend to bask in the sun until the body temperature is raised, usually near to that of man. Because of this ectothermic requirement, reptiles usually live in temperate and tropical climates.

When reptiles first appeared, the dry land was devoid of vertebrates, and the climates were warmer than they are today; thus the reptiles spread rapidly and soon diversified into many different forms. The best known of these were the dinosaurs, which became the dominant creatures on earth. Modern reptiles are survivors of a great past, and many of the 6,000 or so living species are quite successful in coping with their environments.

ORDER TESTUDINES: *Turtles, Tortoises, and Terrapins*

This ancient group of reptiles has existed for 200 million years with little change in the basic body form. Most members may seem slow and cumbersome, but obviously the body form is admirably adapted to protect them from their enemies other than man. Despite their long history, modern turtles constitute only 12 families and about 220 species. Their distribution is cosmopolitan within the Arctic and Antarctic circles and includes oceans, fresh water, and land. Although turtles are ectothermic and may match the temperature of their surroundings, particularly in water, they often bask in the sun and can raise their body temperatures considerably.

Although American herpetologists call all the Testudines "turtles," the British herpetologists restrict this term to the sea dwellers whose limbs are paddlelike; they call the freshwater forms (and some land dwellers) with webs between the toes "terrapins" and the land forms with stumplike limbs with abbreviated toes, "tortoises."*

The typical turtle has a remarkable exoskeleton composed of an upper shell, the carapace, and a lower shell, the plastron. The shell is ordinarily covered with epidermal scutes that are periodically shed; beneath them are bony plates fused to the underlying ribs and vertebrae. Three families are exceptions to this arrangement: the soft-shelled turtles, Trionychidae, which have a leathery skin and little bony plate development; the marine leatherback, *Dermochelys*, which has a leathery skin underlain by a mosaic of small bones, the osteoderms; and a New Guinean and Australian species, *Carettochelys insculpta* (Carettochelyidae), which has a leathery skin and complete bony carapace (this group is also unusual because it has paddlelike limbs with only two claws). In the Northern Hemisphere almost all turtles have specialized neck vertebrae that allow them to draw the head and neck back until they are totally or partially within the shell (most Southern Hemisphere turtles must fold the neck to one side). The limbs of turtles are modified so that they can be tucked in under the carapace. A unique feature is that the pectoral girdle (shoulder blade area) is beneath the rib cage. Turtles have no teeth; the jaws are covered by a keratinized structure, the tomium, which may have toothlike projections.

All turtles lay either leathery or hard-shelled eggs on land. Fertilization is internal, the spermatozoa being placed into the female by a fleshy penis extruded from the cloaca. Diets are varied, some species being carnivores, some herbivores, and some omnivores.

Key to the Turtles of Louisiana

1. Limbs paddlelike, the digits not clearly defined; wrist and ankle joints rigid

   2

   Limbs not paddlelike; feet with free or webbed digits, or elephantine; wrist and ankle joints movable except in *Gopherus*, where modified for digging

   6

2. Shell covered with leathery skin

   Dermochelys coriacea (p. 178)

   Shell covered with horny scutes   3

3. Prefrontal scales in 1 pair

   Chelonia mydas (p. 171)

   Prefrontal scales in 2 pairs   4

4. Costal scutes in 4 pairs; nuchal scute not touching first costal scute

   Eretmochelys imbricata (p. 172)

*Dundee prefers a modified British terminology, Rossman the American usage.

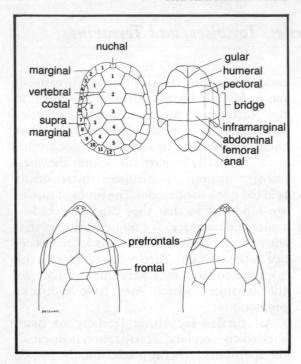

Figure 8. Structural features of turtles: carapace scutes (upper left), plastron scutes (upper right), sea turtle head with two pairs of prefontal scales (lower left), and sea turtle head with one pair of prefrontal scales (lower right).

Costal scutes in 5 pairs; nuchal scute
touching first costal scute   5

5. Bridge with 3 inframarginal scutes; carapace brown or reddish brown
         Caretta caretta (p. 170)
Bridge with 4 inframarginals; carapace gray   *Lepidochelys kempi* (p. 173)

6. Carapace with leathery skin   7
Carapace with horny scutes   8

7. Nostrils round; anterior edge of carapace without tubercles
         Apalone mutica (p. 205)
Each nostril crescentic owing to ridge projecting horizontally from septum; anterior edge of carapace with pronounced tubercles
         Apalone spinifera (p. 207)

8. Hind feet elephantine, unwebbed; forefeet shovel-like, with rigid wrists
         Gopherus polyphemus (p. 204)

All feet more or less webbed; wrists movable   9

9. Plastron small, with lateral projections forming a cross shape; tail more than half the length of the carapace, rough and tuberculate above   10
Plastron large, the lateral projections short and not having cross-shaped appearance; tail less than half the length of the carapace and smooth or only slightly roughened   11

10. A row of supramarginal scutes between marginals and costals; upper jaw strongly hooked; juveniles and adults with 3 strongly developed longitudinal rows of keels on the carapace; underside of tail with numerous small scales
         Macroclemys temminckii (p. 176)
No supramarginal scutes; upper jaw only slightly hooked; juveniles strongly keeled, but adult carapace relatively smooth; tail with only 2 rows of scales below   *Chelydra serpentina* (p. 174)

11. Plastron with only 10 or 11 scutes owing to absence or undivided condition of gular scute; pectoral scute separated from marginal scutes by a few inframarginal scutes   12
Plastron with 12 scutes; pectoral scute in contact with marginals   15

12. Pectoral scutes triangular; plastron relatively broad, with median area narrow and lacking soft skin; 2 transverse hinges, one anterior to, the other posterior to, the abdominal scutes
         Kinosternon subrubrum (p. 199)
Pectoral scutes quadrangular; plastron narrow, with median longitudinal area containing considerable soft skin; a single indistinct hinge just anterior to abdominal scutes   13

13. Side of head with 2 light stripes; carapace scutes not overlapping
         Sternotherus odoratus (p. 203)
Side of head with light stripes absent or some poorly defined lines present; scutes of carapace overlapping   14

14. Gular scute absent; carapace with distinct keel in adults
>*Sternotherus carinatus* (p. 201)

Gular scute present; adult carapace only weakly keeled
>*Sternotherus minor* (p. 202)

15. Plastron with a distinct hinge that allows the anterior end to bend upward 16

Plastron unhinged, rigid 17

16. Carapace rounded above and with a weak or strong median keel; hind foot with 3 or 4 toes; plastron unmarked or, if patterned, without a series of radiating yellow lines
>*Terrapene carolina* (p. 192)

Carapace usually flattened above, unkeeled; 4 toes on each hind foot; plastron and carapace with prominent, radiating yellow lines
>*Terrapene ornata* (p. 196)

17. Head and neck very long, about equal to length of plastron; rear of hind legs prominently marked with vertical light lines
>*Deirochelys reticularia* (p. 181)

Head and neck not exceeding half the length of the plastron; rear of hind legs unmarked or with horizontal or vertical stripes 18

18. Side of head and neck with large, black freckles; scutes of carapace with strongly developed concentric ridges; black knobs present on vertebral scutes *Malaclemys terrapin* (p. 187)

Side of head and neck usually striped but occasionally dark in melanistic specimens; carapace scutes smooth or somewhat roughened, and with or without vertebral knobs 19

19. Vertebral knobs or spines present 20

Vertebral knobs or spines absent 23

20. Costal scutes each with a yellow or orange ring
>*Graptemys oculifera* (p. 183)

Costal scutes without rings, but some yellow lines may be present 21

21. Large, greenish or yellowish blotch behind each eye larger than the orbit in size, or not markedly crescentic in shape *Graptemys pulchra* (p. 186)

Light mark behind each eye smaller than the orbit or markedly crescentic in shape 22

22. Yellow, crescent-shaped mark behind each eye preventing neck stripes from reaching eye; head of large females markedly broadened
>*Graptemys kohnii* (p. 182)

Yellow mark behind each eye abbreviated, neck stripes extending to eye; head always narrow
>*Graptemys pseudogeographica* (p. 184)

23. Carapace with a yellow, orange, or red middorsal stripe; tip of upper jaw with strong notch bordered by toothlike cusps *Chrysemys picta* (p. 180)

Carapace lacking middorsal stripe; upper jaw tip not notched or with shallow notch and poorly developed "teeth" 24

24. Red, or sometimes yellow, line or spot behind each eye and as wide as half the diameter of the eye; plastron with dark spots or entirely dark
>*Trachemys scripta* (p. 197)

Markings behind eye, if present, narrow, no more than one-third the diameter of the eye and yellow in color; plastron cream to dull white and unmarked or with a dark pattern following seams 25

25. Plastron uniformly light colored; second costal scute with light-colored, vertical or somewhat curving lines*
>*Pseudemys floridana* (p. 191)

Plastron with dark pattern along seams, especially well developed in juveniles; second costal scute with a C-shaped light mark
>*Pseudemys concinna* (p. 189)

*The turtles separated by this couplet may be of a single, highly variable species or may include hybrids between the two species, at least in southern Louisiana. This couplet may therefore be inadequate for separating southern Louisiana specimens.

FAMILY CHELONIIDAE
HARD-BACKED SEA TURTLES

The family Cheloniidae contains four genera, three of which definitely occur in Louisiana, and the other possibly does. Only six species are represented in the four genera.

The oceans from the latitude of the northern U.S. border, southern Sweden, and northern Japan, southward to the southern third of South America, the southern tip of Africa, and the shores of Australia and New Zealand, are home to these sea turtles, at least in summer or when they wander along warm oceanic currents. Nesting, however, is confined to the warmer latitudes. These very large turtles may weigh many hundreds of pounds, but human predation has made very large ones now unusual. All the species have flipperlike appendages that provide for strong swimming abilities, and the animals make long annual migrations to and from nesting beaches.

All sea turtles are now protected by federal laws and by various international agreements. These regulations prohibit the taking of the animals or their eggs, as well as the importation and sale of the animals or products derived from them. Not all countries have subscribed to international agreements; thus the turtles remain on endangered and threatened species lists. Much illegal trade in sea turtle products continues, and irregularities in import and export figures indicate that some signatory nations are lax in enforcement. We can only hope that the many studies and efforts to help these turtles survive will save them from extinction.

Caretta caretta (Linnaeus)
Loggerhead
Plate XII

Recognition. A very large marine turtle, average-sized adults weighing about 300 lb (137

Map 48. Distribution of *Caretta caretta.* Solid circles represent specimens examined; hollow circles represent museum specimens not examined or literature records.

kg) and having a carapace length of a yard or more (900+ mm), but the species possibly attaining a carapace length of 84 in. (2,130 mm) and a weight of 1,192 lb (542 kg) (based on extrapolation of measurements of skeletal parts), making it the largest hard-shelled turtle in the world; appendages flipperlike; carapace with five pairs of costal scutes, the first pair in contact with the cervical scute; carapace reddish brown; hatchlings with three dorsal keels on the carapace; bridge between the carapace and plastron with three large, poreless scutes.

Distribution. This marine turtle probably occurs all along the Louisiana coast as a wanderer, but our only known specimens came from the southeastern coast and offshore islands (Map 48). Alfred Smalley showed us a color slide of a dead specimen found on Holly Beach, Cameron Parish, in April 1985. Because of the great decimation of sea turtles by the fishing industries, we cannot be certain that *Caretta* is a bonafide breeding resident of Louisiana today: the most recent nesting record is for 1962. A number of stranding and sighting reports are available (Fuller and Tappan 1986; Schroeder 1986), but such observations were made by lay persons, and specimens are not available to confirm the reports.

Taxonomic comments. Our representative of this species is the Atlantic loggerhead, *Caretta c. caretta* (Linnaeus). No comprehensive taxonomic study has been published.

Habitat and habits. This wide-ranging animal is found in bays and open ocean waters, where it feeds on marine invertebrates such as jellyfish, oysters, clams, squids, and sea urchins and on fishes and marine vegetation. The loggerhead is considered to be rather aggressive and pugnacious for a sea turtle.

Reproduction. The nests contain up to 200 eggs and are excavated on sandy beaches above the high-tide line from late spring through the summer in northern latitudes. But as with any species that occurs in both the northern and southern hemispheres, the nesting season may occur in many months of the year, depending on latitude. Hildebrand (1982) said that B. Melancon gave him a verbal report of loggerhead eggs deposited on Grand Isle, Terrebonne Parish, in the 1930s. The Tulane collection has a set of 25 eggs found in the Chandeleur Islands, where they were deposited on 18 May 1962 (Ogren 1977). The spherical eggs are 35–49 mm in diameter and take about two months to hatch. Survival of sea turtles is always precarious; the eggs are sought for food by people, raccoons, crabs, birds, etc., and the newly hatched young, which measure only 38–50 mm in carapace length, are preyed on by fishes, birds, and mammals. The flesh of adults is not considered a delicacy but is eaten by man; this fact, plus the predation on the eggs, makes the future of the loggerhead precarious. Hopefully, protected nesting beaches can be maintained along the Louisiana coast.

The loggerhead is on the threatened species list and is protected by federal laws and international agreements.

Chelonia mydas (Linnaeus)
Green Turtle
Plate XII

Recognition. A very large marine turtle (average adult carapace 3–4 ft, 910–1,220 mm, long and weight 250–450 lb, 113–204 kg); flipperlike appendages; one pair of prefrontal scutes between the eyes, a strongly serrated margin on the lower jaw, and four pairs of costal scutes, none touching the nuchal scute; carapace brown to olive, sometimes with a mottled, radiating, or wavy pattern of dark markings. The name, green turtle, is deceptive because it refers to the greenish fat of the body. Hatchlings are black and have a middorsal keel. A report in the literature (True 1884) stated that this species may exceed 1,000 lb (454 kg), but Conant (1975) suggests 55+ in. (1,400+ mm) and 650+ lb (295+ kg) as record sizes.

Similar species. The hawksbill (*Eretmochelys imbricata*), a turtle of similar appearance, has overlapping scutes on its carapace.

Distribution. Presumably a visitor and perhaps a nesting species along the entire Louisiana coast, but our only valid records are from Breton Island and the Gulf waters off Grand Terre Island (Map 49). If the green turtle nests in Louisiana, the most probable grounds would be the sandy beaches of Breton Island and the Chandeleur Islands. A number of stranding and sighting reports are available (Fuller and Tappan 1986; Schroeder 1986), but such observations were made by lay persons, and specimens are not available to confirm the reports.

Taxonomic comments. The Louisiana specimens represent the subspecies *Chelonia m. mydas*, the Atlantic green turtle. No comprehensive taxonomic study has been published. Hirth (1980) provided an update of relevant literature.

Habitat and habits. The principal food is vegetation but marine invertebrates and carrion are also eaten. This species is the most

Map 49. Distribution of *Chelonia mydas.* Solid circles represent specimens examined; hollow circles represent museum specimens not examined or literature records.

widely sought of all sea turtles for food; heavy fishing pressure and raids on the nests have reduced its numbers drastically to the point that several countries are at last giving protection to some of the nesting beaches.

Studies on green turtles show that this species makes substantial migrations—the feeding and nesting grounds may be more than 1,000 miles apart. Young turtles are being released at some of the former nesting beaches in an attempt to establish colonies. The young turtles appear able to home in on the release beach. Such behavior offers possibilities for developing nesting grounds in Louisiana.

Green turtles are on the endangered species list for the United States and are protected by federal law and international agreements.

Reproduction. The green turtle may occasionally nest on Florida beaches, but otherwise the nesting grounds are farther south on beaches along the Gulf of Mexico and the

Caribbean Sea, where the eggs are deposited from March to October. Mating occurs during the nesting season in the water near the beaches. Nests are excavated at night above the high-tide line; a single female may nest as many as eight times per season (Pritchard 1967). The eggs are soft, white, and nearly spherical, but the shells harden after a few days. A female may deposit 53 to 226 eggs, the average being 110 or more depending on the locality. Eggs are 35–58 mm in diameter and require 30 to 72 days of incubation. The hatchlings' carapaces are 44–54 mm long and 31–43 mm wide. Hatchlings emerge from the nest at night, a habit that probably helps to reduce predation pressure.

Eretmochelys imbricata (Linnaeus)
Hawksbill
Plate XII

Recognition. A handsome, moderate-sized sea turtle (maximum size about 3 ft, 762 mm, weight to about 280 lb, 127 kg); appendages flipperlike; two pairs of prefrontal scutes; snout elongate and downturned; four pairs of costal scutes, the first not touching the nuchal; the large carapacial scutes overlapping, except in very old animals; scutes, when polished, translucent and brownish olive with lighter and darker streaks creating a "tortoiseshell" pattern.

Distribution. Known to nest in Florida and throughout the Caribbean and along the Central American coast; hence it could be expected anywhere along the Louisiana coast, although no valid records from Louisiana are available. Percy Viosca, who spent many years as a biologist with the Louisiana Department of Wildlife and Fisheries, failed to include the species in several lists of Louisiana amphibians and reptiles, but in 1961, in the *Louisiana Conservationist,* he mentioned the hawksbill as rare along our coast. Viosca most likely saw good evidence of a specimen called to the attention of the department. Fuller and Tappan (1986) reported that a hawksbill was caught in a gill net in Cameron Parish, and Schroeder (1986) stated that a single stranding occurred in Louisiana in 1986. The specimens are not available for confirmation, however, and the observers are not identified in the reports.

Taxonomic comments. The subspecies to be expected in Louisiana is the Atlantic hawksbill, *Eretmochelys i. imbricata* (Linnaeus). No comprehensive taxonomic study has been published.

Habitat and habits. Much like other sea turtles, the hawksbill nests on sandy beaches and feeds on invertebrates and marine vegetation. Although sought for food by man and beast alike, the hawksbill seems to have some propensity for storing toxic substances from its food, thereby making its flesh potentially hazardous to eat.

The handsome polished scutes of the hawksbill turtle have been used for hundreds of years to make various jewelry items, combs, and other novelties. Mounted specimens are sold in stores catering to tourists in places like Mexico. The hawksbill is now on the endangered species list and is protected by federal law and international agreements, yet many tourists arriving in Louisiana from the Yucatan Peninsula of Mexico continue to bring in recently purchased hawksbill materials. Customs officials not only will confiscate the items, but tourists may find themselves fined for illegal importation.

Reproduction. In the United States this species has been known to nest only in Florida, apparently from April to midsummer, but at lower latitudes the nesting season extends to November. Mating takes place in shallow water off the nesting beaches. Nests are dug in the sand above the tidal zone. The spherical, hard-shelled eggs number from 53 to 206 (average 161.1) and average 38 mm in diameter (35–43 mm) (Carr, Hirth, and Ogren 1966). Incubation takes 52 to 74 days, and the

hatchlings have carapaces ranging from 39 to 50 mm in length and 27 to 35 mm in width (Carr, Hirth, and Ogren 1966). Females mature at about three years of age and weigh about 13 kg (Carr, Hirth, and Ogren 1966), but most nesting females are 762 mm or more in length, thus far heavier than 13 kg.

Lepidochelys kempi (Garman)
Atlantic Ridley, Gray Sea Turtle
Plate XII

Recognition. A small sea turtle (record carapace length 29½ in., 749 mm; maximum weight 110 lb, 49.9 kg); flipperlike appendages; five pairs of costal scutes, the anterior pair in contact with nuchal; bridge with four (rarely five) pore-bearing, enlarged scutes; carapace very broad, presenting a roughly circular outline; color gray to olive above and yellow below.

Distribution. The most frequently encountered sea turtle in Louisiana, taken regularly offshore and in bays by fishermen and shrimpers (Map 50). Specimens have been collected in Lake Borgne, St. Bernard Parish, and in 1968 one surfaced alongside a boat occupied by Dundee in the Mississippi River–Gulf Outlet Channel near Violet in St. Bernard Parish. A number of stranding and sighting reports are available (Fuller and Tappan 1986; Schroeder 1986), but such observations were made by lay persons, and specimens are not available to confirm the reports.

Taxonomic comments. No subspecies are recognized now that Pritchard (1969) has established that *Lepidochelys kempi* is distinct from *L. olivacea*.

Habitat and habits. This species is principally carnivorous, feeding mostly on crabs, clams, and snails in shallow waters (Dobie, Ogren, and Fitzpatrick 1961). Liner (1954) reported that stomach analysis of 11 specimens taken in shrimp trawls off the Terrebonne Parish

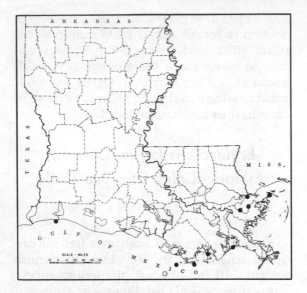

Map 50. Distribution of *Lepidochelys kempi.* Solid circles represent specimens examined; hollow circles represent museum specimens not examined or literature records.

coast revealed crab shells (*Callinectes*) and some barnacles.

This species is subject to the usual predation on its eggs and flesh by people, other mammals, birds, and crabs. Some recent federal estimates suggest that no more than 4,000 Atlantic ridleys now survive, and even these are gravely threatened by persons who seek them for their hides, which are used to make gloves and shoes. The current status of endangered species and protection under federal laws and international agreements may be inadequate to save these turtles because of poaching and because various countries have shown little regard for the seriousness of the situation.

Reproduction. At one time the Atlantic ridley nested on beaches from the southern Texas coast to southern Mexico from April to mid-August. Viosca (1961) stated that it laid eggs on the Chandeleur Islands of Louisiana. Today this species is known to nest only on the coastline of the Mexican state of Tamaulipas (Pritchard 1979). In their better days the ridleys would come ashore in huge numbers within a brief time period; Carr (1967) called such gatherings "arribadas," the Spanish word for "arrivals." Mating takes place offshore from the nesting beach. Unlike other sea turtles, ridleys are diurnal nest excavators. The most detailed information on reproduction is that of Chavez, Contreras, and Hernandez (1968), who reported that females laid an average of 110 eggs (54 to 185) that required 50 to 70 days of incubation. The eggs measured were spherical, averaging 38.9 mm in diameter (35.0–44.5 mm), and soft and white (Chavez, Contreras, and Hernandez 1968). Females may nest up to three times in one year, and one female that had laid 118 eggs was reported to contain another 258 large oviducal eggs (Chavez, Contreras, and Hernandez 1968). Hatchlings had carapacial lengths of 38–46 mm and carapacial widths of 30–40 mm.

FAMILY CHELYDRIDAE
SNAPPING TURTLES

The family Chelydridae, a New World group, comprises two genera, each with a single species, and ranges from southern Canada to Ecuador. Both species occur in Louisiana. One chelydrid, the alligator snapping turtle (*Macroclemys*), possibly attains the greatest weight of any freshwater turtle. Both species in this family have large heads and very powerful jaws.

Chelydra serpentina (Linnaeus)
Snapping Turtle
Plate VIII

Recognition. A large, aquatic turtle reaching 19⅖ in. (494 mm) in carapace length; head large; eyes visible from above; tail long, two-thirds or more the length of the carapace in adults to 1¾ the length of the carapace in juveniles, and saw-toothed above; carapace dark,

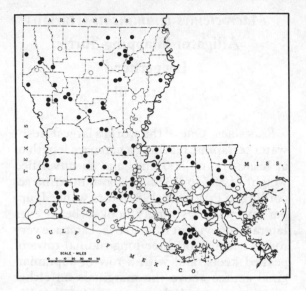

Map 51. Distribution of *Chelydra serpentina*. Solid circles represent specimens examined; hollow circles represent museum specimens not examined or literature records.

with three longitudinal rows of keels (becoming obscure in larger individuals); plastron small, narrow, cross-shaped, and without a hinge; only five pairs of plastral scutes.

Similar species. Juveniles may be confused with alligator snapping turtles (*Macroclemys temminckii*) because of the keels on the back. To distinguish them, note the lack of supramarginal scales above the marginals and observe that the eyes of *Chelydra serpentina* are visible from above.

Distribution. Statewide in fresh water; uncommon in the Marsh (Map 51).

Taxonomic comments. One subspecies, *C. s. serpentina* (Linnaeus), the common snapping turtle, inhabits Louisiana. The most recent taxonomic studies are those of Feuer (1966, 1971).

Habitat and habits. This turtle may be found in almost any kind of freshwater situation, particularly permanent ponds, lakes, and streams. It also enters somewhat brackish waters in marsh areas. Although snapping turtles are highly aquatic, they are quite

mobile on land and occasionally are encountered walking across roads, sometimes far from water. They are active day and night.

Snapping turtles only occasionally bask out of water; if they do bask, the site is likely to be on a mud flat. The typical behavior is to float just below the surface of the water or to lie in or on the bottom mud of shallow places with only the eyes and nostrils exposed. The long neck allows them to lie concealed on the bottom, only occasionally stretching the neck to the surface to breathe.

Snapping turtles have powerful jaws and prey on a wide variety of animals, including sponges, worms, mollusks, insects, crustaceans, fishes, amphibians, reptiles, birds, and mammals. Adults usually lie concealed waiting to ambush prey, but the juveniles forage actively. Lagler's (1943) studies of the food habits of these turtles in Michigan revealed that they also eat a large amount of aquatic vegetation. Carrion also is taken in quantity, and seems to be quite attractive to snapping turtles, a habit exploited by commercial trappers.

The snapping turtle has a well-deserved reputation for viciousness; it must be handled with great caution to avoid a nasty, flesh-tearing bite. The safe way to handle a snapper is to hold it by the hind legs with the plastron toward you and well away from your body. Although the long tail offers an apparently safe handle, this method of holding the snapper is not recommended because it may result in injury to the turtle's vertebral column. When handled, the snapper exudes a strong-smelling musk.

Despite their defensive capabilities, snapping turtles may fall prey to alligators, and the young are eaten by birds, mammals, snakes, and fishes.

Snapping turtles are much maligned because of their alleged depredation of game fishes. Lagler (1943) pointed out that they are far more likely to eat smaller fish species, especially forage types, and because of their limited numbers, he considered the effect of these turtles on game fishes to be of little concern.

Reproduction. Ernst and Barbour (1972), in their description of the reproductive habits of *C. serpentina*, indicated that nesting occurs from May through September and that usually 20 to 30 tough-shelled, spherical white eggs 23–33 mm in diameter are laid in a nest dug on land as far as several hundred meters from the water. Incubation time was reported as being 55 to 125 days and hatchling carapace lengths as 26–31 mm. At Tulane there is a clutch of 26 specimens from St. Landry Parish that were hatched in the laboratory 10 August. Carapace lengths for these animals are 36 mm or more. We have no information to indicate whether these animals were retained and fed prior to preservation.

In Louisiana, snappers are one of the more desirable turtles for the dining table. Retail prices for whole, live snappers in summer, 1982, in New Orleans ran about $2.40 per pound. Adult snapping turtles weigh 10–35 lb (4.5–16 kg) and reach 75 lb (34 kg) or more; thus this species of turtle plays a moderate role in the economics of Louisiana fisheries resources. Heavy fishing pressure on Louisiana snapping turtles has resulted in a decline in the catch, and much of the meat is now being imported from other states.

No accurate data are available on the abundance of the snapping turtle, but Arny (1948) stated that in 1947 K. Myers, the manager of the Delta Wildlife Refuge, Plaquemines Parish, estimated that 35,000 snappers occupied the 45,861-acre tract. This does not seem like a very high density but, of course, Arny did not give any data for the actual livable habitat.

Bennett (1935) described a new species of trematode, *Cercorchis singulare*, from snapping turtles in East Baton Rouge Parish, and Stunkard (1943) described a new trematode, *Dictyangium chelydrae*, from a Louisiana snapping turtle (locality not stated).

Macroclemys temminckii (Harlan)
Alligator Snapping Turtle, Loggerhead
Plate VIII

Recognition. One of the world's largest freshwater terrapins, reaching a carapace length of at least $31\frac{1}{2}$ in. (800 mm) and an unverified weight of 307 lb (137.5 kg), both maxima according to Pritchard (1982); toes webbed; upper jaw with a strongly hooked beak; eyes lateral, not evident from above; carapace very rough because of three longitudinal rows of peaked keels, and with a row of supramarginal scutes above the marginals on either side; carapace dark brown, often heavily coated with algal growth; plastron small, narrow, and cross-shaped because of the long, narrow bridge; only five pairs of plastral scutes.

Similar species. This species, at least the juveniles, may be confused with the common snapping turtle (*Chelydra serpentina*), whose young also have a rough carapace with three rows of keels. If in doubt, look for the presence of supramarginals in the alligator snapper or their absence in the common snapper.

Distribution. Statewide; uncommon in the Marsh (Map 52). Verbal reports for localities not shown on our map are listed by Pritchard (1982).

Taxonomic comments. No subspecies have been described, and only an informal study of variation has been published (Pritchard 1982).

Habitat and habits. Alligator snapping turtles are most commonly discovered in large rivers, canals, lakes, and oxbows, but they also enter swamps near rivers. In the coastal marsh they are most evident in the freshwater lakes and bayous. In Terrebonne Parish they are regularly taken from shallow, brackish, marsh pools near the deeper freshwater habitats, but those animals probably

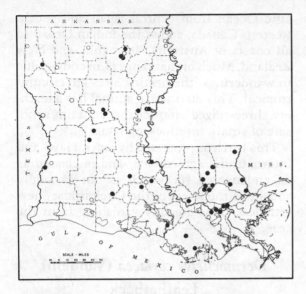

Map 52. Distribution of *Macroclemys temminckii.* Solid circles represent specimens examined; hollow circles represent museum specimens not examined or literature records.

were isolated there by fluctuating tidal flushings and hurricane-driven waters. These turtles are common in the brackish, tidally flushed Manchac area between Lakes Pontchartrain and Maurepas. A small country store in Tangipahoa Parish displays a photo of a 40.5-kg *Macroclemys* that was found in a pool at the highway bridge across the road. The stream forming the pool is perhaps 5 ft (1.5 m) wide and far from any major waterway.

The alligator snapping turtle spends most of its time lying quietly on the bottom, where its dark, rough body is well concealed. Here it performs a remarkable feat of luring fishes into reach by lying with the mouth agape and wriggling a peculiar wormlike appendage that projects from the tongue. Most feeding, however, is probably done by active search, as may be judged by the variety of turtles, fishes, snails, crustaceans, clams, carrion, and even palmetto fruits and acorns that have been found in its stomach.

Although these turtles are wholly aquatic, they must reach the surface to gulp air, but at least one report (E. R. Allen and Neill 1950) suggested that buccopharyngeal breathing may be used under water, thereby allowing long submergence.

Commercial fishermen capture alligator snapping turtles in Louisiana mostly by trotline fishing. Some unusually skilled fishermen work rivers and marsh pools by probing the bottom with a pole—they are able to recognize the feel of the turtle when the pole hits it, and they then capture the animal by using a metal hook to grab it. The large size and formidable jaws of *Macroclemys* create some problems for handling live specimens. The neck, fortunately, is rather short, therefore the animal can be lifted by grasping it at the anterior and posterior ends of the carapace. Grasping the long tail is not a safe method because of the difficulty of suspending so large and heavy a creature safely away from the body, and it may injure the turtle's vertebral column.

Pritchard (1982) said that alligator snapping turtles can be caught on baited hooks from mid-March to mid-October, which probably corresponds to the normal breeding season. He listed two independent reports, one from Manchac, Tangipahoa Parish, indicating that these turtles hibernate in groups of up to 15 animals.

In summer 1981 John Newsome (pers. com.) of the Louisiana Department of Wildlife and Fisheries reported that a 75-kg specimen was taken in lower Concordia Parish.

In 1976 the flesh of the alligator snapper brought more than $2 per pound in the wholesale marketplace at New Orleans, but by 1983 very few of the turtles were coming to market. In early 1985 the price had risen to $4.50 to $8.90 per pound, and much of this meat was being imported from other states.

Reports from various commercial turtle dealers indicate that populations of the alligator snapping turtle in Louisiana are seriously depleted (Pritchard 1982), and the same applies to other southern states. Pritchard (1982) strongly recommended that action be taken to protect and restore this valuable species, but he suggested that, in light of the lack of responsiveness by state agencies, federal action might be in order. A more complete picture of this species' biology, with many reports and statements from Louisiana collectors and dealers, is contained in Pritchard's report.

Reproduction. A major study of alligator snappers in Louisiana (Dobie 1971) indicated that the eggs are laid from mid-April to late May in southeastern Louisiana and from mid-May to early June in the northeastern section of the state. Usually one clutch of eggs is laid yearly, but some females may lay every other year. The large leathery eggs, 34.0–51.8 mm in diameter, number from 16 to 38, and possibly as many as 52. Dobie (1971) described a natural nest that F. R. Cagle discovered on a ridge next to a bayou in St. Charles Parish. Trappers in the Manchac area told Dobie that they had found the females laying at night and in early morning on ridges along canals and bayous. Incubation of the eggs required 80 to 90 days in the laboratory, and hatchlings measured 37–46 mm in carapace length. However, at Tulane, two sets of eggs from St. Charles Parish hatched 19–20 September; incubation time for these is not known. Dobie (1971) ascertained that at least one turtle he examined was at least 36 years old.

FAMILY DERMOCHELYIDAE
LEATHER-BACKED SEA TURTLES

Only one genus containing a single species is represented by the family Dermochelyidae, which has the widest range of all sea turtles. This animal, largest of all modern-day chelonians, has been found from the North Sea to Labrador, to nearly all of the South American and African coasts, and throughout the Pacific Ocean from central Japan and southwestern Canada, across the Indian Ocean to all coasts of Australia, Tasmania, and New Zealand. Much of that range is, of course, due to wanderings; the nesting sites are circumtropical. This distinctive animal has a leathery, three-ridged carapace that contains a mosaic of small, interlocking bones.

This turtle is protected by federal laws and international agreements, and is classed as an endangered species. It is not as avidly sought as members of the Cheloniidae; nevertheless, it is steadily vanishing from the seas.

Dermochelys coriacea (Vandelli)
Leatherback
Plate XII

Recognition. Largest of all living turtles, commonly attaining a length of 4½–5½ ft (1,370–1,675 mm) and a weight of 650–1,200 lb (295–544 kg), and easily recognized by the flipperlike, clawless limbs and a blackish, leathery carapace having seven distinct longitudinal ridges.

Reliable data for maximum size are difficult to establish, but unquestionably these animals might exceed 6 ft (1,830 mm) in carapace length and 1,500 lb (680 kg), perhaps even achieving a ton in weight. In Louisiana we have several modern-day records of note. In 1937, the *Louisiana Conservation Review* (6[2]: 49) reported a specimen 7 ft, 3 in. (2,210 mm) long weighing 700 lb (315 kg). A specimen brought in to Tulane University in the 1950s measured 6 ft, 1½ in. (1,867 mm) from tip of head to end of carapace and weighed 750 lb (337 kg). In 1962, Dundee preserved a specimen caught in a trawl in Timbalier Bay, Terrebonne Parish. This particular animal was 6½ ft (1,981 mm) from end of head to end of carapace and weighed 750 lb (337 kg) some two weeks after capture, death, and subsequent refrigeration.

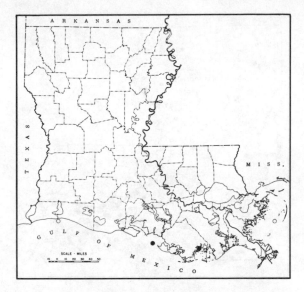

Map 53. Distribution of *Dermochelys coriacea*. Solid circles represent specimens examined; hollow circles represent museum specimens not examined or literature records.

Distribution. This species occurs frequently along the entire Louisiana coast and in bays (Map 53). A number of stranding and sighting reports are available (Fuller and Tappan 1986; Schroeder 1986), but such observations were made by lay persons, and specimens are not available to confirm the reports.

Taxonomic comments. The Atlantic leatherback, *Dermochelys c. coriacea* (Vandelli), is the race found in Louisiana waters. No taxonomic study has been published, but Pritchard (1971) suggested that subspecies should not be recognized.

Habitat and habits. Most specimens have been caught in trawl nets, apparently while basking or sleeping on the surface. The nearest known nesting sites are the Florida coasts, West Indian islands, and Nicaragua.

The diet is remarkable—the leatherback appears to subsist principally on jellyfishes, but also consumes other marine invertebrates and some vegetation.

The flesh of the leatherback is not considered edible, but unfortunately the juveniles

and eggs are eaten by the usual enemies of turtles, such as humans, other mammals, birds, and fishes. Some commercial pressure is exerted on the leatherback for its oils, which are used in cosmetics. Although the leatherback is on the endangered species list and protected by federal laws and international agreements, Dundee saw a store in Puntarenas, Costa Rica, that was selling turtle oil in December 1983. In 1979, New Orleans U.S. Customs officials made 108 seizures of sea turtles and sea turtle products, mostly creams made with turtle oil.

Reproduction. In the United States, this species has been known to nest in Florida; otherwise nesting in the Atlantic region appears to occur primarily on the beaches of the Caribbean Sea from April through November. The eggs, numbering up to 170 or so, are 51–65 mm in diameter. New hatchlings have a carapace length of about 63.5 mm and weigh ±30 g. The growth potential of these juveniles is fantastic, but little is known of the growth beyond the first year and a half or so.

FAMILY EMYDIDAE
LAND AND FRESHWATER
TURTLES

The Emydidae is the most diverse of all turtle families, comprising perhaps 30 genera and 85 species. The primary distribution is the Northern Hemisphere, but a few species range south of the equator in South America and Indonesia. The primary centers of diversity are in the eastern United States and southeastern Asia. Six genera containing 12 or 13 species occur in Louisiana.

If we base common names of turtles on limb structure, the emydids are classed as terrapins, having partial or complete webbing between the toes, even in the almost completely terrestrial box turtles. With such a range of webbing, the family has become adapted to diverse habitats, from land to rivers, ponds, lakes, and freshwater and salt-water marshes.

Chrysemys picta (Schneider)
Painted Turtle
Plate IX

Recognition. A medium-sized freshwater terrapin attaining a carapace length of 6⅛ in. (156 mm) in the race occurring in Louisiana; toes webbed; head, neck, and limbs striped; upper jaw strongly notched, with a toothlike cusp on either side of the notch; carapace smooth, unkeeled except for the middorsal keel in juveniles; carapace color olive brown to black, the scutes with light-colored borders; a prominent red (sometimes yellow) middorsal stripe down the back; plastron plain yellow, perhaps with one or two small black spots.

Distribution. Eastern and northern Louisiana in suitable fresh waters; absent from the Sabine and Calcasieu river drainages except for a single locality in Beauregard Parish that may represent an incorrect locality datum or perhaps a released pet (Map 54). Common only in the lower Mississippi and Atchafalaya drainages.

Taxonomic comments. This is one of our best-studied turtles, and the subspecies found in Louisiana, *Chrysemys picta dorsalis* Agassiz, the southern painted turtle, is well defined. Ernst (1971) provided a thorough literature summary of the species.

Habitat and habits. This is conspicuously a pond-dwelling turtle, but it may be found in very slowly moving waters. Shallow waters are preferred, even pools that dry up periodically. Painted turtles also inhabit sunny open areas in swamps. The major requisites are relatively clear water, a good supply of aquatic vegetation, basking sites, and a soft bottom. These animals forage over the bottom and eat some arthropods such as crawfish and dragonfly nymphs, but the

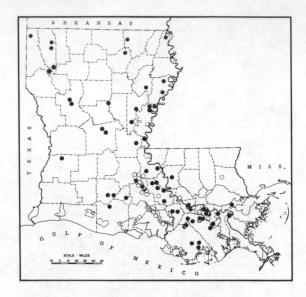

Map 54. Distribution of *Chrysemys picta.* Solid circles represent specimens examined; hollow circles represent museum specimens not examined or literature records.

main items seem to be algae and duckweeds (Marchand 1942). The painted turtle is often seen floating at the surface, where it feeds on floating vegetation.

The greatest numbers of painted turtles in Louisiana have come from the vicinity of Grosse Tete, Iberville Parish, where commercial collectors have been quite active (Cagle 1954); approximately 20 percent of the turtles coming to buyers in the Atchafalaya area were painted turtles (Cagle 1954). The turtles have been sought for the pet trade rather than for their flesh.

Reproduction. Painted turtles lay their eggs in nests excavated away from the water in sandy or loamy soil. Cagle (1954) said *C. picta dorsalis* lays four to ten eggs (six in a Louisiana nest). The eggs are white, bluntly oval, and measure about 32 × 19 mm. Cagle said that few Louisiana painted turtles had large oviducal eggs in June, but the local collectors insisted to him that the eggs are laid from early April to the end of July. Hatching probably occurs after two and a half months. The hatchling turtles usually measure about 25 mm in length, but if they hatch late in the season, they may spend the first winter in the nest—even in Louisiana, according to Cagle's (1954) observations. He further indicated that Louisiana specimens might achieve sexual maturity after the first growing season (i.e., late February through December).

Deirochelys reticularia (Latreille)
Chicken Turtle
Plate IX

Recognition. A medium-sized aquatic terrapin attaining a maximum length of 10 in. (254 mm); feet webbed; an extremely long neck (head plus neck equal to plastral length); vertical yellow stripes on the posterior surface of the hind legs and a broad yellow stripe on the front of the foreleg; carapace usually dark olive with a pattern of lighter-colored reticulate lines and with numerous slender longitudinal ridges; plastron unmarked, but possibly a dark spot or two on the bridge; from above the carapace appearing widest over the hind limbs.

Distribution. Statewide except for the coastal marshes (Map 55).

Taxonomic comments. Two races are known in Louisiana: *Deirochelys r. reticularia* (Latreille), the eastern chicken turtle, which occurs east of the Mississippi River and has a reticulate pattern of very narrow lines on the carapace and an unmarked plastron; and *D. r. miaria* Schwartz, the western chicken turtle, which occurs west of the Mississippi River and has faint, broader reticulate lines on the carapace and dark markings along the plastral scute seams. The most recent taxonomic revision is that by Schwartz (1956).

Habitat and habits. The chicken turtle is almost exclusively a resident of ditches, ponds, and lakes, and it rarely, if ever, occurs in streams. It frequently wanders overland and

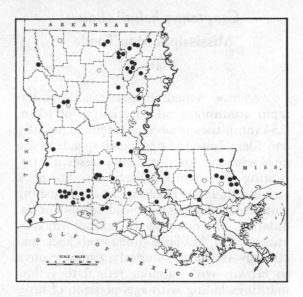

Map 55. Distribution of *Deirochelys reticularia*. Solid circles represent specimens examined; hollow circles represent museum specimens not examined or literature records.

not surprisingly turns up in temporarily flooded woodland pools. Records from Cameron Parish (Sabine Pass and 7 miles west of Holly Beach) appear to be from cheniers; in the Lacassine Refuge the habitat includes cypress trees and hence is essentially fresh water. Little is known about this turtle in Louisiana. Cagle (1950) commented that it is most attracted to trap bait in advanced stages of decay, and in his personal notes he indicated that the large intestine of a hatchling contained a mass of green, fluffy material. Elsewhere the species is omnivorous.

Reproduction. A specimen commented on by Cagle and Tihen (1948) presumably was a Louisiana animal; that animal contained seven eggs in January, three of which had escaped into the abdominal cavity.

In Florida this species lays eggs throughout the year, but on the southeastern coastal plain, *Deirochelys* lays eggs from March to June. We presume that in Louisiana the season is similar or perhaps even longer.

Graptemys kohnii (Baur)
Mississippi Map Turtle
Plate X

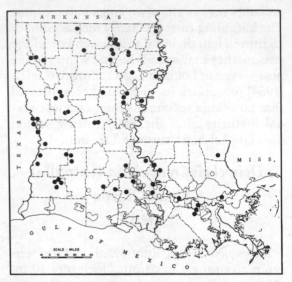

Map 56. Distribution of *Graptemys kohnii*. Solid circles represent specimens examined; hollow circles represent museum specimens not examined or literature records.

Recognition. A medium-sized freshwater terrapin attaining a carapace length of 10 in. (254 mm); toes webbed; head broad (usually considerably so in large females); side of the head with a yellow postorbital crescent interrupting a series of longitudinal yellow neck stripes otherwise reaching the eye; crushing surface of the upper jaw broad, smooth or undulating, but not ridged; carapace smooth, but with a knobbed middorsal keel and strongly serrated posteriorly; carapace olive to brown, with circular reticulate yellow markings fading with age; plastron of juveniles strongly marked with a pattern of mostly longitudinal dark lines fading with age.

Similar species. The Mississippi map turtle is easily confused with the false map turtle, *Graptemys pseudogeographica* (see the description for that species).

Distribution. Probably statewide in suitable freshwater habitat north of the Marsh but poorly known from central Louisiana and the Florida Parishes, areas neglected by turtle collecters (Map 56).

Taxonomic comments. See "Taxonomic comments" under *G. pseudogeographica*, a species with which *G. kohnii* may be conspecific or may hybridize.

Habitat and habits. This species occupies habitats like those preferred by the similar species *G. pseudogeographica*, with which it is frequently found. It occurs along water bodies such as slow-current streams, oxbows, and lakes, usually where vegetation is abundant. Both species are conspicuous as they bask on brush piles and on fallen trees that project from the water. The food habits of *G. kohnii* are much like those of *G. pseudogeographica*, except that juveniles and males seem more omnivorous, consuming more vegetation and mollusks in addition to

aquatic insects. Shively and Vidrine (1984), using the name *G. pseudogeographica* for this species, reported that adult female Mississippi map turtles in parts of the Sabine and Calcasieu river drainages of western Louisiana contained large numbers of freshwater mollusks in their alimentary tracts, the most important component being the recently introduced Asiatic clams of the genus *Corbicula*. Shively and Vidrine suggested that the turtle has shifted from feeding on native mollusks to feeding primarily on *Corbicula* because of the availability of the latter.

Probably relatively few turtles of this species are eaten by human beings. The young are highly prized as pets because of their handsome appearance.

Reproduction. Little is known of the reproductive habits. Carr (1952) mentioned a 1 June laying date at Natchez, Mississippi. The Tulane collections contain two lots of eggs laid 15 June or slightly later by females from Catahoula Parish: one lot of four eggs averaged 39.9 mm long (38.9–41.0 mm) and 21.7

mm wide (20.7–22.6 mm); the other lot of eight eggs averaged 38.1 mm long (36.6–41.0 mm) and 25.6 mm wide (25.3–26.2 mm). Two other lots, containing two shelled eggs each, were dissected from females taken 14–15 June. A group of three eggs dissected from a Catahoula Parish female on 13 June hatched on 28 August. The hatchlings were 35–37 mm in carapace length.

Graptemys oculifera (Baur)
Ringed Map Turtle, Ringed Sawback
Plate X

Recognition. A medium-sized freshwater terrapin attaining a carapace length of 8½ in. (216 mm); toes webbed; head narrow in both sexes; head, neck, and limbs with yellow stripes; a transverse yellow band on the chin, and a yellow postorbital mark; crushing surface of the upper jaw unridged, relatively narrow for the genus; carapace smooth, but with strongly developed spinelike knobs on the middorsal keel and strongly serrated posteriorly; carapace olive to brown, becoming darkened by black pigment with age, and a broad yellow or orange ring on each costal scute, these fading with age; plastron yellow or orange with dark markings along the seams, and without a hinge.

Distribution. The Pearl River and its larger tributaries (Map 57). Said to be in the Tangipahoa River in Tangipahoa Parish, but no specimens are available for proof. Type specimen recorded as being from Mandeville, St. Tammany Parish, but lack of suitable habitat or recent specimens suggests that collection data are erroneous.

The history of this species is quite intriguing. The original description was given by Baur (1890), but the origins of the specimens are questionable; sites such as Pensacola, Florida; Mandeville, Louisiana; and the marshes of southwestern Louisiana were recorded. Eventually some dried animals from the Gustave Kohn collection were discovered

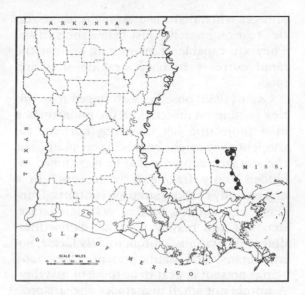

Map 57. Distribution of *Graptemys oculifera*. Solid circles represent specimens examined; hollow circles represent museum specimens not examined or literature records.

in storage in the old Tulane University Museum, and this led Cagle and his students to search the Pearl River, the locality given on the labels of some of the stored animals. Finally, in 1949 the ringed map turtle was rediscovered in Louisiana.

There is cause for concern about the survival of this handsome, endemic resident of the Pearl River system (see remarks under *Graptemys pulchra* for details). As of 28 November 1986, this turtle was listed as a threatened species by the U.S. Fish and Wildlife Service.

Taxonomic comments. No systematic study of this geographically restricted species has been made, but Cagle (1953) examined its relationships to other members of the genus *Graptemys*.

Habitat and habits. Graptemys oculifera is a common turtle in sections of the Pearl and Bogue Chitto rivers where wide sand beaches, narrow channels, and fast currents are characteristic. The ringed map turtle basks on logs and debris over deep water into which it plunges when disturbed. At night, these turtles rest on branches just below the surface. They are capable of swimming against the rapid currents to reach basking sites and food.

Cagle (1953) observed two ringed map turtles feeding on material on the undersurface of a projecting log in strong current. He thought they might be feeding on snails, but the stomach contents that he mentioned included "only fragments of insects." In a closer study of those stomach contents, Dundee found aquatic beetles and their larvae, mayflies and mayfly nymphs, damselflies, dragonfly nymphs, chironomid fly larvae, homopterans, and snails present. The many wings present appear to be those of mayflies. A number of small nematodes also are present in the stomach contents, but these probably are parasites within the turtle. The small quantities of algae present were probably ingested with the prey. Several unidentified, intact globular masses were in two stomachs examined.

Reproduction. Cagle (1953) suggested that early June is the active egg-laying season because numerous trails on a sandy beach and a "trial nest" cavity dug by a female were noted at that time. He reported that two of the three oviducal eggs from the female observed measured 40.3 × 20.6 mm and 40.0 × 21.0 mm. The Tulane collections contain two eggs with the label "July 26, 1956." We cannot ascertain if these were dissected from a female or were laid, but they probably came from a sizable series of turtles taken 7–8 July in Simpson County, Mississippi. The eggs measure 49 × 25 mm and 42 × 23 mm and contain only yolk, thus indicating that the laying season extends well into July.

Hatchling *G. oculifera* have plastron lengths of 22.3–32.7 mm according to Cagle (1953), which extrapolates to carapace lengths of 24.5–36.0 mm.

The only animal that Cagle (1953) mentioned to be a hatchling (TU 11960) no longer

exists, and according to the museum catalog entry it was collected in mid-April. Another hatchling animal collected in that period (TU 12007) has been cleared and stained: it measures 31 mm in carapace length and 25 mm in plastron length. The blank spaces for data in the field catalogs and the scattered fashion in which the numerical entries were made for the hatchlings lead us to suspect that the April entry in the museum catalog is incorrect; certainly that is not a reasonable time to expect hatchlings.

Graptemys pseudogeographica (Gray)
False Map Turtle
Plate X

Recognition. A medium-sized freshwater terrapin attaining a carapace length of 10¾ in. (273 mm), but maximum length in Louisiana 7⅛ in. (180 mm); males substantially smaller than females; toes webbed; head narrow in both sexes of all sizes; side of head with a yellow postorbital mark, and neck with a series of longitudinal yellow stripes, some reaching the eye; crushing surface of the upper jaw broad, smooth or undulating, but not ridged; carapace smooth, but with a knobbed middorsal keel, and strongly serrated posteriorly; carapace color brown to olive green, usually with some yellow oval markings or concentric lines, these fading in older animals; plastron without a hinge; plastron of juveniles with a longitudinal pattern of black lines, but only slightly marked or immaculate in adults.

Similar species. This species may be confused with the Mississippi map turtle (*Graptemys kohnii*), from which it differs in having a postorbital spot rather than a postorbital crescent; the spot in *G. pseudogeographica* does not interrupt all of the neck stripes as does the crescent of *kohnii*. Also, large female *G. kohnii* have broadened heads. Jack-

184

son and Shively (1983) indicated that female *G. kohnii* (which they refer to as *G. pseudogeographica*) in the Calcasieu River system of western Louisiana have larger heads than do females of typical lower Mississippi Valley populations. For more detail on the distinctions, see Dundee (1974c).

Distribution. Probably statewide west of the Mississippi River and north of the Marsh in suitable freshwater habitats, but currently no records are available for central Louisiana (Map 58).

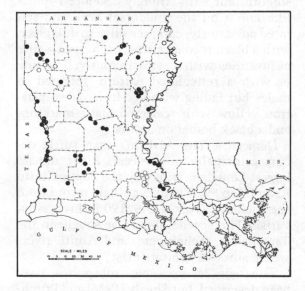

Map 58. Distribution of *Graptemys pseudogeographica*. Solid circles represent specimens examined; hollow circles represent museum specimens not examined or literature records.

Taxonomic comments. Two races are recognized in Louisiana: *G. p. sabinensis* Cagle, the Sabine map turtle, occurs in the Sabine, Calcasieu, and Mermentau river drainages and is characterized by an oval or elongate postorbital mark and from five to nine yellow lines reaching the eye; *G. p. ouachitensis* Cagle, the Ouachita map turtle, occurs in the Ouachita, Red, Mississippi, and Atchafalaya

river drainages and can be recognized by the presence of a rectangular postorbital spot, a yellow spot under the eye and another below it on the upper jaw, and only one to three lines reaching the eye.

Throughout the entire geographic range of the false map turtles and the Mississippi map turtle, there are numerous variations in pattern; some herpetologists (e.g., Vogt 1978, 1980; Dobie 1981) believe that more than two species exist in the complex, whereas others believe that extensive hybridization has occurred. Vogt (1978, 1980), studying Wisconsin examples, considered *G. ouachitensis* to be a distinct species and *G. o. sabinensis* to be one of its races. Dobie (1981) apparently followed Vogt's usage but gave no basis for the interpretation. Ward (1980) thought that separation of *ouachitensis* as a distinct species might be valid but considered his own study inconclusive. Bertl and Killebrew (1983) used the name *G. sabinensis*, but Killebrew informed us that that was a typographical error.

Ward (1980) referred the Sabine map turtle to *G. sabinensis*, stating that it was so unlike any other *Graptemys* that it deserved specific designation. He found the most notable feature to be complete separation of the nasal bones by the prefrontal process of the frontal bone. But Ward presented data for only two specimens of *G. sabinensis*—although he had borrowed nine skulls from Tulane—and did not compare the sexes as he did for most other species. He also failed to determine if there were any ontogenetic differences in any species. His conclusion seems too sweeping for so few data.

Unless future osteological and biochemical studies produce evidence to the contrary, we are still inclined to believe that map turtle relationships are rather well defined in Louisiana, at least to the extent that *G. kohnii* is distinct from *ouachitensis-sabinensis*, and pending a formally published presentation by Vogt, we use the name *G. pseudogeographica*.

Habitat and habits. Graptemys pseudogeographica is a species inhabiting streams with slow to moderate currents, oxbow lakes, ponds, impoundments, and backwaters. These turtles are conspicuous baskers on fallen trees and logs projecting from the water. They prefer deeper water and are not readily trapped because of their seeming reluctance to respond to bait. However, they can be easily secured at night as they rest just below the surface on submerged branches (Chaney and Smith 1950).

Webb (1961) examined stomachs of Ouachita map turtles in Oklahoma and found that the juveniles had fed mostly on aquatic insects but also contained parts of various arthropods, mollusks, and some presumably accidentally ingested vegetation. One of two adult females was gorged with grasshoppers; the other contained much vegetation.

Shively (1982) found that adult female Sabine map turtles from Whiskey Chitto Creek (Sabine River drainage), Louisiana, eat mostly filamentous green algae that they graze off of logs, and that males are insectivorous, actively selecting caddis fly larvae (*Hydropsyche*), as do the juveniles, but juveniles are somewhat more omnivorous.

False map turtles are occasionally eaten by humans, but they are mostly sought for the pet trade because of their attractive markings.

Reproduction. Nesting occurs throughout the spring and summer (Collins 1974), and the nests are made in loose soil in sunny sites. From 6 to 13 eggs are laid, and Webb (1961) estimated the reproductive potential of *G. p. ouachitensis* at 21 eggs, in three clutches or fewer. Webb found oviducal eggs of Oklahoma *G. p. ouachitensis* to measure 32.8–40.3 mm long and 18.7–23.8 mm wide. A set of six eggs of *G. p. sabinensis* taken 6 July in Sabine Parish averages 38.2 mm long (37–39 mm) and 20.75 mm wide (20–22 mm). Hatching takes at least 45 days (Collins 1974). The nearly round hatchlings measure 33–35 mm in carapace length.

Graptemys pulchra Baur
Alabama Map Turtle
Plate X

Recognition. A medium-sized, freshwater terrapin attaining a carapace length of 11½ in. (292 mm); toes webbed; head broad (grotesquely broadened in older females), and with large yellow postorbital blotches connected to a large interorbital yellow blotch; chin with a longitudinal yellow stripe; neck and limbs striped with yellow; carapace smooth, but with strongly developed spinelike knobs on the middorsal keel, and serrated posteriorly; carapace olive to dull green with a black median stripe; each costal scute of juveniles with a semicircular yellow line or with a reticulated pattern, retained in males but fading with age in females; plastron yellow with scattered black markings and a black border on seams.

Distribution. The Alabama map turtle occurs principally in the Pearl River and its largest Louisiana tributary, the Bogue Chitto River (Map 59). There is a single record from the Tickfaw River at U.S. 190 in Livingston Parish. The species should be sought in the Tangipahoa, Tchefuncte, and Amite rivers where suitable habitats exist.

Taxonomic comments. No subspecies have been described, but Shealy (1976) and Pritchard (1979) described differences in populations from different rivers and suggested that subspecific designations might be appropriate.

Habitat and habits. This turtle is associated with *Graptemys oculifera* along moving, deeper waters of the Pearl River system where sand or gravel bottoms and logs and debris for basking sites are available. At night these turtles may venture into shallow water or onto the sandy beaches, but usually they cling to submerged objects just below the surface of the water. Cagle (1952a) said that they preferred to rest on the half-submerged branches of thorny locust trees.

186

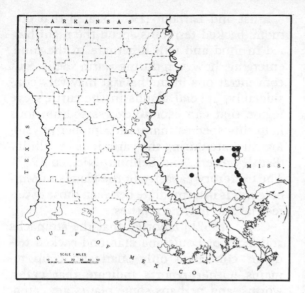

Map 59. Distribution of *Graptemys pulchra.* Solid circles represent specimens examined; hollow circles represent museum specimens not examined or literature records.

The juveniles, young females, and males have relatively weak jaws and feed mostly on insects, but the adult females, with their huge heads and strong jaws, are able to crush and feed on snails and clams.

The largest animal from large recent collections (1950) from the Pearl River system measures 224 mm (Conant [1958] indicated a maximum of 215 mm for the species, but extrapolations by Dundee based on the ratio of plastral length to carapace length indicate that an animal from Florida mentioned by Cagle [1952a] would have been 228–241 mm long). Four specimens collected in the Pearl River in 1901 and deposited at Tulane (data used by Conant 1975) measure 267–292 mm in carapace length. The great size discrepancy over the 50-year interval may reflect alteration of the Pearl River system. Mount (1975) reported a 285-mm female and remarked that removal of snags and logs from streams reduces the available basking places for *G. pulchra.* The modern Pearl River channel is maintained for navigation and receives

industrial effluents, particularly from the paper industries, and we suspect that these alterations may be damaging the habitat and food supply of *G. pulchra,* as well as its close associate, *G. oculifera.* Survival of the latter species, which is restricted to the Pearl River system, is a matter of considerable concern to conservationists.

Reproduction. Nesting occurs in Alabama from late April into August (Mount 1975), and females deposit as many as six or seven clutches per year, averaging four to six eggs each. Courtship activity has been observed in Alabama from September through November (Shealy 1976). Exposed sandbars are the favored nesting sites (Cagle 1952a). Three eggs of a Louisiana female examined by Cagle measured 42.7–46.0 × 25.0–27.0 mm, and five from a Florida female measured 38–40 × 24.2–25.0 mm. The carapace length of the attractive hatchlings ranges from 23.7 to 38.8 mm (extrapolated from plastral lengths given in Cagle 1952a). Crows by day and raccoons at night are major nest predators (Shealy 1976).

Malaclemys terrapin (Schoepff)
Diamond-backed Terrapin
Plate XI

Recognition. A medium-sized terrapin reaching a carapace length of $9\frac{3}{8}$ in. (238 mm); toes webbed; head often greatly broadened in large females; head and limbs gray, heavily freckled with dark spots; carapace with strongly developed concentric grooves and ridges on each scute and a prominent tuberculate middorsal keel; carapace dark brown or black; plastron yellow, often clouded with darker colors.

Distribution. Saline sections of the Marsh (Map 60).

Taxonomic comments. The Louisiana race is *Malaclemys terrapin pileata* (Wied), the Mississippi diamond-backed terrapin. At the western boundary of Louisiana, this race intergrades with the Texas diamond-backed ter-

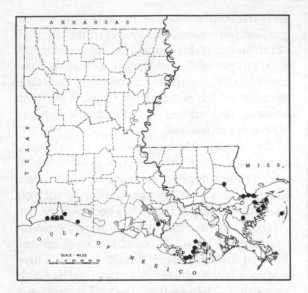

Map 60. Distribution of *Malaclemys terrapin.* Solid circles represent specimens examined; hollow circles represent museum specimens not examined or literature records.

rapin (*M. t. littoralis*), which has a higher, lighter-colored carapace, an almost white plastron, carapace sides that are less parallel than those of *M. t. pileata,* and a more heavily mottled skin. Cagle (1952b), however, considered a large series from Dulac, Terrebonne Parish, to be intermediate between the two races. The last comprehensive taxonomic study of the species is that by Hay (1904). Ernst and Bury (1982) summarized the current systematics.

Habitat and habits. Malaclemys terrapin is a turtle of brackish waters, but within the coastal marsh it prefers the more open channels to the "grassy" flats. Fishermen often take this species in nets (Cagle 1952b). Diamond-backed terrapins may bask on mud flats or float in channels. They are thus not easily captured turtles; the difficulty of walking in the marshlands, combined with the often treacherous tidal draining of marshland channels and pools, makes access to them difficult for the would-be collector.

Ernst and Barbour (1972) stated that diamond-backed terrapins spend the night buried in mud and will hibernate in the mud, emerging, however, during warm spells. Salt concentrations in the habitat may vary considerably; special glands in the turtle's eye region that can excrete excess sodium ions help this species maintain a proper physiological state during the variations in salinity (Bentley, Bretz, and Schmidt-Nielsen 1967). The excretory capacity of the glands in *Malaclemys* is intermediate between those of terrestrial and marine reptiles.

Cagle (1952b) reported that the stomachs and feces of Louisiana diamond-backed terrapins contained only snail and clam remains. Other reports indicate that crabs, worms, and perhaps some plants are eaten.

Along the eastern U.S. coast, diamond-backed terrapins were esteemed as a gourmet's preference in turtle flesh. In the eighteenth century the turtle was abundant enough to serve as a mainstay for the feeding of slaves, but eventually the traffic in turtles so reduced the numbers of the animals that prices in Savannah reached as high as $90 per dozen in 1921. The diamond-backed terrapin only rarely reaches the marketplace in Louisiana today, and in 1976 the retail price was about $4 per turtle.

Reproduction. Growth of *M. terrapin* is rapid; in Louisiana, the females are mature in six years and capable of producing several clutches of 4 to 12 eggs per year. Nests are made in sandy areas above the high tide mark. Ernst and Barbour (1972) indicated that southern races of the diamond-backed terrapin nest from April through July. The Tulane collections include a clutch of five eggs excavated from a gravel beach in Terrebonne Parish on 1 June 1952. The individual eggs measured 38.5–41.0 × 24.0–25.0 mm (averaging 39.7 × 24.3 mm), substantially larger than egg measurements reported (31.1 × 21.2 mm) for a clutch from a northern race (McCauley 1945). Two "no data" shelled eggs at Tulane, stored with some large ovarian eggs, measure 41 × 24 mm and 41 × 25 mm.

Burns and Williams (1972) reported on 11 clutches laid in captivity by females from St. Bernard Parish. They noted that clutches had 5 to 12 eggs, and each female required 9 to 47 days to lay her egg complement. The egg-laying period began 5 July, and some eggs were deposited as late as 10 September. The 95 eggs measured 37.34 mm (34.0–40.1 mm) long and 23.96 mm (21.9–27.0 mm) wide. Hatchlings emerged from 3 of the 90 eggs incubated and measured 29.4–30.4 mm in carapace length and 22.7–24.5 mm in carapace width.

Pseudemys concinna (Le Conte)
River Cooter, Slider, Mobilian
Plate IX

Recognition. A large freshwater terrapin reaching a carapace length in excess of 16 in. (406 mm); toes webbed; head with orange to red stripes on top, bottom, and sides; underside of the chin flat; crushing surface of the upper jaw with a ridge or row of tubercles parallel to the jaw margin; roughened carapace with narrow, curving ridges; carapace with a low middorsal keel and a somewhat serrate posterior margin; second costal scute with a light C-shaped mark; carapace brown with orange-yellow concentric and/or curving lines and bars developed to varying degrees; plastron without a hinge; plastron yellow or orangish yellow, usually with dark markings, especially along the anterior seams, these markings often forming an "X" anteriorly; juveniles more strongly patterned than adults.

Distribution. Apparently statewide in rivers but occurring also in some lake situations such as Lac des Allemands in St. John Parish (Map 61).

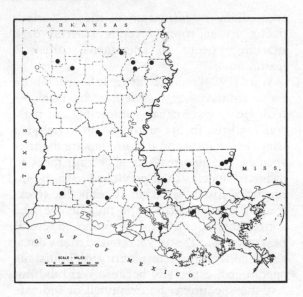

Map 61. Distribution of *Pseudemys concinna*. Solid circles represent specimens examined; hollow circles represent museum specimens not examined or literature records.

Taxonomic comments. This is one of the most enigmatic reptiles in Louisiana; over the years various authors have discussed the relationships of turtles assigned to *Pseudemys concinna* and *P. floridana* (Carr 1952; Crenshaw 1955a; Weaver and Rose 1967; Fahey 1980; Ward 1984). There has been disagreement concerning specific assignment of some races, whether there are two species or one, and whether hybridization is a complicating factor. Diagnostic tools have long involved primarily carapacial patterns, and more recently phalangeal formulae, tarsal osteology, and markings on the marginal scutes of the bridge. With these criteria the consensus seemed to be that *P. concinna* is defined by a "C" mark on the second costal scute and a plastron with dark markings, whereas *P. floridana* has a more-or-less vertical light mark on the second costal scute and few or no dark plastral markings. The confusion in separating the two species results from the variability in carapace markings; all stages of intermediacy in formation of the "C" mark occur. In addition, juvenile plastral dark markings occur in specimens called *P. floridana*.

Ward (1984) reported at great length on the representatives of *Pseudemys:* he used osteological, myological, carapacial, and plastral features in his analysis and concluded that *P. concinna* and *P. floridana* are distinct species. He also reassigned certain races to different species than previous usage; he interpreted much variation as being due to extensive intergradation, and thus he declared some subspecies invalid and proposed several new ones. Ward's study has raised many questions concerning the identity of Louisiana specimens, especially because Ward did not list the specimens he examined or indicate the species or race to which he assigned them; in fact, only in describing the new subspecies did he actually identify particular specimens examined. Additionally, although he showed some poorly defined maps of *P. concinna* distribution, he presented only a verbal description of *P. floridana* distribution, stating that it extended to the Mississippi River.

Because Ward's (1984) paper appeared so recently, we have been unable to do a thoroughly detailed evaluation of Ward's interpretations. Dundee has looked at a modest number of Louisiana specimens to see what Ward's criteria would reveal. Dundee did not use osteological data, which Ward indicated were the best criteria. However, Dundee extracted and evaluated 21 features from Ward's scattered data; each feature supposedly would provide 100 percent separation of the species. Several of the features proved intermediate or did not conform to Ward's description of species differences, for example, anterior width of marginals XII as a percentage of posterior width, carapace height/width, carapace height/length, carapace patterns, presence of a dark spot on the inguinal scute, plastral markings, width of the dorsal cervical scute as a percentage of carapace width, and plastral bulge. There may be some flaws in Dundee's examination because Ward's methods are sometimes ambiguously stated (e.g., he measured carapace length as midline length, whereas most researchers measure overall length, and Ward's method does not indicate if he measured from the base of the anterior and posterior carapacial notches). Although Ward's dissertation (1980) is more detailed than the 1984 paper, it does not resolve our questions.

Ward (1984) challenged Fahey's (1980) interpretation on the basis of specimens that he examined from Louisiana and East Texas. Ward did not, however, examine the Tulane specimens on which Dundee applied Ward's criteria (Ward's statement on p. 9 that he examined specimens from Tulane University is a section carried over from his dissertation [Ward 1980]—he did borrow Tulane *Graptemys* skeletal material, but no *Pseudemys* material). Although Ward may be right that *P. concinna* and *P. floridana* are different species, he has not solved to our satisfaction the status of these turtles in Louisiana.

We are not prepared to make a definitive determination of *Pseudemys* in Louisiana at this time; an extensive examination of material is required. We do not feel that Ward's erection of *P. concinna metteri* (which he shows as occurring in northwestern Louisiana) is justified, and we find such an extensive area of intergradation among the races of *concinna* as that proposed by Ward difficult to accept. Ward said that dark pigment on the inguinal scute will distinguish 99 percent of the *concinna* from 98 percent of the *floridana*. However, that feature does not work well in Louisiana, judging from the specimens examined by Dundee. We note especially that Fahey (1980) found southern Louisiana specimens to show complete gradations in carapace and bridge markings, plastral patterns and tarsal osteology to exhibit ontogenetic changes, and variations in characters to be great in individuals hatched from single clutches of eggs.

Carr (1952) considered *P. floridana* and *P. concinna* to be conspecific, but Crenshaw (1955a) considered them to be distinct species that occasionally hybridize. Ditch and sluggish-water *Pseudemys* in Louisiana tend to fulfill the descriptive criteria for *P. floridana*, but those in northern Louisiana trend toward having the intricate, fine-line scrollwork patterns on the carapace that characterize *concinna*. Many carapace patterns from the Pearl River near Varnado appear to be intermediate, as do those of south-central Louisiana juveniles. We agree with Fahey (1980) that if the relationships of *P. concinna* and *P. floridana* were to be based on Louisiana material, those from southern Louisiana would appear to be representatives of a single, highly variable species.

If we were to accept *P. concinna* as a valid species, we would recognize two races in Louisiana: *P. c. mobilensis* (Holbrook), the Mobile cooter of southern Louisiana, and *P. c. hieroglyphica* (Holbrook), the hieroglyphic river cooter, of northern Louisiana. This is the nomenclature advocated by Ernst and Barbour (1972). This scheme allows us to retain *P. floridana* as a widespread Louisiana species. In view of Fahey's (1980) findings, we would consider *P. c. mobilensis* to represent hybrids between *concinna* and *floridana*. If *mobilensis* is a valid race of *concinna*, then the best distinction between the two races seems to be that *hieroglyphica* often has a constriction of the carapace at the level of the sixth marginal scute (i.e., in front of the hind limbs); *hieroglyphica* also has a lower carapace profile. There is enough intermediacy to suggest that most Louisiana specimens are intergrades.

Habitat and habits. Pseudemys concinna predominantly inhabits streams with moderate currents and is fond of basking on logs projecting from the water. Cooters are capable of remaining submerged for two or more hours and walk along the bottom to seek food. The juveniles are said to be carnivorous or herbivorous or both, but adults are conspicuously consumers of varied aquatic vegetation.

The "Mobilian" is well known for its flesh in Louisiana, but that name, as used by fishermen, includes *P. floridana*. These turtles are not particularly desirable for the table both because they contain much dark meat and because the low yield (about 15 percent of the total weight) makes them uneconomical to flesh out.

Reproduction. Cagle (notes) hatched several sets of *P. c. mobilensis* eggs from southern Louisiana. The eggs numbered 7 to 15 per clutch and were elliptical, measuring approximately 37–44 mm long and 26–29 mm in diameter. Hatchlings had carapace lengths of 33–36 mm. Cagle was not clear on the dates of deposition, but one set of oviducal eggs taken from a turtle from Waggaman, Jefferson Parish, on 12 June hatched 6 August in the laboratory.

Fahey (1980) retrieved 7 to 16 oviducal eggs from southern Louisiana specimens. Mount (1975) reported that in Alabama the eggs are laid in sandy soil above nearby water.

Pseudemys floridana (Le Conte)
Cooter
Plate IX

Recognition. A large freshwater terrapin reaching a foot (305 mm) in length; toes webbed; head with numerous yellow stripes (often broken or twisted) on top, bottom, and sides; underside of the chin flat; crushing surface of the upper jaw with a ridge or row of tubercles parallel to the jaw margin; roughened carapace with narrow, curving ridges and a low middorsal keel, and with the posterior margin somewhat serrate; second costal scute with a transverse light bar occasionally forked medially and/or laterally; dorsum brownish with straight and curved yellow lines; plastron without a hinge; plastron yellow or orange-yellow, usually without dark markings; juveniles more strongly patterned than adults.

Similar species. Carr (1952) said a median notch present in the upper jaw separates this turtle from most *Pseudemys concinna hieroglyphica*, but we do not see that the notch is always developed, especially in younger animals; hence it is not a useful character. This species is difficult to distinguish from *P. concinna*, with which it apparently hybridizes.

Distribution. Apparently statewide in sluggish or silted streams, ponds, lakes, and ditches (Map 62).

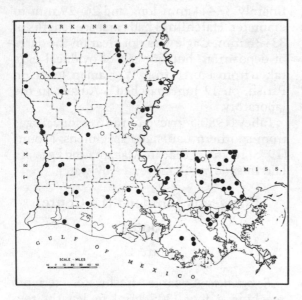

Map 62. Distribution of *Pseudemys floridana*. Solid circles represent specimens examined; hollow circles represent museum specimens not examined or literature records.

Taxonomic comments. The Louisiana specimens are allocated to *P. floridana hoyi* (Agassiz), the Missouri cooter. For further comment, see the *P. concinna* account.

Habitat and habits. In stream situations, *P. floridana* prefers sluggish or unmoving waters. We have not seen it often in turbid, standing pools; it seems to prefer clearer waters. This preference may be attributable to its primarily vegetarian diet because much aquatic growth develops in clear waters. Some insects, sponges, and bryozoans also are eaten (D. R. Hart, pers. com.). This species is fond of basking on logs during sunny periods.

A group of *Pseudemys* from Lake Pontchartrain referred to as *floridana* by Cagle (his notes describe some as having immaculate plastrons, but the specimens are now osteological and lack scutes) were grazing on "bottom grass" and had guts full of the grass. The gonads of large females in this lot, collected 30 July, revealed that the breeding season was over for most, but two animals had enlarged ova that presumably could have been deposited later that year.

This species is used for food in Louisiana (see the *P. concinna* account).

Reproduction. Little is known of the reproductive habits of *P. floridana hoyi*. Collins (1974), presumably referring to Kansas populations, reported that 12 to 29 eggs are laid in June.

Terrapene carolina Linnaeus
Eastern Box Turtle
Plate XI

Recognition. A medium-sized land terrapin reaching a carapace length of 8½ in. (216 mm) in one Louisiana race, less in the other race (see "Taxonomic comments"); toes only slightly webbed; hind foot usually with three, sometimes four, toes; carapace rather high domed and usually with a median keel; carapace plain brown or with a variable pattern of yellow or orange spots, blotches, or radiating lines, depending on degree of union of the markings; plastron with a divided gular scute, without a bridge, and with a hinge between pectoral and abdominal scutes, thus forming two movable lobes capable of enclosing the entire body and legs within the shell; plastron patternless or without well-defined markings, but with a dark area in juveniles.

Similar species. The western box turtle (*Terrapene ornata*) has a bold pattern of narrow radiating yellow lines on both carapace and plastron, and its carapace is flattened dorsally and lacks a keel or has only a very low keel on the posterior surface. Western box turtles usually have four toes on each hind foot, with the inner nails of males being turned inward.

Blaney (1968) reported hybridization between *T. carolina* and *T. ornata* in Cameron and Caddo parishes. Although *T. ornata* is known from Cameron Parish (Rossman 1965b), the Caddo Parish report poses an interesting problem. The nearest reported record for pure *ornata* in Texas is Marion County (Raun and Gehlbach 1972), which is about 31 miles northwest of Blaney's locality. The nearest Arkansas record is 110 miles north, and Dundee has seen *ornata* near Idabel, McCurtain County, Oklahoma (farther east than recorded in the literature), a distance of 130 miles. Hybrids between the two species have been reported from Missouri, Illinois, and Indiana, but despite the large overlap of the ranges of *carolina* and *ornata*, the frequency of hybridization is low. Most reports are from the perimeter of the range of *ornata*, which, of course, appears to be the case for Blaney's report. Blaney suggested that perhaps ecological segregation breaks down in the peripheral ecotonal zone. But, although prairie and woodland ecotones are common from Kansas into Texas, hybrids have not been reported from those states.

The interpretation of what constitutes a hybrid between *T. carolina* and *T. ornata* is difficult. For example, a specimen (TU 19339) from DeSoto County, Mississippi, near Memphis, Tennessee, came from a locality more than 100 miles east of the nearest recorded *ornata* range limit, yet it has inter-

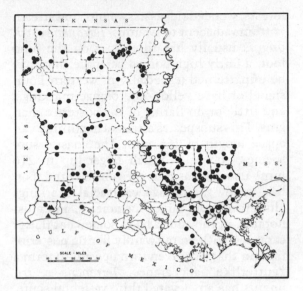

Map 63. Distribution of *Terrapene carolina.* Solid circles represent specimens examined; hollow circles represent museum specimens not examined or literature records; solid triangles represent hybrid specimens.

mediate markings, a flattened, keelless carapace, and is four-toed (the locality is in the zone of intergradation for *T. c. carolina*, a four-toed race, and *T. c. triunguis*). Most features of the Mississippi specimen are more nearly *ornata*, according to criteria given by Milstead (1969). Moreover, there is a *T. carolina* from Alabama (TU 15925.1) whose plastral pattern strongly resembles that of some *ornata*. An intensive search for *ornata* is needed in Caddo Parish; if pure *ornata* does occur there, the probability that hybrids are also present is much greater.

Distribution. Statewide, but absent from the Marsh except on cheniers (Map 63).

Taxonomic comments. This is a wide-ranging species represented by six living races. In Louisiana we have two subspecies, *T. c. triunguis* Agassiz, the three-toed box turtle, which inhabits most of the state except for the low coastal areas, and *T. c. major* Agassiz, the Gulf Coast box turtle of the eastern Louisiana coastal regions, which inhabits damp forests, wooded ridges in swamps, and stream bottoms adjacent to swamps. *Terrapene c. triunguis* usually has three toes on the hind foot, a fairly high-domed carapace that may be unpatterned (especially in western Louisiana) or have yellow and orange markings, and little or no flaring of the posterior margins. This subspecies attains a maximum carapace length of 165 mm. The coastal subspecies, *major*, is much larger (up to 216 mm), usually has four toes on the hind foot, has yellow or orange carapacial markings (duller in many larger specimens), and most notably, in the adults has a somewhat flatter carapace with an outwardly flaring posterior margin that may even turn upward to form a "gutterlike" appearance. *Terrepene c. triunguis* has an elevated third vertebral scute, and *major* has a convex fifth vertebral scute. Intermediates between *major* and *triunguis* are rarely seen because the two races seem to be ecologically segregated.

Considerable controversy exists concerning the status of the species of *Terrapene*. Milstead (1967, 1969) considered *T. carolina* to consist of a number of races and found the material he examined from southeastern Louisiana to represent intergrades between *T. c. triunguis* and *T. c. major*. But Ward (1980) regarded the Gulf Coast box turtle to be a distinct species, *T. major*, ranging from Florida to the Mississippi River. Ward did not use the same characters to define each of the different *Terrapene* species he recognized, nor did he always compare the same characters as Milstead. Ward included contradictory statements; for example, he described the anterior plastral lobe length of *T. carolina* as being 55–61 percent the length of the posterior plastral lobe, but in Table 10 he shows a mean of 68±5.6, an unresolvable inconsistency (Ward 1980:292). Additionally, Ward (1980:293) claimed that the intermediates noted by Milstead (1969) and Mount (1975) that he examined fell within the limits of variation found in either *major* or *triunguis* and

showed no intermediacy of characters or combinations of characters, but Ward presented no definitive data to support such a statement. Ward's claim for the specific distinctness of *T. major* is based partly on skull characters, but he examined only nine skulls, all from eastern Florida.

Because of the above-mentioned discrepancies, Dundee visited a woodland near Boutte, St. Charles Parish, west of the Mississippi River and definitely in low coastal country. A number of males that he had seen in that area had the deep plastral concavity characteristic of *T. c. major*. The four females collected on that trip range from 158 to 169 mm in carapace length (exceptionally large for *triunguis*), each has four toes on the hind foot (which disagrees with Ward's definition of *triunguis*) and has anterior plastral lobes that were 63–67 percent the lengths of the posterior lobes (too high for *triunguis* if Ward's range of 55–61 percent is correct).

We are more in accord with Milstead's (1969) interpretation that *major* is a race of *T. carolina*, certainly in Louisiana. Although Milstead cited several features that he considered intermediate in southeastern Louisiana material, the large size, the plastral concavity in males, the absence of a humped third vertebral scute, presence of a convex fifth vertebral scute, the tendency for a flaring, upwardly turned posterior margin on the carapace, and the consistently four-toed condition support the identification of the St. Charles Parish population as *T. c. major*, and we suspect that other coastal samples may also prove to be *major*.

Habitat and habits. Eastern box turtles primarily inhabit open woodlands but also turn up in fields wherever forests are nearby. The three-toed box turtle is occasionally seen as it crosses highways. The Gulf Coast box turtle is rarely if ever encountered away from woods, perhaps indicating that it is associated with more humid and shaded habitats. During cool months, these box turtles may be found under logs, but as the season warms they roam over the forest floor by day. In very hot weather they may lie in the shallow water of pond margins.

Large numbers of eastern box turtles are picked up and brought home as pets. Many are sold in pet stores. These pressures, plus roadway mortality and the clearing and burning of woodlands, are causing eastern box turtles to become less common, and they may eventually need protection.

Virtually every eastern box turtle found is an adult. Juveniles or newly hatched animals are rarely seen, probably because they have subterranean proclivities and use rodent burrows or forage under leaf litter.

During winter months, eastern box turtles hibernate in burrows or under deep leaf litter. Penn and Pottharst (1940) studied captive *T. c. major* taken in Orleans and Jefferson parishes and concluded that those animals entered a period of torpor when air temperatures dropped to roughly 65°F (18°C), emerging periodically from their burrows during the winter months when temperatures climbed to 60°–70°F (15.5°–21°C). During the warmer months, activity observed by Penn and Pottharst was mainly from dawn to 8:00 A.M. and from sunset to dark. During the day, especially when temperatures were above 90°F (32°C), the animals refused food that they would normally have eaten five to six hours earlier or later.

Eastern box turtles usually have small, well-defined home ranges. They are noted also for their longevity, which certainly reaches 80 years, perhaps a century or more.

Eastern box turtles are omnivorous feeders, taking all kinds of plants, fungi, and smaller animals, as well as carrion. Cagle (notes) found that the stomach contents of three specimens from northern Louisiana contained plant and insect fragments and an enormous number of nematodes (most likely parasites of the turtle—our interpretation).

Reproduction. Courtship and mating usually occur in the spring but may extend into autumn (Ernst and Barbour 1972). Penn and Pottharst (1940) indicated that their captive *T. c. major* would mate over a lengthy period of the year, especially when temperatures were between 70° and 80°F (21° and 26.7°C), but within a range of 50°–90°F (10°–32°C), and when humidities were relatively high. Some of the matings actually occurred in water (on one occasion when air temperatures had fallen to 56°F [13.3°C], but the water had retained its higher temperature). On 17 March 1986 Dundee found a pair copulating in a shallow pool (15 mm deep) in St. Charles Parish. Air temperature was 80°F (26.7°C), water 72°F (22.2°C). The larger male was lying on its back but had a secure hold on the female's body with his hind limbs. Rossman noted a pair of *T. c. triunguis* mating in Franklin Parish in late afternoon on 24 April 1971.

Various reports indicate that nesting occurs from May to July; the eggs are deposited in excavations 3–4 in. (76–100 mm) deep and then covered.

The four females from Boutte, St. Charles Parish, mentioned under "Taxonomic comments" were retained in a sand-bottomed pen from their capture on 2 July until mid-October. In mid-September four eggs were found; the eggs were either broken or partially dehydrated, and none contained embryos. The eggs measured 34.5 × 22.5 mm, 34.4 × 22.4 mm, 40.2 × 25.1 mm, and 42.5 × ? mm. The date(s) of deposition is (are) unknown.

Tulane has several sets of eggs and hatchlings, some with good data; others have conflicting catalog and jar data or with no adequate data available, but these probably are Louisiana-collected material. From these we find that two female *T. c. triunguis* from Catahoula Parish laid two and three eggs, respectively. Another label indicates a set of dataless *triunguis* eggs laid between 6:00 P.M. and 8:00 A.M. on 12–13 October. These measure 36.1–38 mm in length and 20.4–21.4 mm in diameter. The eggs allegedly from the Catahoula Parish animals are part of a batch of eggs measuring 30.5–40.1 mm in length and 19.4–23.0 mm in diameter.

Hatching dates are recorded as August through September 1937, 30 August 1937, and 20 October 1935, all probably for *major* inasmuch as the data are from Penn, who had studied *major* (see Penn and Pottharst 1940). The Tulane Natural History Museum contains an uncataloged set of five eggs from east of Boutte (very likely from a *major*) that were laid 8 July. Those failed to hatch, and on 9 September one was opened. It contained a juvenile with a carapace 27.5 mm long, with a yellow spot in the center of each costal scute and double yellow spots down each vertebral scute. The egg measured 18.5 × 29 mm.

One Tulane specimen is a hatchling *T. c. major* from Jefferson County in the Florida Panhandle. That animal was from an egg removed from a female 8 June 1953 and hatched 5 August (59 days incubation). It measures 32.8 mm in carapace length, 23.9 mm in carapace width, and has a yolk mass attached. The keel has pronounced broad, yellow knobs. The caruncle or egg tooth is prominently obvious on the snout. Juveniles that hatched in late summer or fall, but were preserved in late May, no longer had the caruncle and had relatively much broader carapaces.

Terrapene ornata Agassiz
Western Box Turtle, Ornate Box Turtle
Plate XI

Recognition. A small land terrapin reaching a carapace length of just over 6 in. (154 mm); toes only slightly webbed; hind foot with four toes, the innermost turned inward at a sharp angle in males; carapace flattened on top, rarely with a median keel; carapace with a bold pattern of radiating yellow lines on a brown to black ground color and often with a middorsal yellow stripe; plastron with a divided gular scute, without a bridge, and with a hinge between abdominal and pectoral scutes, thus forming two movable lobes capable of enclosing the entire body within the shell; plastron with a strong pattern of yellow lines on a dark ground color.

Similar species. May be confused with *Terrapene carolina*, with which it sometimes hybridizes.

Distribution. Southwestern Louisiana on the coastal prairies; possibly extreme northwestern Louisiana (see "Similar species" for *T. carolina*) (Map 64). Specimens may turn up almost anywhere in the state, but such animals probably represent released pets obtained elsewhere.

Taxonomic comments. Only the nominate subspecies, *T. o. ornata* Agassiz, the ornate box turtle, occurs in Louisiana. The most recent taxonomic study is that by Milstead (1969).

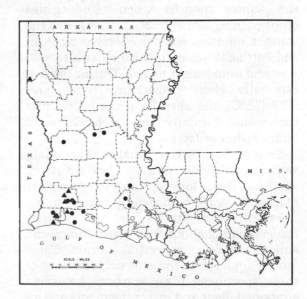

Map 64. Distribution of *Terrapene ornata*. Solid circles represent specimens examined; hollow circles represent museum specimens not examined or literature records; solid triangles represent hybrid specimens.

Habitat and habits. The western box turtle is principally an inhabitant of prairies and savannas. Although this is a rare species in Louisiana, it is very abundant in states such as Kansas, Oklahoma, and Texas, where it may appear in large numbers on roads after early summer rains. We know little about it in Louisiana, but elsewhere it burrows to hibernate or to escape high temperatures or cool nights and is thus often found under stones. In hot weather western box turtles may gather in large numbers to lie in shallow ponds.

Although the western box turtle eats some vegetation, it is primarily a carnivore, feeding especially on insects. It is adept at catching insects as they fly or walk by.

Reproduction. According to a summary of habits in Ernst and Barbour (1972), this species may court and nest primarily in the spring and nest from early May to mid-July. The two to eight eggs are laid in shallow cavities and covered with dirt. About two months of incubation are required before the eggs hatch.

Like the eastern box turtle (*T. carolina*), juvenile and subadult western box turtles are rarely encountered. The young probably are rather subterranean, using rodent burrows. But Legler (1960) said that juveniles are not as rare as most observers believe. He stated that juveniles are often covered with mud or cow dung and blend well with the substrate; thus he usually discovered them only when he was scrutinizing the ground rather carefully. Legler estimated that these turtles may live to an age of 50 years.

Trachemys scripta (Schoepff)
Slider
Plate IX

Recognition. A medium-sized freshwater terrapin reaching a length of 11 in. (279 mm); toes webbed; side of the head usually with a broad, red stripe behind the eye, sometimes

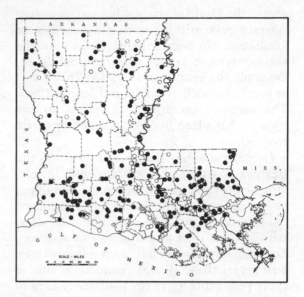

Map 65. Distribution of *Trachemys scripta.* Solid circles represent specimens examined; hollow circles represent museum specimens not examined or literature records.

widened to form a reddish spot; underside of the chin rounded; crushing surface of the upper jaw with a smooth or finely serrate ridge, not with coarse tubercles on the ridge; roughened carapace with narrow, curving ridges and a low middorsal keel; posterior margin of the carapace somewhat serrate; dorsal pattern variable with age, juveniles green with fine yellow lines (primarily transversely arranged), adults olive or brown with yellow lines less obvious; old males melanistic with almost total loss of carapace, plastron, and head patterns; plastron yellow with paired, dark blotches; plastral blotches of juveniles sometimes black-edged.

Distribution. Statewide, in virtually all freshwater habitats; also entering brackish waters such as Lake Pontchartrain and coastal marsh ponds (Map 65).

Taxonomic comments. One subspecies, *Trachemys scripta elegans* (Wied), the red-eared slider, occurs in Louisiana. An eastern race, *T. s. scripta,* may have some minor genetic influence on specimens from the Pearl River area of the Florida Parishes, but not enough to warrant recognition of that subspecies in Louisiana. No comprehensive study on the taxonomy of this species has been published. We apply the generic designation *Trachemys* as recommended by Seidel and Smith (1986). The name *Pseudemys*, long applied to this species, has often been challenged by turtle researchers.

Habitat and habits. Trachemys scripta is the freshwater turtle of Louisiana and, in fact, almost the only freshwater turtle sold in pet stores (see p. 199). It is exceedingly abundant in all sorts of pond, lake, and ditch habitats. A trip down almost any highway in southern Louisiana on a warm day, even in midwinter, will reveal these turtles crowded on almost every projecting log in the roadside ditches to bask in the sunshine. Many are crushed by cars as they cross roads. This species utilizes moving waters, but only occasionally. The sheer abundance of *T. s. elegans* in Louisiana has resulted in the red-eared slider being one of the most studied of turtles; it is the principal turtle used for anatomical dissection and physiological experimentation. As pets they have been sold by the millions, and the release of pets has resulted in scattered colonies in many areas where the species might otherwise not occur. Cagle (1950) considered *T. scripta* to constitute 80 percent of the turtle population in Louisiana fresh waters.

The major source of ecological information on red-eared sliders is a series of studies by Cagle, one of which (1950) included numerous data for Louisiana. Although *T. scripta* is a basking turtle, at night it usually lies quietly at the bottom or just below the surface on submerged limbs; sometimes it sleeps while floating at the surface. It feeds when water temperatures are above 50°F (10°C). Minyard (1947), who examined 110 stomachs from two localities near New Orleans, found that neither size nor sex had any bearing on food selection. Availability was the main factor, and plants, both aquatic and terrestrial, were taken more than animals.

Crawfish, small crustaceans, and insects were the usual animal food; only a few vertebrate items were included. In contrast, juvenile red-ears from Lafourche Parish near New Orleans were found to be principally carnivorous, feeding especially on insects, but older and larger turtles were found to eat more vegetation (Hart 1983). Hart concluded that the dietary shift with size was paralleled by a shift from shallow to deeper water; thus juvenile-adult and male-female dietary differences could be explained by plastron length relationships to plant consumption and habitat choice. Juvenile red-ears are principally carnivorous, but with age more vegetation is taken—practically any animal small enough and many kinds of aquatic plants are eaten. In captivity the turtles are thorough omnivores, eating such things as canned dog food, lettuce, bananas, and watermelon.

Trachemys scripta has a strong homing instinct, and the turtles will return to their usual haunts if removed and released some distance away.

In nature, the life of the red-eared slider is precarious. Huge numbers of nests are dug up and the eggs eaten by skunks, raccoons, and snakes. All kinds of animals eat the young and adult turtles, but probably the greatest enemy is man, who either wantonly destroys the turtles or seeks them for the pet trade or food market, or to use as laboratory animals. In one way, however, humans have actually given *Trachemys scripta* a big boost because of the pet trade demand. During the 1950s and the early 1960s, there were many turtle "farmers" in southern Louisiana. Such operators would capture adult turtles and confine them around artificial ponds of an acre or so in size. During the laying season the eggs would be removed from nests, placed in cans of moist soil in a small shed to incubate, and then harvested at hatching time. This reduced annual pressure on wild populations. The wholesale market value during the early 1960s was $11 to $22 per hundred hatchlings.

The turtle-farming era had been brought almost to a standstill by 1975. Epidemiologists, searching for the source of numerous *Salmonella* (a type of food poisoning) infections in young children found that the common denominator was the much-loved pet turtle. The adult turtles were being fed on lettuce refuse, moldy bread, etc., by the turtle farmers. The decayed food developed *Salmonella* growth, but the turtles, though serving as reservoirs for the infection, were not themselves injured by it. The infection was passed on to the juvenile turtles, which when kissed by their doting fanciers, provided a source of contact transmission. Today, strict federal requirements for proving that turtles are free of *Salmonella* have reduced the turtle trade to a miniscule volume. The red-eared turtle trade once was so great that Dundee was amazed when he sought native turtles in an East African pet store only to find that the only turtle they sold was *Trachemys scripta.*

Although federal regulations prohibit sale of the hatchlings in the United States, export to foreign countries still is legal. Warwick (1984) reported that there were about 25 turtle farms in Louisiana and about 25 in the rest of the United States, and that the farm operators were taking up to 100,000 mature redears every year. Mary Anderson of Roanoke, Virginia (pers. com.), told Dundee that Warwick said some Louisiana farmers were buying their breeding stock from Arkansas and Mississippi because of the decreasing supply in Louisiana. Warwick (1984) also reported that the turtle farmers were trying to perfect a system of selling cleaned red-ear hatchlings packaged in sterile plastic bubbles. This latest idea is alarming because many turtles surely will die if sealed without food, water, or adequate air.

Bennett (1935) described two new trematode parasites, *Cercorchis singulare* and *Protenes vitellosus,* from red-eared turtles taken in East Baton Rouge Parish.

Reproduction. Courtship occurs in spring and fall, and in Louisiana the eggs are deposited from late March to mid-July. Cagle (1950) found that in southern Louisiana clutch size varied from 2 to 19 eggs, averaging 7, and Arny (1948) reported a female with 20 oviducal eggs. The elliptical, leathery, white eggs were 23.5–44.2 mm long (average, 37.7 mm) and 18.4–24.6 mm wide (average, 22.6 mm). The eggs are placed in a small excavation above the water, then covered with dirt. At 30°C (86°F) eggs hatch in 68 to 70 days. Newly hatched young are 20–35 mm long. Sexual maturity is reached in two to five years, and Cagle (1950) believed that these turtles may live for 50 to 75 years.

Surprisingly few reports on turtles use weight as a criterion of growth—carapace and plastron lengths are the usual values given. Based on a limited perusal of major works on this species, the greatest weight is 2,050 g; the female with 20 oviducal eggs mentioned above weighed 2,430 g, according to Arny (1948).

FAMILY KINOSTERNIDAE
MUD AND MUSK TURTLES

The family Kinosternidae is a New World group of four genera comprising about 22 species, mostly Central American. The family members occur from southern Canada to northern South America. Some herpetologists have considered the kinosternids to be a specialized branch of the Chelydridae, but biochemical and structural evidence suggests that this is not a tenable classification. All kinosternids are small to medium-sized freshwater species, most of which are prone to wander on land. Two genera containing four species occur in Louisiana.

Kinosternon subrubrum (Lacépède)
Eastern Mud Turtle, Stinkpot
Plate VIII

Recognition. A small, semiaquatic terrapin not exceeding 4⅞ inches (124 mm) in carapace length; toes webbed; carapace smooth in adults, but with a middorsal keel and two weak lateral keels in the young; carapace olive to black; plastron with two transverse hinges in adults and with five pairs of large horny scutes plus a single small scute at the anterior end; pectoral scutes distinctly triangular; plastron yellowish brown to dark brown in adults, red in hatchlings.

Distribution. Statewide, but definite records lacking for the Mississippi River alluvial plain in northern Louisiana (Map 66).

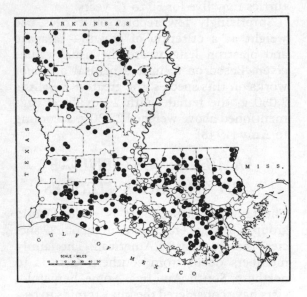

Map 66. Distribution of *Kinosternon subrubrum*. Solid circles represent specimens examined; hollow circles represent museum specimens not examined or literature records.

Taxonomic comments. West of the Mississippi River, the mud turtles have two light lines on either side of the head and are identifiable as the Mississippi mud turtle, *Kinosternon subrubrum hippocrepis* Gray. East of the Mississippi River, the head tends to be mottled or spotted; these animals are considered to be intermediate between *K. s. hippocrepis* and the eastern mud turtle, *K. s. subrubrum* (Lacépède). No taxonomic study of *K. sub-*

rubrum has been published, but Iverson (1977) summarized pertinent studies.

Habitat and habits. Mud turtles are associated with the shallow waters of ditches, ponds, swamps, bayous, and other bodies of water where the bottom is soft and there is little water movement. They are particularly abundant in the Marsh, often frequenting distinctly brackish water. *Kinosternon subrubrum* is often encountered on roadways, and hundreds of them may be seen, especially on roads such as State Highway 82 in Cameron and Vermilion parishes. Mud turtles do not bask very often; usually they crawl about on the bottom when in water. Many of the waters utilized are temporary, and when the pool dries the mud turtle may burrow into the mud and estivate. Occasionally they burrow into rotting logs or lie beneath the logs to estivate or hibernate.

Mud turtles, on being disturbed, may produce a foul-smelling musk from glands on the bridge of the shell.

Mahmoud (1968) reported that mud turtles are omnivorous feeders. The only stomach from Louisiana for which we have data was filled with small snails. In captivity we have observed mud turtles killing and eating leopard frogs that were confined with them in aquaria.

Byrd (1936) described a new trematode parasite, *Cercorchis kinosterni*, from a mud turtle taken near Raceland, Lafourche Parish.

Reproduction. The reproductive season is quite long; eggs have been found in the New Orleans area as early as 15 January, and evidence of eggs ready for deposition, or of turtles apparently digging nests, exists for dates as late as 29 July. Some eggs collected in December were of questionable age and condition (Cagle notes). The brittle-shelled eggs from Louisiana specimens range from 23.8 to 30.8 mm × 12.7 to 17.0 mm and are in nests dug in the ground, under boards, or in decaying logs. Fourteen clutches of oviducal and newly deposited eggs examined by Cagle and us contained two to four eggs (average 2.64), but Arny (1948) reported five eggs in a nest in Plaquemines Parish. A clutch laid in the laboratory on 26 March took until 30 July to hatch, an interval of 127 days (Cagle notes). The new hatchlings measured 20–27 mm in carapace length.

Sexual maturity in Oklahoma females occurs at carapace lengths of 80–120 mm, according to Mahmoud (1967); however, Cagle noted that many Louisiana females 70.2–79.2 mm had large oviducal eggs or gonadal evidence that eggs had probably been laid.

Sternotherus carinatus (Gray)
Razor-backed Musk Turtle

Plate VIII

Recognition. A small, aquatic terrapin reaching a carapace length of 5⅞ in. (149 mm); toes webbed; head variously marked, usually spotted, never with distinct stripes; barbels present on chin only; carapace with a prominent middorsal keel in adults and often with smaller lateral keels in juveniles; scutes of the carapace, especially the vertebrals, tending to overlap those behind; carapace light brown, with dark spots and streaks; plastron with a single hinge and with only five pairs of large horny scutes, the gular scute being absent; pectoral scutes roughly square.

Distribution. Statewide but absent from the Marsh (Map 67).

Taxonomic comments. No subspecies are recognized. Tinkle (1958) wrote the most recent account of the systematics of *Sternotherus carinatus.*

Habitat and habits. *Sternotherus carinatus* is principally a river-dwelling turtle; lakes it inhabits are usually associated with streams that have been dammed or are old oxbows. Otherwise, it occurs in the great swamp areas, such as that of the Atchafalaya River basin.

Razor-backed musk turtles bask more than

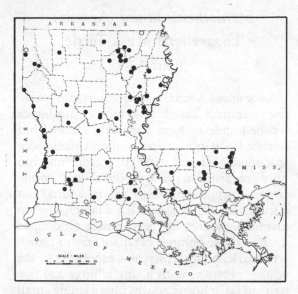

Map 67. Distribution of *Sternotherus carinatus.* Solid circles represent specimens examined; hollow circles represent museum specimens not examined or literature records.

the other two species of *Sternotherus* with which they may occur. They are quite shy and not easily taken in traps. Although capable of producing foul-smelling musk from glands, they do not often do so. They find their food—mostly insects, snails, clams, crawfish, and vegetation—principally by bottom prowling.

Reproduction. Little is known of the reproductive habits. The only nest found was on a steep bank of the Pearl River (Tinkle 1958). Tinkle (1958) indicated that females had oviducal eggs in early April and early June, and probably lay an average of 7.3 eggs per season in two clutches. Mahmoud (1969) reported that Oklahoma hatchlings from a mountain stream were 23–31 mm in carapace length. Included in a lot of 34 hatchlings taken 16 March 1955 from Bayou Desiard, Ouachita Parish, is a 22.5-mm animal and many others under 31 mm. Considering that the growing season in Ouachita Parish probably is longer than in Oklahoma, juveniles may hatch at sizes as small as 20 mm.

Sternotherus minor (Agassiz)
Loggerhead Musk Turtle

Plate VIII

Recognition. A small, aquatic terrapin reaching a carapace length of 4½ in. (114 mm); toes webbed; side of head variously marked but without distinct stripes; side of neck conspicuously striped; barbels present on chin only; carapace with a vertebral keel sometimes disappearing with age in adults, but flanked on either side with a lateral keel in juveniles; scutes of the carapace tending to overlap those behind; carapace gray or brown with dark spots and streaks, especially in the young; plastron with a single hinge and five pairs of large horny scutes plus a single small scute at the anterior end; pectoral scutes roughly square.

Similar species. Caution must be exercised to avoid confusing this species with the stinkpot, *Sternotherus odoratus*, which has stripes on the side of the head and barbels on the chin and throat.

Distribution. Known only from the Louisiana-Mississippi border in the Pearl River drainage (Map 68). An 1857 record for New Orleans may represent an animal obtained at the marketplace. A verbal report for the Tangipahoa River is unsubstantiated by a specimen.

Taxonomic comments. Two or three subspecies of this species are recognized, depending on the authority consulted. For the Louisiana area, however, the race, *S. minor peltifer* Smith and Glass, the stripe-necked musk turtle, is accepted without dispute. The most recent systematic study is that by Tinkle (1958).

Habitat and habits. Sternotherus minor is primarily a stream dweller that may inhabit quieter waters such as oxbows connected to streams.

Like other species of musk turtles, the stripe-necked is a bottom prowler that thrives on insects, snails, crawfish, algae, and

Map 68. Distribution of *Sternotherus minor.* Solid circles represent specimens examined; hollow circles represent museum specimens not examined or literature records.

other animal and plant life. It produces a strong musk from glands under the edge of the carapace. Stripe-necked musk turtles are rarely seen basking.

Reproduction. Little is known of the reproductive habits; Tinkle (1958) determined that females could potentially lay an average of seven eggs per year, substantially more than the other race(s) might produce. Carr (1952) reported finding *S. m. minor* eggs in shallow burial spots at the bases of trees and beside logs close to a creek on 14 April. Estridge (1970) observed that a brittle-shelled egg 32.0 × 16.4 mm laid 16 June by a *S. m. depressus* (= *S. depressus*) hatched on 16 October. The hatchling measured 25 × 20 mm. A specimen of *S. m. peltifer* found by Dundee in May in Alabama measured 27 × 26 mm.

Sternotherus odoratus (Latreille)
Stinkpot, Common Musk Turtle
Plate VIII

Recognition. A small, aquatic terrapin attaining a maximum carapace length of 5½ in. or 139 mm (based on a female from Lake Glendale, Illinois, mentioned in Cagle's notes); toes webbed; head usually with two conspicuous white or yellow stripes on either side; barbels present on both chin and throat; carapace smooth in adults, but with a prominent middorsal keel and smaller keels on each side in juveniles; scutes of the carapace nonoverlapping; carapace olive brown to black, often with dark spots or streaks; plastron with a single hinge and five pairs of large horny scutes plus a single small scute at the anterior end; pectoral scutes roughly square.

Distribution. Statewide but absent from brackish areas of the Marsh (Map 69).

Taxonomic comments. Various studies (e.g., Tinkle 1961) have explored selected aspects of the taxonomy, but a comprehensive taxonomic study has not been published. Reynolds and Seidel (1982) reviewed pertinent literature.

Habitat and habits. Sternotherus odoratus occurs in a variety of fresh waters; the principal criteria are that the water be permanent, currents absent or slow, and the bottom soft. The stinkpot is thoroughly aquatic and only occasionally climbs out of water to bask. It is able to prowl or rest on the bottom for long periods of time. The name "stinkpot" is well earned because of the vile-smelling musk exuded by glands on either side of the body just beneath the carapace.

Stinkpots are omnivorous and find most of their food by prowling the bottom, but at least one observer told of them capturing slugs on land.

Reproduction. Southern stinkpots mature earlier and at smaller sizes than their northern counterparts, and as might be expected, they produce their eggs earlier in the year

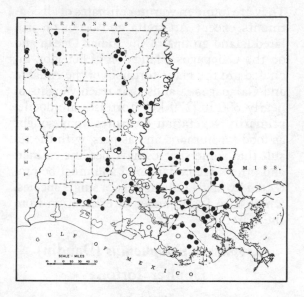

Map 69. Distribution of *Sternotherus odoratus*. Solid circles represent specimens examined; hollow circles represent museum specimens not examined or literature records.

(March through July) than do stinkpots in the North (Tinkle 1961). The brittle-shelled eggs (24.0–31.0 × 14.2–17.0 mm) are deposited in dug nests, in the open, under debris, or in decaying logs; the one to four eggs (average, 2.2) are less than half the average complement laid by northern stinkpots, but whether more than one clutch per season is produced in the South is unknown. Incubation is 60 to 75 days, but at least one Louisiana clutch retained by Cagle (notes) required from 8 May to 1 August to hatch (85 days), and another took from 8 June to 27 August (81 days). The newly hatched young are elongate to broadly oval in shape and measure 17–25 mm in carapace length.

FAMILY TESTUDINIDAE
TORTOISES

The family Testudinidae is an assemblage of 10 genera and about 40 species of terrestrial chelonians whose hind feed are elephantine, having a stumplike base with very short toes.

They are found in warmer climates of all continents except Australia and occur on isolated island groups in the Indian Ocean and on the Galapagos Islands off of Ecuador. Included are the giant tortoises of the Aldabra and Galapagos islands that reach weights of nearly 600 lb (270 kg). Tortoises are docile, primarily vegetarian creatures, long sought as food for humans and as pets, with the result that some species have become extinct, and others are endangered and must be protected by law. Louisiana has a single species, which also is in danger of extirpation from the state.

Gopherus polyphemus (Daudin)
Gopher Tortoise
Plate XI

Recognition. A large terrestrial tortoise attaining almost 16 in. (400 mm) in carapace length; hind feet stumpy and elephantine, front feet shovel-like; toes not evident on either set of feet, but the toenails, especially on the front feet, well developed; carapacial scutes usually with strongly developed growth rings but becoming smoother in old age; carapacial scutes brown in adults, yellow centered with brown margins in young animals; plastron unhinged and with strongly projecting gular scutes.

Distribution. Longleaf pine forest uplands of the eastern Florida Parishes, but one population also known from near Slidell, St. Tammany Parish (Map 70). See also the third paragraph of "Habitat and habits."

Taxonomic comments. No subspecies are currently recognized. Auffenberg (1976) provided the most comprehensive summary of certain variational features.

Habitat and habits. Auffenberg and Franz (1982) provided our most comprehensive account of the status of the gopher tortoise in Louisiana. They noted that this species, fast vanishing in Louisiana, excavates burrows in well-drained, loamy soils of high clay content

Map 70. Distribution of *Gopherus polyphemus.* Solid circles represent specimens examined; hollow circles represent museum specimens not examined or literature records.

near the crests of hills. The soil mounds at the burrow mouths are usually compacted into a hard cement. The burrows are usually shallow and may collapse if humans walk on them or automobiles drive over them. The preferred habitat is relatively open forest where the grasses and forbs utilized for food are common. In the areas that Auffenberg and Franz surveyed, the number of active and inactive burrows observed had a mean density of 2.76 per acre (1.12 per hectare). Most burrows were inactive; the colonies were nonrandomly distributed and the populations small—they actually observed only 9 active and 14 inactive burrows in six different localities. The highest density observed in Louisiana was 6 per acre (2.43 per hectare).

A gopher tortoise usually inhabits the burrow it excavates throughout its life. Many other animals—insects, spiders, frogs, other reptiles, and mammals—may share the burrow or take over abandoned ones. The tortoise may roam away from the hole for some distance during feeding and may construct some alternate burrows within the home range. Males have strong territorial behavior and will fight intruding males by ramming them with the gular projection. Captive specimens eat a wide variety of garden vegetables and foliage not found in the natural habitat.

The decimation of the original longleaf pine forests and their replacement with densely planted tree farms or pastures has been a major factor in the decline of the gopher tortoise. Serious damage may be done when the areas are denuded by burning, but burning often is conducive to the development of forage plants eaten by the tortoises. The gopher tortoise probably never was particularly abundant in Louisiana, but in Florida, especially, individuals were once routinely captured and eaten by rural people. The docility of the gopher tortoise has made it a favorite among pet fanciers, and this also has contributed to its decline. For these reasons, we believe that the gopher tortoise in Louisiana should be placed on the endangered species list. Such legislation has already been enacted in several southern states, and in Florida a bag limit has been established. The U.S. Fish and Wildlife Service placed western populations of gopher tortoises (including Louisiana populations) on the threatened species list in July 1987. A recent in-house report by Lohoefener and Lohmeier (1984) discussed habitats and the status of gopher tortoises in Louisiana.

Gopher tortoises turn up from time to time outside the eastern Florida Parishes. Such specimens may occasionally be *Gopherus polyphemus*, but are more often *G. berlandieri*, a species often picked up on southern Texas roads by vacationers who bring them home as pets and subsequently discard them.

Reproduction. The gopher tortoise constructs its nests in the mound in front of its burrow or some distance away. From four to seven white, brittle-shelled, spherical eggs, 38–46 mm in diameter, are laid from late April to mid-July. Hatching occurs in August and September,

and the hatchlings average about 43 mm in length. A 305-mm female found in Slidell, St. Tammany Parish, laid an egg on 3 July and four more eggs on 11 July. On 12 August she laid still another egg; on 22 August, two more. Another arrived between 30 August and 3 September, and one more on 16 October. The eggs were 41–45 mm in diameter, averaging 42.7 mm, and weighed 42.3–45.6 g, averaging 43.5 g.

FAMILY TRIONYCHIDAE
SOFT-SHELLED TURTLES

A soft-shelled turtle, as the common name implies, has a soft, flexible carapace, but the family name, Trionychidae, reflects the fact that these turtles have only three claws on each foot. Soft-shelled turtles comprise six genera and 23 species and occur from southern Canada to northern Mexico in the New World, and from the Mideast throughout Africa and into Southeast Asia and western Indonesia. All are thoroughly aquatic and represent a highly specialized but ancient group of turtles. In Louisiana we have a single genus and two species.

Apalone mutica (Le Sueur)
Smooth Softshell
Plate XII

Recognition. A moderately large, flattened aquatic turtle reaching 14 in. (356 mm*); toes extensively webbed and equipped with long claws; snout extended in tubular form; openings of nostrils circular, lacking projecting ridges internally; body covered with a soft, gray or brown leathery shell lacking horny scutes; carapace essentially smooth, lacking spines or tubercles, especially on the anterior edge.

*The largest *A. m. calvata* reported is 287 mm long (Mount 1975).

205

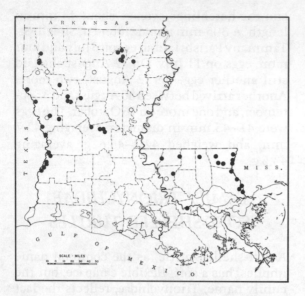

Map 71. Distribution of *Apalone mutica*. Solid circles represent specimens examined; hollow circles represent museum specimens not examined or literature records.

Distribution. Possibly statewide, but based on current knowledge, absent from the Marsh, the Prairie, and most of the Atchafalaya Basin (Map 71).

Taxonomic comments. We are applying the generic name *Apalone*, which was resurrected by Meylan (1987). Previous generic designations such as *Amyda* and *Trionyx* may be more familiar to many of our readers. Webb (1962), who published the most recent systematic study of the species, considered it to be divisible into two races, *Apalone m. mutica* (Le Sueur), the midland smooth softshell, which occurs west of the Mississippi River in Louisiana, and the Gulf Coast smooth softshell, *A. m. calvata* (Webb), which occurs in the Florida Parishes. The two forms are morphologically similar and differ principally in the markings of juveniles and males, but no intermediate animals are available from anywhere in the range. The subspecies *mutica* has a juvenile pattern of dusky dots and short lines on the carapace; adults have pale stripes on the dorsal surface of the snout and postocular stripes with black borders less than half their width. The subspecies *calvata* has a juvenile pattern of large circular spots, sometimes black bordered; adults lack stripes on the snout, and the postorbital stripes have black borders that are approximately half the width of the stripe, at least in adult males.

The absence of intergrade specimens and the allopatric distributions of the two forms (*calvata* is absent from the Mississippi River drainage system, and *mutica* does not occur in streams entering the Gulf of Mexico east of the Mississippi) provide a basis for speculation that *mutica* and *calvata* may be different species. Intensive collecting in Louisiana's Florida Parishes should provide the additional data to determine whether intergrades exist. The Mississippi alluvial plain does separate many other amphibian and reptile populations, either completely or at least in the southern portions of their ranges (*Deirochelys reticularia, Sceloporus undulatus, Carphophis amoenus, Micrurus fulvius, Pituophis melanoleucus,* and *Scaphiopus holbrookii* at the subspecific level; *Cnemidophorus sexlineatus, Eumeces anthracinus, Cemophora coccinea, Lampropeltis calligaster, Masticophis flagellum, Virginia striatula, V. valeriae, Plethodon glutinosus,* and *Rana palustris* in part or without racial distinction).

Habitat and habits. The extensively webbed feet of this agile turtle allow it to occupy large streams that have moderate to fast currents. *Apalone m. calvata* is known only from the riverine habitats, but the midland smooth softshell also occurs in lakes and impoundments. Smooth softshells are thoroughly aquatic; they do bask on beaches or mud flats, but more often they lie buried in the bottom at a depth where the tip of the snout can still reach the surface. From this buried position they can ambush their prey, which includes all kinds of aquatic animals, such as worms, fishes, crawfishes, and insects. Otherwise they prowl the bottom seeking out less mobile animals and perhaps some plant material. While lying beneath the surface, the smooth softshell can obtain oxygen directly from the water by pharyngeal and cloacal absorption. Fishery biologists who use rotenone, a gill artery constrictor, to stun fishes say that softshells also are affected by the rotenone.

Softshells have long necks and require cautious handling because of their ability to reach far around to bite; they also kick furiously, thus creating an additional hazard from their sharp claws.

Softshells are eaten by human beings, but seldom found in Louisiana marketplaces.

Reproduction. According to Ernst and Barbour (1972), the smooth softshell nests from late May through July, producing clutches of 4 to 33 eggs. The eggs are white, spherical, hard-shelled, and 20–33 mm in diameter. Nest holes are made in loose soils in sunny places within 60 ft (18 m) of water. P. K. Anderson (1958) found nests in open sandbars along the Pearl River from 17 May to 13 June, and the eggs hatched 4–15 August. He calculated that the incubation period was 67 to 77 days. The newly hatched young were 34–45 mm (average, 41.3 mm) in carapace length.

Apalone spinifera (Le Sueur)
Spiny Softshell
Plate XII

Recognition. A medium-sized to large, flattened aquatic turtle reaching 21¼ in. (540 mm) in carapace length; toes extensively webbed and equipped with long claws; snout extended in tubular form; opening of the nostril with an internal ridge projecting from the septum; body covered with a soft, leathery shell without horny scutes; carapace usually gritty-feeling because of numerous small projections, the anterior edge with conical projections or spines.

Distribution. Statewide, but absent from saline sections of the Marsh (at least one rec-

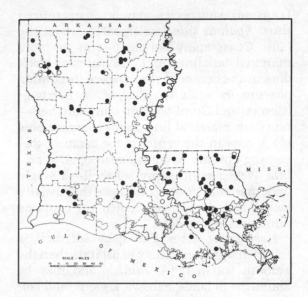

Map 72. Distribution of *Apalone spinifera.* Solid circles represent specimens examined; hollow circles represent museum specimens not examined or literature records; a hexagon in the middle of a parish represents a literature record for the parish with no specific locality stated.

ord, however, from brackish water in Cameron Parish) (Map 72).

Taxonomic comments. We are applying the generic name *Apalone,* which was resurrected by Meylan (1987). Previous generic designations such as *Amyda* and *Trionyx* may be more familiar to many of our readers. Webb (1962) interpreted the wide-ranging spiny softshell as comprising six subspecies, three of which show their influence in Louisiana. The lower Mississippi drainage is a vast area in which most specimens must be considered intergrades; "pure" representatives of each race can be identified within the Mississippi drainage, as well as in the adjacent areas. But if we adhere to the biological concept that populations rather than individuals define the race, then some version of geographic range of each race can be presented, as was done by Webb (1973). Identification to race is complicated by the variations between juvenile, male, and female patterns. The

Louisiana subspecies may be characterized thus: *Apalone spinifera aspera* (Agassiz), the Gulf Coast spiny softshell—two or more marginal dark lines on the carapace and black dots in the center of the carapace (becoming obscure in adult females); *A. s. hartwegi* (Conant and Goin), western spiny softshell—one dark marginal line on the carapace plus black dots in the center of the carapace (becoming obscure in adult females); *A. s. pallida* Webb, pallid spiny softshell—a single dark marginal line on a carapace that usually lacks black dots in the center, but contains numerous white dots.

Habitat and habits. The spiny softshell is found in a greater variety of habitats than the smooth softshell (*A. mutica*) and may be abundant in lakes, oxbows, lagoons, and borrow pits, as well as in rivers. In New Orleans *A. spinifera* even occurs in drainage ditches. The basic habits are very much like those of the smooth softshell. Baited hoop nets, box traps, and basking traps are good ways to capture softshells; otherwise they may be caught by hand as they lie on the bottom in shallow water, often partly concealed under sand or mud, and they will take fishing lures, even fly-rod surface bugs.

Reproduction. Nesting occurs from May into August. The females produce clutches of 4 to 32 eggs, probably several times a year. The spherical, hard-shelled eggs average 28 mm in diameter (24–32 mm) and hatch from late August to October. The newly hatched young are 30–40 mm in carapace length.

ORDER SQUAMATA: *Lizards, Amphisbaenians, and Snakes*

The cosmopolitan members of the order Squamata, along with the lizardlike tuatara of New Zealand, are the living representatives of the Lepidosauria, an ancient reptilian lineage related to—but distinct from—the Archosauria, which produced the dinosaurs, pterosaurs, crocodilians, and birds. Amphisbaenians (wormlike burrowing squamates most closely related to lizards) do not occur in Louisiana and will not be discussed further.

Suborder Lacertilia: Lizards

At present the more than 3,000 species of lizards are classified in some 18 to 20 families, but the higher classification of lizards is in flux (Estes and Pregill 1988). Most lizards—including all of the species in Louisiana—are carnivores but, unlike the snakes, almost none of them have evolved venom to help subdue their prey (the Gila monster and Mexican beaded lizard are the exceptions). One major evolutionary trend in lizards is toward a reduction of the limbs, a trend that culminates in such lizards as our *Ophisaurus*, which have lost the limbs altogether. Male lizards have paired, hollow, eversible copulatory organs, the hemipenes, one of which is inserted into the cloaca of the female during mating. Most lizards lay eggs, although some (none of the Louisiana species) do give birth directly to living young. The hatchlings are miniatures of the adults, but some may have a brighter color pattern. In many lizard species, the tail will break off very easily and, as it wriggles, may distract a predator from the lizard's body. As they grow, lizards shed the outer layer of the skin, which usually comes off in patches. Nearly all Louisiana lizards (the introduced Mediterranean gecko is an exception) are active almost exclusively during the day.

KEY TO THE LIZARDS OF LOUISIANA

1. Legs present   3
   Legs absent   2
2. Dark lines present below lateral fold
       Ophisaurus attenuatus (p. 210)
   Dark lines absent below lateral fold
       Ophisaurus ventralis (p. 212)
3. Moveable eyelids present   4
   Eyelids fused to form transparent spectacle   *Hemidactylus turcicus* (p. 212)
4. Belly scales large and quadrangular, in 8 longitudinal rows
       Cnemidophorus sexlineatus (p. 223)
   Belly scales not as above   5
5. Body scales smooth, flat, and overlapping   6
   Body scales granular, or keeled and overlapping   11
6. Dorsum brown with a pair of dark dorsolateral stripes; light stripes absent; snout-vent length rarely exceeding 50 mm   *Scincella lateralis* (p. 222)
   Dorsum brown or black; light stripes present (except in large males of some species); snout-vent length often exceeding 50 mm   7
7. Dorsum brown with a pair of broad, dark

dorsolateral stripes bordered by narrow light stripes 8
Dorsum brown or black with 5 light stripes on body (except in large males), 2 on head 9
8. Dark dorsolateral stripe 2½ to 4 scales wide; 1 postmental scale
Eumeces anthracinus (p. 218)
Dark dorsolateral stripe 2 scales wide; 2 postmental scales
Eumeces septentrionalis (p. 221)
9. Median row of subcaudal scales noticeably wider than adjacent rows 10
Median row of subcaudal scales not noticeably widened
Eumeces inexpectatus (p. 219)
10. Usually 7 supralabials; 2 relatively large postlabials; usually less than 30 scale rows at midbody; snout-vent length not exceeding 85 mm
Eumeces fasciatus (p. 218)
Usually 8 supralabials; usually 1 large postlabial, 2 small postlabials, or none; 30 or more scale rows at midbody; snout-vent length often exceeding 85 mm   *Eumeces laticeps* (p. 220)
11. Body noticeably broad and flattened; head with a series of backward-projecting spines
Phrynosoma cornutum (p. 216)
Body not noticeably flattened; head without spines 12

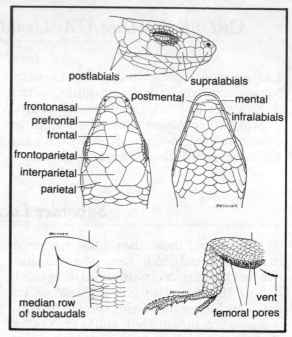

Figure 9.   Structural features of lizards: lateral, dorsal, and ventral views of the head (upper); ventral view of skink tail scales (lower left); and ventral view of the fence lizard hindleg (lower right).

12. Body scales large, keeled, and overlapping   *Sceloporus undulatus* (p. 217)
Body scales granular 13
13. Toes expanded, padlike; femoral pores absent   *Anolis carolinensis* (p. 214)
Toes unexpanded; femoral pores present
Crotaphytus collaris (p. 215)

FAMILY ANGUIDAE

The relatively small family Anguidae comprises seven genera and 75 species (Dowling and Duellman 1978). It has an essentially worldwide distribution (absent from Australia), but exhibits its greatest diversity in the New World. One anguid genus, *Ophisaurus* (the limbless lizards), comprising two species, occurs in Louisiana.

Ophisaurus attenuatus Baird
Slender Glass Lizard
Plate XIII

Recognition. A very elongated (up to 42 in.; 1,067 mm), legless lizard with a fold of skin along the side of the body and a pattern of narrow dark stripes (including some below the fold) extending onto the very long tail. The presence of external ear openings, movable eyelids, and a tail, if unbroken, more than twice as long as the body permits these animals to be recognized as lizards rather than snakes.

Distribution. Statewide except for the Mississippi alluvial plain and the Marsh (but present on Avery Island and the Cameron Parish cheniers). Apparently very rare in the Florida Parishes (Map 73).

Map 73. Distribution of *Ophisaurus attenuatus.* Solid circles represent specimens examined; hollow circles represent museum specimens not examined or literature records.

Taxonomic comments. Two very weakly differentiated subspecies may occur in Louisiana: *Ophisaurus a. attenuatus,* the western slender glass lizard, characterized by having the unregenerated tail less than 2.4 times longer than the snout-vent length, and *O. a. longicaudus* McConkey, the eastern slender glass lizard, characterized by having the unregenerated tail 2.4 or more times longer than the snout-vent length. The former oc-

curs west of the Mississippi River; the latter may occur in the Florida Parishes (Conant 1975) although earlier researchers (McConkey 1954; Holman 1971) indicated that it did not enter Louisiana. Too few specimens with unregenerated tails are known from the Florida Parishes to make a determination at this time. The most recent taxonomic study is that by McConkey (1954).

Habitat and habits. Slender glass lizards are more abundant in the coastal cheniers of Cameron Parish than in any other part of Louisiana. There the lizards may be encountered actively prowling about or concealed beneath boards or other cover. Fitch (1949) reported finding seven specimens in west-central Louisiana during the spring and early summer of 1948. He encountered them in "grassland where grass is thick and high, and not frequently burned, as where adjacent to brush or moist bottomlands" (Fitch 1949:89). In September 1971, Gerhard Kuehnhanss (pers. com.) observed a slender glass lizard at a garbage dump near Flatwoods, Rapides Parish. Dundee has found slender glass lizards under logs in damp woods adjacent to the marshes in St. Tammany Parish, in open pinewoods in central Louisiana, and in a stump with an *O. ventralis* in southern Mississippi.

Lizards of the genus *Ophisaurus* get their common name from the fact that their tails are very fragile and readily break off in one or more pieces if the animals are restrained. The wriggling sections of tail may then serve to distract a predator from the body of the lizard, which is rapidly moving away in another direction. Should the lizard escape, it will grow a new tail.

The food of the slender glass lizard in Louisiana is not known. In Kansas, it reportedly feeds on insects, spiders, snails, and the eggs of other reptiles (Collins 1974).

Reproduction. We have no reproductive data for Louisiana specimens, but an *O. attenuatus* from Pearlington, Mississippi, deposited five eggs on 13 May 1959. The eggs ranged in size from 19.5 to 21.8 mm × 9.3 to 10.4 mm. Fitch (1985) reported that 53 clutches from elsewhere numbered from 5 to 17 eggs.

Ophisaurus ventralis (Linnaeus)
Eastern Glass Lizard
Plate XIII

Recognition. A very elongated (up to 42½ in.; 1,080 mm), legless lizard with a fold of skin along the side of the body and a pattern of narrow dark stripes in juveniles and subadults, but no stripes below the fold (adults with a very fine checkered pattern, no stripes). The presence of external ear openings, movable eyelids, and a tail, if unbroken, more than twice as long as the body permits these animals to be recognized as lizards rather than snakes.

Distribution. The Florida Parishes and the extreme lower portion of the Mississippi alluvial plain (Map 74).

Taxonomic comments. No subspecies of *Ophisaurus ventralis* have been described. The most recent taxonomic study is that by McConkey (1954).

Habitat and habits. Extremely little ecological information is available for this species in Louisiana. Percy Viosca (notes) collected two eastern glass lizards in pinewoods near Mandeville, St. Tammany Parish, in August 1914. P. K. Anderson et al. (1952) found two in a pipeline ditch where it cut through an area of dense grass near Angie, Washington Parish. Dundee captured one near Pearlington, Mississippi, in a stump that it shared with an *O. attenuatus.*

P. W. Smith (1961) maintained a captive *O. ventralis* that fed on other lizards, small snakes, and crickets.

Reproduction. No information is available on the reproductive habits of the eastern glass lizard in Louisiana. Mount (1975) reported finding two brooding females in Alabama

with clutches of seven and eight eggs, respectively.

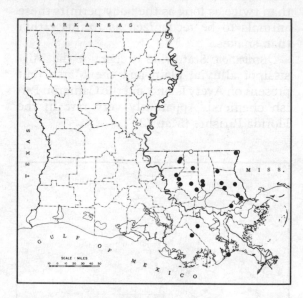

Map 74. Distribution of *Ophisaurus ventralis.* Solid circles represent specimens examined; hollow circles represent museum specimens not examined or literature records.

FAMILY GEKKONIDAE

The family Gekkonidae, which is widely distributed throughout the warmer parts of the world, comprises 84 genera and 667 species (Dowling and Duellman 1978). No geckos occur naturally in Louisiana, but the Old World species *Hemidactylus turcicus* has been introduced and is well established in several cities.

Hemidactylus turcicus (Linnaeus)
Mediterranean Gecko
Plate XIII

Recognition. A small to medium-sized (to 5 in.; 127 mm) lizard with scattered dark spots on a light-colored, warty dorsum; belly pale,

212

nearly transparent; eyes large and lidless, with vertical pupils; toes with large pads.

Distribution. Introduced and established in several southern Louisiana cities (Map 75).

Map 75. Distribution of *Hemidactylus turcicus.* Solid circles represent specimens examined; hollow circles represent museum specimens not examined or literature records.

Taxonomic comments. Only the nominate subspecies, *Hemidactylus t. turcicus,* occurs in Louisiana. No recent taxonomic study of this species has been published.

Habitat and habits. In this country, the introduced Mediterranean gecko is almost exclusively associated with structures constructed by humans; in the Old World the species also has been found beneath flat rocks on the ground. Hiding in cracks or behind drainpipes, loose bricks, or plaster by day, the geckos become active at night and then may be seen on the walls of buildings, on window screens, and on glass window panes, particularly when light shines through them, attracting the insects on which the lizards feed. Geckos occasionally can be seen scurrying across sidewalks.

Where the geckos occur they are often abundant; Dundee has counted as many as 36 individuals on his house during a five-minute search. Rose and Barbour (1968) found the species to reach its greatest population densities in the aboveground cemeteries throughout New Orleans.

According to Etheridge (1952), *H. turcicus* was first discovered in Louisiana in the summer of 1949 and probably was accidentally introduced by ships bringing cargo to the port of New Orleans. However, Viosca (1957) reported the species to have been in New Orleans as early as 1945. The lizard's ability to hide in crevices (or even enter buildings) permits colonies to survive the brief periods of subfreezing winter weather that occasionally affect the southern part of Louisiana. The lowest temperature at which activity has been noted is 42°F or 3.3°C (Rose and Barbour 1968; Dundee, pers. observation). Most of the introductions outside of New Orleans have been deliberate, a practice conservationists generally frown upon—and with good reason, because an introduced species may displace some member of the native fauna. Fortunately, no native vertebrate species seems to have occupied the Mediterranean gecko's ecological niche, that of a nocturnal insect-feeder that lives on the sides of buildings. The gecko's most likely ecological counterpart would be one or more species of spider, and the gecko populations are neither so large nor so widely distributed as to pose any competitive threat to the spiders.

Rose and Barbour (1968) found that *H. turcicus* feeds on a wide variety of insects (such as tent caterpillars, ants, small beetles, earwigs, mosquitoes, and homopterans) and even an occasional spider. Dundee has often watched the geckos capturing moths.

Reproduction. Rose and Barbour (1968) observed a pair of geckos copulating on 1 June 1965. They also determined that a female may produce two hard-shelled eggs per clutch and two or three clutches per year. The only natural clutch they discovered was beneath a

213

small (20 mm high) mound of debris on the floor of a small unused closet; a dozen captive females also built nests. The earliest date for observed egg deposition was 9 June, but a female containing shelled oviducal eggs on 24 May had only small yellow ovarian follicles 14 days later (7 June). On 30 July 1974, Dundee found more than 30 eggs, all but four of them broken, in the folds of a large piece of nylon parachute in his garage. Rose and Barbour (1968) found the newly deposited eggs to measure about 11 × 9 mm and the average incubation period to be 40 (37 to 45) days. Allowing for Rose and Barbour's data (1968) for the female with large oviducal eggs on 24 May, and assuming a minimum incubation time of 37 days, eggs could perhaps be laid as early as 30 June in New Orleans. The latest hatching date noted by Rose and Barbour was 22 September. The hatchlings average about 26 mm in snout-vent length. Dundee measured a juvenile taken on his home on 7 July as 47 mm in total length, 26 mm in snout-vent length; at the same time he measured a specimen 40 mm in snout-vent length. The latter presumably represents an animal born late the preceding year.

FAMILY IGUANIDAE

The almost exclusively New World family Iguanidae (one genus occurs in the Fiji Islands, two in Madagascar) consists of 56 genera comprising 635 species (Dowling and Duellman 1978). Four genera comprising four species, two of which may be introduced, occur in Louisiana.

Anolis carolinensis (Voigt)
Green Anole
Plate XIII

Recognition. A moderate-sized (to 8 3/16 in.; 208 mm), green or gray-brown lizard (individuals can change color); males with exten-

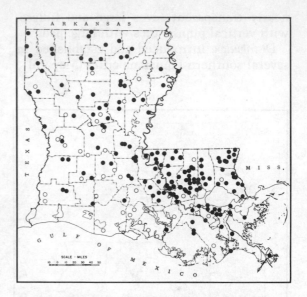

Map 76.   Distribution of *Anolis carolinensis.* Solid circles represent specimens examined; hollow circles represent museum specimens not examined or literature records.

sible pink throat fan; scales small and granular.

Distribution. Statewide, but apparently occurring in the Marsh only on cheniers and natural levees (Map 76).

Taxonomic comments. Only the nominate subspecies, *Anolis c. carolinensis*, occurs in Louisiana. No comprehensive taxonomic study of this species has ever been published.

Habitat and habits. The green anole is probably the most common lizard in Louisiana—certainly it is the most conspicuous. Anoles do occur deep in forests, but seem to prefer to live in dense shrubbery in more open areas. Sizable populations occur in towns and cities, where the animals are found on fences, in backyards, on the sides of buildings, and even inside houses. In the winter, anoles may retreat (often in large numbers) under flat boards, beneath the bark on dead trees, in rotting logs, and in the bases of palmettos. During a two-day period in December 1953, 525 *Anolis*, 100 *Scincella*, and numerous

214

Hyla squirella were collected from palmetto bases near New Orleans (Tinkle 1959). Biological supply houses sell large numbers of anoles, most of them collected near New Orleans.

The anole's ability to change color has earned it the nickname "chameleon," although *Anolis* is not related to the true chameleons of the Old World. Louisiana anoles feed on insects and, presumably, other small arthropods.

Reproduction. As early as February male anoles exhibit territorial behavior, doing "push-ups" and extending their pink dewlaps to intimidate any other males that approach their perches too closely. The defender of the territory will also approach the intruder and often pursue him for some distance after he almost invariably retreats. In an encounter observed at the Thistlethwaite Game Management Area, St. Landry Parish, on 23 March 1986, the resident anole was ousted from his vertically oriented wild grapevine when the intruder managed to dodge around him and "capture the high ground." Once in this position, the intruder turned sidewise to his opponent and displayed his dewlap. After a moment's hesitation, the defender retreated down the vine and shortly thereafter leaped onto a nearby palmetto frond.

Tinkle (1959) observed mating in mid-April at the Sarpy Wildlife Refuge in St. Charles Parish. Hamlett (1952) discovered that the two ovaries of a female alternate in producing eggs, which are laid singly under leaves, logs, or other debris, and Dundee has found eggs that were merely dropped on the surface amid garden plants. The eggs are deposited at two-week intervals throughout the breeding season. The eggs are about 12–14 mm long and 10 mm in diameter, and the hatchlings average about 24 mm in snout-vent length (Tinkle 1959). Growth is rapid; individuals reach sexual maturity in less than a year and breed the first spring following hatching (Cagle 1948b).

Crotaphytus collaris (Say)
Collared Lizard
Plate XIII

Recognition. A large (to 14 in.; 356 mm), big-headed lizard with a pair of black crossbands forming a "collar" on neck; body scales granular, tail scales larger; tail extremely long.

Distribution. We are uncertain if *Crotaphytus collaris* is native to Louisiana's lizard fauna or even if there are any populations established in the state at the present time. In either case, only the northwestern quarter of the state appears to provide suitable habitat (Map 77).

Taxonomic comments. Only the nominate subspecies, *C. c. collaris*, the eastern collared lizard, has been reported from Louisiana. The last taxonomic revision of the entire species is that by Burt (1928).

Map 77. Distribution of *Crotaphytus collaris.* Solid circles represent specimens examined; hollow circles represent museum specimens not examined or literature records.

Habitat and habits. Frierson (1927a) reported *C. collaris* from the vicinity of a gas well at Taylortown (Bossier Parish) and suggested that the species may have been introduced in oil well pipes (presumably brought in from Texas). More recently (7 June 1968) Dan Leslie collected a collared lizard at Boone's Landing on the Toledo Bend Reservoir southwest of Negreet (Sabine Parish). Outside Louisiana the species usually occurs in dry, rocky, hilly areas.

When moving at top speed, collared lizards will usually run on their hind legs alone. They are active predators, feeding on a variety of arthropods and small lizards.

Reproduction. No data are available on the reproductive activity of the collared lizard in Louisiana, but in Kansas breeding occurs in May and June, and the eggs are deposited in June or early July (Fitch 1956b). Fitch found the clutch size to range from 2 to 11 eggs (mean, 7.6), and the hatchlings to measure about 40 mm in snout-vent length.

Phrynosoma cornutum (Harlan)
Texas Horned Lizard

Plate XIII

Recognition. A medium-sized (to 7⅛ in.; 181 mm), rough-scaled, very broad and flat-bodied lizard with a dorsal pattern consisting of irregular dark brown spots on a lighter brown ground color; rear margin of the head with prominent spines; tail very short.

Distribution. Whether *Phrynosoma cornutum* is native to Louisiana's lizard fauna, or even if there are any populations established in the state at the present time, is not known. In either case, only the western border of the state would seem to provide suitable habitat (Map 78). Because of the horned lizard's popularity in the pet trade, it is frequently released outside of its natural range, particularly near large population centers.

Taxonomic comments. No subspecies of *P. cornutum* have been described. The most recent taxonomic study is that by Reeve (1952).

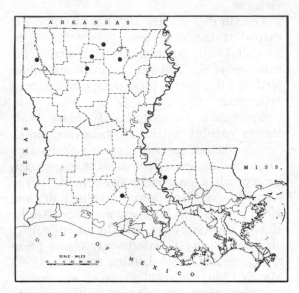

Map 78. Distribution of *Phrynosoma cornutum*. Solid circles represent specimens examined; hollow circles represent museum specimens not examined or literature records.

Habitat and habits. Frierson (1927b) found a horned lizard on a sandbar of the Red River near Gayles (Caddo Parish) during the summer of 1925 and another in Shreveport in August 1927. Whether they represented natural populations, an expansion of the colony established at Forbing (Caddo Parish) in 1918 (Strecker and Frierson 1926), or fresh introductions cannot be determined. No other ecological data are available for Louisiana. Elsewhere in its range the species seems to prefer dry, sandy habitat and feeds largely, though not exclusively, on ants.

Reproduction. No data are available on reproductive activity in Louisiana, but elsewhere the females lay 13 to 47 eggs (Fitch 1985).

Sceloporus undulatus (Latreille)
Eastern Fence Lizard

Plate XIII

Recognition. A moderately large (to 8¼ in.; 210 mm), rough-scaled, gray-brown lizard with a pattern of narrow, undulating, dark crossbands; belly of females predominantly white, males with prominent black-bordered blue or green patches on each side of the belly.

Distribution. Statewide except for the Marsh and the lower part of the Mississippi alluvial plain (Map 79). The species is apparently very rare in the middle and upper portions of the Mississippi alluvial plain.

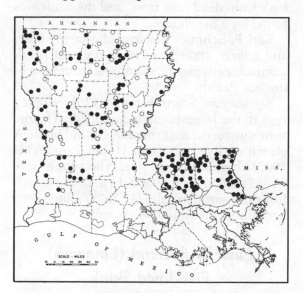

Map 79. Distribution of *Sceloporus undulatus.* Solid circles represent specimens examined; hollow circles represent museum specimens not examined or literature records.

Taxonomic comments. Two weakly differentiated subspecies occur in Louisiana: *Sceloporus u. undulatus*, the southern fence lizard, characterized by its darker color and fewer middorsal scales (averaging 36 in Louisiana specimens, counting from the back of

the head to the back edge of the hind legs), and *S. u. hyacinthinus* (Green), the northern fence lizard, characterized by its lighter color and more numerous middorsal scales (averaging more than 40 in Louisiana specimens). The former occurs in the Florida Parishes, the latter west of the Mississippi River. The most recent taxonomic study of the populations in our area is that by Morgan (1972).

Habitat and habits. The fence lizard is an animal of forested regions; although it shows a particular affinity for pinewoods, specimens are occasionally encountered in the purely hardwood forests of the Blufflands. Both Strecker and Frierson (1926) and Walker (1963) noted that *S. undulatus* is particularly abundant in cutover woodlands where fallen trees and brush piles are plentiful. The lizards are usually seen resting on logs, stumps, or sides of trees, and during the breeding season, adult males can be observed doing "push-ups" to display the bright color of their lower sides. When disturbed, a fence lizard usually attempts to escape by scurrying to the side of the log or tree opposite the pursuer.

The diet of the fence lizard in Louisiana has not been recorded. Elsewhere it is reported to feed upon various arthropods, ants being a particular favorite.

Reproduction. A clutch of fence lizard eggs dug up from beneath 5–6 in. (127–152 mm) of dirt in a Baton Rouge garden earlier in the month hatched on 30 September 1976. Crenshaw (1955b) reported 11 clutches of 6 to 10 eggs each from southwestern Georgia; the earliest date of deposition was 2 May and hatching occurred from 21 June to 5 September. The hatchlings measured 38.5–61.5 mm in total length. Fitch (1985) found clutch size in *S. u. undulatus* to range from 6 to 11, and in *S. u. hyacinthinus*, from 4 to 12. In the vicinity of Houston, Texas, a single female may deposit as many as five clutches in a year's time (Kennedy in Fitch 1970).

FAMILY SCINCIDAE

The worldwide family Scincidae consists of approximately 75 genera comprising 600 species (Dowling and Duellman 1978). Two genera comprising six species occur in Louisiana.

Eumeces anthracinus (Baird)
Coal Skink
Plate XIV

Recognition. A medium-sized (to 7 in.; 178 mm), shiny brown lizard with a pair of dark, light-bordered dorsolateral stripes, the dark stripes two and a half to four scales wide (young with a very dark dorsum and a blue tail); usually a single postmental scale; scales flat and smooth.

Distribution. Statewide except for the Marsh and the Mississippi alluvial plain (Map 80).

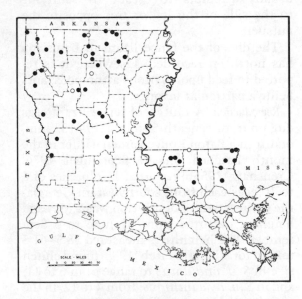

Map 80. Distribution of *Eumeces anthracinus*. Solid circles represent specimens examined; hollow circles represent museum specimens not examined or literature records.

Taxonomic comments. Only the subspecies *Eumeces anthracinus pluvialis* Cope, the southern coal skink, occurs in Louisiana. The most recent taxonomic study is that by P. W. Smith and H. M. Smith (1952).

Habitat and habits. The relatively uncommon coal skink is found in forested areas, often beneath logs, boards, or other ground cover. *Eumeces anthracinus* has been taken in fairly dry situations in western Louisiana, but also near a farm pond in Union Parish and on wooded hillsides near water in Jackson Parish. In the latter region, Walker (1963:96) found the species to exhibit arboreal tendencies—a juvenile "retreated up a small pine tree, the subadults were caught by stripping bark from dead pine trees, and the adult was found on a beech tree."

Karl P. Schmidt discovered a large spider and a large cranefly larva in the coal skink stomach contents he examined from Natchitoches Parish.

Reproduction. Schmidt found 13 developing eggs in the largest female he collected sometime during the first three weeks in March. A clutch of five eggs from Union Parish (TU 19028) hatched on 30 June; the young were 55–57 mm in total length. In a second clutch from the same parish (TU 15297), the seven hatchlings measured 48–54 mm.

Eumeces fasciatus (Linnaeus)
Five-lined Skink
Plate XIV

Recognition. A moderately large (to 8$\frac{1}{16}$ in.; 205 mm), shiny lizard with a pattern, in small specimens, of a blue tail and narrow yellow or white stripes on a black background (large adults with brown body and gray tail, the stripes dull); head orange-red and swollen in jaw region of large males during breeding season; scales flat and smooth; scales in median row beneath tail wider than those in adjacent

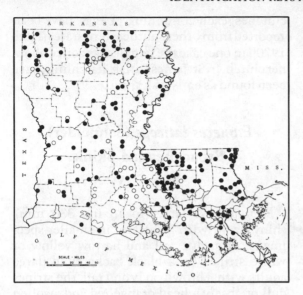

Map 81. Distribution of *Eumeces fasciatus.* Solid circles represent specimens examined; hollow circles represent museum specimens not examined or literature records.

rows; 26 to 30 rows of scales at midbody; usually seven supralabials; two enlarged postlabial scales. Occasional specimens may have characteristics of both *Eumeces fasciatus* and *E. laticeps* and defy identification.

Distribution. Statewide, but apparently occurring in the Marsh only on cheniers and natural levees (Map 81).

Taxonomic comments. No subspecies of *E. fasciatus* have been proposed. The most recent available taxonomic study is that by Taylor (1935); a much more comprehensive work by Davis (1968) exists only in the form of an unpublished doctoral dissertation.

Habitat and habits. The five-lined skink is a common species that seems to be equally at home in hardwood and pine forests, and may often be found at the same localities as its close relatives *E. inexpectatus* and *E. laticeps.* The ecological factors that minimize competition and permit such structurally similar species to coexist are not well understood and are worthy of investigation. Five-

lined skinks are often found on the sides of living trees; on, in, and under logs; beneath bark on stumps and dead trees; under slabs and chips in sawdust piles; and beneath assorted debris in trash piles.

An adult *E. fasciatus* collected in a pile of asbestos shingles in western Rapides Parish on 15 March 1973 was eating a wood roach when it was uncovered. Collins (1974) reported that the species feeds on a wide variety of arthropods and small vertebrates.

Reproduction. Tinkle (1959) observed a pair of five-lined skinks copulating on 8 May 1954. He collected a brooding female and her clutch of seven eggs beneath a board on a swamp ridge in St. Charles Parish on 17 June 1954. The eggs hatched on 5 July. Other females with their clutches (seven to nine eggs) have been taken as early as 6 June and as late as 3 August, other hatchlings as early as 8 June. Fitch (1954) recorded three other Louisiana clutches as hatching between 19 and 26 July. He found that in Kansas the newly hatched young average 23–27 mm in snout-vent length.

Eumeces inexpectatus Taylor
Southeastern Five-lined Skink
Plate XIV

Recognition. A moderately large (to 8½ in.; 216 mm), shiny lizard with a pattern, in smaller specimens, of a blue tail and narrow yellow or white stripes on a black background (large adults with brown body and gray tail, the stripes dull); head stripes orange, especially in younger individuals; head red-orange and swollen in the jaw region of large males during breeding season; scales flat and smooth; scales in the median row beneath the tail no wider than those in adjacent rows.

Distribution. Confined to the Florida Parishes (Map 82).

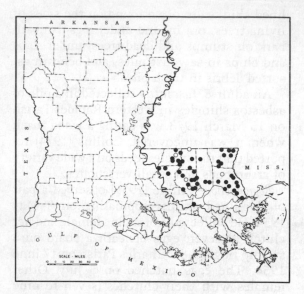

Map 82. Distribution of *Eumeces inexpectatus*. Solid circles represent specimens examined; hollow circles represent museum specimens not examined or literature records.

Taxonomic comments. No subspecies of *E. inexpectatus* has been proposed. The most recent available taxonomic study is that by Taylor (1935); a much more comprehensive work by Davis (1968) exists only in the form of an unpublished doctoral dissertation.

Habitat and habits. Eumeces inexpectatus is a creature of the pine woods, where it is found most often in or under rotten logs or beneath the bark of dead trees and stumps.

No dietary information has been published for Louisiana specimens. Presumably their diet is similar to that of *E. fasciatus* and *E. laticeps.*

Reproduction. Two females and their clutches were discovered beneath logs near Varnado, Washington Parish, on 1 and 5 June. A third female was found with her clutch at Enon, Washington Parish, on 9 June; the eggs hatched on 10 July, and the three hatchlings measured 63.5–67 mm in total length. Two

clutches, each containing 11 eggs, have been reported from other southeastern states (Fitch 1970); in one case the female was coiled about her clutch. In St. James Parish, hatchlings have been found as early as 13 June.

Eumeces laticeps (Schneider)
Broad-headed Skink
Plate XIV

Recognition. A large (to 13 in.; 330 mm), shiny lizard with a pattern, in smaller specimens, of a blue tail and narrow yellow or white stripes on a black background (large adults with a brown body and tail, the stripes dull or absent); head orange-red and swollen in the jaw region of large males during breeding season; scales flat and smooth; scales in the median row beneath the tail wider than those in adjacent rows; 30 to 32 rows of scales at midbody; usually eight supralabials; no enlarged postlabial scales. Occasional specimens may have characteristics of both *Eumeces laticeps* and *E. fasciatus* and defy identification.

Distribution. Statewide except for the Marsh (Map 83). The species is apparently extremely rare in southwestern Louisiana.

Taxonomic comments. No subspecies of *E. laticeps* have been proposed. The most recent available taxonomic study is that by Taylor (1935); a much more comprehensive work by Davis (1968) exists only in the form of an unpublished doctoral dissertation.

Habitat and habits. Eumeces laticeps is the most arboreal of our skinks and shows a definite preference for hardwood trees, at least in Louisiana, often taking up residence in hollow limbs or other cavities. During winter and early spring, these skinks can be found under the bark of logs and standing dead trees. The large males are impressive with their red heads and swollen jaws, and not a spring goes by in Baton Rouge without Loui-

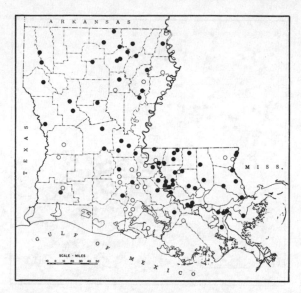

Map 83. Distribution of *Eumeces laticeps*. Solid circles represent specimens examined; hollow circles represent museum specimens not examined or literature records.

Eumeces septentrionalis (Baird)
Prairie Skink
Plate XIV

Recognition. A moderately large (to 8⅛ in.; 206 mm), shiny brown lizard with a pair of light-bordered, dark dorsolateral stripes, the dark stripes no more than two scales wide (young with blue tail); usually two postmental scales, rarely one; scales flat and smooth.

Distribution. Confined to the extreme northwestern corner of Louisiana (Map 84).

Map 84. Distribution of *Eumeces septentrionalis*. Solid circles represent specimens examined; hollow circles represent museum specimens not examined or literature records.

siana State University's Museum of Natural Science receiving several telephone inquiries, referring to *E. laticeps*, from callers wondering what kind of strange beast has turned up in their backyard or carport. These lizards can inflict a painful bite but will not do so unless they are restrained. They are nonpoisonous and not at all dangerous to humans, so they should not be harmed.

The feeding habits of *E. laticeps* in Louisiana are yet to be recorded. Apparently they will eat almost anything small enough to capture, including other vertebrates as well as arthropods (Collins 1974).

Reproduction. Almost no reproductive data are available for the broad-headed skink in Louisiana. Elsewhere clutch size ranges from 6 to 16 eggs (Mount 1975). Females often remain with their eggs. A hatchling from Pointe Coupee Parish was collected on 17 June.

Taxonomic comments. Only the subspecies *Eumeces septentrionalis obtusirostris* Bocourt, the southern prairie skink, occurs in Louisiana. The most recent taxonomic study is that by H. M. Smith and Slater (1949).

Habitat and habits. The first specimen of the prairie skink to be collected in Louisiana was taken in a cornfield near open pastureland in mid-April; four additional specimens were collected beneath logs in wooded areas during the summer (Morizot and Douglas 1967).

There are no data on feeding habits of the prairie skink in Louisiana. In Kansas, lizards of this species are reported to feed on insects, snails, spiders, and smaller lizards (Collins 1974).

Reproduction. There are no data on reproductive activity of *E. septentrionalis* in Louisiana. Collins (1974) has reported that in Kansas 6 to 10 eggs are deposited in late June. Two clutches from Texas (10 and 9 eggs, respectively) noted by McAllister (1987) were deposited in May; the hatchlings measured 24–26 mm in snout-vent length.

Scincella lateralis (Say)
Ground Skink
Plate XIV

Recognition. A small to medium-sized (to 5¾ in.; 145 mm), shiny brown lizard with a pair of dark dorsolateral stripes that lack light borders; belly white or light yellow; scales flat and smooth.

Distribution. Statewide (Map 85).

Taxonomic comments. No subspecies have been proposed, and no taxonomic study of this species has been published.

Habitat and habits. The ground skink is one of the two most common and abundant lizards in Louisiana. It occurs in practically every environment that will support lizards, from deep in forests to backyards in cities. In backyards, ground skinks are most apt to be discovered beneath boards or other debris, but in wooded habitats—although they are often found under logs—the lizards may be observed prowling about on the surface amid dead leaves and clumps of grass. At such times they may press their legs, especially the forelimbs, back against the body and proceed with an almost snakelike, undulating motion.

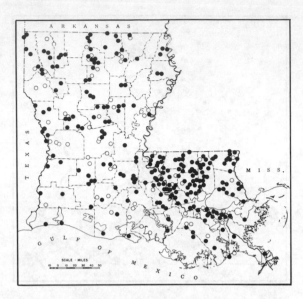

Map 85. Distribution of *Scincella lateralis*. Solid circles represent specimens examined; hollow circles represent museum specimens not examined or literature records.

We have no information on the feeding habits of this species in Louisiana. Elsewhere *Scincella lateralis* has been reported to feed on small insects, spiders, and earthworms (Collins 1974; P. W. Smith 1961).

Reproduction. Johnson (1953) observed a pair of ground skinks copulating beneath a board on 25 July 1950. The earliest date for field-collected eggs in Louisiana is 12 May (Johnson 1953), the latest 28 July (Arny 1948); Johnson provided evidence suggesting that eggs may be deposited as late as September. Both Johnson and Arny found clutch size to vary from one to five eggs. Field-collected clutches from the Delta National Wildlife Refuge in Plaquemines Parish hatched on 24 July and 6 August 1947, respectively (Arny 1948). The hatchlings measured 47–50 mm in total length.

FAMILY TEIIDAE

The 40 genera and 198 species of the family Teiidae are confined to the New World (Dowling and Duellman 1978). A single species occurs in Louisiana.

Cnemidophorus sexlineatus (Linnaeus)
Six-lined Racerunner

Plate XIV

Recognition. A moderately large to large (to 10½ in.; 267 mm) lizard with six narrow light stripes on a dark dorsum, often with a green tint overlying the stripes and ground color on the sides of the body; dorsal scales tiny and granular, ventral scales large and rectangular; tail long and whiplike.

Distribution. Statewide except for the Mississippi alluvial plain and the Marsh (but present on cheniers in the western portion; Map 86).

Taxonomic comments. Louisiana racerunners belong to the nominate subspecies, *Cnemidophorus s. sexlineatus*. The most recent comprehensive taxonomic study is that by Burt (1931), although subsequent papers have dealt with the species in a limited portion of its range.

Habitat and habits. Although racerunners occur throughout most of Louisiana, the distribution is discontinuous because of their preference for open, well-drained habitats—sandy areas in particular. In northern Louisiana, Walker (1963:96) found the largest populations "in cut-over woodlands used for pasture land or for planting pine trees," habitats characterized by scattered trees and brush piles. Both Walker (1963) and Strecker and Frierson (1926) reported the species to be abundant in open areas near ponds and along sandy country roads. Strecker and Frierson (1926) noted that racerunners will burrow under bushes, and Percy Viosca (notes) said that he observed the lizards taking refuge in holes

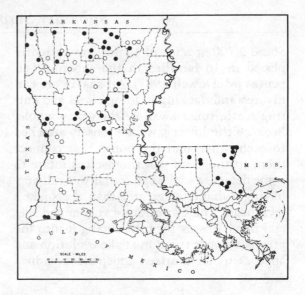

Map 86. Distribution of *Cnemidophorus sexlineatus.* Solid circles represent specimens examined; hollow circles represent museum specimens not examined or literature records.

in the cliff banks north of Bastrop, Morehouse Parish. A sun-loving species, *C. sexlineatus* will usually take cover under boards or logs on overcast days. During its periods of greatest activity, the racerunner is easily our fastest-moving lizard.

No information is available on the feeding habits of *C. sexlineatus* in Louisiana, but presumably arthropods constitute the chief items in the diet here as elsewhere in the range of the species.

Reproduction. Fitch (1985) reported clutch size to range from one to eight eggs in samples from throughout the racerunner's range. Hatchlings measure 32–35 mm in snout-vent length (Fitch 1958). We have no specific information concerning Louisiana specimens.

Suborder Serpentes: Snakes

Some 2,700 species of snakes are currently placed in 16 families in the suborder Serpentes (McDowell 1987). All snakes are carnivores and, lacking holding claws and cutting teeth, must swallow their prey whole. Because the lower jaws are loosely attached to each other, and the bones that connect them to the skull can themselves rotate to some degree, a snake can actually engulf prey having a diameter greater than the snake's own head. The evolution of venom and special mechanisms for introducing it into the prey is a major trend in snake evolution and appears to have arisen independently in a number of groups. Nonvenomous snakes kill their prey by constriction, pin it down with their body, or simply swallow it struggling. Like the lizards, male snakes have paired hemipenes for copulation. Although many snakes do lay eggs, a substantial number (most North American species) are live bearers. Unlike the lizards, only a few species of snakes can easily detach the tail. As they grow, snakes shed the outer layer of the skin in one piece from the snout backward—like removing a stocking. Most species of snakes are as likely to be active after dark as during the day, some species even more so.

KEY TO THE SNAKES OF LOUISIANA

1. Large pit present between eye and nostril
2

   Facial pit absent
6
2. Horny rattle (or "button" in juveniles) present on tail
3

   Rattle absent
5
3. Top of head covered with large scales
   Sistrurus miliarius (p. 268)

   Top of head covered with many small scales
4
4. Dorsum with diamond-shaped blotches
   Crotalus adamanteus (p. 265)

   Dorsum with dark crossbands (interrupted anteriorly)
   Crotalus horridus (p. 266)
5. Subocular series complete, no supralabial in border of orbit
   Agkistrodon contortrix (p. 262)

   Subocular series incomplete, 1 supralabial in border of orbit
   Agkistrodon piscivorus (p. 264)
6. Dorsal scales at midbody smooth
7

   Dorsal scales keeled (sometimes weakly)
23
7. Anal plate single
8

   Anal plate divided
11

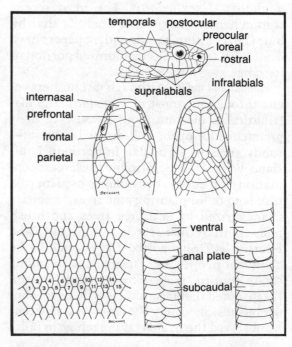

Figure 10. Structural features of snakes: lateral, dorsal, and ventral views of the head (upper); dorsal view of the body showing the method of counting scale rows (lower left); and ventral view of the anal region (lower right).

8. Dorsum white or yellow with black-edged red blotches or bands 9
   Dorsum tan, gray, or black; no bright red markings 10
9. Belly white, unmarked
   Cemophora coccinea (p. 228)
   Belly with light-and-dark pattern
   Lampropeltis triangulum (p. 238)
10. Dorsum black, most scales with small light spots or dorsum with narrow light crossbands
    Lampropeltis getulus (p. 237)
    Dorsum tan or gray with reddish brown or dark brown blotches (often virtually indistinguishable in adults from Florida Parishes)
    Lampropeltis calligaster (p. 236)
11. Dorsum spotted, blotched, or crossbanded 12
    Dorsum not spotted, blotched, or crossbanded except on neck 14
12. Dorsum with black, yellow, and red crossbands *Micrurus fulvius* (p. 261)
    Black, yellow, and red crossbands absent 13
13. Dorsal scales in 15 rows immediately anterior to vent
    Coluber constrictor (p. 229)
    Dorsal scales in 13 rows immediately anterior to vent
    Masticophis flagellum (p. 239)
14. Dorsum black or gray, a yellow ring on neck *Diadophis punctatus* (p. 230)
    Yellow neck ring absent 15
15. Dorsal scales in 17 or more rows at midbody 16
    Dorsal scales in fewer than 17 rows at midbody 21
16. Dorsal scales in 19 rows at midbody 17
    Dorsal scales in 17 rows at midbody 18
17. Dorsum black with 3 narrow, longitudinal red stripes
    Farancia erytrogramma (p. 234)
    Dorsum black, unstriped, but with vertical red bars ventrolaterally
    Farancia abacura (p. 233)
18. Size large (exceeding 400 mm); juveniles

and subadults blotched 19
Size small (not exceeding 400 mm); pattern never blotched 20
19. Dorsal scales in 15 rows immediately anterior to vent
    Coluber constrictor (p. 229)
    Dorsal scales in 13 rows immediately anterior to vent
    Masticophis flagellum (p. 239)
20. Supralabials 7 on each side; dark line extending through eye
    Rhadinaea flavilata (p. 252)
    Supralabials 6 on each side; no dark line extending through eye
    Virginia valeriae (p. 260)
21. Dorsal scales in 15 rows at midbody 22
    Dorsal scales in 13 rows at midbody
    Carphophis amoenus (p. 227)
22. Head black, neck with black ring
    Tantilla coronata (p. 254)
    Head slightly darker than body, neck without black ring
    Tantilla gracilis (p. 255)
23. Anal plate entire 24
    Anal plate divided 27
24. Dorsum with dark blotches; prefrontals 4 *Pituophis melanoleucus* (p. 248)
    Dorsum with 3 longitudinal light stripes; prefrontals 2 25
25. Light lateral stripe on second and third dorsal scale rows
    Thamnophis sirtalis (p. 258)
    Light lateral stripe on third and fourth dorsal scale rows 26
26. Dark pigment of dorsum extending well onto belly scutes; light parietal spots small and separate, or lacking; supralabials usually 7 on each side
    Thamnophis sauritus (p. 257)
    Dark pigment of dorsum extending only slightly, if at all, onto belly scutes; light parietal spots large and usually fused; supralabials usually 8 on each side *Thamnophis proximus* (p. 256)
27. Dorsum uniformly green (bluish gray in preservative)
    Opheodrys aestivus (p. 247)

Dorsum not uniformly green   28

28. Snout protruding, keeled, and slightly upturned
    Heterodon platyrhinos (p. 235)
Snout not so modified   29

29. Belly scutes more than 200   30
Belly scutes less than 200   31

30. Dark neck stripes joining on head to form "spearpoint" between eyes; dark stripe from eye to corner of jaw extends onto neck; underside of tail striped
    Elaphe guttata (p. 231)
Head without "spearpoint"; if present, dark stripe from eye extends only to edge of upper lip; underside of tail usually unstriped
    Elaphe obsoleta (p. 232)

31. Dorsal scales in 21 or more rows at midbody   32
Dorsal scales in fewer than 21 rows at midbody   37

32. Suboculars present, no supralabials entering orbit
    Nerodia cyclopion (p. 241)
Suboculars absent, supralabials entering orbit   33

33. Dorsum tan or grayish brown with narrow, dark, chainlike markings
    Nerodia rhombifera (p. 245)
Dorsum crossbanded, blotched, or striped   34

34. Dorsum crossbanded or striped; belly light with large rectangular blotches or dark with row of light spots   35
Dorsum virtually unpatterned, or crossbanded anteriorly and blotched posteriorly; belly light with small crescentic spots or unmarked   36

35. Dorsum crossbanded; belly light with large rectangular blotches
    Nerodia fasciata (p. 244)

Dorsum striped; belly dark with row of light spots   *Nerodia clarkii* (p. 240)

36. Dorsum in adults usually uniformly dark brown or dark gray, in juveniles always distinctly patterned; belly unmarked, or with inconspicuous spots (wider than long) confined to anterior margin of ventral scutes
    Nerodia erythrogaster (p. 242)
Dorsum distinctly patterned in adults as well as juveniles; belly always patterned, the spots (usually longer than wide) in 2 median rows
    Nerodia sipedon (p. 246)

37. Dorsal scales in 19 rows at midbody   38
Dorsal scales in fewer than 19 rows at midbody   39

38. Light lateral stripe on first, second, and third dorsal scale rows; belly with single row of dark spots or unmarked
    Regina grahamii (p. 249)
Light lateral stripe on first dorsal scale row; belly with double row of dark spots   *Regina rigida* (p. 250)

39. Dorsal scales in 17 rows at midbody; no light spot on supralabials below eye   40
Dorsal scales in 15 rows at midbody; light spot on supralabials below eye
    Storeria occipitomaculata (p. 254)

40. Prefrontal not in border of orbit; supralabials 7 on each side
    Storeria dekayi (p. 252)
Prefrontal in border of orbit; supralabials 5 or 6 on each side   41

41. Dorsal scales very weakly keeled or smooth; internasals 2; supralabials 6
    Virginia valeriae (p. 260)
Dorsal scales noticeably keeled; internasal 1; supralabials 5
    Virginia striatula (p. 259)

FAMILY COLUBRIDAE

The enormous, cosmopolitan family Colubridae contains approximately 291 genera comprising 1,500 species (Dowling and Duellman 1978). It is well represented in Louisiana by 18 genera composed of 32 species.

Carphophis amoenus (Say)
Worm Snake
Plate XV

Recognition. A very short (to 14¾ in.; 375 mm), brown or black snake; belly pink, the color extending onto the lower rows of dorsal scales; dorsal scales smooth, in 13 rows; anal plate divided.

Distribution. Widespread in the Florida Parishes, but west of the Mississippi River the only records are from the Red River valley near Shreveport and from the Bastrop Hills and Macon Ridge in northeastern Louisiana (Map 87). The record from St. Bernard Parish is highly questionable on ecological grounds, but one of the collectors (John Boley) recalls picking up an egg in the woods behind Shell Beach that hatched out the specimen in question (TU 10759).

Taxonomic comments. Two subspecies of the worm snake occur in Louisiana: *Carphophis amoenus helenae* (Kennicott), the Midwest worm snake, characterized by a brown dorsum, the pink ventral coloration extending only onto the two lower rows of dorsal scales, and the absence of internasal scales; and *C. a. vermis* (Kennicott), the western worm snake, characterized by a black dorsum, the pink coloration extending onto the third row of dorsal scales, and the presence of a pair of internasal scales. The former occurs in the Florida Parishes, the latter in northwestern Louisiana. Specimens from the northeastern part of the state are intermediate and represent an intergrade population (Rossman 1973).

Habitat and habits. The worm snake occurs

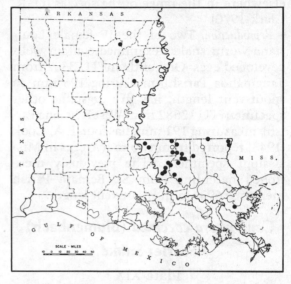

Map 87. Distribution of *Carphophis amoenus.* Solid circles represent specimens examined; hollow circles represent museum specimens not examined or literature records.

in both hardwood and pine forests in both hill country and flatwoods (although we have relatively fewer records from the latter habitat). Except for Strecker and Frierson's (1926) report that occasional specimens were plowed up in the vicinity of Gayles (Caddo Parish), specific information on microhabitat in Louisiana is lacking. Worm snakes are rarely encountered in the open, although one was found dead on the road in the Tunica Hills (West Feliciana Parish). A second Tunica Hills specimen was active after dark in the leaf litter near the base of a ravine on 16 September 1983, and on the night of 22 August 1914 Percy Viosca discovered one beneath an electric light in Mandeville (St. Tammany Parish). In Mississippi, F. A. Cook (1943) found this species to occur principally in and under rotten logs and leaves. Worm snakes are active burrowers and can escape rather quickly if the collector is not alert.

There are no data available on the food of *C. amoenus* in Louisiana; presumably it consists primarily of earthworms, as is the case elsewhere in the range of the species (D. R. Clark 1970).

Reproduction. Two of the 19 female Louisiana worm snakes examined contain well-developed eggs. One of them (TU 3302 from Tangipahoa Parish), measuring 196 mm in snout-vent length, has five eggs; the other specimen (TU 12582 from West Feliciana Parish), measuring 191 mm, has four. F. A. Cook (1943) reported from two to five eggs in Mississippi specimens. The previously mentioned hatchling from St. Bernard Parish measures 69 mm in snout-vent length.

Cemophora coccinea (Blumenbach)
Scarlet Snake
Plate XIX

Recognition. A moderately short to medium-sized (to 32½ in.; 826 mm) snake with a pattern of black-bordered, red saddle-shaped blotches on a white or light yellow ground color (the snout red); belly cream colored; rostral scale enlarged and projecting beyond the lower jaw; dorsal scales smooth, in 19 rows; anal plate undivided.

Similar species. *Lampropeltis triangulum* and *Micrurus fulvius* have somewhat similar dorsal patterns, but each of them possesses a boldly patterned belly.

Distribution. Flatwoods of St. Tammany Parish and the hill country of northern Louisiana (Map 88). A few records are from floodplain forest adjacent to the hill country. Most records are from Longleaf Pine Forest and Pine-Oak-Hickory Forest.

Taxonomic comments. *Cemophora coccinea copei* Jan, the northern scarlet snake, is the only subspecies that occurs in Louisiana. The most recent taxonomic study is that by Williams and Wilson (1967).

Habitat and habits. Relatively little is known about the ecology of this moderately rare species in Louisiana. Walker (1963) reported that an adult male was collected at midday in a

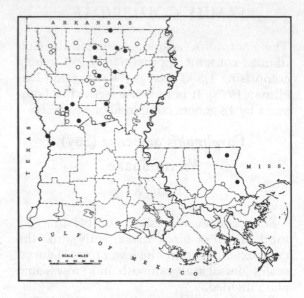

Map 88.   Distribution of *Cemophora coccinea.* Solid circles represent specimens examined; hollow circles represent museum specimens not examined or literature records.

sandy garden in Jackson Parish in June 1962. Williams and Wilson (1967) collected six specimens in two nights in Natchitoches Parish during June 1966. Those specimens were taken on blacktop roads at night and, to our knowledge, constitute by far the largest series of scarlet snakes taken in Louisiana in such a short period of time. The scarlet snake is known to burrow on occasion, and the compact skull and protruding snout appear to be morphological adaptations for such activity (Williams and Wilson 1967).

No records of feeding behavior have been noted from this state, but elsewhere the scarlet snake is known to feed primarily on small lizards and snakes and on reptile eggs, the latter perhaps being slit by the enlarged, saberlike, posterior maxillary teeth (Williams and Wilson 1967). Insects, small amphibians, and young mammals have also appeared in the diet.

Reproduction. An adult female (Northeast

Louisiana University 20287) collected alive on the road near Fairbanks in Ouachita Parish on 14 July 1968 contained four eggs. An apparent hatchling (TU 18023) collected 19 September 1960 in Union County, Arkansas, very close to the Louisiana state line, measures 138 mm in total length.

Coluber constrictor Linnaeus
Racer
Plate XVII

Recognition. A long (to 75¼ in.; 1,911 mm), glossy snake with a uniformly black, gray, brown, tan, olive green, or blue dorsum (the latter often with a variable number of light spots); belly white, grayish white, light yellow, grayish blue, slate gray, or black; dorsal scales smooth, in 17 rows; anal plate divided. Young individuals have a series of dark middorsal blotches on a gray dorsum; in this respect they are very different in appearance from the adults.

Distribution. Statewide (Map 89). Within the Marsh, racers are largely confined to the cheniers and natural levees.

Taxonomic comments. Five subspecies of the racer occur in Louisiana: *Coluber constrictor priapus* Dunn and Wood, the southern black racer, characterized by a black dorsum and a slate gray or black venter; *C. c. latrunculus* Wilson, the black-masked racer, characterized by a slate gray dorsum, a bluish gray venter, and a broad black stripe behind the eye; *C. c. flaviventris* Say, the eastern yellow-bellied racer, characterized by an olive green dorsum and a light yellow venter; *C. c. etheridgei* Wilson, the tan racer, characterized by a light tan dorsum with some light spotting and a grayish white venter; and *C. c. anthicus* (Cope), the buttermilk racer, characterized by a blue, blue-black, or blue-green dorsum with a variable amount of light spotting and a grayish white venter. *Coluber c. priapus* occurs in the Florida Parishes, in-

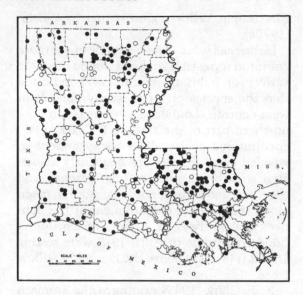

Map 89. Distribution of *Coluber constrictor.* Solid circles represent specimens examined; hollow circles represent museum specimens not examined or literature records.

tergrading with *C. c. latrunculus* at the eastern border of the Mississippi alluvial plain. *Coluber c. latrunculus* occupies the lower Mississippi alluvial plain (and perhaps the upper plain as well—too few specimens are available from that area for confirmation) and intergrades with *C. c. flaviventris* and *C. c. anthicus* along the western border of the plain. *Coluber c. flaviventris* is found in the western portion of the Marsh and in the Prairie; it intergrades with *C. c. etheridgei* to the northwest and *C. c. anthicus* to the north. *Coluber c. etheridgei* is confined to the western portion of the Longleaf Pine Forest in Calcasieu, Beauregard, and Vernon parishes; it intergrades with *C. c. anthicus* to the north and east. *Coluber c. anthicus* is widespread throughout central and northern Louisiana, intergrading with either *C. c. priapus* or *C. c. latrunculus* along the western margin of the Mississippi alluvial plain. The most recent taxonomic study on the racers of the lower

Mississippi Valley region is that by Wilson (1970a).

Habitat and habits. The racer, one of our more common terrestrial snakes, is found in a wide variety of habitats. Fitch (1949) indicated that the species preferred grassy uplands in west-central Louisiana, whereas in the northern part of the state R. F. Clark (1949) encountered nearly all of his specimens in wooded areas. Racers are frequently associated with brush piles or briar patches, and they are good climbers. Two adults taken along the railroad embankment at the Bonnet Carre Spillway, St. Charles Parish, during flood conditions in April 1973 were resting 10–12 ft (3–4 m) above the ground in willow trees.

R. F. Clark (1949) examined the stomach contents of northern Louisiana racers and found mice in 25 stomachs, rats in 5, fence lizards (*Sceloporus undulatus*) in 8, leopard frogs (*Rana sphenocephala*) in 7, and birds in 2. A large *Coluber* discovered dead on the road in bottomland hardwood forest in Madison Parish on 24 April 1971 contained a large skink (*Eumeces* sp.).

Reproduction. A mating pair of racers was observed at Chalmette, St. Bernard Parish, on 11 June 1949 (data on tag of TU 5848). Clutches containing from 6 to 18 granular white eggs have been found from 9 June through 18 September in such places as soft moist soil beside decaying logs, in a decaying pile of wood pulp, in a slight depression at the base of a clump of grass, beneath a piece of newspaper, and under a small thin board (Arny 1948; R. F. Clark 1949; Liner 1949; Tinkle 1959). Hatching dates range from 24 July through 20 September. The eggs discovered by Arny measured 32–37 × 19–20 mm; they hatched on 13 August 1947, and the hatchlings measured 282–326 mm in total length. The eggs reported by Liner (1949) hatched 20–22 July 1947, and the hatchlings measured 299–310 mm. Five additional sets of hatchlings in the Tulane collection have the following ranges:

287–315 mm, 295–320 mm, 296–331 mm, 278–295 mm, and 256–306 mm.

Diadophis punctatus (Linnaeus)
Ring-necked Snake
Plate XV

Recognition. A moderately short (to 30 in.; 762 mm*), black or slate gray snake with a bright yellow neck band; belly yellow, usually with small black spots; dorsal scales smooth, in 15 rows; anal plate divided.

Distribution. Statewide except for the Marsh, but apparently very rare in the Prairie, the Atchafalaya and Tensas basins, and the Longleaf Pine Forest south of the Red River (Map 90).

Taxonomic comments. Only a single subspecies, *Diadophis punctatus stictogenys* Cope, the Mississippi ring-necked snake, occurs in Louisiana. The most recent comprehensive taxonomic study is that by Blanchard (1942), although several subsequent papers have dealt with the species in a limited portion of its range.

Habitat and habits. The ring-necked snake is an inhabitant of forested regions, and most Louisiana specimens are found in or under rotten logs. Others have been taken in stumps or beneath boards, railroad ties, bark on fallen trees, and brick piles. One individual was discovered beneath a large flat rock in the middle of a dry, sandy stream bottom in the Tunica Hills (West Feliciana Parish); the soil beneath the rock was moist. When picked up, a specimen from Madison Parish coiled its tail and displayed the bright undersurface.

No information is available on the diet of *D. punctatus* in Louisiana. Brode and Allison (1958) reported that Mississippi ring-necked

---

*Ring-necked snakes reach a considerably greater size in the far West than they do in this part of the country. The record length for *Diadophis punctatus stictogenys* is 18½ in. (470 mm) according to Conant (1975).

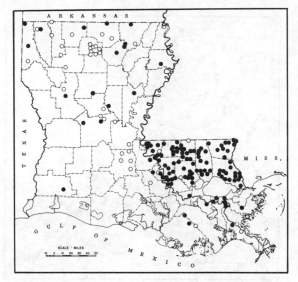

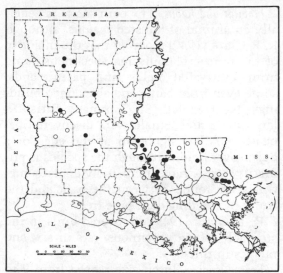

Map 90. Distribution of *Diadophis punctatus*. Solid circles represent specimens examined; hollow circles represent museum specimens not examined or literature records.

Map 91. Distribution of *Elaphe guttata*. Solid circles represent specimens examined; hollow circles represent museum specimens not examined or literature records.

snakes feed on earthworms and insect larvae. F. A. Cook (1954) indicated that Mississippi specimens also feed on small lizards and salamanders.

Reproduction. No data are available on reproductive activity in Louisiana, but F. A. Cook (1954) stated that female ring-necked snakes in Mississippi lay two to five oblong eggs (27.5 × 6 mm), which the female broods. Fitch (1985) recorded clutch sizes elsewhere as ranging from 1 to 10 eggs.

Elaphe guttata (Linnaeus)
Corn Snake
Plate XVI

Recognition. A long (to 72 in.; 1,829 mm), brightly marked snake with a dorsal pattern of red or brown blotches on an orange or gray background; belly white, checkered with black; dorsal scales very weakly keeled, in 27 rows; anal plate divided.

Distribution. Statewide except for the Marsh, the Prairie, and most of the Mississippi alluvial plain (Map 91).

Taxonomic comments. Two subspecies of the corn snake occur in Louisiana: *Elaphe g. guttata*, characterized by red blotches on an orange or light brown background and a solid black subocular bar, and *E. g. emoryi* (Baird & Girard), the Great Plains rat snake, characterized by brown or reddish brown blotches on a gray or gray-brown background and a light center in the subocular bar. *Elaphe g. guttata* is generally thought to occur in and adjacent to the Florida Parishes and along the western margin of the lower Atchafalaya Basin, and to intergrade with *E. g. emoryi* in central Louisiana. Thomas (1974) and Raymond and Hardy (1983) concluded that all the other Louisiana populations also are intergrades between *guttata* and *emoryi*, but we think a case could be made for considering those from the northwestern portion of the state to be *emoryi* rather than intergrades.

Habitat and habits. The corn snake is generally an animal of forested regions, although R. F. Clark (1949) reported that the majority of his northern Louisiana specimens came from cultivated fields and pasturelands, some even from barns and abandoned buildings. Near Slidell, St. Tammany Parish, a large male and female were discovered beneath a fallen signboard at the edge of a burnt-over field. Although the species is primarily terrestrial, small individuals sometimes are found between the bark and the trunk of standing dead pine trees.

R. F. Clark (1949) discovered birds in the stomachs of six specimens, rats in six, and rabbits in three.

Reproduction. Clutch size ranged from 9 to 27 in the two instances known from Louisiana. In the former clutch the eggs were deposited on 7 June 1968 and measured 27–33 × 15–16 mm. Thirteen hatchlings from the latter clutch averaged 308 mm in total length.

Elaphe obsoleta (Say)
Rat Snake
Plate XVI

Recognition. A very long (to 101 in.; 2,565 mm) snake with a uniformly black dorsum or a pattern of large dark blotches on a gray-brown or yellowish brown background (all juveniles blotched); belly mottled or checkered; dorsal scales weakly keeled, in 25 to 27 rows; anal plate divided.

Distribution. Statewide (Map 92).

Taxonomic comments. Two subspecies of the rat snake occur in Louisiana: *Elaphe o. obsoleta*, the black rat snake, characterized by a uniformly black dorsum or at least a very dark background that contrasts very little with the blotches, and *E. o. lindheimeri* (Baird & Girard), the Texas rat snake, characterized by dark blotches on a gray-brown or yellowish brown background. The former oc-

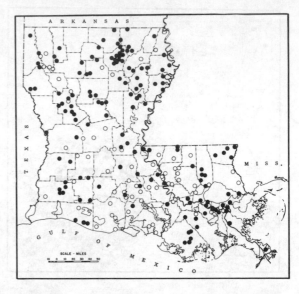

Map 92. Distribution of *Elaphe obsoleta*. Solid circles represent specimens examined; hollow circles represent museum specimens not examined or literature records.

curs in north-central Louisiana, the latter in the southern half of the state and, apparently, along the Mississippi alluvial plain into northeastern Louisiana. Intergradation occurs over a broad area, and even populations that are predominantly *E. o. obsoleta* may have an occasional individual that appears to be an *E. o. lindheimeri*. No recent taxonomic study of this species has been published.

Habitat and habits. The rat snake, one of our most common and widespread snakes, is found in a wide variety of habitats. In northern Louisiana, R. F. Clark (1949) recorded *E. obsoleta* as occurring on roads and in swamps, wooded areas, pastures, briar patches, cultivated fields, open sandy places, houses, and barns. The majority of Liner's (1954) southern Louisiana specimens were collected near barns and houses. Arny (1948) collected an adult female 12 ft (3½ m) up in the branches of a willow tree in the Delta National Wildlife Refuge, Plaquemines Parish, during flood conditions in the spring of 1947. All four rat snakes that Tinkle (1959) collected from the Sarpy Wildlife Refuge, St. Charles Parish, were at least 4 ft (1¼ m) above the ground in trees or bushes. Viosca (notes) caught an *E. obsoleta* in a tree on Cheniere au Tigre, Vermilion Parish, just after it had eaten a bird. Several Louisiana herpetologists have observed rat snakes swimming in bayous and rivers. When cornered, rat snakes often pull their bodies into a tight coil and rapidly vibrate their tails. If they are lying in dead leaves, the resulting sound somewhat resembles the "buzz" of a rattlesnake and may cause undue concern to any humans viewing the performance. Rat snakes are, nonetheless, harmless and should not be killed.

R. F. Clark (1949) found mice in 35 stomachs, rats in 20, rabbits in 18, birds in 17, and squirrels in 10. Lizards probably make up a significant portion of the diet in juveniles; Kennedy (1964) found an *Anolis* and an *Anolis* egg in a subadult *E. obsoleta* from eastern Texas.

Reproduction. We have no data on reproduction in Louisiana specimens. Fitch (1985) recorded clutch sizes ranging from 6 to 44 eggs from many localities scattered across the range of the species.

Farancia abacura (Holbrook)
Mud Snake
Plate XVIII

Recognition. A very long (to 81 in.; 2,057 mm), glossy black snake; belly bright red, the color extending onto the lower sides of the body as irregular bars; dorsal scales smooth, in 19 rows; anal plate divided.

Distribution. Statewide (Map 93).

Taxonomic comments. The western subspecies, *Farancia abacura reinwardtii* Schlegel, the western mud snake, occurs in Louisiana. The most recent taxonomic study is that by H. M. Smith (1938).

Habitat and habits. The mud snake, one of the two most thoroughly aquatic snakes in

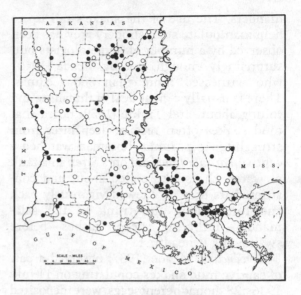

Map 93. Distribution of *Farancia abacura*. Solid circles represent specimens examined; hollow circles represent museum specimens not examined or literature records.

Louisiana, is rarely seen out of water except when it crosses roads. With the first really heavy rain of spring, mud snakes may be commonly encountered on the road between Boutte and New Orleans in willow swampland. Occasional specimens may be found in or under rotten logs or in burrows along the banks of small streams (R. F. Clark 1949; Hahn and Wilson 1966); adult females coiled about their eggs are those most often found in these situations. When picked up, newly captured *Farancia* never attempt to bite and often are as limp as a piece of rope. Occasionally one will poke the collector's hand with the sharp tip of its tail; for this reason *F. abacura* is sometimes called the "stinging snake" or "horn snake." Despite the name, however, the tail tip is incapable of even breaking the skin. Sometimes a mud snake will hide its head beneath its coils and display the brightly colored underside of its tightly coiled tail.

Adult mud snakes feed almost exclusively on *Amphiuma* and *Siren*, large eel-like salamanders. The use of the snake's tail tip to help manipulate such slippery prey has been observed by a number of herpetologists but, surprisingly enough, not by Meade (1940), who witnessed more than 300 feedings. There is usually a great deal of thrashing and rolling about, and Tinkle (1959) noted that mud snakes often receive deep bites from struggling *Amphiuma*. Rossman watched a captive *Farancia* feeding on a *Siren* in a tank of water; the snake coiled about and constricted its prey. It chewed vigorously back and forth along the trunk of the salamander—inflicting deep gashes—before swallowing it headfirst.

Reproduction. Meade (1937) observed a pair of captive mud snakes copulating on 11 July 1936; 28 nonadherent eggs were deposited eight weeks later and hatched on 30 October. Clutch sizes recorded for Louisiana specimens range from 16 (R. F. Clark 1949) to 50 eggs (Hahn and Wilson 1966). Frequently the female will remain coiled about her clutch throughout the period of incubation, leaving only for short periods to feed, defecate, or shed her skin. A clutch of 27 eggs deposited on 5 August 1954 averaged approximately 32 × 21 mm (Tinkle 1959). Hatching may occur as early as mid-September; the hatchlings average about 217 mm in total length (Hahn and Wilson 1966).

Farancia erytrogramma (Palisot de Beauvois)
Rainbow Snake
Plate XVIII

Recognition. A long (to 66 in.; 1,676 mm), glossy black snake with three red stripes and yellow on the lower sides just above the belly; belly red with three rows of black spots, the median row often weakly developed; dorsal scales smooth, in 19 rows; anal plate divided.

Map 94. Distribution of *Farancia erytrogramma*. Solid circles represent specimens examined; hollow circles represent museum specimens not examined or literature records.

Distribution. Confined to the Florida Parishes (Map 94).

Taxonomic comments. Only the nominate subspecies, *Farancia e. erytrogramma*, occurs in Louisiana. The most recent taxonomic study is that by Neill (1964).

Habitat and habits. Most Louisiana rainbow snakes have been collected in or near clear, cool streams with sand and gravel bottoms. A few specimens have been taken in the Pearl River swamps and along a deep bayou in a marshy area between forests just above Lake Pontchartrain. F. A. Cook (1943) reported that in adjacent Pearl River County, Mississippi, specimens have been found coiled on a sand bank near the water and coiled under a large overhanging rock about 6 ft (2 m) from the water. Another Mississippi rainbow snake, when disturbed, attempted to hide its head in the sand and leaves, and it struck at its tormentor with its tail.

On 9 August 1947 a 1,098-mm rainbow snake was collected at 10 A.M. on a sandy beach about 3 ft (1 m) from the edge of Darling's Creek (St. Helena Parish), where it was feeding on a 356- to 406-mm eel. Neill (1964) considered eels to be the primary food of adult *F. erytrogramma*. F. A. Cook (1943) related an account of a Mississippi specimen found swallowing an *Amphiuma*, a large eel-like salamander.

Reproduction. In Florida, rainbow snakes deposit 22 to 52 eggs in a "nest" 8–18 in. (203–457 mm) below the surface in sandy soil (Neill 1964). Egg laying in Florida occurs from early to mid-July, and 5 September is recorded as a hatching date. The hatchlings burrow to the surface through the sand. The three Louisiana hatchlings available for study (LSUMZ 11772-73, 42185) measure 143–172 mm in total length.

Heterodon platyrhinos Latreille
Eastern Hog-nosed Snake

Plate XVIII

Recognition. A medium-sized to moderately long (to 45½ in.; 1,156 mm), heavy-bodied snake with an upturned snout and a highly variable dorsal pattern, occasionally uniformly black but more often consisting of large dark spots on a lighter ground color; underside of the tail usually lighter than the belly; dorsal scales keeled, in 25 rows; anal plate divided.

Distribution. Statewide, but apparently rare or absent from the eastern portion of the Marsh (Map 95).

Taxonomic comments. No subspecies of *Heterodon platyrhinos* are currently recognized. The most recent study of geographic variation in this species is that by Edgren (1961).

Habitat and habits. The hog-nosed snake occurs in a wide variety of habitats in Louisiana but seems to be most abundant in relatively dry, upland situations. When disturbed, this snake will flatten its neck to spread an almost cobralike hood and will hiss loudly;

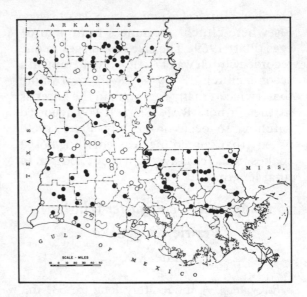

Map 95. Distribution of *Heterodon platyrhinos*. Solid circles represent specimens examined; hollow circles represent museum specimens not examined or literature records.

such behavior has earned this snake the name of spreading adder or puff adder. Despite its ferocious appearance, however, a hog-nosed snake will rarely bite. If the other animal refuses to be intimidated, the snake will roll over on its back, writhe around with its mouth open and its tongue hanging out, and finally lie still. If righted the snake will immediately roll over on its back again, instinctively behaving as if this is the only proper position for a "dead" snake.

Toads are the principal dietary item of *H. platyrhinos*. The upturned snout appears to be an adaptation for digging toads out of sandy soil, but this snake also eats frogs and salamanders. A specimen collected by L. D. Wilson near Georgetown, Grant Parish, on 27 March 1966 regurgitated a live *Ambystoma texanum*.

Reproduction. Louisiana hog-nosed snakes have been observed copulating as early as 16 April (R. F. Clark 1949). Egg deposition has been seen as early as 8 June and as late as 1

October; clutch size ranges from 9 to 25 eggs. Elsewhere clutch size ranges from 4 to 61 eggs (Platt 1969). The size of the eggs in one recorded clutch was 17–19 × 33–40 mm, in a second clutch 17–19 × 28–35 mm (more than twice as many eggs were in the latter as in the former). R. F. Clark (1949) reported hatching to occur 4–12 July. Platt (1969) noted that hatchling eastern hog-nosed snakes from Texas averaged about 200 mm in total length.

Lampropeltis calligaster (Harlan)
Prairie Kingsnake
Plate XIX

Recognition. A moderately long (to 53⅜ in.; 1,356 mm) snake with alternating dorsal and lateral series of black-bordered brownish or reddish blotches on a gray or tan ground color, the pattern often obscured by dark pigment in large adults; belly usually with a checkerboard pattern; dorsal scales smooth, in 21 to 27 rows; anal plate divided.

Similar species. Some specimens of *Lampropeltis calligaster* superficially resemble the corn snake, *Elaphe guttata,* but the latter has a more prominent head, very weakly keeled dorsal scales, and a divided anal plate.

Distribution. Statewide except for the Marsh, the Mississippi alluvial plain, and, apparently, the western half of the Florida Parishes (Map 96).

Taxonomic comments. Two subspecies of *L. calligaster* occur in Louisiana: *L. c. calligaster,* the prairie kingsnake, characterized by 25 to 27 dorsal scale rows and lateral blotches only slightly wider than long, and *L. c. rhombomaculata* (Holbrook), the mole kingsnake, characterized by 21 to 23 dorsal scale rows and lateral blotches much wider than long. The former occurs west of the Mississippi alluvial plain, the latter in the Florida Parishes. The most recent published taxonomic study is that by Blanchard (1921).

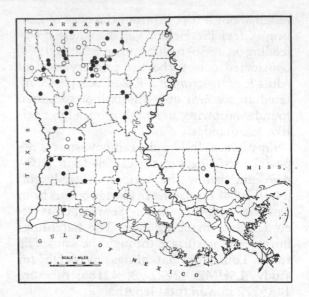

Map 96. Distribution of *Lampropeltis calligaster.* Solid circles represent specimens examined; hollow circles represent museum specimens not examined or literature records.

Habitat and habits. Both Fitch (1949) and Walker (1963) reported finding the prairie kingsnake in mixed pine-hardwood forest areas. A few specimens have been collected in the Prairie region of the state. Considering the relative abundance of the species in north-central Louisiana in recent years, we are surprised that R. F. Clark (1949) encountered only a single specimen during his extensive field work in that region during the mid-1920s.

No data are available on the feeding habits of Louisiana specimens of *L. calligaster.* Elsewhere the species is said to feed on small rodents, snakes, lizards, and young birds.

Reproduction. No data are available on reproductive activity in Louisiana. F. A. Cook (1954) reported a clutch of four eggs in a female *L. c. rhombomaculata* from southern Mississippi. Elsewhere clutches ranging from 5 to 17 eggs have been deposited from 19 June to 22 July and hatched during August or early September (Fitch 1970, 1985).

Lampropeltis getulus (Linnaeus)
Common Kingsnake
Plate XIX

Recognition. A long (to 82 in.; 2,083 mm), shiny, black snake with a pattern of small, light-colored spots (usually one per scale), some dorsal spots fused to form narrow crossbands in all juveniles and in some adults; belly usually light with black markings; dorsal scales smooth, in 21 to 23 rows; anal plate undivided.

Distribution. Statewide (Map 97).

Taxonomic comments. A single subspecies, *Lampropeltis getulus holbrooki* Stejneger, the speckled kingsnake, occurs in Louisiana. Crossbands are present in adults much less frequently in western Louisiana than in other parts of the state. Specimens from the Marsh in southwestern Louisiana often are spotted with bright orange pigment rather than with the somewhat paler colors in evidence elsewhere. The most recent taxonomic study is by Blaney (1977).

Habitat and habits. The speckled kingsnake occurs throughout Louisiana in all types of habitat, although it is probably most abundant in moist situations. Ridges or levees that border or extend into marshes or swamps seem to support substantial populations. Usually considered to be a terrestrial snake, *L. getulus* has been observed swimming across a canal deep in the marsh (Arny 1948), and its eggs have been found in a muskrat house (Penn 1943). Kingsnakes will actively prowl about during daylight hours, but are just as likely to be found under logs, boards, or other debris. One 4-ft (1,219-mm) specimen collected in West Feliciana Parish on 17 April 1971 was inside a partially buried, hollow log on the bank of a dry creek bed.

Kingsnakes do kill (by constriction) and eat poisonous snakes, but their reputation for doing so is rather exaggerated. In northern Louisiana, R. F. Clark (1949) found their most

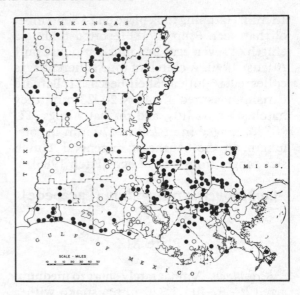

Map 97. Distribution of *Lampropeltis getulus.* Solid circles represent specimens examined; hollow circles represent museum specimens not examined or literature records.

common prey to be mice, followed in decreasing frequency of occurrence in stomach contents by rats, *Nerodia fasciata, N. rhombifera, Masticophis flagellum, Heterodon platyrhinos, Agkistrodon contortrix,* birds, unidentified snakes, *Agkistrodon piscivorus, Opheodrys aestivus, Thamnophis sirtalis, Crotalus horridus,* and *Micrurus fulvius.*

Percy Viosca (notes) observed a kingsnake eating a *Virginia valeriae* near Covington, St. Tammany Parish, on 7 April 1918. Arny (1948) found turtle eggs (*Kinosternon* and *Pseudemys*) in the stomachs of snakes from the Delta National Wildlife Refuge in Plaquemines Parish, and Tinkle (1959) reported the eggs of *Trachemys scripta* and of the lizards *Anolis carolinensis* and *Scincella lateralis* in the diet of St. Charles Parish kingsnakes.

Reproduction. Meade (1932) described copulation between a pair of captive Louisiana kingsnakes in May 1931. The female deposited nine eggs on 17 July, which averaged 32 ×

13 mm. Hatching took place on 24 September of that year. Penn (1943) reported finding a clutch of seven eggs in a muskrat house on 1 August 1940. A clutch of nine adherent eggs collected 16 July at Shell Beach, St. Bernard Parish, measured 37–42 × 20–23 mm; they hatched on 31 July, and the hatchlings (TU 10743) ranged from 250 to 270 mm in total length. In the Southeast in general, clutch size ranges from 5 to 17 eggs (Fitch 1985).

Lampropeltis triangulum (Lacépède)
Milk Snake
Plate XIX

Recognition. A moderately short to medium-sized (to 52 in.; 1,320 mm*) snake with a series of black-bordered red bands or rings on a yellow or white background; the belly patterned as the dorsum, or the rings incomplete midventrally; dorsal scales smooth, in 19 to 21 rows; anal plate undivided.

Similar species. The scarlet snake (*Cemophora coccinea*) and coral snake (*Micrurus fulvius*) each have a dorsal pattern somewhat similar to that of *Lampropeltis triangulum*, but the scarlet snake has an unpatterned belly, and the coral snake's red and yellow rings are in contact.

Distribution. Statewide, but apparently rare or absent from the Prairie, much of the Marsh, and much of the western Louisiana hill country (Map 98).

Taxonomic comments. Two subspecies of *L. triangulum* occur in Louisiana: *L. t. amaura* Cope, the Louisiana milk snake, characterized by a predominantly black snout, usually 21 dorsal scale rows, and usually two anterior temporals on either side of the head; and *L. t. elapsoides* (Holbrook), the scarlet kingsnake, characterized by a red snout, 19

*In the southeastern part of the U.S., *Lampropeltis triangulum* does not attain as large a size as it does in some other areas. Conant (1975) reported the record length for *L. t. amaura* to be 31 in. (787 mm) and for *L. t. elapsoides* to be 27 in. (686 mm).

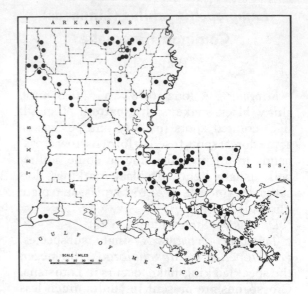

Map 98. Distribution of *Lampropeltis triangulum*. Solid circles represent specimens examined; hollow circles represent museum specimens not examined or literature records.

dorsal scale rows, and usually one anterior temporal. The former occurs west of the Mississippi alluvial plain, the latter in the northern part of the Florida Parishes. According to the most recent taxonomic study of this species (Williams 1978), the snakes occupying the alluvial plain from the Arkansas border to the mouth of the Mississippi are intergrades between *L. t. amaura* and *L. t. syspila* (Cope), the red milk snake, which is the race of *L. triangulum* present through most of Arkansas. Snakes from the eastern border of the alluvial plain and the southern portion of the Florida Parishes are said to be intergrades between *L. t. amaura*, *L. t. syspila*, and *L. t. elapsoides*. The influence of *L. t. syspila* is seen primarily in the ventral and subcaudal counts of the alluvial plain specimens, which are higher than those of either Louisiana *L. t. amaura* or *L. t. elapsoides*, but agree with (subcaudals), or are less than (ventrals), those of typical *L. t. syspila*.

Habitat and habits. Williams (1978) stated that in Louisiana, *L. t. elapsoides* occurs almost exclusively in pine woods, a conclusion with which we concur. Meade (1945) reported that a juvenile scarlet kingsnake was plowed up in a field near Baton Rouge on Christmas Eve, 1941. On 1 August 1968 another East Baton Rouge Parish specimen was discovered more than 4 ft (1.25 m) above the ground on the brick wall of a house south of Deerford. In contrast to *L. t. elapsoides*, *L. t. amaura* and the Mississippi alluvial plain milk snake population are primarily inhabitants of bottomland hardwood forest, where during the winter and early spring, they are often found some distance (at least as much as 8 ft or 2.4 m) above the ground beneath the bark of dead trees or in the heart of rotten ones. More often than not, these dead trees are standing in several feet of water; milk snakes have been collected rather frequently under such conditions along the eastern margin of the Atchafalaya Basin in Iberville Parish and near the Bonnet Carre Spillway in St. Charles Parish. On 19 June 1977 a partially melanistic adult *L. t. amaura* was discovered swimming in Lake Maurepas about 2 or 3 miles offshore. A juvenile was found under a log in Iberville Parish on 30 March 1971, and 10 days later an adult was collected beneath a brick pile in shaded woods near Coushatta, Red River Parish. Strecker and Frierson (1926) found one specimen in the crevice of a log and a number of others in cotton fields bordering a bayou in the northwestern corner of the state. R. F. Clark (1949) noted that a north-central Louisiana milk snake was plowed up near an old stump.

No data are available on the food of *Lampropeltis triangulum* in Louisiana, but Dundee found that captive specimens from southern Louisiana would eat anoles, whereas those from the northern part of the state would take only baby mice. Elsewhere the diet consists primarily of lizards and small snakes, although young mice, earthworms, and some insects are also reputed to be eaten.

Reproduction. No information is available on the reproductive habits of the species in Louisiana. Elsewhere clutch size ranges from three to nine eggs in the subspecies found in Louisiana (Fitch 1985). Eggs are deposited from early June to early July, and hatching occurs from early August to early September (Williams 1978). W. M. Palmer (1961) reported that three hatchling *L. t. elapsoides* from North Carolina measured 146–159 mm in total length nine days after hatching.

Masticophis flagellum (Shaw) Coachwhip

Plate XVIII

Recognition. A very long (to 102 in.; 2,591 mm) snake with the head and anterior one-third to three-quarters of the body dark brown to black, the posterior part tan to reddish brown (the juvenile pattern of banding lost with increase in size); venter dark brown anteriorly, grading to cream posteriorly; dorsal scales smooth, in 17 rows (reducing to 13 just in front of the vent); anal plate divided.

Distribution. Largely confined to the Shortleaf Pine-Oak-Hickory Forest and Longleaf Pine Forest in the Florida Parishes and western Louisiana (Map 99). Wilson (1970b) stated that a few coachwhips have been collected in the Prairie in southwestern Louisiana, but the specific localities appear to be in the Flatwoods.

Taxonomic comments. Only the nominate subspecies, *Masticophis f. flagellum*, the eastern coachwhip, occurs in Louisiana. The most recent taxonomic study is that by Wilson (1970b).

Habitat and habits. Fitch (1949) found the coachwhip to be one of the more frequently encountered snake species on the roads in western Louisiana, occurring in all habitats but particularly in dry uplands, often near cultivated areas. R. F. Clark (1949) also mentioned the coachwhip's affinity for cultivated fields and pastures in north-central Louisiana. He stressed that in these circum-

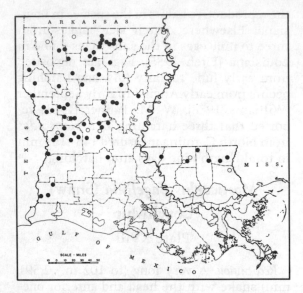

Map 99. Distribution of *Masticophis flagellum.* Solid circles represent specimens examined; hollow circles represent museum specimens not examined or literature records.

stances there was always a nearby briar patch or underbrush into which the snake would flee when pursued. On one occasion he discovered a 5-ft (1.5-m) specimen resting in the branches at the top of an oak tree 20 ft (6 m) above the ground. In contrast to the experience of Fitch and Clark, Strecker and Frierson (1926) found *M. flagellum* to be rare in Caddo and De Soto parishes. One specimen was collected at the edge of the woods near Wallace Bayou and another was dug from a hole in the bank of the bayou. On 16 October 1971 a large adult was observed sunning itself along a jeep trail in the Sicily Island Hills (Catahoula Parish); the snake escaped into a hole in a gully that led from the trail into dense hardwood forest.

R. F. Clark (1949) found unidentified birds in 12 coachwhip stomachs he examined, unidentified mice in 18 others. He also reported that two hatchling coachwhips were eaten by a larger individual of the same species. Elsewhere *M. flagellum* has also been recorded as

feeding on lizards and insects, particularly grasshoppers and cicadas.

Reproduction. R. F. Clark (1949) found a clutch of 15 coachwhip eggs on 7 June 1926 along a rail fence separating a cultivated field from a pasture; two of them hatched on 14 June. On 4 August 1926 Clark removed 14 eggs from the body of an adult female.

Nerodia clarkii Baird & Girard
Salt Marsh Snake
Plate XX

Recognition. A medium-sized (to 36 in.; 914 mm), moderately heavy-bodied snake with five light stripes on a dark background; belly light with two rows of large dark spots; dorsal scales keeled, in 21 rows; anal plate divided.

Similar species. Garter snakes and ribbon snakes (genus *Thamnophis*) resemble the salt marsh snake somewhat, but have only three light stripes on a dark background and no large spots on the belly.

Distribution. Confined to the Marsh (Map 100).

Taxonomic comments. Only the nominate subspecies, *Nerodia c. clarkii*, the Gulf salt marsh snake, occurs in Louisiana. Long considered to be only a distinctive race of *N. fasciata*, the salt marsh snake recently has been shown to have such limited genetic exchange with its freshwater relative as to justify considering it a separate species (Lawson 1985). Some hybridization does occur, particularly where human beings or hurricanes have disturbed the habitat. Not all instances where the striped pattern is partially broken up into bands necessarily reflect hybridization, however, inasmuch as the southern Florida race, *N. clarkii compressicauda*, is normally banded throughout. Occasionally the appearance of bands in *N. c. clarkii* may simply be a partial expression of the ancestral color pattern.

240

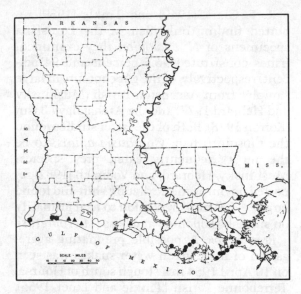

Map 100. Distribution of *Nerodia clarkii*. The circles represent *clarkii*; the triangles represent *clarkii × fasciata* hybrids; the hexagons represent localities where both *clarkii* and hybrids have been collected.

Habitat and habits. As its name implies, the salt marsh snake is adapted for living in salt water—a rather harsh habitat not fully utilized by any other Louisiana snake. *Nerodia clarkii* can survive in this environment partly because it obtains metabolic water from the food it eats; the snake does not drink salt water (Pettus 1958).

Because of the general inaccessibility of the preferred habitat of this species, we have relatively little information on the behavior or diet of *N. clarkii* in Louisiana. On 18 January 1985, Philip M. Hall excavated an inactive juvenile from a muskrat lodge in brackish water marsh in Iberia Parish. During the warmer months of the year, the species seems to be most active at dusk or after dark. Mount (1975) reported the diet of Alabama salt marsh snakes to consist of small fish and, occasionally, crabs.

Reproduction. No data are available for Louisiana specimens. Elsewhere brood sizes ranging from 2 to 44 have been recorded (Mount 1975).

Nerodia cyclopion (Duméril, Bibron, & Duméril)
Western Green Water Snake
Plate XX

Recognition. A moderately long (to 50 in.; 1,270 mm), heavy-bodied, olive brown snake with an indistinct pattern of narrow dark crossbars, the ones on the back alternating with those on the sides; belly dark brown marked with light spots or crescents; dorsal scales keeled, in 23 to 27 rows; subocular scales present; anal plate divided.

Distribution. Statewide, but apparently absent from the upper three-quarters of the Florida Parishes and from the hill country of western Louisiana, except near large lakes and in the floodplains of major streams (Map 101).

Taxonomic comments. No subspecies of *Nerodia cyclopion* are currently recognized. The most recent taxonomic study is an unpublished thesis by Sanderson (1983), who recognized the western (*N. cyclopion*) and the Florida (*N. floridana*) green water snakes as separate species. His conclusions were based on morphological data and supported by Lawson's (1985) biochemical studies.

Habitat and habits. One of the most aquatic of the North American *Nerodia*, the green water snake is seldom, if ever, found away from the immediate vicinity of water (specimens encountered on roads are generally moving from one body of water to another). It prefers still or very slow-moving water; specimens have been collected or observed in lakes, ponds, canals, ditches, bayous, rivers, swamps, marshes, rice fields, and even in flooded woods. The green water snake may be extremely abundant under favorable conditions. Field crews have found them in large

241

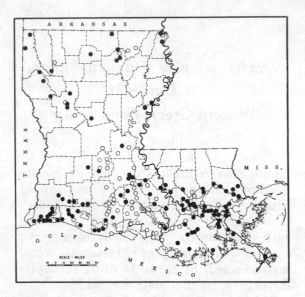

Map 101. Distribution of *Nerodia cyclopion*. Solid circles represent specimens examined; hollow circles represent museum specimens not examined or literature records.

numbers on roads through the marshes in Cameron and Vermilion parishes, particularly during or after a rain. Percy Viosca (notes) observed more than 80 individuals basking in the sun along the London Avenue canal in the Gentilly section of New Orleans between 6:30 and 9:30 A.M. on 7 April 1915, and on 18 June 1922 he collected 119 specimens on Delacroix Island in St. Bernard Parish. *Nerodia cyclopion* was found to be the second most abundant water snake in the Atchafalaya Basin (Kofron 1978) and at an Ascension Parish site (Mushinsky, Hebrard, and Walley 1980).

Mushinsky, Hebrard, and Walley (1980) found *N. cyclopion* to be the only water snake in Ascension Parish that was active year-round, although it reached a peak abundance in June and July. They found it to be primarily a diurnal basking snake from November through March and predominantly nocturnal and aquatic during the warmer months of the year.

R. F. Clark (1949) and Tinkle (1959) reported finding only fish in the Louisiana specimens of *N. cyclopion* they examined; fishes constituted 96.5 percent and 94 percent, respectively, of the gut contents in large samples from Ascension Parish (Mushinsky and Hebrard 1977) and the Atchafalaya Basin (Kofron 1978). Both of the latter studies found the mosquito fish, *Gambusia affinis*, to be the most frequently eaten prey species; Mushinsky, Hebrard, and Vodipich (1982) reported on ontogenetic dietary shift and found large (> 700 mm) *cyclopion* to feed primarily on sunfish (*Lepomis*) and bass (*Micropterus*).

Reproduction. A possible pre-mating aggregation of male green water snakes was seen on 10 April 1954 in a slough south of Houma, Terrebonne Parish (Tinkle and Liner 1955), and Meade (1934) observed that *N. cyclopion* held in an outdoor cage mated during the first three weeks of April—one of his snakes gave birth to seven young on 11 August. Kofron (1979a) found that females of this species in the Atchafalaya Basin ovulate from late April through June and give birth to an average of 18.4 young from late July through September. Data on eight broods in the Tulane collection reveal a brood size of 11 to 34 (average, 17); the broods were born from 14 July to 4 August. In three broods the newborn young ranged from 250 to 305 mm in total length; one brood (TU 10730) ranged from 187 to 264 mm.

Nerodia erythrogaster (Forster)
Plain-bellied Water Snake
Plate XX

Recognition. A moderately long (to 62 in.; 1,575 mm), relatively heavy-bodied snake with a pattern of alternating dorsal and lateral dark blotches readily visible, partially obscured, or totally lacking on a gray or dark brown background (the pattern always visible in juveniles); belly some shade of yellow with relatively few dark markings; dorsal scales keeled, in 23 to 27 rows; anal plate usually divided.

Similar species. Juvenile *Nerodia erythrogaster* are sometimes confused with young *N. sipedon,* but the latter have prominent red or black crescents on the belly, and the anterior dorsal blotches are fused with the lateral ones to form crossbands.

Distribution. Statewide, but apparently rare or absent from much of the Marsh (Map 102).

Taxonomic comments. Two subspecies of *N. erythrogaster* occur in Louisiana: *N. e. flavigaster* (Conant), the yellow-bellied water snake, characterized by its adult dorsal pattern, which is visible only as narrow middorsal bars if visible at all, and *N. e. transversa* (Hallowell), the blotched water snake, which is characterized by retention in the adults of the blotched pattern found in all juveniles. *Nerodia e. flavigaster* occurs throughout most of Louisiana; *N. e. transversa* occurs only in the Prairie. Specimens clearly referable to *N. e. transversa* have been taken as far east as 8 miles northeast of Abbeville, Vermilion Parish. Intergradation is extensive, and there is some indication that the Louisiana population of *N. e. transversa* is being swamped genetically by *N. e. flavigaster.* Certain specimens from Calcasieu Parish in the McNeese State University collection can be assigned to *N. e. transversa,* whereas others appear to be intergrades or perhaps even *N. e. flavigaster.* Conant (1949) reviewed the taxonomy of the species, but a thorough revisionary study is still needed.

Habitat and habits. Nerodia erythrogaster is as apt to be found in the ponds, sloughs, bayous, streams, rivers, lakes, and swamps in the hill country of Louisiana as in the drainage ditches and flooded rice fields of the lowlands. It is more likely to wander some distance from water than the other species of *Nerodia.* Mushinsky, Hebrard, and Walley (1980) found this species to be primarily nocturnal, especially during the summer

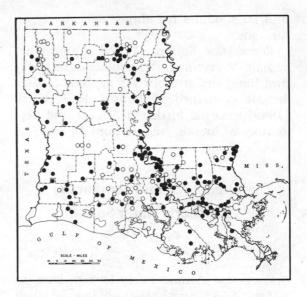

Map 102. Distribution of *Nerodia erythrogaster.* Solid circles represent specimens examined; hollow circles represent museum specimens not examined or literature records.

months, and to bask very rarely. The same authors designated May through July as the period of peak abundance in Ascension Parish. Kofron (1978) and Mushinsky, Hebrard, and Walley (1980) found *N. erythrogaster* to be by far the least abundant species of water snake in the Atchafalaya Basin and Ascension Parish, respectively.

Liner (1954) observed yellow-bellied water snakes feeding on small fish (*Gambusia affinis* and *Mollienesia latipinna*) in a drying borrow pit near Houma, Terrebonne Parish. In northern Louisiana, R. F. Clark (1949) found fish to be the most prevalent item in the diet, followed by crawfish and leopard frogs; in his Atchafalaya Basin sample, Kofron (1978) found only anuran remains in the five guts containing food. Mushinsky and Lotz (1980) reported an ontogenetic change in food preferences of the *N. erythrogaster* they studied in Ascension Parish: the young snakes showed a marked preference for fish, and large adults fed almost exclusively on anurans.

Reproduction. Kofron (1979a) found that female *N. erythrogaster* ovulate during May and June, and give birth in September. One female contained 22 fetuses. R. F. Clark (1949) reported births in August and September of broods ranging from 14 to 27 in number.

Nerodia fasciata (Linnaeus)
Southern Water Snake
Plate XX

Recognition. A moderately long to long (to 62½ in.; 1,588 mm*), relatively heavy-bodied snake with broad dark bands on a tan or yellow background (the dorsum almost black in some individuals and rather light in others); belly light with large squarish dark blotches; dorsal scales keeled, in 21 to 25 rows; anal plate divided.

Similar species. In its "light phase," *Nerodia fasciata* may be confused with *N. sipedon* (and perhaps some limited hybridization does occur), but *N. fasciata* has squarish blotches, rather than crescentic spots, on the belly; a pattern of crossbands throughout the length of the dorsum rather than alternating dorsal and lateral blotches posteriorly; and a dark band running from the eye to the angle of the jaw (no such band in *sipedon*).

Distribution. Statewide, except for high-salinity parts of the Marsh (Map 103).

Taxonomic comments. Only the western subspecies, *N. f. confluens* (Blanchard), the broad-banded water snake, occurs in Louisiana. The most recent review of the taxonomic problems in this species is that by

*Conant (1975) indicated that the maximum length for *Nerodia f. confluens* is 45 in. (1,143 mm), but R. F. Clark (1949) gave 60 in. as the maximum for his northern Louisiana specimens. Clark's material is no longer extant, so his record cannot be confirmed.

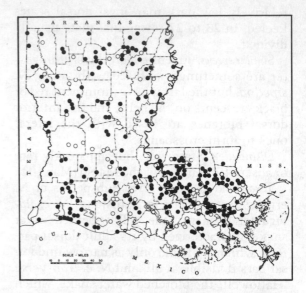

Map 103. Distribution of *Nerodia fasciata*. Solid circles represent specimens examined; hollow circles represent museum specimens not examined or literature records.

Conant (1963), but a thorough revisionary study is urgently needed. See the *N. sipedon* account for a brief discussion of the controversy surrounding its relationship to *N. fasciata.*

The relatively narrow bands (which frequently are brown rather than black) of some *N. f. confluens* make the whole animal appear to be rather light in coloration. Such individuals may turn up anywhere in the state, but the highest incidence appears to be in the western part of the Florida Parishes (although similar specimens may have been what R. F. Clark [1949] was calling *N. f. fasciata*). These snakes probably merely represent the "light phase" of *confluens* (both of the eastern races, *N. f. fasciata* and *N. f. pictiventris* [Cope]), have such a phase). Of course, some influence from *N. f. fasciata* is perhaps being expressed in the Florida Parishes (as Blaney and Blaney [1979] asserted), although if that were the case one would expect to find intergrades in St. Tammany and Washington parishes rather than farther west. We have not seen any Louisiana snakes we would identify as *N. f. fasciata* × *confluens* intergrades.

Habitat and habits. Nerodia fasciata occurs in all aquatic situations, except salt marsh, where it is replaced by *N. clarkii*. Mushinsky, Hebrard, and Walley (1980) found that *N. fasciata* basked more frequently than the other water snakes, that it did not become predominantly nocturnal until June, and that its abundance was relatively uniform from April through July. Kofron (1978) and Mushinsky, Hebrard, and Walley (1980) found *N. fasciata* to be the third most abundant species of water snake in the Atchafalaya Basin and Ascension Parish, respectively.

This snake feeds on a variety of fishes (especially *Gambusia affinis* and *Heterandria formosa*) and anurans (including *Rana sphenocephala, R. clamitans, R. catesbeiana, Pseudacris triseriata, Hyla cinerea*, and *Bufo* species). Mushinsky, Hebrard, and Vodipich (1982) found that anurans form an important part of the diet only in large (> 500 mm) individuals. In addition to fishes and frogs, R. F. Clark (1949) reported finding squirrels in 10 and birds in 7 of the 350 guts examined from northern Louisiana, but such food items must be considered extremely unusual in the diet of *N. fasciata* if, indeed, Clark's records were not in error.

Reproduction. Meade (1934) observed that *N. fasciata* held in an outdoor cage mated during the first three weeks in April. Kofron (1979a) found females of this species to ovulate from early May to mid-June and to give birth from July to September. Six broods from southern Louisiana in the Tulane collection were born from 25 July to 15 August, the 7 to 19 newborn young ranged from 198 to 252 mm in total length. R. F. Clark (1949) reported on 10 broods from northern Louisiana (12 to 39 young), and Tinkle (1959) found the number to vary from 10 to 27 in 11 sets of follicles and embryos from St. Charles Parish.

Nerodia rhombifera (Hallowell)
Diamond-backed Water Snake
Plate XX

Recognition. A long (to 63 in.; 1,600 mm), heavy-bodied, tan to gray-brown snake with a pattern of dark brown to black chainlike markings; belly yellow (but occasionally dusky brown), marked with small, dark crescents; dorsal scales keeled, usually in 25 to 27 rows; no subocular scales; anal plate divided.

Distribution. Statewide, but apparently absent from the Marsh except at a few localities in Cameron Parish (Map 104).

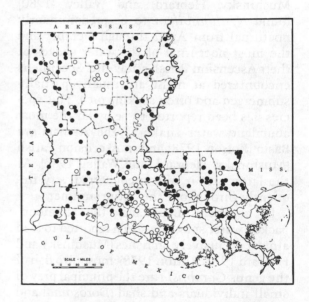

Map 104. Distribution of *Nerodia rhombifera*. Solid circles represent specimens examined; hollow circles represent museum specimens not examined or literature records.

Taxonomic comments. Only the nominate subspecies, *Nerodia r. rhombifera*, occurs in Louisiana. The most recent taxonomic study (Conant 1969) deals almost exclusively with the Mexican populations. Very dark specimens with dusky venters have been confused with *N. taxispilota* (Holbrook) by Wright and Wright (1957) and others. That species occurs east of Mobile Bay, Alabama.

Habitat and habits. Like its relative, the green water snake, *N. rhombifera* primarily inhabits still or slow-moving waters, where individuals may often be seen during the day basking in the overhanging branches of small trees, from which they drop into the water if disturbed. The species also occurs, however, in such fast-moving rivers as the Amite, Tangipahoa, Bogue Chitto, and Pearl. In northern Louisiana, R. F. Clark (1949) found diamond-backed water snakes most frequently in drift-wood and logjams, slightly less frequently in ponds, and about half as often in sloughs. Mushinsky, Hebrard, and Walley (1980) found *N. rhombifera* to be predominantly nocturnal from April through October and the most nocturnal of the water snakes at their Ascension Parish study site. Specimens encountered at night are usually partially submerged and often seeking prey. This species has been reported to be by far the most abundant water snake in the Atchafalaya Basin (Kofron 1978) and in Ascension Parish (Mushinsky, Hebrard, and Walley 1980). At the latter site it was encountered very frequently throughout the entire summer.

In southern Louisiana, the diamond-backed water snake has been reported to feed almost exclusively on fishes (Mushinsky and Hebrard 1977; Kofron 1978); mosquito fish of the genus *Gambusia* are the principal prey of small individuals and shad (*Dorosoma*) and catfish (*Ictalurus*) the principal prey of large (> 800 mm) adults (Mushinsky, Hebrard, and Vodipich 1982). In northern Louisiana, R. F. Clark (1949) examined the gut contents of 250 specimens and found that 97 contained fishes, 85 contained leopard frogs (*Rana sphenocephala*), 57 contained bronze frogs (*R. clamitans*), and 11 contained birds. Clark did not, unfortunately, determine the type of bird involved, so we cannot speculate how

such a peculiar prey for a water snake would have been included in the diet.

Reproduction. Meade (1934) observed that *N. rhombifera* held in an outdoor cage mated during the first three weeks of April. Kofron (1979a) found females of this species to ovulate from early May to late July and to give birth from early August to late October. R. F. Clark (1949) reported broods of 11 to 30 from northern Louisiana. A female 1,200 mm long (TU 6321) from Cameron Parish gave birth to 18 young on 6 September 1947; the newborn young were 276–315 mm in total length.

Nerodia sipedon (Linnaeus)
Northern Water Snake
Plate XX

Recognition. A moderately long (to 53 in.; 1,346 mm), tan to gray-brown snake with red to black crossbands on the neck and alternating dorsal and lateral blotches thereafter (rarely banded throughout); belly white or cream with two irregular rows of red or black crescents; no dark stripe from the eye to the angle of the jaw; dorsal scales keeled, in 21 to 23 rows; anal plate divided.

Distribution. Confined to the Florida Parishes (Map 105).

Taxonomic comments. Only the southern subspecies, *Nerodia sipedon pleuralis* (Cope), the midland water snake, occurs in Louisiana. The most recent variational study is an unpublished doctoral dissertation by Morris (1987).

Conant (1963) considered *N. sipedon* and *N. fasciata* to be separate species, but Blaney and Blaney (1979) presented data that they interpreted to demonstrate that intergradation occurs between *N. sipedon* and *N. fasciata* in southern Mississippi and the Florida Parishes, thus refuting Conant's conclusions. A subsequent analysis of alleged intergrade populations in the Bogue Chitto River and

Map 105. Distribution of *Nerodia sipedon.* Solid circles represent specimens examined; hollow circles represent museum specimens not examined or literature records.

sympatric populations in the Tchefuncte River revealed no biochemically intermediate individuals (Schwaner, Dessauer, and Landry 1980). Furthermore, Rossman has examined the external diagnostic features of the same Bogue Chitto specimens that Blaney and Blaney concluded were intergrades and decided that only two specimens out of a series of 49 cannot readily be identified as either *N. sipedon* or *N. fasciata.* He concurs with Schwaner, Dessauer, and Landry (1980) that the two forms generally maintain their species integrity in Louisiana, but that they do occasionally hybridize.

Habitat and habits. All Louisiana specimens of *N. sipedon* have been collected in or near clear, cool, sand-and-gravel-bottomed streams. Although midland water snakes are occasionally encountered during daylight hours, they are far more abundant at night, when they are often found prowling about in the shallow water near sandbars searching for

food. No reports have been published concerning the feeding habits of *N. sipedon* in Louisiana. Mount (1975) reported that in Alabama the midland water snake feeds on fishes, frogs, tadpoles, and salamanders.

Reproduction. No data are available on the reproductive habits of *N. sipedon* in Louisiana. In Alabama, females bear 12 to 30 young from July to early September (Mount 1975). The young in three broods from Alabama and Mississippi (Tulane collection) range from 182 to 246 mm in total length.

Opheodrys aestivus (Linnaeus)
Rough Green Snake
Plate XVIII

Recognition. A medium-sized (to 45⅝ in.; 1,159 mm), extremely slender, green (usually appearing blue in preservative) snake; belly white or yellow; dorsal scales keeled, in 17 rows; anal plate divided.

Distribution. Statewide (Map 106).

Taxonomic comments. Only the nominate subspecies, *Opheodrys a. aestivus,* occurs in Louisiana. The most recent taxonomic study is that by Grobman (1984).

Habitat and habits. The rough green snake is an excellent climber and is usually found in vines, bushes, or small trees, frequently near streams or lakes. Tinkle (1959) collected a specimen from the upper fronds of a cattail in shallow water at the Sarpy Wildlife Refuge (St. Charles Parish) on 30 October 1954. A young-of-the-year that Rossman observed on 6 November 1971 in the Tunica Hills (West Feliciana Parish) was crawling on dead leaves along a trail in dense upland hardwood forest. When disturbed it escaped by crawling under the leaves. Nearly invisible when entwined in vines, green snakes are often overlooked when they are lying motionless, even against a contrasting background. Such was the case

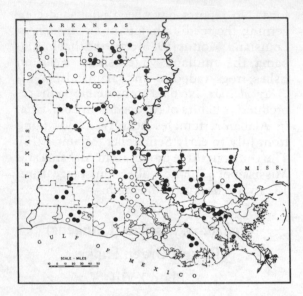

Map 106. Distribution of *Opheodrys aestivus.* Solid circles represent specimens examined; hollow circles represent museum specimens not examined or literature records.

with an adult discovered on a stretch of dry, sandy creek bottom in the Tunica Hills on 29 March 1972. Two of the three members of the party walked past the snake without seeing it. Gerhard Kuehnhanss reported finding five specimens under boards along Little Chenier (Cameron Parish) on 28 February 1971; none were encountered in the open that day.

R. F. Clark (1949) reported finding grasshoppers, katydids, and crickets in the stomachs of green snakes from northern Louisiana, although captive specimens would accept only grasshoppers. Late one summer Abe Oliver (pers. com.) came upon an *Opheodrys aestivus* in a persimmon tree with a praying mantis in its mouth; the mantis, in turn, was grasping a fall webworm.

Reproduction. A specimen collected 3 May 1968 in Greenwood Park (East Baton Rouge Parish) deposited five eggs on 13 June. The dimensions of the eggs were 8–9 × 22–26 mm. One of the five eggs R. F. Clark (1949) dis-

covered on 25 July 1926 in a mossy depression along the side of a decaying log in northern Louisiana hatched four days later. The hatchling measured 114 mm.

Pituophis melanoleucus (Daudin)
Pine Snake
Plate XVI

Recognition. A very long (to 108 in.; 2,743 mm*), moderately heavy-bodied snake with a series of large, dark brown blotches on a white or yellowish tan background, or the pattern almost completely obscured by black pigment; rostral scale enlarged; dorsal scales keeled, in 27 to 33 rows; anal plate undivided.

Distribution. Confined to the Longleaf Pine Forests in west-central Louisiana and to the northeastern corner of the Florida Parishes (Map 107).

Taxonomic comments. Two subspecies of the pine snake occur in Louisiana: *Pituophis melanoleucus ruthveni* Stull, the Louisiana pine snake, characterized by its distinct pattern, and *P. m. lodingi* Blanchard, the black pine snake, characterized by its predominantly black coloration. The former occurs in west-central Louisiana, the latter in Washington Parish. The two reported Louisiana specimens of *P. m. lodingi* were thought to show some influence from *P. m. ruthveni* (Conant 1956; Crain and Cliburn 1971); if so, it reflects intergradation during a time long past because the ranges are now separated by considerable distance and unsuitable habitat, as was previously pointed out by Fugler (1955). The most recent taxonomic study of these two subspecies is by Conant (1956).

Habitat and habits. The pine snake is rarely encountered in Louisiana; most specimens

---

*The pine snakes occurring in this part of the country apparently do not reach as great a length as their relatives in adjoining areas. Conant (1975) reported the record for *Pituophis melanoleucus lodingi* to be 74 in. (1,880 mm) and *P. m. ruthveni* to be 70¼ in. (1,784 mm).

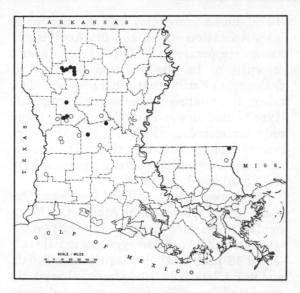

Map 107. Distribution of *Pituophis mela-noleucus*. Solid circles represent specimens examined; hollow circles represent museum specimens not examined or literature records.

have been associated with sandy soil and second-growth longleaf pine forest. Some specimens of *P. m. ruthveni* have been found adjacent to areas of longleaf pine in blackjack oak woodlands (Walker 1965). A number of *P. m. ruthveni* were either lying near or emerging from pocket gopher burrows (Conant 1956); presumably *P. m. lodingi* utilizes gopher tortoise (*Gopherus*) and armadillo (*Dasypus*) burrows (Jennings and Fritts 1983). Pine snakes often hiss quite loudly when threatened or restrained.

There are no records of the food of the pine snake in Louisiana. Elsewhere the species is known to feed on rodents, rabbits, and birds and their eggs.

Reproduction. No data are available on reproductive activity in Louisiana. F. A. Cook (1954), in her study on the snakes of Mississippi, said that female pine snakes lay from one to two dozen eggs. Fitch (1985) recorded clutch sizes ranging from 6 to 13 eggs in the eastern United States.

Regina grahamii Baird & Girard
Graham's Crayfish Snake
Plate XXI

Recognition. A medium-sized to moderately long (to 47 in.; 1,194 mm), small-headed brown snake with a dark-bordered cream or light gray stripe on the three lower dorsal scale rows (occasionally a pale, dark-bordered vertebral stripe); belly cream or yellow, either unmarked or with a medial row of dark spots, occasionally forming a stripe; dorsal scales keeled, in 19 to 21 rows (always 19 at midbody); anal plate divided.

Distribution. Statewide, but extremely rare or absent from the Longleaf Pine Forest, the Flatwoods, and the Blufflands (Map 108). The East Baton Rouge Parish record from the Amite River drainage at Indian Mound is represented by two specimens (TU 5505) Viosca collected, but no mention of them appears in his field notes. Because this locality is the only one in the Florida Parishes outside the Mississippi River alluvial plain, the occurrence of *Regina grahamii* there requires confirmation.

Taxonomic comments. No subspecies are recognized, and no taxonomic study of this species has been published.

Habitat and habits. Mushinsky, Hebrard, and Walley (1980) reported that in their Ascension Parish study area, *R. grahamii* was predominantly a diurnal basking snake in March at the peak of its abundance, was equally diurnal and nocturnal during April through May, and virtually disappeared during the rest of the year. Hebrard and Mushinsky (1978) suggested that this species may feed in crawfish burrows and thus be largely overlooked when not basking. Graham's crayfish snake is frequently encountered at night in borrow pits west of the Mississippi River levee at Baton Rouge and in similar circumstances in the Bonnet Carre Spillway southeast of La Place (St. Charles Parish). In

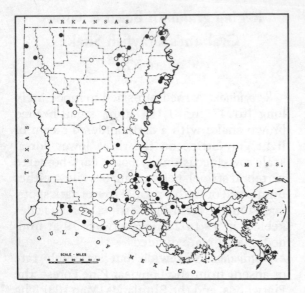

Map 108. Distribution of *Regina grahamii*. Solid circles represent specimens examined; hollow circles represent museum specimens not examined or literature records.

southwestern Louisiana, *R. grahamii* is often associated with flooded rice fields and ditches, and Liner (1954) reported collecting a specimen as it was feeding on trapped fish in a nearly dry pond in Lafayette Parish. In the northern part of the state, R. F. Clark (1949) found approximately one-fourth of his specimens during the day near or in small, swift spring runs. He collected most of those snakes at night in the masses of water weeds that he raked out of small ponds.

Regina grahamii, like the other species of *Regina*, is docile and rarely attempts to bite, in marked contrast to the behavior of the water snakes of the genus *Nerodia*, which frequently utilize the same habitat as the crayfish snakes.

The literature is contradictory regarding the food habits of this species. R. F. Clark (1949) found nothing but fish (the largest of which was a 152.4-mm catfish) in the guts he examined in northern Louisiana, whereas Mushinsky and Hebrard (1977) and Kofron

(1978) found only crawfish in specimens from Ascension Parish and the Atchafalaya Basin, respectively. Hall (1969) found crawfish to be the principal food of *R. grahamii* in Kansas, but other prey would be taken if crawfish were scarce. Burghardt (1968) found newly born *R. grahamii* to be more interested in crawfish than in any other type of food he offered to them. The snakes seem to prefer molting crawfish to those having a hard exoskeleton.

Reproduction. Kofron (1979a) found that females of this species in the Atchafalaya Basin ovulate from late April to late July. Arny (1948) found 23 ovarian eggs in a female collected 13 June 1947 in Plaquemines Parish, and R. F. Clark (1949) discovered nine poorly developed young in a female collected 5 July 1926 in north-central Louisiana. A female collected on the Tulane campus gave birth to six young in September (Beyer 1898). Elsewhere litters have ranged from 4 to 39 (Fitch 1985). Kennedy (1964) reported that newly born (10 August 1961) *R. grahamii* from Houston, Texas, averaged 197.6 mm in snout-vent length and 38.1 mm in tail length.

Regina rigida (Say)
Glossy Crayfish Snake
Plate XXI

Recognition. A moderately short to medium-sized (to 31⅜ in.; 797 mm), small-headed, shiny brown snake with a light stripe on the first dorsal scale row; belly light with two rows of black spots; dorsal scales keeled, in 19 rows; anal plate divided.

Distribution. Statewide, but extremely rare or absent from the eastern half of the Marsh and the hilly portions of the Florida Parishes (Map 109).

Taxonomic comments. Two weakly differentiated subspecies of *Regina rigida* occur in Louisiana: *R. r. sinicola* (Huheey), the Gulf

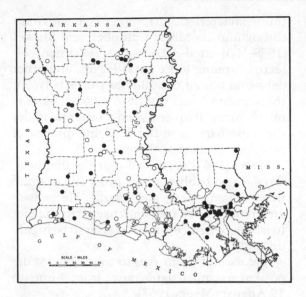

Map 109. Distribution of *Regina rigida*. Solid circles represent specimens examined; hollow circles represent museum specimens not examined or literature records.

crayfish snake, characterized by two preoculars on both sides of the head, and *R. r. deltae* (Huheey), the Delta crayfish snake, usually characterized by a single preocular on at least one side of the head. *Regina r. sinicola* has fewer ventrals and more subcaudals on the average than *R. r. deltae*, but there is considerable overlap in both features. *Regina r. sinicola* occurs across the south-central United States, *R. r. deltae* only in the southeastern quarter of Louisiana; intergradation occurs in the Pearl River valley and, presumably, the Atchafalaya Basin. The most recent taxonomic study is that by Huheey (1959). Several melanistic specimens have been collected in Orleans and St. Tammany parishes. At one site in eastern New Orleans, the entire population seems to be melanistic.

Habitat and habits. Regina rigida is a highly aquatic snake; with the exception of one specimen collected in an upland woods of sandjack oak (Fitch 1949), all glossy crayfish snakes for which habitat data are available were discovered either in water or immediately adjacent to it. The 18 specimens R. F. Clark (1949) collected in north-central Louisiana were all in small running streams, where most of them lay partially hidden under sunken logs or bark. In the same part of the state (Jackson Parish), Walker (1963) collected a single *R. rigida* under roots in a spillway. David Sever found a glossy crayfish snake under wet leaves along the edge of a pool left by a drying stream in a St. Tammany Parish pine forest. Tinkle (1959) reported finding two specimens on the Sarpy Wildlife Refuge (St. Charles Parish) during the course of his studies there; one was taken from a ditch beside a shell road, the other from beneath a board. In the early spring, young individuals are often found in moderate numbers under logs, boards, and other debris along the western levees of the Atchafalaya Basin in St. Martin Parish. Kofron (1978) also found a juvenile specimen amid water hyacinths.

R. F. Clark (1949) reported finding fish, leopard frogs, cricket frogs, and crawfish in the guts of the northern Louisiana specimens he examined. One of the St. Charles Parish snakes Tinkle (1959) collected regurgitated a crawfish; Huheey (1959) cited several reports of crawfish in the diet of *R. rigida* from North Carolina; and Rossman (1963a) suggested that the stout, chisel-like teeth of this species are adaptations for feeding on hardshelled crawfish. Rojas and Godley (1979) have shown that these teeth are actually hinged at the base and function as a ratchet mechanism to help draw the crawfish into the mouth.

Reproduction. Kofron (1979a) found that females of this species in the Atchafalaya Basin ovulate during May and June. Brood size ranges from 6 (TU 1256) to 14 (Huheey 1959). A brood of 11 from St. Charles Parish, born 31 July, range from 188 to 202 mm in total length. The smallest individuals Huheey (1959) examined measured 174 mm in total length.

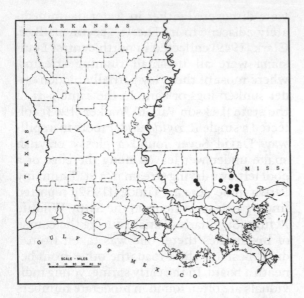

Map 110. Distribution of *Rhadinaea flavilata*. Solid circles represent specimens examined; hollow circles represent museum specimens not examined or literature records.

Rhadinaea flavilata (Cope)
Pine Woods Snake
Plate XV

Recognition. A short (to 15⅞ in.; 403 mm), golden brown snake with a dark head and often a narrow, indistinct, dark vertebral stripe and lateral stripe; belly white or pale yellowish green; dorsal scales smooth, in 17 rows; anal plate divided.

Distribution. Confined to the southeastern quarter of the Florida Parishes (Map 110).

Taxonomic comments. No subspecies of *Rhadinaea flavilata* have been proposed. The most recent taxonomic study is that by Myers (1967).

Habitat and habits. Very little is known of the ecology of this species in Louisiana. All but a few localities lie within the Flatwoods (the others are in the Longleaf Pine Forest),

the characteristic habitat of *R. flavilata* throughout its range. Campbell and Stickel (1939:105) cited a Louisiana specimen collected "among loose bark, leaves, and other debris on one of the alluvial ridges between the swamps," but the pine woods snake is much more frequently encountered under the loose bark or in the decaying interior of pine logs or stumps (Myers 1967).

Myers (1967) suggested that the diet of *R. flavilata* probably consists primarily of small frogs, salamanders, and lizards. He considered reports of snakes and insects in the diet to be unconfirmed, and the latter to be highly unlikely.

Reproduction. From two to four eggs are deposited; recorded dates range from 4 June to 19 August (Myers 1967).

Storeria dekayi (Holbrook)
Brown Snake
Plate XXII

Recognition. A short (to 20¾ in.; 527 mm), light brown or gray-brown snake with a relatively broad, indistinct, pale vertebral stripe, bordered or crossed by dark spots (occasionally with a pair of light lateral stripes in southwestern Louisiana); belly white or with a pinkish cast; dorsal scales keeled, in 17 rows; supralabials seven on each side; anal plate divided.

Distribution. Statewide (Map 111).

Taxonomic comments. Three subspecies of *Storeria dekayi* have been reported to occur in Louisiana: *S. d. limnetes* Anderson, the marsh brown snake, characterized by a usually unbarred dorsum, the lack of a dark mark along the suture between supralabials six and seven, and a longitudinal dark line through the middle of the anterior temporal; *S. d. texana* Trapido, the Texas brown snake, characterized by an unbarred dorsum, a dark mark along the suture between supralabials six and

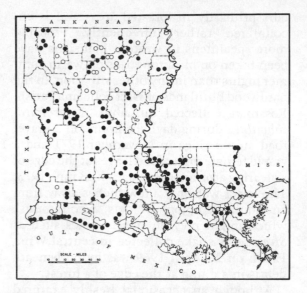

Map 111. Distribution of *Storeria dekayi*. Solid circles represent specimens examined; hollow circles represent museum specimens not examined or literature records.

seven, and no longitudinal line through the middle of the anterior temporal (but sometimes one along the upper edge); and *S. d. wrightorum* Trapido, the midland brown snake, characterized by dark crossbars on the anterior dorsum, a dark mark along the sutures between supralabials six and seven, and a dark vertical bar on the anterior temporal. Specimens fitting the description of *S. d. limnetes* are found throughout the Marsh and, west of the Atchafalaya Basin, they occur at least as far north as Lafayette; intermediates between *S. d. limnetes* and *S. d. wrightorum* have been taken along the western edge of the Atchafalaya Basin in St. Martin and St. Landry parishes. The latter race (*wrightorum*) occupies the Florida Parishes and most of central and northern Louisiana. The status of *S. d. texana* in Louisiana remains to be determined; we have seen specimens having the characteristics of *texana* from Bossier, Caddo, Natchitoches, Rapides, and Vernon parishes, but apparently "good"

wrightorum also are known from Bossier, Natchitoches, and Rapides parishes, and we have seen specimens exhibiting characteristics intermediate between *texana* and *wrightorum* from Natchitoches and Rapides parishes. The most recent taxonomic study of *S. dekayi* in the lower Mississippi Valley region is that by Sabath and Sabath (1969).

Habitat and habits. The brown snake occurs in a wide variety of habitats in Louisiana, from natural levees and muskrat houses in the Marsh (P. K. Anderson 1961) to rocky ravines in the northern hill country (R. F. Clark 1949) and backyards in uptown New Orleans. During the day *Storeria dekayi* is usually secretive and most commonly found beneath logs, rocks, boards, or other debris, but it apparently emerges at dusk and wanders some distance because brown snakes are occasionally found crossing paved roads on warm nights.

Although food records are lacking for wild-caught Louisiana specimens, captives have taken earthworms, slugs, and snails; the latter the snakes extract from their shells (P. Myer, pers. com.). Elsewhere the species is also known to eat soft-bodied insects, spiders, and, rarely, small amphibians.

Reproduction. Kofron (1979b) found that female brown snakes in Louisiana usually ovulate during April, and most births occur during the latter half of June and July. Projected litter size in his sample (based on follicles and embryos) ranged from 5 to 24 (mean, 14.9). R. F. Clark (1949) reported four northern Louisiana litters of 11 to 17 offspring, which apparently were born in late July or early August. One litter of 11 from New Orleans, born 11 June 1957, ranges from 78 to 96 mm in total length; a second litter (12) from the same area measures 100–111 mm; 16 young in a litter from Washington Parish (born 23–24 June) measure 87–100 mm; and a litter of 25 from East Baton Rouge Parish (born 25 June 1986) measure 99–107 mm (mean, 103.6).

Storeria occipitomaculata (Storer)
Red-bellied Snake
Plate XXII

Recognition. A short (to 16 in.; 406 mm), brown or gray snake with three light spots or a light collar on the neck, and a light spot on supralabial five; belly varying shades of yellow, orange, or red; dorsal scales keeled, in 15 rows; supralabials six on each side; anal plate divided.

Distribution. Statewide except for the Marsh; apparently rare or absent from the Mississippi alluvial plain (Map 112).

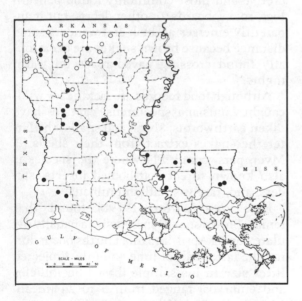

Map 112. Distribution of *Storeria occipito-maculata.* Solid circles represent specimens examined; hollow circles represent museum specimens not examined or literature records.

Taxonomic comments. Only the southern subspecies, *Storeria occipitomaculata obscura* Trapido, the Florida red-bellied snake, occurs in Louisiana. The most recent taxonomic study is that by Rossman and Erwin (1980). The "common" name is inappropriate in our state, where the belly is rarely red.

Habitat and habits. The red-bellied snake oc-

curs primarily in forested areas and is encountered rather infrequently. Probably more specimens in western Louisiana have been taken on blacktop roads on warm summer nights than in any other situation. In the hardwood Blufflands of West Feliciana Parish, Rossman collected an adult *S. occipitomaculata* during daylight hours on a gravel road atop a ridge in November 1971 and a gravid female under dead leaves at the edge of a clearing atop another ridge on 23 June 1973. The latter was only a few inches away from an adult scorpion (*Vejovis carolinianus*), which might prey on small snakes such as *Storeria*. A snake collected in central Winn Parish on 26 April 1969 was found beneath debris in a dump at the edge of a forest.

Although an occasional freshly captured individual will roll its upper lip back in a "sneer"—thus exposing the teeth of the upper jaw—red-bellied snakes do not bite. Apparently the behavior only serves to intimidate a potential predator.

A specimen forestry students collected in East Feliciana Parish regurgitated three slugs. Captives have also taken earthworms and snails; the latter the snakes extract from their shells (P. Myer, pers. com.). Semlitsch and Moran (1984) found only slugs in the stomachs of 10 South Carolina *S. occipitomaculata*. Elsewhere the diet is reputed to also include earthworms, snails, sowbugs, millipedes, and insect larvae.

Reproduction. The gravid female collected in the Tunica Hills Nature Preserve on 23 June 1973 gave birth to 10 young on 22 July. They ranged from 78 to 93 mm (average, 87.8 mm) in total length. Elsewhere litter size ranges from 1 to 18 (Fitch 1985).

Tantilla coronata Baird & Girard
Southeastern Crowned Snake
Plate XV

Recognition. A very short (to 13 in.; 330 mm), tan snake with a black head, a light collar

Map 113. Distribution of *Tantilla coronata*. Solid circles represent specimens examined; hollow circles represent museum specimens not examined or literature records.

across the back of the head, and a black band on the neck; belly white; dorsal scales smooth, in 15 rows; anal plate divided.

Distribution. Confined to the Florida Parishes (Map 113).

Taxonomic comments. No subspecies of *Tantilla coronata* are currently recognized. The most recent taxonomic study is that by Telford (1966).

Habitat and habits. Most Louisiana records of this species are from the Longleaf Pine Forest, the others from the Flatwoods. This is a secretive form; specimens have been taken from beneath pine logs and under debris in garbage dumps. P. K. Anderson, Liner, and Etheridge (1952) discovered a crowned snake that had fallen into a pipeline ditch running through a truck garden adjacent to a pine forest. Telford (1966) noted that Louisiana and Mississippi snakes were frequently collected from rotten stumps in seasonally flooded flatwoods. Other Mississippi specimens were collected under logs and chunks of wood and among dry, shaded, dead leaves in mixed

woods on hills and in bottomlands (F. A. Cook 1943) and in the roots of a palmetto (P. W. Smith and List 1955).

No data are available on the food of *T. coronata* in Louisiana. F. A. Cook (1943) observed some Mississippi specimens feeding on earthworms.

Reproduction. Reproductive data are also lacking from Louisiana. Elsewhere the southeastern crowned snake apparently matures at about 130 mm snout-vent length (Telford 1966) and is known to deposit a clutch of three eggs (Fitch 1970). A newly hatched specimen discovered on 23 October 1960 in St. Tammany Parish had a yellowish orange collar and superficially resembled a small *Diadophis punctatus.*

Tantilla gracilis Baird & Girard
Flat-headed Snake
Plate XV

Recognition. A very short (to 9⅝ in.; 244 mm), gray to reddish brown snake with a darker brown head; belly pink medially, white anteriorly and laterally; dorsal scales smooth, in 15 rows; anal plate divided.

Distribution. Confined to northern Louisiana west of the Mississippi alluvial plain (Map 114).

Taxonomic comments. No subspecies of *Tantilla gracilis* are currently recognized. The most recent comprehensive taxonomic study (Kirn, Burger, and Smith 1949) did recognize two geographic races, but its conclusions were convincingly refuted by two subsequent papers (Dowling 1957; Hardy and Cole 1968).

Habitat and habits. The vast majority of flat-headed snakes collected to date in Louisiana have been taken in Natchitoches Parish. Clyde Fisher (pers. com.) found them to be fairly abundant under boards near an old house northwest of Natchitoches during the spring of 1969. In the same area on 11 April 1969, he discovered two *T. gracilis* beneath a rotten 6-by-6-in. beam and another under a

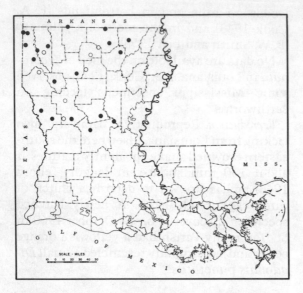

Map 114. Distribution of *Tantilla gracilis*. Solid circles represent specimens examined; hollow circles represent museum specimens not examined or literature records.

small log in pine woods. Over the years, field crews from several universities have collected flat-headed snakes beneath rocks on the slopes near Longleaf Vista in the Red Dirt Wildlife Management Area south of Derry (Natchitoches Parish). On no occasion has more than a single specimen been collected and even that usually only after the expenditure of many man hours. On 8 August 1971, Gerhard Kuehnhanss discovered a *T. gracilis* under debris in a garbage dump in the Red Dirt area. Strecker and Frierson (1926) found a single specimen under rotten wood in a pine forest near Mansfield, De Soto Parish.

No information is available on the diet of this species in Louisiana. Force (1935) observed the flat-headed snake to feed on insects, centipedes, spiders, sow bugs, and slugs in Oklahoma.

Reproduction. A specimen collected at Sibley Lake (Natchitoches Parish) on 9 June 1968 deposited two eggs on 14 June (Fisher 1973). The eggs measured 19 × 16 mm and 29 × 15 mm. No other reproductive data are available

from Louisiana. Elsewhere clutches of one to four eggs (usually two or three) have been laid between 13 June and 9 July, and hatching has occurred between 7 and 22 September. The gray hatchlings range from 77.5 to 92 mm in total length.

Thamnophis proximus (Say)
Western Ribbon Snake
Plate XXI

Recognition. A moderately long (to 48½ in.; 1,232 mm), slender, olive brown to black snake with a gold or orange vertebral stripe and a yellowish lateral stripe on the third and fourth dorsal scale rows; dark coloration of back not extending onto lateral margins of belly scutes; paired parietal spots fairly large and fused together medially; dorsal scales keeled, in 19 (or rarely 21) rows; supralabials usually eight on each side; anal plate undivided.

Similar species. Many specimens of *Thamnophis proximus* bear a superficial resemblance to the common garter snake, *T. sirtalis*, but they are easily distinguished by the position of the light lateral stripe.

Distribution. Statewide (Map 115).

Taxonomic comments. Two subspecies of the western ribbon snake occur in Louisiana: *T. p. proximus*, characterized by a black dorsum and a narrow orange vertebral stripe, and *T. p. orarius* Rossman, the Gulf Coast ribbon snake, characterized by an olive brown dorsum and a broad gold vertebral stripe. The former occurs in northern Louisiana, the latter in and adjacent to the Marsh. The width of the zone of intergradation is not adequately delimited at present because of the lack of series of living specimens from many localities. Specimens that have been in preservative for any length of time often become discolored and thus are of only limited use in determining subspecific identities. The most recent taxonomic study is that by Rossman (1963b).

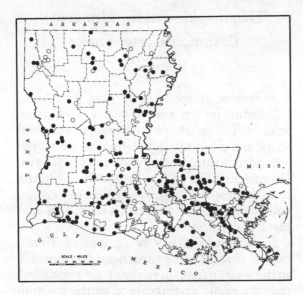

Map 115. Distribution of *Thamnophis proximus*. Solid circles represent specimens examined; hollow circles represent museum specimens not examined or literature records.

Habitat and habits. The western ribbon snake is among the most commonly encountered and abundant snake species occurring in Louisiana, where it is found in or near ditches, ponds, lakes, streams, swamps, rice fields, and even flooded jeep trails. These situations may occur in open areas or dense forest, and the snakes may be found under boards or other cover, in rotten logs, basking on mats of cattails or blackberries, or actively foraging on the ground or in low vegetation. On 31 May 1914, Percy Viosca observed western ribbon snakes swimming around some pilings near an old sunken barge at Shell Beach, St. Bernard Parish.

The food of the western ribbon snake consists primarily of fishes and adult and larval amphibians (Rossman 1963b). Like its close relative the eastern ribbon snake, *T. proximus* will not eat earthworms or adult toads.

Reproduction. Tinkle (1957) found *T. proximus* in southeastern Louisiana to reach sexual maturity in approximately two years and at minimum snout-vent lengths of 485 mm

in females and 410 mm in males. Gravid females have been found as early as 28 February and young have been born on dates ranging from 5 July through 2 October. Litter size in Louisiana ranges from 4 to 24; the newly born young range from 222 to 268 mm in total length.

Thamnophis sauritus (Linnaeus)
Eastern Ribbon Snake
Plate XXI

Recognition. A medium-sized (to 40 in.; 1,016 mm), slender, reddish brown snake with a golden yellow vertebral stripe and a light yellow lateral stripe on the third and fourth dorsal scale rows; brown coloration of back extending onto lateral margins of belly scutes; paired parietal spots small and separated or absent; dorsal scales keeled, in 19 rows; supralabials usually seven on each side; anal plate undivided.

Similar species. Where the eastern ribbon snake and its close relative *Thamnophis proximus* occur together in the southeastern corner of the Florida Parishes, they have remarkably similar coloration and may be confused if given only a hasty examination. Maximum emphasis should be placed on the presence or absence of brown pigment on the lateral margins of the belly scutes, minimum emphasis on the number of supralabials. Ventral counts are useful in double checking the identification; *sauritus* usually have fewer than 164, *proximus* usually have more.

Distribution. Confined to the Florida Parishes north of the marshes bordering Lake Pontchartrain (Map 116).

Taxonomic comments. Only the nominate subspecies, *Thamnophis s. sauritus*, occurs in Louisiana. The most recent taxonomic study is that by Rossman (1963b).

Habitat and habits. Very little information is available about the ecology of this species in Louisiana. Two specimens from St. Tam-

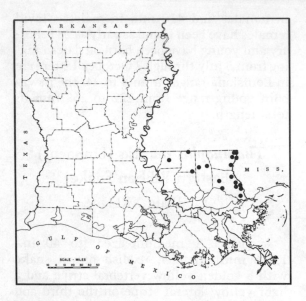

Map 116. Distribution of *Thamnophis sauritus*. Solid circles represent specimens examined; hollow circles represent museum specimens not examined or literature records.

many Parish were collected in pine flatwoods, one in or near a roadside ditch and the other under a slab of concrete in a pile of debris along a bulldozed road. The latter was taken on 6 March 1971; the temperature was approximately 65°F (18°C) and light rain was falling intermittently.

The food of the eastern ribbon snake consists primarily of fishes and adult and larval amphibians (Rossman 1963b). Unlike its relative the common garter snake (*T. sirtalis*), *T. sauritus* will not eat earthworms or adult toads.

The ecological relationships of *T. sauritus* and *T. proximus* where they occur together in the Florida Parishes merit investigation.

Reproduction. Outside Louisiana, broods range from 3 to 26, and average about 11 (Rossman 1963b). Newly born *T. sauritus* vary considerably in size; the average snout-vent length ranges from a low of 135 mm to a high of 172.6 mm (Rossman 1963b).

Thamnophis sirtalis (Linnaeus)
Common Garter Snake
Plate XXI

Recognition. A moderately long (to 52 in.; 1,321 mm), brown, gray, or nearly black snake with a yellowish or red-orange vertebral stripe and a light yellow lateral stripe on the second and third dorsal scale rows (with two alternating rows of black spots between the light stripes); dorsal scales keeled, in 19 rows; supralabials usually seven on each side; anal plate undivided.

Similar species. Many specimens of *Thamnophis sirtalis* bear a superficial resemblance to the western ribbon snake, *T. proximus*, but they are easily distinguished by the position of the light lateral stripe.

Distribution. Statewide (Map 117), but extremely rare or absent from the Marsh and from the part of Louisiana lying west of the Red River valley and the Teche Ridge (the latter forms a natural western boundary of the Atchafalaya Basin).

Taxonomic comments. Only the nominate subspecies, *T. s. sirtalis*, the eastern garter snake, has been reported from Louisiana. The presence of a red-orange vertebral stripe in some individuals may reflect genetic influence from *T. s. annectens* Brown, the Texas garter snake, but there seems to be no geographic consistency in its occurrence, and the yellowish stripe occurs in the same areas. Rossman has seen living garter snakes with a red-orange stripe from localities as widely separated as Angie (Washington Parish) and Cheniere Brake (Ouachita Parish), and Beyer (1898) reported collecting red-striped garter snakes in New Orleans in 1892 and 1893.

No comprehensive taxonomic study of *T. sirtalis* has appeared since Ruthven's monograph in 1908; one is urgently needed.

Habitat and habits. Relatively little ecological information is available on this species in Louisiana. R. F. Clark (1949) reported that all

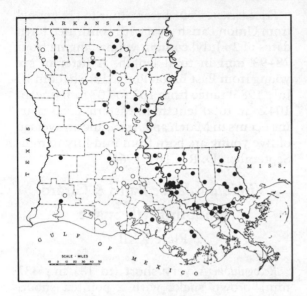

Map 117. Distribution of *Thamnophis sirtalis.* Solid circles represent specimens examined; hollow circles represent museum specimens not examined or literature records.

the specimens he encountered in north-central Louisiana were in heavily wooded areas along the banks of small streams. Two of them escaped by taking to the water and hiding under projecting roots. Gerhard Kuehnhanss found four *T. sirtalis* on 21 February 1971 under boards in the tidal wrack along the western shore of Lake Pontchartrain at the Bonnet Carre Spillway. Two other garter snakes from the Bonnet Carre Spillway were discovered beneath trash in a dump on 14 April 1973. At localities where the common garter snake and western ribbon snake both occur, the former is usually much less frequently encountered than the latter.

Throughout its range the common garter snake is a generalized feeder, its diet consisting primarily of earthworms and amphibians, but also including small mammals, fish, leeches, other snakes, crawfish, snails and slugs, birds, sowbugs, and insects. The insects that appear in stomach contents are

usually believed to have been present in the amphibians eaten by the snake, rather than to have been the direct prey. Stomach contents of Louisiana specimens have included *Rana sphenocephala* and an unidentified toad, fish, and insects (R. F. Clark 1949). On 19 March 1963 Dundee observed an 838-mm garter snake eating an adult *Bufo valliceps.*

Reproduction. R. F. Clark (1949) observed two captive northern Louisiana *T. sirtalis* mating on 15 April 1926. Between 17 and 19 July, 27 young were born. Meade (1934) reported that a specimen held in an outdoor cage gave birth to 21 young on 25 June and that a brood of 15 born to a St. Charles Parish female on 17 June 1971 ranged from 160 to 180 mm in total length. Fitch (1985) reported litter size in the Southeast to range from 9 to 38 young.

Virginia striatula (Linnaeus)
Rough Earth Snake
Plate XXII

Recognition. A very short (to 12¾ in.; 324 mm), brown snake with a pointed snout, occasionally with an indistinct pale band across the back of the head; belly white or pink; dorsal scales keeled, in 17 rows; a single internasal; supralabials five on each side; anal plate divided.

Distribution. Statewide except for the Marsh and, apparently, the Mississippi alluvial plain (Map 118).

Taxonomic comments. No subspecies of *Virginia striatula* have been proposed. No taxonomic study of this species has been published.

Habitat and habits. Although frequently found under logs and loose bark in the woods (usually pine forest), rough earth snakes seem to occur in greatest abundance in areas disturbed by humans. These snakes are found under boards in pastures and vacant lots, under cardboard and other debris in trash dumps, and in the plant litter of flower gar-

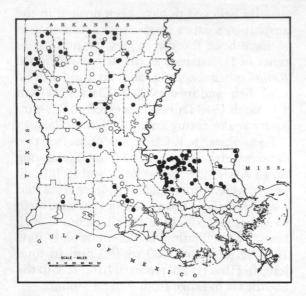

Map 118. Distribution of *Virginia striatula.* Solid circles represent specimens examined; hollow circles represent museum specimens not examined or literature records.

dens adjacent to houses. The Louisiana State University Museum of Natural Science receives telephone calls early each spring from Baton Rouge householders concerned about the numerous small brown snakes (usually, and incorrectly, calling them "ground rattlers," a term properly applied only to *Sistrurus miliarius*) they encounter when preparing their gardens. Almost invariably, the cause of all the furor turns out to be the completely harmless *Virginia striatula*! Brode and Allison (1958) found this species to be a common inhabitant of rotten pine stumps in southern Mississippi. On 9 March 1952 two collectors from Tulane found 45 rough earth snakes in pine stumps in Hancock County, Mississippi, near the Louisiana state line.

No information is available on the diet of this species in Louisiana. Brode and Allison (1958) reported that in Mississippi it preferred earthworms and larvae [presumably of insects]. Blem and Blem (1985) found only small pieces of red annelids in Virginia specimens.

Reproduction. Four litters (four to six young) from Union Parish (two with confirmed birth dates of 28 July) contain young ranging from 78–93 mm in total length. A litter of six young from East Baton Rouge Parish (born 10 July 1986) range from 103 to 107 mm (mean, 104.3) in total length. In eastern Texas mating occurs in March and April, and an average of five young are born from mid-July to mid-September (D. R. Clark 1964).

Virginia valeriae Baird & Girard
Smooth Earth Snake
Plate XXII

Recognition. A very short (to 13¼ in.; 337 mm), brown snake with a pointed snout; belly white or pale yellow; dorsal scales very weakly keeled, in 17 rows; two internasals; supralabials six on each side; anal plate divided.

Distribution. The Florida Parishes and the hill country of northern Louisiana (Map 119).

Taxonomic comments. Only the western subspecies, *Virginia valeriae elegans* Kennicott, the western earth snake, occurs in Louisiana. The most recent taxonomic study is that by Blanchard (1923).

Habitat and habits. Although sharing most of the same habitat preferences as its congener, *V. striatula*, the smooth earth snake is not nearly as abundant. Certainly it is rarely encountered near human habitation, a situation in which *V. striatula* thrives. Louisiana specimens of *V. valeriae* have been collected under logs, boards, a paper sack, a rock, and a pile of leaves.

Although there are no recorded observations on the food of the smooth earth snake in Louisiana, F. A. Cook (1954) reported that it eats insect larvae, slugs, and worms in Mississippi. Blem and Blem (1985) found only small pieces of red annelids in Virginia specimens.

Reproduction. A female from Washington Parish gave birth to five young on 30 June

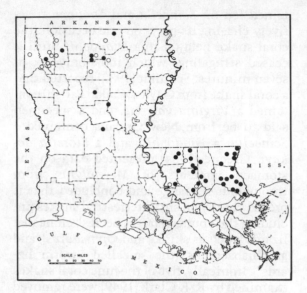

Map 119. Distribution of *Virginia valeriae*. Solid circles represent specimens examined; hollow circles represent museum specimens not examined or literature records.

1949; they measure 76–80 mm in total length. Elsewhere the average litter size is 6.6 (Fitch 1970). A female from Hattiesburg, Mississippi, gave birth to four young on 4 July 1959. They were opalescent gray in color, in contrast to the dark golden brown of their mother.

FAMILY ELAPIDAE

The family Elapidae comprises 62 genera and 244 species of fixed-fang venomous snakes that are worldwide in distribution in tropical and subtropical regions (Dowling and Duellman 1978). Only a single genus and species, *Micrurus fulvius*, occurs in Louisiana.

Micrurus fulvius (Linnaeus)
Eastern Coral Snake
Plate XXIII

Recognition. A medium-sized to moderately long (to 47½ in.; 1,207 mm), small-headed snake with a pattern of alternating black, yellow, and red rings—the yellow and red rings in contact (the tip of the snout black); belly marked as dorsum; dorsal scales smooth, in 15 rows; anal plate divided.

Similar species. Lampropeltis triangulum and *Cemophora coccinea* exhibit somewhat similar dorsal patterns, but they have the red and black bands in contact rather than the red and yellow. Moreover, *Cemophora* usually has an unmarked belly.

Distribution. Statewide except for the Marsh and the Mississippi alluvial plain (Map 120). Coral snakes are rare in the Florida Parishes.

Taxonomic comments. Two subspecies of the eastern coral snake occur in Louisiana: *Micrurus f. fulvius,* characterized by its relatively few black markings within the red rings and those often forming a pair of relatively large spots, and *M. f. tenere* (Baird & Girard), the Texas coral snake, characterized by its more numerous black markings, which do not form spots, within the red rings. The former occurs in the eastern Florida Parishes, the latter west of the Mississippi River. No detailed taxonomic study of this species has been published; the most recent review is by Roze and Tilger (1983).

Habitat and habits. Coral snakes are primarily inhabitants of forested areas, although Walker (1963) found two Jackson Parish specimens in open pasture in late afternoon, and Fitch (1949) collected one in open grassland in an area formerly pine woods in west-central Louisiana. Fitch encountered another *Micrurus* crossing a road in swampy, wooded bottomland. R. F. Clark (1949) reported finding coral snakes near an old log and an old stump in virgin pine forests and under decaying logs in dense forest. A Winn Parish specimen was collected at midmorning as it was crawling into a hardwood stump in mixed hardwood-pine forest in a dry bottomland in rolling hill country. F. A. Cook (1954) reported that coral snakes were found in and on old logs on sand ridges in Mississippi, and Richard Blaney discovered a spec-

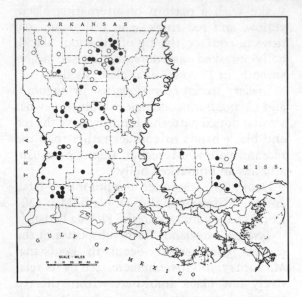

Map 120. Distribution of *Micrurus fulvius*. Solid circles represent specimens examined; hollow circles represent museum specimens not examined or literature records.

imen under similar conditions near the Sabine River in Beauregard Parish.

Coral snakes often have a mild disposition and may not attempt to bite even when freely handled. Nonetheless, when they do bite a human, the consequences may be quite serious; the venom is more potent than that of any other poisonous snake species in our area (Russell 1980). Coral snake venom attacks the nervous system (whereas that of the others is primarily hemotoxic), and *Micrurus fulvius* does not deliver a single strike, but chews vigorously, forcing venom into the multiple wounds.

R. F. Clark (1949) examined stomach contents of two coral snakes from northern Louisiana; both contained skinks (*Eumeces*). Captive snakes that he maintained would feed only on lizards; his specimens refused small snakes, which constitute a significant portion of the coral snake's diet throughout its range. A captive specimen Dundee main-

tained fed on *Scincella* and *Diadophis*, actively chasing its prey; on one occasion, the coral snake held on to a *Diadophis* until it ceased struggling, which took only six or seven minutes. Schmidt (1932) reported that a coral snake from Gayles (Caddo Parish) contained a *Virginia valeriae*, and a specimen said to be from New Orleans contained a *Scincella*, a *Diadophis*, and a *Storeria dekayi*. Greene (1984) presented data on the stomach contents of *M. fulvius* from throughout its range and concluded that it preyed chiefly on small terrestrial snakes (including the young of large species), elongated lizards (such as skinks and *Ophisaurus*), and amphisbaenians (the so-called "worm lizards"). Ironically, five of the nine coral snakes examined by R. F. Clark (1949) were removed from the guts of speckled kingsnakes.

Reproduction. Coral snakes deposit 5 to 9 elongate eggs in June (Fitch 1970). No data are available concerning time of hatching or size of the hatchlings.

FAMILY VIPERIDAE

The nearly cosmopolitan family Viperidae consists of 18 genera comprising 180 species of folding-fanged venomous snakes (Dowling and Duellman 1978). It is represented in Louisiana by three genera with five species.

Agkistrodon contortrix (Linnaeus) Copperhead

Plate XXIII

Recognition. A moderately long (to 53 in.; 1,346 mm), heavy-bodied, tan snake with a pattern of broad reddish brown crossbands, much narrower middorsally—sometimes to the point of being interrupted—than laterally; belly light brown marked with darker brown blotches; juveniles with sulfur-yellow tail tip; a narrow dark line from the eye to the angle of the jaw; a pair of dark parietal spots; a deep pit in the side of the head between the eye and the nostril; dorsal scales keeled, in 23 to 27 rows; subcaudal scales in only one row except toward the tail tip; anal plate undivided.

Distribution. Statewide except for the Marsh (Map 121).

Taxonomic comments. Only the nominate subspecies, *Agkistrodon c. contortrix*, the southern copperhead, occurs in Louisiana. The most recent comprehensive taxonomic study is that by Gloyd and Conant (1943), although several subsequent papers have dealt with the species in limited portions of its range.

Habitat and habits. The copperhead is usually encountered in wooded areas, occasionally in moderately large numbers. A field crew from Tulane collected 20 individuals from stumps in St. Charles Parish one January, and R. F. Clark (1949) once found 11 adult specimens under rocks in an abandoned quarry in Winn Parish. Despite the fact that *A. contortrix* is sometimes called the "highland moccasin," in Louisiana it seems to occur just as frequently on lowland situations as in hill country, and is even found on low ridges in swamps. Walker (1963) observed one of these snakes swimming across a pond in Jackson Parish. Copperheads are usually active at night; during the day they are most often discovered beneath logs, boards, or other cover. Occasionally one may be seen prowling about in broad daylight, as was the case with a very large individual encountered in August 1973 at midday at the edge of a clearing atop a ridge in the Tunica Hills of West Feliciana Parish. On another occasion, a Tunica Hills copperhead found after dark vibrated its tail in dead leaves, creating a sound somewhat similar to that of a rattlesnake.

The copperhead apparently is responsible for more bites than any other poisonous snake species in eastern North America; for-

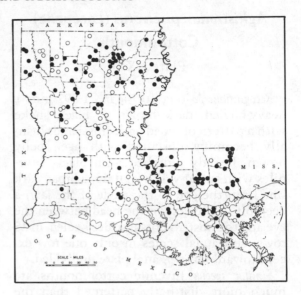

Map 121. Distribution of *Agkistrodon contortrix*. Solid circles represent specimens examined; hollow circles represent museum specimens not examined or literature records.

tunately, its venom is by far the least potent (Russell 1980).

In northern Louisiana, R. F. Clark (1949) examined the stomach contents of 55 copperheads and found that 22 contained southern leopard frogs (*Rana sphenocephala*), 7 contained green frogs (*Rana clamitans*), one contained a bullfrog (*Rana catesbeiana*), 15 contained mice, and 10 contained birds. Liner (1954) discovered a pair of adult copperheads in a wood rat (*Neotoma*) nest in Lafayette Parish; whether they came there for shelter or food was not determined.

Reproduction. Broods ranging in number from 5 to 10 have been born from 10 September to 4 October in northern Louisiana (R. F. Clark 1949). On the basis of gravid females he examined, Clark indicated that young might be born as early as mid-August or as late as mid-October. Fitch (1960) reported that young copperheads from Kansas ranged from 203 to 264 mm in snout-vent length (total length not given).

Agkistrodon piscivorus (Lacépède)
Cottonmouth
Plate XXIII

Recognition. A long (to 74½ in.; 1,892 mm*), heavy-bodied, dark brown or black snake with a pattern of broad dark crossbands (usually becoming obscured with age); belly brown, heavily blotched with black; juveniles with sulfur yellow tail tip; a broad dark line from the eye to the angle of the jaw; a deep pit in the side of the head between the eye and the nostril; dorsal scales keeled, in 25 rows; subcaudal scales in only one row except toward tail tip; anal plate undivided.

Similar species. Juvenile cottonmouths are much more distinctly patterned than the adults and consequently are frequently misidentified as copperheads. The latter are much lighter in color, however, and have a narrow (rather than broad) dark line from the eye to the angle of the jaw, and crossbands that are much narrower middorsally.

Distribution. Statewide (Map 122).

Taxonomic comments. Only the western subspecies, *Agkistrodon piscivorus leucostoma* (Troost), the western cottonmouth, occurs in Louisiana. The most recent comprehensive taxonomic study is that by Gloyd and Conant (1943), although subsequent papers have dealt with the species in limited portions of its range.

Habitat and habits. Cottonmouths can be found in virtually every permanent or temporary aquatic situation in the state, including such seemingly unlikely places as tiny, intermittent hill-country creeks and city drainage ditches. In larger bodies of water they are commonly seen basking on logs, brush piles, the roots of fallen trees, or limbs overhanging the water (at least as high as 8 ft [2.4 m] above the surface). Along shell roads in the margins

*The western cottonmouth does not attain as large a size as the eastern subspecies. Conant (1975) cited 55½ in. (1,410 mm) as the record length for *Agkistrodon p. leucostoma*.

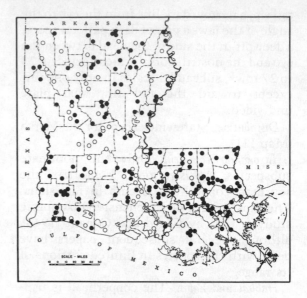

Map 122. Distribution of *Agkistrodon piscivorus.* Solid circles represent specimens examined; hollow circles represent museum specimens not examined or literature records.

of the Atchafalaya Basin, small and medium-sized individuals are abundant beneath boards and logs. On 7 June 1922, Percy Viosca collected 114 cottonmouths on Delacroix Island in St. Bernard Parish. Although *A. piscivorus* usually occurs in the immediate vicinity of water, Kofron (1978) found the majority of his Atchafalaya Basin specimens in bottomland forests. Rossman encountered a cottonmouth on a hillside several hundred yards from the nearest creek in the Tunica Hills of West Feliciana Parish.

Unquestionably the most abundant and frequently encountered poisonous snake in Louisiana, the cottonmouth also may be the most ill-tempered; both factors contribute to its being the leading source of snakebite in southern Louisiana (Liner 1954). Its venom, while more potent than that of *A. contortrix*, is less potent than that of the rattlesnakes and coral snake (Russell 1980). When the cottonmouth is disturbed and has no route of retreat readily available, it will frequently pull itself into a compact coil with its head in the center and open its mouth widely, as if defying the intruder to come any closer. The white lining of the mouth, so prominently displayed under such circumstances, has given rise to the snake's most frequently used common name.

Cottonmouths apparently take any vertebrate prey that is small enough to be swallowed, although fish are the principal item in the diet. R. F. Clark (1949) found catfish, spotted bass, frogs (*Rana clamitans, R. sphenocephala*), cricket frogs (*Acris crepitans*), southern water snakes (*Nerodia fasciata*), birds, and squirrels in specimens from northern Louisiana. Arny (1948) was able to identify the remains of muskrats (*Ondatra zibethicus*) and ground skinks (*Scincella*) in *Agkistrodon piscivorus* collected in the Delta National Wildlife Refuge in Plaquemines Parish. Percy Viosca (notes) found minnows, sunfish, a tadpole, a garter snake (*Thamnophis*), and a western green water snake (*Nerodia cyclopion*) in seven cottonmouths he collected near New Orleans on 22 April 1915. The previous year, a 978-mm specimen he examined contained a 1,219-mm king snake (*Lampropeltis getulus*) and a 610-mm southern water snake (*N. fasciata*). According to Kofron (1978), Atchafalaya Basin cottonmouths contained six species of fish (the catfish *Ictalurus melas* being the most frequent), *N. fasciata, N. rhombifera, Regina rigida, Thamnophis proximus*, and the short-tailed shrew, *Blarina brevicauda*. Penn (1943) reported that an adult female *A. piscivorus* had eaten two young individuals of the same species; presumably such examples of cannibalism are rare.

Reproduction. Kofron (1979b) found that females of this species ovulate at least during May and give birth at least during August. Beyer (1898) observed a pair of cottonmouths copulating near New Orleans on 10 March 1893; the female gave birth to nine young on 17 August. Another female he collected on Avery Island gave birth to eight young on 25 August 1894. Viosca's embryo counts on gravid females ranged from 5 to 20. R. F. Clark (1949) reported two embryo counts of 16 each, and Penn (1943), four counts ranging from 2 to 7. Fitch (1985) noted a range of 2 to 15 young in 21 litters of the western cottonmouth. Burkett (1966) noted that newly born western cottonmouths range from 225 to 290 mm in total length.

Crotalus adamanteus Beauvois
Eastern Diamond-backed Rattlesnake
Plate XXIII

Recognition. A very long (to 96 in.; 2,438 mm), heavy-bodied, gray-brown or olive snake with a pattern of brown diamond-shaped blotches, each blotch having a broad black border enclosed, in turn, by a narrow yellow border; belly cream colored with indistinct dark blotches; broad, light-bordered dark line from the eye to the angle of the jaw; a deep pit in the side of the head between the eye and the nostril; dorsal scales keeled, in 29 rows; tip of tail with horny rattle or button; anal plate undivided.

Distribution. Confined to the eastern Florida Parishes (Map 123).

Taxonomic comments. No subspecies of *Crotalus adamanteus* have been proposed, and no taxonomic studies of this species have been published.

Habitat and habits. Although Beyer (1900) reported the eastern diamond-backed rattlesnake from St. Tammany Parish, until recently the only existing specimens were two dried skins (LSUMZ 7721-22) of snakes that had been collected in Washington Parish during the summer of 1949. Then, nearly 30 years later in 1977, Henry Harrison killed another specimen at the edge of a swamp just north of Angie, also in Washington Parish. The most recent find occurred on 20 September 1980, when Rita Davis and John Cornwell discovered a freshly killed adult (LSUMZ 39100) at 11:30 P.M. on the shoulder of Interstate 12, three-quarters of a mile west

Map 123. Distribution of *Crotalus adamanteus*. Solid circles represent specimens examined; hollow circles represent museum specimens not examined or literature records.

of Interstate 55 in Tangipahoa Parish. The animal had had its rattles cut off, but it was still moving. Isolated records such as this one are always suspect, but the habitat in that area is appropriate for the species, and it seems unlikely that someone would pick up a large rattlesnake in Mississippi and carry it in the car for several hours before killing and discarding it alongside a highway in Louisiana in the middle of the night. Beyer (1900:5) said that he found eastern diamond-backed rattlesnakes chiefly "in the hummock lands which border the pine-flats on the one side and the water-courses on the other." More specifically, he reported catching several near Madisonville (St. Tammany Parish) in hummocks along the margins of gum swamps. He also allegedly observed *C. adamanteus* along the eastern bank of the Mississippi River, but this record seems somewhat dubious. Beyer (1900) attributed the increasing rarity of the eastern diamond-backed rattlesnake to progressive deforestation and draining of the swamps; F. A. Cook reached a more-or-less

similar conclusion regarding the species in Mississippi, although *C. adamanteus* is as yet by no means rare in that state. F. A. Cook (1954:36) said that eastern diamond-backed rattlesnakes occupy "the hillsides where there are gopher holes, caves, or large rocks, which afford a certain amount of shelter and warmth. During hot mid-summer days, they seek out shady spots near water, and then return in the fall to the dry hills where they winter in gopher holes and other natural recesses." Through much of its range, the eastern diamond-backed rattlesnake is frequently associated with the gopher tortoise, *Gopherus polyphemus*, in whose burrows the snake often takes refuge.

The eastern diamond-backed rattlesnake has the most potent venom of any pit viper occurring in Louisiana (Russell 1980); this fact, plus the snake's large size and usually irritable disposition, makes *C. adamanteus* an animal to be treated with extreme caution.

Conant (1975) reported rabbits, rodents, and birds as the main prey of *C. adamanteus*.

Reproduction. No reproductive data are available on *C. adamanteus* in Louisiana. Elsewhere the species has been reported to give birth to 7 to 21 young (Klauber 1956). Mount (1975) reported that newborns average about 355 mm in total length, but the brood of a specimen Dundee collected in the Florida Panhandle averaged 388 mm.

Crotalus horridus Linnaeus
Timber Rattlesnake

Plate XXIII

Recognition. A very long (to 74½ in., 1,892 mm), heavy-bodied, gray-brown or yellowish gray snake with a pattern of relatively narrow black crossbands—sometimes interrupted laterally—and an ill-defined, rust-colored middorsal stripe; tail black; venter gray or cream, mottled with dark pigment; a broad dark line from the eye to the angle of the jaw;

a deep pit in the side of the head between the eye and the nostril; dorsal scales keeled, in 25 to 27 rows; tip of the tail with horny rattle or button; anal plate undivided.

Distribution. Statewide except for the Marsh and, apparently, the Longleaf Pine Forest in the Florida Parishes (Map 124). It appears to be absent or very rare in much of southwestern Louisiana.

Taxonomic comments. Only the southern subspecies, *Crotalus horridus atricaudatus* Latreille, the canebrake rattlesnake, occurs in Louisiana. On the basis of a morphometric analysis of geographic variation in this species, Pisani, Collins, and Edwards (1972) concluded that no subspecies should be recognized. They largely ignored color pattern, however, and their conclusions were not accepted by Conant (1975), who continued to recognize the canebrake rattlesnake as a distinct subspecies. On the basis of differences in adult size, color pattern, number of dorsal scale rows, and number of ventrals, Brown and Ernst (1986) concluded that *C. h. atricaudatus* is a valid form east of the Appalachians. Pending a thorough analysis throughout the range of the species, we are inclined to recognize the canebrake rattlesnake as a distinct entity.

Habitat and habits. The canebrake rattlesnake is most frequently encountered in areas where hardwood forest predominates, or at least once did. The species seems equally at home in the forests and cane fields of the Mississippi alluvial plain and in the hill country. Although specimens have been collected in the spring (when they were found basking along an old railroad spur on the Tulane University Riverside Campus), canebrake rattlesnakes seem to occur much more frequently in the summer and fall. Walker (1963) noted that they were most often reported in Jackson Parish by hunters in October, and Liner (1954) stated that they were killed quite often by sugarcane harvesters in Terrebonne Parish from October through December. In the Baton Rouge area, *C. horridus*

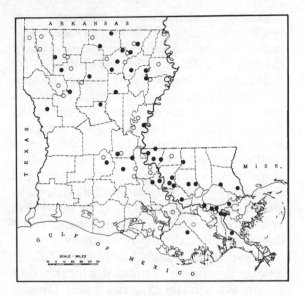

Map 124. Distribution of *Crotalus horridus.* Solid circles represent specimens examined; hollow circles represent museum specimens not examined or literature records.

seems to be particularly active in August and September, when a number of the snakes have been reported from the eastern part of the city. Walker (1963) observed a specimen swimming across a lake in Jackson Parish.

Certainly a dangerous snake because of its large size and potent venom, *C. horridus* nonetheless does not seem to be particularly aggressive and may not rattle even when closely approached by a human. A 5-footer (1,524 mm), which was crawling over a cedar log at the edge of a clearing atop a ridge in the Tunica Hills at high noon on 28 July 1973, did not rattle until after it had retreated beneath a brush pile. A somewhat smaller specimen, which was coiled in a sunny patch of honeysuckle on the side of the same ridge on 17 March 1974, took refuge beneath a log when persistently disturbed. A third specimen, which was collected 31 August 1974 on the side of the same ridge, was coiled on dead leaves alongside a log and neither rattled nor struck, despite the fact that two people inadvertently placed a foot within 5 in. of the snake. This same animal remained calm while it was being prodded into a sack, transported to another locality, and dumped out of the sack. F. A. Cook (1954) and Collins (1974) noted the tendency of this species to seek retreat rather than stay and fight; Collins also commented on the frequently silent rattle. The tendency of *C. horridus* to coil alongside logs was first noted in Louisiana by Beyer (1900) and has been studied in more detail in Pennsylvania by Reinert, Cundall, and Bushar (1984), who found that a rattlesnake would stay by a particular log for more than seven hours waiting to ambush the small rodents that used the log as a runway.

A specimen from Chicot State Park in Evangeline Parish contained a nearly full-grown fox squirrel (*Sciurus niger*). Dundee and Marlin Perkins found a 1,676-mm female near Sorrento (Ascension Parish) that contained a swamp rabbit (*Sylvilagus aquaticus*); this snake was stretched out and did not move or rattle until handled. In northern Louisiana, R. F. Clark (1949) found that ten snakes contained rabbits, eight contained mice, six contained rats, one contained a squirrel, and five contained quail (*Colinus virginianus*). This agrees with the findings of F. A. Cook (1954), who reported the food of the canebrake rattlesnake in Mississippi to include wood rats, mice, chipmunks, squirrels, rabbits, and birds.

Reproduction. R. F. Clark (1949) found from 7 to 11 fetuses in three northern Louisiana females examined in late August and early September. Elsewhere in the range of *C. h. atricaudatus*, litter sizes of 7 to 16 have been reported (Fitch 1985).

Sistrurus miliarius (Linnaeus)
Pygmy Rattlesnake
Plate XXIII

Recognition. A moderately short to medium-sized (to 31 in.; 787 mm), gray or tan snake with a pattern of narrow, dark bars and fre-quently an ill-defined, rust-colored middorsal stripe; tail banded; belly pale, mottled with black; a broad dark line from the eye to the angle of the jaw; a deep pit in the side of the head between the eye and the nostril; dorsal scales keeled, in 21 to 23 rows; tip of tail with very small horny rattle or button; anal plate undivided.

Distribution. Apparently statewide, but definite records are lacking from the Mississippi alluvial plain above New Orleans and from the Marsh in southwestern Louisiana (Map 125).

Taxonomic comments. Only the western subspecies, *Sistrurus miliarius streckeri* Gloyd, the western pygmy rattlesnake, has been reported from Louisiana, but it may intergrade with *S. m. barbouri* (Gloyd), the dusky pygmy rattlesnake, in the eastern Florida Parishes. The most recent comprehensive study is that by Gloyd (1940), although subsequent papers have dealt with the species in limited portions of its range.

Habitat and habits. In most parts of Louisiana the pygmy rattlesnake is encountered infrequently and in small numbers. The species appears to be most abundant south of New Orleans; Tulane University has large series from Lake Perez in Plaquemines Parish and Shell Beach in St. Bernard Parish. This observation is also borne out by the fact that Percy Viosca (notes) collected 103 pygmy rattlesnakes on Delacroix Island, St. Bernard Parish, during a 12-day period in June 1922 (49 on 11 June alone). The snakes had been driven onto the levees by severe flooding. Although *S. miliarius* is frequently associated with moist habitat in Louisiana and elsewhere in its range, it is occasionally found in rather dry situations as well. On 17 October 1971 a juvenile was collected under a rock in mixed pine-hardwood forest in the Chalk Hills of Catahoula Parish, and on 20 April 1974 an adult was taken beneath a log on a rocky hillside in Longleaf Pine Forest in the Red Dirt Wildlife Management Area, Natchitoches Parish. During the summer

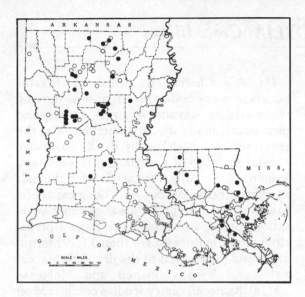

Map 125. Distribution of *Sistrurus miliarius.* Solid circles represent specimens examined; hollow circles represent museum specimens not examined or literature records.

months specimens occasionally turn up on roads at night, particularly in the hill country of central Louisiana and the Florida Parishes.

Pygmy rattlesnakes usually will vibrate their rattles, but the noise often can scarcely

be heard. The venom of this species is about as potent as that of *Crotalus horridus* (Russell 1980), but because this snake can inject only a small amount, human fatalities from *Sistrurus* bites probably are extremely rare. The venom is much more effective on smaller creatures—a frog that was bitten died in three minutes (R. F. Clark 1949).

Stomach contents R. F. Clark (1949) examined consisted primarily of frogs; *Acris, Rana sphenocephala,* and *R. clamitans* were present in that order of frequency. One snake contained a bird. Elsewhere pygmy rattlesnakes are reported to feed also on mice, lizards, and snakes.

Reproduction. R. F. Clark (1949) removed six developing embryos from the body of a 381-mm female, and Beyer (1900) reported that a female from Avery Island, Iberia Parish, gave birth to six young on 12 August 1894. Two females from Shell Beach, St. Bernard Parish, gave birth to six and four young on 12 and 25 August, respectively. The newly born snakes measured 121–146 mm in total length. Fitch (1985) reported that litter size in nine Texas females ranged from 3 to 32 young, although he noted that the litter of 32 was remarkably large.

Only 21 species of the order Crocodylia are still in existence, and several of these are facing extinction because of human activities. All crocodilians are aquatic carnivores, and all of them are egg layers. The males have a single solid copulatory organ.

FAMILY CROCODYLIDAE

The largely circumtropical family Crocodylidae contains eight genera comprising 21 species (Dowling and Duellman 1978). Only a single species, *Alligator mississippiensis*, occurs in Louisiana.

Alligator mississippiensis (Daudin)
American Alligator
Plate XXIV

Recognition. A very large (to 230 in.; 5,842 mm*), lizardlike reptile with tough leathery skin overlying bony plates on back and tail; ventral scales more or less quadrangular; snout long and broadly rounded; eyes and nostrils protruding; vent opening longitudinal; dorsum uniformly dark in adults, black with yellow crossbands in juveniles.

Distribution. Statewide, but apparently absent from the hill country except near large lakes and in the floodplains of major streams (Map 126).

Taxonomic comments. No subspecies are recognized. No taxonomic study of this species has been published.

*This size record for the species was an old male killed 2 January 1890 in Bayou Cock near the point where it enters Vermilion Bay, Vermilion Parish (McIlhenny 1935). There is considerable sexual dimorphism in size in the American alligator, and the males attain the larger size. The largest female McIlhenny (1935) measured was 109½ in. (2,781 mm) long. According to the Louisiana Department of Wildlife and Fisheries, no alligator exceeding 168 in. (4,267 mm) in length has been taken since the state reopened legal trapping in 1972.

Habitat and habits. The American alligator occurs in many bodies of still or slow-moving water—lakes, bayous, swamps, canals, and even occasionally drainage ditches—but the species is most abundant in the extensive coastal marshes of Louisiana (McNease and Joanen 1978). Alligators will enter the salt marsh on occasion but will not nest there. Juveniles seem to prefer areas of dense vegetation, perhaps to lessen the risk of predation, but alligators longer than 3 ft (914 mm) are found more often in the deeper lakes, canals, and bayous (Joanen and McNease 1972a). Radiotelemetry studies conducted on the Rockefeller Refuge (Cameron Parish) have revealed both sex- and age-related differences in the movements of alligators: adult females had a maximum home range of 41 acres (16.6 ha) and a maximum daily movement of 1,500 ft or 457.3 m (Joanen and McNease 1970); adult males had a maximum home range of 12,560 acres (5,083 ha) and a maximum daily movement of 27,750 ft (8,460 m) (Joanen and McNease 1972b); and immatures of both sexes had a maximum home range of about 1,500 acres (607 ha) (McNease and Joanen 1974). The latter study found seasonal differences in the daily movement of immatures, but the maximum average daily distance achieved was 2,500 ft (762 m). The greatest distance covered by any alligator studied at the Rockefeller Refuge was 33 air-line miles by an adult male between 17 May and 10 October (Joanen and McNease 1972b). McIlhenny (1935) found that alligators would often travel considerable distances (1–2 miles) overland.

In a swamp or marsh, alligators will dig holes 4–10 ft (1–3 m) in diameter and 4–6 ft (1–2 m) deep that are connected to the underground dens they construct (McIlhenny 1935). During periods of drought, these alligator holes may be the only sources of sur-

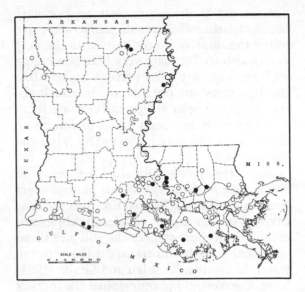

Map 126. Distribution of *Alligator mississippiensis.* Solid circles represent specimens examined; hollow circles represent museum specimens not examined or literature records.

face water in the marshes. The dens may be as long as 40 ft (12 m) and serve primarily as a retreat for the winter, when the alligators are largely inactive. Along streams or lakes the dens are excavated in the muddy banks.

Alligators are voracious predators and will feed on virtually any animal they can capture and crush with their powerful jaws. McIlhenny (1935) has noted that the nature of the prey tends to reflect the size of the alligator: hatchlings feed chiefly on insects and small fish; juveniles add crawfish, crabs, small frogs, and small reptiles to their diet; and individuals more than 3 ft (1 m) long will eat anything they can catch and swallow. The prey of these larger animals includes snakes, turtles, small alligators, fishes (including the alligator gar), crabs, crawfish, shrimp, birds (especially ducks, coots, and herons), and mammals—especially muskrats (Kellogg 1929; McIlhenny 1934) and nutria (McNease and Joanen 1977). Even large domesticated animals, such as dogs, hogs, and in a few instances, cattle, have been attacked and killed

(McIlhenny 1935). The alligator seizes animals too large to swallow whole by a limb and then rolls and twists violently to immobilize the prey through shock or drowning and to tear off the limb so it can be swallowed. Unprovoked attacks on humans are, somewhat surprisingly, extremely rare; E. A. McIlhenny knew of only one instance during all of his many years' experience with alligators in southern Louisiana. Nevertheless, alligators will attack if provoked (if their nests are approached too closely or their hatchlings molested, for instance), and even a relatively small individual has jaws so powerful that one would be extremely foolish not to use extreme caution when in their vicinity. In Florida, where the pressure of land development has thrown man and alligator into ever more frequent contact, the incidence of attacks has also increased (Hines and Keenlyne 1976).

Alligator skins are of commercial value in the leather trade, and when no controls existed, alligators were killed in such great numbers that biologists feared the species might become extinct (McIlhenny [1935] estimated that 3–3.5 million were killed in southern Louisiana alone between 1880 and 1933). For that reason, the state closed the alligator season in 1963 and banned all legalized trapping. With this protection the alligator populations recovered so quickly that by 1972 Louisiana was able to open a limited trapping season for alligators in certain southern parishes. The enactment of the federal Endangered Species Act late in 1973, which included the alligator under its protection, prevented the state from holding a season in 1974, but successful negotiations with the U.S. Fish and Wildlife Service permitted reestablishment of an annual season beginning in 1975. Alligator trapping is strictly regulated through a special tagging and licensing system, and trapping outside the designated areas or even in those areas other than during the specific season would violate both state and federal laws.

Reproduction. Female alligators apparently do not breed until they are nearly 10 years old and at least 6 ft (1.8 m) long (McIlhenny 1935; Joanen and McNease 1975). Courtship and mating occur in April and May, nest building and egg laying from 20 May to the first week in July (McIlhenny 1935; Joanen 1969). During the breeding season, male alligators are territorial and frequently make a roaring or bellowing sound that can be heard (by human ears) at distances up to a mile away. At this time males also emit a powerful sweet-smelling scent from two musk glands on their lower jaws. Mating takes place in the water.

In southwestern Louisiana female alligators construct their nest mounds from marsh vegetation that they strip from an area within 8 ft (2.4 m) of the mound. McIlhenny (1935) reported that nest mounds were usually 5–7 ft (1.5–2.1 m) in diameter by 2½–3 ft (0.8–0.9 m) in height; the nests studied by Joanen (1969) averaged 6 ft (1.8 m) in diameter by 2 ft (0.6 m) in height. The eggs, numbering from 2 to 58 (mean 39), are deposited in a more or less oval cavity 9 in. (229 mm) in diameter, the top of which lies 7 in. (178 mm) below the top of the mound (Joanen 1969). The female stays near the mound for the 62 to 65 days the eggs are incubating, presumably to protect them against such nest robbers as raccoons, opossums, bears, hogs, and humans. Joanen (1969) found the temperature inside the nest cavity to average only 4½°F (8°C) less than the outside air temperature, but to fluctuate much less than the outside temperature. He found the relative humidity within the nest cavity also to fluctuate very little, averaging 98.5 percent, some 20 percent higher than the less constant outside air. Interestingly, the temperature at which the eggs are incubated recently has been found to determine the sex of developing embryos (Ferguson and Joanen 1982).

When the young alligators are ready to hatch, they begin to call. Their mother hears them and removes the covering over the nest cavity with her mouth so the hatchlings can emerge. In some instances she will pick them up in her mouth and transport them to the water. In Florida, Kushlan and Simon (1981) have observed and photographed the mother alligator removing unhatched eggs from her nest and rolling them about between her tongue and palate to assist the hatching process. According to McIlhenny (1935), upon emergence the hatchlings, 9–9½ in. (229–241 mm) long, follow their mother to her den and remain with her through the winter, striking out on their own in the spring when they have reached a length of 16–18 in. (406–457 mm). Growth in alligators is rapid; individuals average about a foot increase each year for the first five years. Males continue to grow at this rate through their ninth year, but the growth rate in females decreases henceforth (McIlhenny 1934).

GLOSSARY

A–1, A–2. Abbreviations for anterior tooth rows in tadpole mouths (i.e., the upper set of rows).

A–2 GAP RATIO. The ratio between the length of one side of tooth row A–2 and the gap between the two sides of the tooth row.

ACUTE. Pointed by virtue of forming a narrow angle.

ADPRESSED. To press close, as to lay one toe against another, or, in the case of salamanders, to rotate the forelimb backward along the side and the hindlimb forward along the side.

ALLOPATRIC. Occupying a geographic range separated from that of another population.

AMPLEXUS. A sexual embrace in amphibians wherein the male usually grasps the female with his forelimbs between the axilla and groin.

ANAL PLATE. The scale that covers the vent.

ANGULATE. Running at an angle to the horizontal.

AXILLA. The armpit region.

BAND. A colored area, different from the ground color, that extends across the back to, or nearly to, the edge of the ventral surface. Also, sometimes used to refer to a ring or to a widened, elongated, longitudinal colored area, often appearing as a widened stripe.

BARBEL. A short, fleshy, whiskerlike projection or filament on the chin or throat of a turtle.

BARRED. Having a vertical pattern of contrasting colors, usually on the side of the body.

BLOTCHES. Relatively large, rounded or squarish areas of pattern (often with irregular margins).

BODY WIDTH/BASAL WIDTH. Ratio of the widest part of a tadpole body to the width at the base of its fleshy tail.

BRIDGE. The bony section connecting the upper and lower shells of a turtle.

CARAPACE. The upper shell of a turtle.

CAUDAL. Referring to the tail.

CERVICAL. Referring to the neck.

CHROMATOPHORE. A cell containing pigments, other than brown or black, that give color to an animal.

CIRRI. Short, cylindrical downgrowths from the nasal region of some salamanders.

CLINE. A character gradient usually correlated with an environmental gradient.

CLOACA. An internal chamber at the base of the tail that receives the digestive, urinary, and genital tracts. Its external opening is correctly termed "vent," not "anus."

COMPRESSED. Flattened from side to side.

CONCENTRIC. Arranged in an increasingly larger series of circles.

COSTAL. *adj.* Referring to the rib area. *n.* In turtles, one of several scutes of the dorsolateral section of the carapace.

CRANIAL. Referring to the head region or skull.

CREST. A raised, ridgelike area on the head region, especially in toads.

CROSSBANDS. Transverse dorsal bands that may extend onto the belly but do not cross it.

CRYPTIC SPECIES. Closely related species that are reproductively isolated but morphologically identical or nearly so. Synonym is "sibling species."

CUSP. A pointed, or sometimes rounded, toothlike projection in the mouth or on a tooth.

DEPRESSED. Flattened from the top toward the bottom.

DEWLAP. A brightly colored fold of skin on the throat of male anole lizards that is extended vertically during territorial displays.

DIPLOID. Containing the normal complement of chromosomes in a body cell.

DISC, ADHESIVE. An expanded, suction cup—like structure at the end of the toes in certain frogs.

DISC, ORAL. The collective term for the lips that surround the mouth in tadpoles.

DORSAL. Pertaining to the back. Not to be confused with the small scales on the backs of snakes and lizards.

DORSALS. Longitudinally arranged rows of scales that cover the dorsal surface of the body.

DORSOLATERAL. Pertaining to the area along the side of the back.

DORSUM. The upper surface (back) of the body.

ECTOTHERM. An animal whose body temperature is largely produced by external environmental factors and that generates little or no internal body heat through its metabolism. *See* "poikilotherm," a synonym.

ELECTROPHORETIC. Referring to a technique used to separate proteins by causing them to move in response to electric currents.

ELEPHANTINE. Referring to elephantlike limbs in turtles; therefore, having a rounded foot and short toes.

ENDEMIC. Restricted to a specific geographic region.

ERYTHROCYTE. A red blood cell.

ESTIVATE. To spend a period of the warm season in a state of torpor. Because some mammals (e.g., bats) may enter a torpid state during the warm season (but will become active at night), the application of "estivate" to both the ectothermic amphibians and reptiles and the endothermic mammals poses a semantic problem for biologists.

EVERSIBLE. Capable of being turned inside out like a glove.

FEMORAL. Referring to the thigh region.

FLAGELLUM. A free section of tail projecting beyond the end of the musculature in some hylid frogs.

FIMBRIAE. The finest branches on the external gills of salamanders.

FIN. In amphibians, the membranous or sometimes fleshy vertical projections above and below the tail and posterior section of the back.

FOLD, INTERCOSTAL. A bulging mass of flesh lying between adjacent ribs of salamanders and made evident by grooves between the folds.

FOLD, LATERAL. A longitudinal fold of skin on the lower side of the body in glass lizards (*Ophisaurus*).

FOSSORIAL. Pertaining to burrowing.

GILL FILAMENT. A vernacular term for a fimbria (*See* FIMBRIAE).

GILL RAMI. The central axes from which the gill filaments (fimbriae) project.

GILL SLIT. Opening on the side of the neck of salamanders, usually concealed between bushy external gills.

GLAND, HEDONIC. One of several glands on the heads of salamanders and which is involved in sexual stimulation.

GLAND, MENTAL. A hedonic gland on the underside of the chin in salamanders.

GLAND, PAROTOID. A large, roughened, poison-producing gland atop the posterolateral side of a toad's head.

GRAVID. Pregnant or containing a mass of enlarged eggs almost ready to lay.

GROIN. The crotch area between hind limbs and side of body.

GROOVE, COSTAL. One of a series of vertical grooves on the side of the trunk of a salamander. Each represents the position of a rib.

GROOVE, NASOLABIAL. A small groove running downward from each external nostril opening to the upper lip in transformed plethodontid salamanders.

GULAR. Pertaining to the throat.

HEMIPENIS. The paired, eversible, thin-walled copulatory organ of male lizards and snakes used to convey sperm to the oviduct openings in the female.

HIBERNATE. To spend the winter in a state of torpor. Although this term is widely applied to amphibians and reptiles, the condition is not the same as that occurring in certain mammals during their winter dormancy. Some biologists, therefore, object to the use of "hibernation" to describe the wintering habits of amphibians and reptiles.

HINGE. A flexible joint between different sections of the lower shell in certain turtles.

HOLARCTIC. Pertaining to Eurasia and North America north of tropical Mexico.

HYBRID. A cross between two different species.

INFOLDED. In tadpoles, a reference to the lips being indented at the sides.

INFRAMARGINAL. *adj.* Referring to under the edge or margin. *n.* In turtles, one of several small scutes that may occur on the lower part of the bridge.

INTERNASALS. Dorsally situated scale or scales lying between the narial openings but not in contact with those openings.

INTERORBITAL. Between the eyes.

JAW. In reference to tadpoles, a widened, black structure above or below the mouth opening.

KEEL. A narrow, elongated ridge.

KERATINIZED. Containing a horny substance, keratin; hence, usually darkened, dry, and rough.

LABIAL. Referring to the lip region.

LABIUM. Technical term for the lip.

LARVA. The immature form of an amphibian, usually equipped with fins and gills.

LATERAL. Referring to the side.

LATERAL LINE. In amphibian larvae a canal, usually evident as white areas perforated by small pores, and located along the sides and on the head and chest regions.

LATERAL LINE PORE (= MUCIFEROUS CRYPT). One of the openings into the lateral line.

LICHENLIKE. Having a shape with many small, slender lobes at the margin.

LOBULATED. Having a shape with a few broadened lobes projecting.

LOREAL (FACIAL) PIT. A deep pit in the loreal scale, lying between eye and nostril and somewhat below an imaginary line between them. Present in certain poisonous snakes and sensitive to infrared wavelengths of light (hence, heat-detecting).

MEDIAL. Referring to the middle.

MELANISTIC. Black in color.

MELANOPHORE. A cell containing black pigment.

METAMORPHOSIS. Process wherein an amphibian undergoes a drastic change in body form and structure in transforming from the larval to the adult stage.

METATARSAL. The region just anterior to the heel.

METATARSAL SPADE. A hardened, spadelike projection near the heel of a toad.

MONOTYPIC. A genus that contains only a single species.

MORPHOLOGICAL. Referring to anatomical structures.

MOTTLED. An indefinite pattern of spots of various sizes.

MUCIFEROUS CRYPT (= LATERAL LINE PORE).

NARIS. The nostril opening.

NEOTENIC. A somewhat loosely applied term describing a salamander that attains sexual maturity but retains the appearance of a larva. In actuality the term is applicable to any larval feature that is retained in the adult.

NEOTENOUS. Being neotenic for a brief period, or having a number of larval features.

NEOTENY. The state of being neotenic (*See* NEOTENIC).

NICTITATING MEMBRANE. A transparent third eyelid found beneath the conventional opaque eyelids of certain amphibians.

NUCHAL. *adj.* Referring to the dorsal neck area just behind the head. *n.* In some lizards, the posteriormost pair of dorsal head scales; in turtles, the small scute at the middle front margin of the carapace.

NUCLEOLI. Plural of nucleolus, a small, dense body found within the nucleus of a cell.

ORBIT. Pertaining to the eye socket.

ORBITONASAL. Pertaining to the region between eye and nostril.

OVIPAROUS. Laying eggs outside of the body.

OVOVIVIPAROUS. Retaining eggs within the body almost until the time of hatching.

P–1, P–2. Abbreviations for posterior tooth rows in tadpole mouths (i.e., the lower set of rows).

P–2 GAP. A space devoid of teeth in the second posterior row of teeth in tadpoles.

PAPILLA. A small, fleshy protuberance in the tissue surrounding a tadpole mouth.

PARAPATRIC. Having a geographic range abutting that of another population.

PARAVOMERINE. Referring to a bone in the medial section of the posterior roof of a salamander's mouth.

PECTORAL. *adj.* Pertaining to the lower chest region. *n.* In turtles, a scute in the chest region of the plastron.

PEDICEL. A stemlike support found in certain salamander tongues, much like the "stem" of a mushroom.

PLASTRON. The lower shell of a turtle.

PLICA. One of the folds of tissue between the grooves of certain salamander tongues.

PLINTH. An amphibian egg mass that is somewhat flattened and rectangular in shape.

POIKILOTHERM. An animal having a variable body temperature that is principally produced by external environmental factors. Synonym is "ectotherm." Although the term "cold blooded" is often applied to such creatures, they may actually be quite warm if the surroundings are warm.

PORES, FEMORAL. A series of small openings in the scales (one per scale) on the underside of the thigh in some species of lizards.

POSTLABIALS. Small scales lying between the last supralabial and the ear opening in certain lizard species (especially *Eumeces fasciatus*).

POSTMENTAL. The scale in certain lizard species that lies in the midline directly behind the mental, which is the anteriormost scale on the chin.

POSTORBITAL. Behind the eye.

PREFRONTALS. Paired scales that lie on the dorsal surface of the head immediately anterior to the large unpaired frontal.

RETICULATE. Netlike in appearance.

RIDGE, DORSOLATERAL. A longitudinal fleshy ridge on either side of some frogs' backs; may run the length of the body or may be limited to the area just behind the head.

RINGS. Transverse bands that completely encircle the body.

RUGOSE. Roughened, especially in a wrinkled fashion.

SCALE. A thin keratinized structure forming part of the covering of most reptile skins. May be small, circular, and humped, but usually flattened. In turtles, it may be adherent to an underlying bony plate and not the skin. Sometimes with a small bony core in lizards or crocodilians.

SCUTE (= SCALE). Term usually applied to relatively large scales.

SEPTUM. A thin dividing wall.

SERRATE. Saw-toothed.

SIBLING SPECIES. *See* CRYPTIC SPECIES.

SNOUT-VENT LENGTH. In snakes and lizards, the distance between the tip of the snout to the posterior end of the scute that covers the cloacal aperture. In salamanders, the distance is measured to the posterior end of the elongated vent opening. Most easily measured if the animal is lying on its back.

SPADE, METATARSAL. *See* METATARSAL SPADE.

SPECTACLE. The transparent covering of the eye in snakes and those lizards that lack movable eyelids.

SPERMATHECA. A small chamber in the roof·

of the cloaca of a female salamander that stores spermatozoa.

SPERMATOPHORE. A stalklike structure produced from the cloacal glands of male salamanders that is used to hold a mass of spermatozoa.

SPIRACLE. A small opening, usually on the left side of a tadpole's head, into a gill chamber.

SPIRACULAR TUBE. A tubelike projection from the side of a tadpole's head that contains the spiracle at its free end.

SPOTS. Relatively small, rounded areas of pattern (often with fairly regular margins).

SPOTS, PARIETAL. Relatively small, usually light-colored spots on the parietal scales near their common suture.

SPUR. A raised, solid projection turning off at an angle from a longer axis.

STRIPE, LATERAL. Any longitudinal line that is situated on the side of the body.

STRIPE, VERTEBRAL. A longitudinal line that is confined to the middorsal region of the body.

SUBARTICULAR. Under a toe joint.

SUBCAUDAL SCALES. The scales that cover the underside of the tail.

SUBMARGINAL. Below the edge.

SUBOCULARS. Small scales beneath the eye that separate it from the supralabials.

SUBORBITAL. Below the eye.

SUPRALABIALS. The scales that border the upper lip posterior to the rostral.

SUPRAMARGINAL. *adj.* Above the edge or margin. *n.* In the alligator snapping turtle, one of several small scutes lying above the bridge.

SYMPATRIC. Occupying the same geographic range, or having broadly overlapping ranges.

TERRAPIN. A term sometimes restricted to turtles that have partially webbed feet.

TETRAPLOID. Having a duplicate set of the normal complement of chromosomes; hence, twice the diploid (2N) number, being thus 4N.

TIBIAL. Referring to the shin region.

TORTOISE. A term used to describe land turtles that have stumpy, elephantlike feet.

TRANSFORM. To change from larval to adult form during amphibian metamorphosis.

TRANSVERSE. Running at a right angle to the long axis; hence, across the body.

TUBERCLE. A projecting knob or bump on the skin.

TUBERCULATE. Covered with tubercles.

TURTLE. A term sometimes restricted (usually by the British) to those turtles that have flipperlike feet, i.e., only the sea turtles.

TYMPANUM. The rounded eardrum on the side of the head of many reptiles and amphibians.

TYPE LOCALITY. The site at which the specimen that is used to fix the identity of a new species or subspecies was discovered.

VASA DEFERENTIA. The ducts that convey spermatozoa from the testes of animals.

VENT. The external opening of the cloaca; hence, the outlet for digestive, urinary, and reproductive tracts in amphibians and reptiles.

VENTER. The bottom side; the belly.

VENTRAL. Referring to the underside.

VENTRALS. The belly scales, which are widened in snakes to form a single longitudinal series.

VERTEBRAL. *adj.* Referring to the vertebral column (backbone, spine); hence, the area down the middle of the back. *n.* In turtles, one of several scutes covering the midline of the carapace.

VITELLUS. The yolk in the center of an egg.

VOMERINE. Referring to the vomer, a bone lying in the anterior roof of the mouth and usually containing the internal nostril openings or notched to accommodate part of the openings.

WART. A raised, often spiny or hardened, tubercle on the skin.

LITERATURE CITED

Allen, E. R., and W. T. Neill. 1950. The alligator snapping turtle, *Macrochelys temminckii*, in Florida. *Special Publication Ross Allen's Reptile Institute* (4):1–15.

Allen, M. J. 1932. A survey of the amphibians and reptiles of Harrison County, Mississippi. *American Museum Novitates* (542):1–20.

Altig, R. 1970. A key to the tadpoles of the United States and Canada. *Herpetologica* 26:180–207.

Anderson, J. D. 1967a. *Ambystoma maculatum. Catalogue of American Amphibians and Reptiles*: 51.1–51.4.

———. 1967b. *Ambystoma opacum. Catalogue of American Amphibians and Reptiles*: 46.1–46.2.

Anderson, P. K. 1954. Studies in the ecology of the narrow-mouthed toad, *Microhyla carolinensis carolinensis. Tulane Studies in Zoology* 2:15–46.

———. 1958. The photic responses and water approach behavior of hatchling turtles. *Copeia* 1958:211–15.

———. 1961. Variation in populations of brown snakes, genus *Storeria*, bordering the Gulf of Mexico. *American Midland Naturalist* 66:235–49.

Anderson, P. K., E. A. Liner, and R. E. Etheridge. 1952. Notes on amphibian and reptile populations in a Louisiana pineland area. *Ecology* 33:274–78.

Arny, S. A. 1948. A survey of the reptiles and amphibians of the Delta National Wildlife Refuge. M.S. thesis, Tulane University, New Orleans, Louisiana.

Ashton, R. E., Jr., and R. Franz. 1979. *Bufo quercicus. Catalogue of American Amphibians and Reptiles*: 222.1–222.2.

Auffenberg, W. 1976. The genus *Gopherus* (Testudinidae): Pt. 1. Osteology and relationships of extant species. *Bulletin of the Florida State Museum, Biological Sciences* 20:47–110.

Auffenberg, W., and R. Franz. 1982. The status and distribution of the gopher tortoise (*Gopherus polyphemus*). In *North American Tortoises: Conservation and Ecology*, ed. R. B. Bury, 95–126. U.S. Fish and Wildlife Service, Wildlife Research Report 12.

Baker, C. L. 1947. The species of amphiumae. *Journal of the Tennessee Academy of Science* 22:9–21.

Ball, S. C. 1936. The distribution and behavior of the spadefoot toad in Connecticut. *Transactions of the Connecticut Academy of Arts and Sciences* 32:351–79.

Barton, B. S. 1808. Some account of the *Siren lacertina*, and other species of the same genus of amphibious animals. Philadelphia, Pennsylvania.

Baur, G. 1890. Two new species of tortoises from the South. *Science*, new series, 16:262.

Bayless, L. E. 1966. Comparative ecology of two sympatric species of *Acris* (Anura; Hylidae) with emphasis on interspecific competition. Ph.D. dissertation, Tulane University, New Orleans, Louisiana.

Bennett, H. J. 1935. Four new trematodes from reptiles. *Journal of Parasitology* 21:83–90.

Bentley, P. J., W. L. Bretz, and K. Schmidt-Nielsen. 1967. Osmoregulation in the diamondback terrapin, *Malaclemys terrapin centrata. Journal of Experimental Biology* 46:161–67.

Bertl, J., and F. C. Killebrew. 1983. An osteological comparison of *Graptemys caglei* Haynes and McKown and *Graptemys versa* Stejneger (Testudines: Emydidae). *Herpetologica* 39:375–82.

Beyer, G. E. 1898. Observations on the life

histories of certain snakes. *American Nat uralist* 32:17–24.

———. 1900. Louisiana herpetology with a check-list of the batrachians and reptiles of the state. *Proceedings of the Louisiana Society of Naturalists for 1897–99:* 25–46.

Bishop, S. C. 1941. The salamanders of New York. *New York State Museum Bulletin* (324):1–365.

———. 1943. *Handbook of Salamanders.* Ithaca, New York.

Blair, A. P., and H. L. Lindsay. 1961. *Hyla avivoca* (Hylidae) in Oklahoma. *Southwestern Naturalist* 6:202.

Blair, W. F., ed. 1972. *Evolution in the Genus "Bufo."* Austin, Texas.

Blanchard, F. N. 1921. A revision of the king snakes: Genus *Lampropeltis. Bulletin, United States National Museum* (114):1–260.

———. 1923. The snakes of the genus *Virginia. Papers of the Michigan Academy of Sciences, Arts, and Letters* 3:343–65.

———. 1942. The ring-neck snakes, genus *Diadophis. Bulletin of the Chicago Academy of Sciences* 7:5–144.

Blaney, R. M. 1968. Hybridization of the box turtles *Terrapene carolina* and *T. ornata* in western Louisiana. *Proceedings of the Louisiana Academy of Sciences* 31:54–57.

———. 1977. Systematics of the common kingsnake, *Lampropeltis getulus* (Linnaeus). *Tulane Studies in Zoology and Botany* 19:47–103.

Blaney, R. M., and P. K. Blaney. 1979. The *Nerodia sipedon* complex of water snakes in Mississippi and southeastern Louisiana. *Herpetologica* 35:350–59.

Blem, C. R. 1979. *Bufo terrestris. Catalogue of American Amphibians and Reptiles:* 223.1–223.2.

Blem, C. R., and L. B. Blem. 1985. Notes on *Virginia* (Reptilia: Colubridae) in Virginia. *Brimleyana* (11):87–95.

Boyd, C. E., and D. H. Vickers. 1963. Distribution of some Mississippi amphibians and reptiles. *Herpetologica* 19:202–205.

Bragg, A. N. 1953. A study of *Rana areolata* in Oklahoma. *Wasmann Journal of Biology* 11:273–318.

———. 1954. *Bufo terrestris charlesmithi,* a new subspecies from Oklahoma. *Wasmann Journal of Biology* 12:245–54.

Brimley, C. S. 1923. The dwarf salamander at Raleigh, North Carolina. *Copeia* (120):81–83.

Brode, W. E., and P. Allison. 1958. Burrowing snakes of the panhandle counties of Mississippi. *Herpetologica* 14:37–40.

Brown, C. A. 1945. *Louisiana Trees and Shrubs.* Baton Rouge, Louisiana.

Brown, C. W., and C. H. Ernst. 1986. A study of variation in eastern timber rattlesnakes, *Crotalus horridus* Linnae [sic] (Serpentes: Viperidae). *Brimleyana* (12):57–74.

Bruce, R. C. 1968. Life history studies of the salamanders of the genus *Pseudotriton* (Caudata: Plethodontidae). Ph.D. dissertation, Duke University, Durham, North Carolina.

———. 1970. The larval life of the three-lined salamander, *Eurycea longicauda guttolineata. Copeia* 1970:776–79.

———. 1972. The larval life of the red salamander, *Pseudotriton ruber. Journal of Herpetology* 6:43–51.

———. 1974. Larval development of the salamanders *Pseudotriton montanus* and *P. ruber. American Midland Naturalist* 92:173–90.

———. 1975. Reproductive biology of the mud salamander, *Pseudotriton montanus,* in western South Carolina. *Copeia* 1975:129–37.

———. 1982. Larval periods and metamorphosis in two species of salamanders of the genus *Eurycea. Copeia* 1982:117–27.

Burger, W. L., P. W. Smith, and H. M. Smith. 1949. Notable records of reptiles and amphibians in Oklahoma, Arkansas, and Texas. *Journal of the Tennessee Academy of Science* 24:130–34.

Burghardt, G. M. 1968. Chemical preference studies on newborn snakes of three sympatric species of *Natrix. Copeia* 1968: 732–37.

Burkett, R. D. 1966. Natural history of cottonmouth moccasin, *Agkistrodon piscivorus* (Reptilia). *University of Kansas Publications, Museum of Natural History* 17:435–91.

Burns, T. A., and K. L. Williams. 1972. Notes on the reproductive habits of *Malaclemys terrapin pileata. Journal of Herpetology* 6:237–38.

Burt, C. E. 1928. The synonymy, variation, and distribution of the collared lizard, *Crotaphytus collaris* (Say). *Occasional Papers of the Museum of Zoology, University of Michigan* (196):1–10.

———. 1931. A study of the teiid lizards of the genus *Cnemidophorus*, with special reference to their phylogenetic relationships. *Bulletin, United States National Museum* (154):1–286.

Byrd, E. E. 1936. A new trematode parasite from the mud turtle *Kinosternon subrubrum hippocrepis. Journal of Parasitology* 22:413–15.

Cagle, F. R. 1948a. Observations on a population of the salamander, *Amphiuma tridactylum* Cuvier. *Ecology* 29:479–91.

———. 1948b. A population of the Carolina anole. *Natural History Miscellanea* (15): 1–5.

———. 1950. The life history of the slider turtle, *Pseudemys scripta troostii* (Holbrook). *Ecological Monographs* 20:31–54.

———. 1952a. The status of the turtles *Graptemys pulchra* Baur and *Graptemys barbouri* Carr and Marchand, with notes on their natural history. *Copeia* 1952:223–34.

———. 1952b. A Louisiana terrapin population (*Malaclemys*). *Copeia* 1952:74–76.

———. 1953. The status of the turtle *Graptemys oculifera* (Baur). *Zoologica* 38: 137–44.

———. 1954. Observations on the life cycles of painted turtles (genus *Chrysemys*). *American Midland Naturalist* 52:225–35.

Cagle, F. R., and J. Tihen. 1948. Retention of

eggs by the turtle *Deirochelys reticularia. Copeia* 1948:66.

Caldwell, J. P. 1982. *Hyla gratiosa. Catalogue of American Amphibians and Reptiles*: 298.1–298.2.

Camp, C. D., and L. L. Bozeman. 1981. Foods of two species of *Plethodon* (Caudata: Plethodontidae) from Georgia and Alabama, U.S.A. *Brimleyana* (6):163–66.

Campbell, G. R., and W. H. Stickel. 1939. Notes on the yellow-lipped snake. *Copeia* 1939:105.

Carr, A. F. 1940. A contribution to the herpetology of Florida. *University of Florida Publications, Biological Science Series* (3):1–118.

———. 1952. *Handbook of Turtles: The Turtles of the United States, Canada, and Baja California*. Ithaca, New York.

———. 1967. *So Excellent a Fishe*. Garden City, New York.

Carr, A. F., and C. J. Goin. 1943. Neoteny in Florida salamanders. *Proceedings of the Florida Academy of Sciences* 6:37–40.

Carr, A. F., H. Hirth, and L. Ogren. 1966. The ecology and migrations of sea turtles, part 6. The hawksbill turtle in the Caribbean Sea. *American Museum Novitates* (2248): 1–29.

Cash, M. N., and J. P. Bogart. 1978. Cytological differentiation of the diploid-tetraploid species pair of North American treefrogs (Amphibia, Anura, Hylidae). *Journal of Herpetology* 12:555–58.

Chandler, A. C. 1923. Three new trematodes from *Amphiuma means. Proceedings of the United States National Museum* 63, Article 3:1–7.

Chaney, A. H. 1949. The life history of *Desmognathus fuscus auriculatus*. M.S. thesis, Tulane University, New Orleans, Louisiana.

———. 1951. The food habits of the salamander *Amphiuma tridactylum. Copeia* 1951:45–49.

———. 1958. A comparison of Louisiana and Arkansas populations of *Desmognathus fuscus.* Ph.D. dissertation, Tulane University, New Orleans, Louisiana.

Chaney, A. H., and C. L. Smith. 1950. Methods for collecting map turtles. *Copeia* 1950:323–24.

Chavez, H. M., G. Contreras, and T. P. E. Hernandez D. 1968. On the coast of Tamaulipas, II. *International Turtle and Tortoise Society Journal* 2(5):16–19, 27–34.

Clark, D. R., Jr. 1964. Reproduction and sexual dimorphism in a population of the rough earth snake, *Virginia striatula. Texas Journal of Science* 16:265–95.

———. 1970. Ecological studies of the worm snake *Carphophis vermis* (Kennicott). *University of Kansas Publications, Museum of Natural History* 19:85–194.

Clark, R. F. 1949. Snakes of the hill parishes of Louisiana. *Journal of the Tennessee Academy of Science* 24:244–61.

Collins, J. T. 1974. Amphibians and reptiles in Kansas. *University of Kansas Museum of Natural History, Public Education Series* No. 1.

Conant, R. 1949. Two new races of *Natrix erythrogaster. Copeia* 1949:1–15.

———. 1956. A review of two rare pine snakes from the Gulf Coastal Plain. *American Museum Novitates* (1781):1–31.

———. 1958. *A Field Guide to Reptiles and Amphibians of the United States and Canada East of the 100th Meridian.* Boston, Massachusetts.

———. 1963. Evidence for the specific status of the water snake *Natrix fasciata. American Museum Novitates* (2122):1–38.

———. 1969. A review of the water snakes of the genus *Natrix* in Mexico. *Bulletin of the American Museum of Natural History* 142:3–140.

———. 1975. *A Field Guide to Reptiles and Amphibians of Eastern and Central North America.* 2nd ed. Boston, Massachusetts.

Cook, F. A. 1943. *Snakes of Mississippi.* Survey Bulletin, Mississippi Game and Fish Commission, Jackson, Mississippi.

———. 1954. *Snakes of Mississippi.* State Game and Fish Commission, Public Relations Department, Jackson, Mississippi.

Cook, M. L., and B. C. Brown. 1974. Variation in the genus *Desmognathus* (Amphibia: Plethodontidae) in the western limits of its range. *Journal of Herpetology* 8:93–105.

Cope, E. D. 1869. A review of the species of the Plethodontidae and Desmognathidae. *Proceedings of the Academy of Natural Sciences of Philadelphia* 21:93–118.

———. 1889. The Batrachia of North America. *Bulletin, United States National Museum* (34):1–525.

Crain, J. L., and J. W. Cliburn. 1971. *Pituophis melanoleucus* from the western part of its range. *Southwestern Naturalist* 15:495–505.

Crenshaw, J. W. 1955a. The ecological geography of the *Pseudemys floridana* complex in the southeastern United States. Ph.D. dissertation, University of Florida, Gainesville.

———. 1955b. The life history of the southern spiny lizard, *Sceloporus undulatus undulatus* Latreille. *American Midland Naturalist* 54:257–98.

Culley, D. D., Jr., S. P. Meyers, A. J. Doucette, and B. Spain. 1976. Growth response of bullfrog larvae in an intensive culture system. Unpublished manuscript, School of Forestry and Wildlife Management, Louisiana State University, Baton Rouge.

Cuvier, M. LeBon. 1827. Sur le genre de reptiles batraciens, nommé *Amphiuma,* et sur une nouvelle espèce de ce genre (*Amphiuma tridactylum*). *Mémoires du Muséum d'Histoire Naturelle, Paris* 14:1–14.

Daudin, F. M. 1803. *Histoire Naturelle des Reptiles.* Vol. 2. Paris.

Davis, D. M. 1968. A study of variation in North American lizards of the *fasciatus* group of the genus *Eumeces* (Scincidae). Ph.D. dissertation, Duke University, Durham, North Carolina.

Delcourt, H. D., and P. A. Delcourt. 1975.

The blufflands: Pleistocene pathway into the Tunica Hills. *American Midland Naturalist* 94:385–400.

Dobie, J. L. 1971. Reproduction and growth in the alligator snapping turtle, *Macroclemys temmincki* (Troost). *Copeia* 1971:645–58.

———. 1981. The taxonomic relationship between *Malaclemys* Gray, 1844 and *Graptemys* Agassiz, 1857 (Testudines: Emydidae). *Tulane Studies in Zoology and Botany* 23:85–102.

Dobie, J. L., L. H. Ogren, and J. F. Fitzpatrick. 1961. Food notes and records of the Atlantic ridley turtle (*Lepidochelys kempi*) from Louisiana. *Copeia* 1961:109–10.

Dowling, H. G. 1957. A review of the amphibians and reptiles of Arkansas. *Occasional Papers, University of Arkansas Museum* (3):1–51.

Dowling, H. G., and W. E. Duellman. 1978. *Systematic Herpetology: A Synopsis of Families and Higher Categories.* New York.

Duellman, W. E., and A. Schwartz. 1958. Amphibians and reptiles of southern Florida. *Bulletin of the Florida State Museum, Biological Sciences* 3:181–324.

Dundee, H. A. 1968. First record of the four-toed salamander, *Hemidactylium scutatum*, in Mississippi, with comments on its disjunct distribution in Arkansas and Louisiana. *Journal of Herpetology* 1:101–103.

———. 1974a. Rediscovery of *Ambystoma tigrinum* in eastern Louisiana, with comments on the biology of the species. *Journal of Herpetology* 8:265–67.

———. 1974b. Recognition characters for *Rana grylio. Journal of Herpetology* 8:275–76.

———. 1974c. Evidence for specific status of *Graptemys kohni* and *Graptemys pseudogeographica. Copeia* 1974:540–42.

———. In press. *Ambystoma tigrinum* locality records—be wary! *Herpetological Review.*

Dunn, E. R. 1923. Mutanda herpetologica. *Proceedings of the New England Zoölogical Club* 8:39–40.

———. 1926. *The Salamanders of the Family Plethodontidae.* Northampton, Massachusetts.

———. 1940. The races of *Ambystoma tigrinum. Copeia* 1940:154–62.

Edgren, R. A. 1961. A simplified method for analysis of clines; geographic variation in the hognose snake *Heterodon platyrhinos* Latreille. *Copeia* 1961:125–32.

Ernst, C. H. 1971. *Chrysemys picta.* Catalogue of American Amphibians and Reptiles: 106.1–106.4.

Ernst, C. H., and R. W. Barbour. 1972. *Turtles of the United States.* Lexington, Kentucky.

Ernst, C. H., and R. B. Bury. 1982. *Malaclemys, M. terrapin.* Catalogue of American Amphibians and Reptiles: 299.1–299.4.

Estes, R., and G. Pregill, eds. 1988. *Phylogenetic Relationships of the Lizard Families.* Stanford, California.

Estridge, R. E. 1970. The taxonomic status of *Sternothaerus depressus* (Testudinata, Kinosternidae) with observations on its ecology. M.S. thesis, Auburn University, Auburn, Alabama.

Etheridge, R. E. 1952. The warty gecko, *Hemidactylus turcicus turcicus* (Linnaeus), in New Orleans, Louisiana. *Copeia* 1952:47–48.

Fahey, K. M. 1980. A taxonomic study of the cooter turtles *Pseudemys floridana* (Le-Conte) and *Pseudemys concinna* (Le-Conte), in the lower Red River, Atchafalaya River, and Mississippi River basin. *Tulane Studies in Zoology and Botany* 22:49–66.

Ferguson, M. W. J., and T. Joanen. 1982. Temperature of egg incubation determines sex in *Alligator mississippiensis. Nature* 296:850–53.

Feuer, R. C. 1966. Variation in snapping turtles, *Chelydra serpentina* Linnaeus: A study in quantitative systematics. Ph.D.

dissertation, University of Utah, Salt Lake City.

———. 1971. Intergradation of the snapping turtles *Chelydra serpentina serpentina* (Linnaeus, 1758) and *Chelydra serpentina osceola* Stejneger, 1918. *Herpetologica* 27:379–84.

Fisher, C. B. 1973. Status of the flat-headed snake, *Tantilla gracilis* Baird and Girard, in Louisiana. *Journal of Herpetology* 7: 136–37.

Fitch, H. S. 1949. Road counts of snakes in western Louisiana. *Herpetologica* 5: 87–90.

———. 1954. Life history and ecology of the five-lined skink, *Eumeces fasciatus*. *University of Kansas Publications, Museum of Natural History* 8:1–156.

———. 1956a. Temperature responses in free-living amphibians and reptiles of northeastern Kansas. *University of Kansas Publications, Museum of Natural History* 8:417–76.

———. 1956b. An ecological study of the collared lizard, *Crotaphytus collaris*. *University of Kansas Publications, Museum of Natural History* 8:213–74.

———. 1958. Natural history of the six-lined racerunner (*Cnemidophorus sexlineatus*). *University of Kansas Publications, Museum of Natural History* 11: 11–62.

———. 1960. Autecology of the copperhead. *University of Kansas Publications, Museum of Natural History* 13:85–288.

———. 1970. Reproduction in lizards and snakes. *University of Kansas Museum of Natural History, Miscellaneous Publication* (52):1–247.

———. 1985. Variation in clutch and litter size in New World reptiles. *University of Kansas Museum of Natural History, Miscellaneous Publication* (76):1–76.

Folkerts, G. W. 1968. The genus *Desmognathus* Baird (Amphibia: Plethodontidae) in Alabama. Ph.D. dissertation, Auburn University, Auburn, Alabama.

Force, E. R. 1925. Notes on reptiles and amphibians of Okmulgee County, Oklahoma. *Copeia* (141):25–27.

———. 1935. A local study of the opisthoglyph snake *Tantilla gracilis* Baird and Girard. *Papers of the Michigan Academy of Sciences, Arts, and Letters* 20: 645–59.

Fortman, J. R., and R. Altig. 1974. Characters of F1 hybrid frogs from six species of *Hyla* (Anura: Hylidae). *Herpetologica* 30: 221–34.

Fouquette, M. J., Jr., and J. Delahoussaye. 1966. Noteworthy herpetological records from Louisiana. *Southwestern Naturalist* 11:137–39.

Frierson, L. S., Jr. 1927a. *Crotaphytus collaris collaris* at Taylor Town, Louisiana. *Copeia* (165):113–14.

———. 1927b. *Phrynosoma cornutum* (Harlan) in Louisiana. *Copeia* (165):114.

Fugler, C. M. 1955. New locality records for the Louisiana pine snake, *Pituophis catenifer ruthveni* Stull. *Herpetologica* 11:24.

Fuller, D. A., and A. M. Tappan. 1986. The occurrence of sea turtles in Louisiana coastal waters. Louisiana State University, Coastal Fisheries Institute, Report LSU-CFI-86-28, Baton Rouge.

Gartside, D. F. 1980. Analysis of a hybrid zone between chorus frogs of the *Pseudacris nigrita* complex in the southern United States. *Copeia* 1980:56–66.

Gloyd, H. K. 1940. The rattlesnakes, genera *Sistrurus* and *Crotalus*. *The Chicago Academy of Sciences, Special Publication* (4):1–266.

Gloyd, H. K., and R. Conant. 1943. A synopsis of the American forms of *Agkistrodon* (copperheads and moccasins). *Bulletin of the Chicago Academy of Sciences* 7: 147–70.

Goin, C. J. 1938. The status of *Amphiuma tridactylum*. *Herpetologica* 1:127–30.

———. 1947a. Notes on the eggs and early larvae of three Florida salamanders. *Natural History Miscellanea* (10):1–4.

———. 1947b. Studies on the life history of

Eleutherodactylus ricordii planirostris (Cope) in Florida. *University of Florida Studies, Biological Sciences Series* 4(2):1–66.

———. 1949. The peep order in peepers; a swamp water serenade. *Quarterly Journal of the Florida Academy of Sciences* 11(2–3):59–61.

———. 1957. Description of a new salamander of the genus *Siren* from the Rio Grande. *Herpetologica* 13:37–42.

Goin, C. J., and M. G. Netting. 1940. A new gopher frog from the Gulf Coast, with comments upon the *Rana areolata* group. *Annals of the Carnegie Museum* 28:137–68.

Gordon, R. E. 1953. A population of Holbrook's salamander, *Eurycea longicauda guttolineata* (Holbrook). *Tulane Studies in Zoology* 1:55–60.

Gosner, K. L., and D. A. Rossman. 1960. Eggs and larval development of the treefrogs *Hyla crucifer* and *Hyla ocularis*. *Herpetologica* 16:225–32.

Gowanloch, J. N. 1935. Frog industry in Louisiana. *Louisiana Department of Conservation Division of Fisheries, Bulletin* (26):1–44.

Green, D. M. 1982. Mating call characteristics of hybrid toads (*Bufo americanus × B. fowleri*) at Long Point, Ontario. *Canadian Journal of Zoology* 60:3293–97.

Green, J. 1831. Description of two new species of salamander. *Journal of the Academy of Natural Sciences of Philadelphia* 6(pt. 2):253–55.

Greene, H. W. 1984. Feeding behavior and diet of the eastern coral snake, *Micrurus fulvius*. In *A Tribute to Henry S. Fitch*, ed. R. A. Seigel, L. E. Hunt, J. L. Knight, L. Malaret, and N. L. Zuschlag, 147–62. Lawrence, Kansas.

Grobman, A. B. 1984. Scutellation variation in *Opheodrys aestivus*. *Bulletin of the Florida State Museum* 29:153–70.

Hahn, D. E., and L. D. Wilson. 1966. Variation in two broods of *Farancia abacura reinwardti* Schlegel (Serpentes: Colubri-dae) from Louisiana. *Journal of the Ohio Herpetological Society* 5:159–60.

Hall, R. J. 1969. Ecological observations on Graham's watersnake (*Regina grahami* Baird and Girard). *American Midland Naturalist* 81:156–63.

Hamlett, G. W. D. 1952. Notes on breeding and reproduction in the lizard *Anolis carolinensis*. *Copeia* 1952:183–85.

Hardy, J. D., and R. J. Borroughs. 1986. Systematic status of the spring peeper, *Hyla crucifer* (Amphibia: Hylidae). *Bulletin of the Maryland Herpetological Society* 22:68–89.

Hardy, L. M., and C. J. Cole. 1968. Morphological variation in a population of the snake, *Tantilla gracilis* Baird and Girard. *University of Kansas Publications, Museum of Natural History* 17:613–29.

Hardy, L. M., and L. R. Raymond. 1980. The breeding migration of the mole salamander, *Ambystoma talpoideum*, in Louisiana. *Journal of Herpetology* 14:327–35.

Harper, F. 1937. A season with Holbrook's chorus frog (*Pseudacris ornata*). *American Midland Naturalist* 18:260–72.

———. 1939. A southern subspecies of the spring peeper (*Hyla crucifera*). *Notulae Naturae* (27):1–4.

———. 1955. A new chorus frog (*Pseudacris*) from the eastern United States. *Natural History Miscellanea* (150):1–6.

Harrison, J. R. 1973. Observations on the life history and ecology of *Eurycea quadridigitata* (Holbrook). *HISS News-Journal* 1:57–58.

Hart, D. R. 1983. Dietary and habitat shift with size of red-eared turtles (*Pseudemys scripta*) in a southern Louisiana population. *Herpetologica* 39:285–90.

Hay, W. P. 1904. A revision of *Malaclemys*, a genus of turtles. *Bulletin, U.S. Bureau of Fisheries* (24):1–20.

Hebard, J. J., and H. R. Mushinsky. 1978. Habitat use by five sympatric water snakes in a Louisiana swamp. *Herpetologica* 34:306–11.

Hecht, M. K., and B. L. Matalas. 1946. A review of Middle American toads of the genus *Microhyla. American Museum Novitates* (1315):1–21.

Hedges, S. B. 1986. An electrophoretic analysis of Holarctic hylid frog evolution. *Systematic Zoology* 35:1–21.

Highton, R. 1956. The life history of the slimy salamander, *Plethodon glutinosus,* in Florida. *Copeia* 1956:75–93.

———. 1962. Revision of North American salamanders of the genus *Plethodon. Bulletin of the Florida State Museum, Biological Sciences* 6:235–367.

Highton, R., and T. P. Webster. 1976. Geographic protein variation and divergence in populations of the salamander *Plethodon cinereus. Evolution* 30:33–45.

Hildebrand, H. H. 1982. A historical review of the status of sea turtle populations in the western Gulf of Mexico. In *Biology and Conservation of Sea Turtles,* ed. K. A. Bjorndal, 447–53. Washington, D.C.

Hill, I. 1954. The taxonomic status of the mid-Gulf Coast *Amphiuma. Tulane Studies in Zoology* 1:191–215.

Hines, T. C., and K. D. Keenlyne. 1976. Alligator attacks on humans in Florida. *Proceedings of the Annual Conference of the Southeastern Association of Fish and Wildlife Agencies* 30:358–61.

Hirth, H. F. 1980. *Chelonia mydas. Catalogue of American Amphibians and Reptiles*: 249.1–249.4.

Holman, J. A. 1971. *Ophisaurus attenuatus. Catalogue of American Amphibians and Reptiles*: 111.1–111.3.

Huheey, J. E. 1959. Distribution and variation in the glossy water snake, *Natrix rigida* (Say). *Copeia* 1959:303–11.

Iverson, J. B. 1977. *Kinosternon subrubrum. Catalogue of American Amphibians and Reptiles*: 193.1–193.4.

Jackson, J. F., and S. H. Shively. 1983. A distinctive population of *Graptemys pseudogeographica* from the Calcasieu River system. *Association of Southeastern Biologists Bulletin* 30:64 (abstract).

Jacobs, J. F. 1987. A preliminary investigation of geographic genetic variation and systematics of the two-lined salamander, *Eurycea bislineata* (Green). *Herpetologica* 43:423–46.

Jennings, R. D., and T. H. Fritts. 1983. The status of the black pine snake, *Pituophis melanoleucus lodingi,* and the Louisiana pine snake, *Pituophis melanoleucus ruthveni.* Unpublished report, U.S. Fish and Wildlife Service.

Joanen, T. 1969. Nesting ecology of alligators in Louisiana. *Proceedings of Twenty-third Annual Conference of Southeastern Association of Game and Fish Commissioners*: 141–51.

Joanen, T., and L. McNease. 1970. A telemetric study of nesting female alligators on Rockefeller Refuge, Louisiana. *Proceedings of Twenty-fourth Annual Conference of Southeastern Association of Game and Fish Commissioners*: 175–93.

Joanen, T., and L. McNease. 1972a. Population distribution of alligators with special reference to the Louisiana coastal marsh zones. *Symposium, American Alligator Council* (Lake Charles, Louisiana), 1–12.

Joanen, T., and L. McNease. 1972b. A telemetric study of adult male alligators on Rockefeller Refuge, Louisiana. *Twenty-sixth Annual Meeting, Southeastern Association of Game and Fish Commissioners* (Knoxville, Tennessee), 1–38.

Joanen, T., and L. McNease. 1975. Notes on the reproductive biology and captive propagation of the American alligator. *Proceedings of the Southeastern Association of Game and Fish Commissioners Conference* 29:407–15.

Johnson, R. M. 1953. A contribution on the life history of the lizard *Scincella laterale* (Say). *Tulane Studies in Zoology* 1:11–27.

Karlin, A. A., and S. I. Guttman. 1981. Hybridization between *Desmognathus fuscus* and *Desmognathus ochrophaeus* (Amphibia: Urodela: Plethodontidae) in northeastern Ohio and northwestern Pennsylvania. *Copeia* 1981:371–77.

Karlin, A. A., and S. I. Guttman. 1986. Systematics and geographic isozyme variation in the plethodontid salamander *Desmognathus fuscus* (Rafinesque). *Herpetologica* 42:283–301.

Keiser, E. D., Jr., and P. J. Conzelman. 1969. The red-backed salamander, *Plethodon cinereus* (Green) in Louisiana. *Journal of Herpetology* 3:189–91.

Keiser, E. D., Jr., and L. D. Wilson. 1979. Checklist and key to the herpetofauna of Louisiana, second edition. *Lafayette Natural History Museum Bulletin*, Lafayette, Louisiana.

Kellogg, R. 1929. The habits and economic importance of alligators. *U.S. Department of Agriculture Technical Bulletin* (147): 1–36.

Kennedy, J. P. 1964. Natural history notes on some snakes of eastern Texas. *Texas Journal of Science* 16:210–15.

Kirn, A. J., W. L. Burger, and H. M. Smith. 1949. The subspecies of *Tantilla gracilis*. *American Midland Naturalist* 42:238–51.

Klauber, L. M. 1956. *Rattlesnakes, Their Habits, Life Histories, and Influence on Mankind.* Berkeley and Los Angeles, California.

Kofron, C. P. 1978. Foods and habitats of aquatic snakes (Reptilia, Serpentes) in a Louisiana swamp. *Journal of Herpetology* 12:543–54.

———. 1979a. Reproduction of aquatic snakes in south-central Louisiana. *Herpetologica* 35:44–50.

———. 1979b. Female reproductive biology of the brown snake, *Storeria dekayi*, in Louisiana. *Copeia* 1979:463–66.

Kushlan, J. A., and J. C. Simon. 1981. Egg manipulation by the American alligator. *Journal of Herpetology* 15:451–54.

Lagler, K. F. 1943. Food habits and economic relations of the turtles of Michigan with special reference to game management. *American Midland Naturalist* 29: 257–319.

Lamb, T. 1984. The influence of sex and breeding condition on microhabitat selection and diet in the pig frog *Rana grylio*. *American Midland Naturalist* 111: 311–18.

Lawson, R. 1985. Molecular studies of thamnophiine snakes. Ph.D. dissertation, Louisiana State University, Baton Rouge.

Legler, J. M. 1960. Natural history of the ornate box turtle, *Terrapene ornata ornata* Agassiz. *University of Kansas Publications, Museum of Natural History* 11: 527–669.

Liner, E. A. 1949. Notes on the young of the blue racer, *Coluber constrictor flaviventris*. *Copeia* 1949:230.

———. 1954. The herpetofauna of Lafayette, Terrebonne, and Vermilion parishes, Louisiana. *Proceedings of the Louisiana Academy of Sciences* 17:65–85.

Livezey, R. L. 1952. Some observations on *Pseudacris nigrita triseriata* (Wied) in Texas. *American Midland Naturalist* 47: 372–81.

Livezey, R. L., and A. H. Wright. 1947. A synoptic key to the salientian eggs of the United States. *American Midland Naturalist* 37:179–222.

Lohoefener, R., and L. Lohmeier. 1984. The status of *Gopherus polyphemus* (Testudines, Testudinidae) west of the Tombigbee and Mobile rivers. Research report to U.S. Fish and Wildlife Service, Jackson, Mississippi.

Mahmoud, I. Y. 1967. Courtship behavior and sexual maturity in four species of kinosternid turtles. *Copeia* 1967:314–19.

———. 1968. Feeding behavior in kinosternid turtles. *Herpetologica* 24:300–305.

———. 1969. Comparative ecology of the kinosternid turtles of Oklahoma. *Southwestern Naturalist* 14:31–66.

Manion, J. J., and L. Cory. 1952. Comparative ecological studies on the amphibians of Cass County, Michigan and vicinity. Ph.D. dissertation, University of Notre Dame, Notre Dame, Indiana.

Marchand, L. J. 1942. A contribution to a knowledge of the natural history of certain freshwater turtles. M.S. thesis, University of Florida, Gainesville.

Martof, B. S. 1956. Growth and development of the green frog *Rana clamitans* under natural conditions. *American Midland Naturalist* 55:101–17.

———. 1975a. *Pseudotriton montanus. Catalogue of American Amphibians and Reptiles*: 166.1–166.2.

———. 1975b. *Pseudotriton ruber. Catalogue of American Amphibians and Reptiles*: 167.1–167.3.

———. 1975c. *Hyla squirella. Catalogue of American Amphibians and Reptiles*: 168.1–168.2.

Martof, B. S., W. M. Palmer, J. R. Bailey, and J. R. Harrison III. 1980. *Amphibians and Reptiles of the Carolinas and Virginia.* Chapel Hill, North Carolina.

McAllister, C. T. 1987. Life history notes: *Eumeces septentrionalis obtusirostris* (Southern Prairie Skink). Reproduction. *SSAR Herpetological Review* 18(4):75.

McCauley, R. H. 1945. *The Reptiles of Maryland and the District of Columbia.* Hagerstown, Maryland.

McConkey, E. H. 1954. A systematic study of the North American lizards of the genus *Ophisaurus. American Midland Naturalist* 51:133–71.

McDowell, S. B. 1987. Systematics. In *Snakes: Ecology and Evolutionary Biology*, ed., R. A. Seigel, J. T. Collins, and S. S. Novak, 3–50. New York.

McIlhenny, E. A. 1934. Notes on incubation and growth of alligators. *Copeia* 1934:80–88.

———. 1935. *The Alligator's Life History.* Boston.

McNease, L., and T. Joanen. 1974. A study of immature alligators on Rockefeller Refuge, Louisiana. *Twenty-eighth Annual Meeting, Southeastern Association of Game and Fish Commissioners* (White Sulphur Springs, West Virginia), 1–21.

McNease, L., and T. Joanen. 1977. Alligator diets in relation to marsh salinity. *Proceedings of the Annual Conference of the Southeastern Association of Fish and Wildlife Agencies* 31:36–40.

McNease, L., and T. Joanen. 1978. Distribution and relative abundance of the alligator in Louisiana coastal marshes. *Proceedings of the Annual Conference of the Southeastern Fish and Wildlife Agencies* 32:182–86.

Meade, G. P. 1932. Notes on the breeding habits of Say's king snake in captivity. *Bulletin of the Antivenin Institute of America* 5(3):70–71.

———. 1934. Some observations on captive snakes. *Copeia* 1934:4–5.

———. 1937. Breeding habits of *Farancia abacura* in captivity. *Copeia* 1937:12–15.

———. 1940. Maternal care of eggs by *Farancia. Herpetologica* 2:15–20.

———. 1945. Further observations on Louisiana captive snakes. *Copeia* 1945:73–75.

Means, D. B. 1974. The status of *Desmognathus brimleyorum* Stejneger and an analysis of the genus *Desmognathus* (Amphibia: Urodela) in Florida. *Bulletin of the Florida State Museum, Biological Sciences* 18:1–100.

Mecham, J. S. 1954. Geographic variation in the green frog, *Rana clamitans. Texas Journal of Science* 6:1–24.

———. 1960. Introgressive hybridization between two southeastern treefrogs. *Evolution* 14:445–57.

———. 1967. *Notophthalmus viridescens. Catalogue of American Amphibians and Reptiles*: 53.1–53.4.

Meylan, P. A. 1987. The phylogenetic relationships of soft-shelled turtles (Family Trionychidae). *Bulletin of the American Museum of Natural History* 186(1):1–101.

Milstead, W. W. 1967. Fossil box turtles (*Terrapene*) from central North America, and box turtles of eastern Mexico. *Copeia* 1967:168–79.

———. 1969. Studies on the evolution of box turtles (genus *Terrapene*). *Bulletin of the Florida State Museum, Biological Sciences* 14:1–113.

Minyard, V. 1947. The food habits of *Pseudemys scripta troostii*. M.S. thesis, Tulane University, New Orleans, Louisiana.

Mittleman, M. B. 1967. *Manculus. Manculus quadridigitatus. Catalogue of American Amphibians and Reptiles*: 44.1–44.2.

Mohlenbrock, R. H. 1959. A floristic study of a southern Illinois swampy area. *Ohio Journal of Science* 59(2):89–100.

Morgan, E. C. 1972. The distribution of the subspecies of *Sceloporus undulatus* (Sauria: Iguanidae) in Louisiana. *Southwestern Naturalist* 17:67–72.

Morizot, D. C., and N. H. Douglas. 1967. New records and range extensions of an amphibian and two reptiles from northern Louisiana. *Herpetologica* 23:132–33.

Morizot, D. C., and N. H. Douglas. 1970. Notes on *Pseudacris streckeri streckeri* in northwest Louisiana. *Bulletin of the Maryland Herpetological Society* 6(2):18.

Morris, Michael A. 1975. Systematics and distribution of the northern water snake, *Nerodia sipedon* (Linnaeus), with comparisons to *Nerodia fasciata*. Ph.D. dissertation, Southern Illinois University, Carbondale.

Mount, R. M. 1975. *The Reptiles and Amphibians of Alabama*. Auburn, Alabama.

Mulcare, D. J. 1966. The problem of toxicity in *Rana palustris*. *Proceedings of the Indiana Academy of Science* 75:319–24.

Mushinsky, H. R., and J. J. Hebrard. 1977. Food partitioning by five species of water snakes in Louisiana. *Herpetologica* 33:162–66.

Mushinsky, H. R., J. J. Hebrard, and D. S. Vodipich. 1982. Ontogeny of water snake foraging ecology. *Ecology* 63:1624–29.

Mushinsky, H. R., J. J. Hebrard, and M. G. Walley. 1980. The role of temperature on the behavioral and ecological associations of sympatric water snakes. *Copeia* 1980: 744–54.

Mushinsky, H. R., and K. H. Lotz. 1980. Chemoreceptive responses of two sympatric water snakes to extracts of commonly ingested prey species, ontogenetic and ecological considerations. *Journal of Chemical Ecology* 6:523–35.

Myers, C. W. 1967. The pine woods snake, *Rhadinaea flavilata* (Cope). *Bulletin of the Florida State Museum, Biological Sciences* 11:47–97.

Neill, W. T. 1950. Taxonomy, nomenclature, and distribution of southeastern cricket frogs, genus *Acris*. *American Midland Naturalist* 43:152–56.

———. 1957. The status of *Rana capito stertens* Schwartz and Harrison. *Herpetologica* 13:47–52.

———. 1958a. The occurrence of amphibians and reptiles in saltwater areas, and bibliography. *Bulletin of Marine Science, Gulf and Caribbean* 8:1–97.

———. 1958b. The varied calls of the barking treefrog, *Hyla gratiosa* LeConte. *Copeia* 1958:44–46.

———. 1963. *Hemidactylium scutatum. Catalogue of American Amphibians and Reptiles*: 2.1–2.2.

———. 1964. Taxonomy, natural history, and zoogeography of the rainbow snake, *Farancia erytrogramma* (Palisot de Beauvois). *American Midland Naturalist* 71:257–95.

Nelson, C. E. 1972. Systematic studies of the North American microhylid genus *Gastrophryne*. *Journal of Herpetology* 6: 111–37.

Newton, M. B., Jr. 1972. *Atlas of Louisiana: A Guide for Students*. Baton Rouge, Louisiana.

Ogren, L. 1977. Survey and reconnaissance of sea turtles in the northern Gulf of Mexico. National Marine Fisheries Service, Panama City, Florida.

Oplinger, C. S. 1963. The life history of the northern spring peeper, *Hyla crucifer crucifer* Wied at Ithaca, New York. Ph.D. dissertation, Cornell University, Ithaca, New York.

———. 1967. Food habits and feeding activity of recently transformed and adult *Hyla crucifer crucifer* Wied. *Herpetologica* 23: 209–17.

Pace, A. E. 1974. Systematic and biological studies of the leopard frogs (*Rana pipiens* complex) of the United States. *Miscellaneous Publications, Museum of Zoology, University of Michigan* (148):1–140.

Palmer, M. E. 1939. Amphibia of southeast Louisiana. M.S. thesis, Louisiana State University, Baton Rouge.

Palmer, W. M. 1961. Notes on eggs and young of the scarlet king-snake, *Lampropeltis doliata doliata. Herpetologica* 17:65.

Pearse, A. S. 1911. Concerning the development of frog tadpoles in sea water. *Philippine Journal of Science* 6:219–20.

Penn, G. H., Jr. 1943. Herpetological notes from Cameron Parish, Louisiana. *Copeia* 1943:58–59.

Penn, G. H., Jr., and K. E. Pottharst. 1940. The reproduction and dormancy of *Terrapene major* in New Orleans. *Herpetologica* 2:25–29.

Petranka, J. W. 1982. Geographic variation in the mode of reproduction and larval characteristics of the small-mouthed salamander (*Ambystoma texanum*) in the east-central United States. *Herpetologica* 38:475–85.

Pettus, D. 1958. Water relationships in *Natrix sipedon. Copeia* 1958:207–11.

Pisani, G. R., J. T. Collins, and S. R. Edwards. 1972. A re-evaluation of the subspecies of *Crotalus horridus. Transactions of the Kansas Academy of Science* 75:255–63.

Platt, D. R. 1969. Natural history of the hognose snakes *Heterodon platyrhinos* and *Heterodon nasicus. University of Kansas Publications, Museum of Natural History* 18:253–420.

Plotkin, M., and R. Atkinson. 1979. Geographic distribution: *Eleutherodactylus planirostris planirostris. SSAR Herpetological Review* 10:59.

Pope, C. H. 1947. Amphibians and reptiles of the Chicago area. *Chicago Natural History Museum.*

Porter, K. R. 1970. *Bufo valliceps. Catalogue of American Amphibians and Reptiles*: 94.1–94.4.

Pritchard, P. C. H. 1967. *Living Turtles of the World.* Jersey City, New Jersey.

———. 1969. Studies of the systematics and reproductive cycles of the genus *Lepidochelys.* Ph.D. dissertation, University of Florida, Gainesville.

———. 1971. The leatherback or leathery turtle, *Dermochelys coriacea. IUCN Monograph, Marine Turtle Series* (1):1–39.

———. 1979. *Encyclopedia of Turtles.* Neptune, New Jersey.

———. 1982. The biology and status of the alligator snapping turtle (*Macroclemys temmincki*) with research and management recommendations. *Report to World Wildlife Fund*: 1–124.

Ralin, D. B. 1968. Ecological and reproductive differentiation in the cryptic species of the *Hyla versicolor* complex (Hylidae). *Southwestern Naturalist* 13:283–300.

———. 1970. Genetic compatibility and a phylogeny of the temperate North American hylid fauna. Ph.D. dissertation, University of Texas, Austin.

Raun, G. G., and F. R. Gehlbach. 1972. Amphibians and reptiles in Texas. *Dallas Museum of Natural History Bulletin* (2):1–61.

Raymond, L. R., and L. M. Hardy. 1983. Taxonomic status of the corn snake, *Elaphe guttata* (Linnaeus) (Colubridae), in Louisiana and eastern Texas. *Southwestern Naturalist* 28:105–107.

Reed, C. F. 1956. *Hyla cinerea* in Maryland, Delaware, and Virginia, with notes on the taxonomic status of *Hyla cinerea evittata. Journal of the Washington Academy of Sciences* 46:328–32.

Reeve, W. L. 1952. Taxonomy and distribution of the horned lizards, genus *Phrynosoma. University of Kansas Science Bulletin* 34(pt. 2):817–960.

Reinert, H. K., D. Cundall, and L. M. Bushar. 1984. Foraging behavior of the timber rattlesnake, *Crotalus horridus. Copeia* 1984:976–81.

Reynolds, S. L., and M. E. Seidel. 1982. *Sternotherus odoratus. Catalogue of American Amphibians and Reptiles*: 287.1–287.4.

Rojas, N. N., and J. S. Godley. 1979. Tooth morphology in crayfish-eating snakes, genus *Regina*. In *Abstracts, Joint Annual Meeting, Herpetologists' League, Society for the Study of Amphibians and Reptiles, University of Tennessee* (Knoxville), 52.

Rose, F. L. 1966a. Reproductive potential of *Amphiuma means. Copeia* 1966:598–99.

———. 1966b. Homing to nests by the salamander *Desmognathus auriculatus. Copeia* 1966:251–53.

Rose, F. L., and C. D. Barbour. 1968. Ecology and reproductive cycles of the introduced gecko, *Hemidactylus turcicus*, in the southern United States. *American Midland Naturalist* 79:159–68.

Rossman, D. A. 1959. Chorus frog (*Pseudacris nigrita* ssp.) intergradation in southwestern Illinois. *Herpetologica* 15: 38–40.

———. 1960. Herpetofaunal survey of the Pine Hills area of southern Illinois. *Quarterly Journal of the Florida Academy of Sciences* (1959) 22:207–25.

———. 1963a. Relationships and taxonomic status of the North American natricine snake genera *Liodytes, Regina*, and *Clonophis. Occasional Papers of the Museum of Zoology, Louisiana State University* (29):1–29.

———. 1963b. The colubrid snake genus *Thamnophis*: A revision of the Sauritus group. *Bulletin of the Florida State Museum, Biological Sciences* 7:99–178.

———. 1965a. Rediscovery of the tiger salamander, *Ambystoma tigrinum*, in Louisiana. *Proceedings of the Louisiana Academy of Sciences* 27:17–20.

———. 1965b. The ornate box turtle, *Terrapene ornata*, in Louisiana. *Proceedings of the Louisiana Academy of Sciences* 28:130–31.

———. 1973. Evidence for the conspecificity of *Carphophis amoenus* (Say) and *Carphophis vermis* (Kennicott). *Journal of Herpetology* 7:140–41.

———. 1984. Distribution of the tarantula *Dugesiella hentzi* (Girard) in Louisiana. *Proceedings of the Louisiana Academy of Sciences* 47:52–53.

Rossman, D. A., and R. L. Erwin. 1980. Geographic variation in the snake *Storeria occipitomaculata* (Storer) (Serpentes: Colubridae) in southeastern United States. *Brimleyana* (4):95–102.

Rossman, D. A., and A. J. Meier. 1979. Geographic distribution: *Plethodon dorsalis. SSAR Herpetological Review* 10:23.

Roze, J. A., and G. M. Tilger. 1983. *Micrurus fulvius. Catalogue of American Amphibians and Reptiles*: 316.1–316.4.

Russell, F. E. 1980. *Snake Venom Poisoning*. Philadelphia, Pennsylvania.

Ruthven, A. G. 1908. Variations and genetic relationships of the garter-snakes. *Bulletin, United States National Museum* (61):1–201.

Sabath, M. D., and L. E. Sabath. 1969. Morphological intergradation in Gulf Coast brown snakes *Storeria dekayi* and *Storeria tropica. American Midland Naturalist* 81:148–55.

Sanders, O. 1986. The heritage of *Bufo woodhousei* Girard in Texas (Salientia: Bufonidae). *Occasional Papers of the Strecker Museum*, (1):1–28.

Sanderson, W. E. 1983. Systematics of the water snakes of the *Nerodia cyclopion* complex. M.S. thesis, Louisiana State University, Baton Rouge.

Schaaf, R. T., Jr., and P. W. Smith. 1970. Geographic variation in the pickerel frog. *Herpetologica* 26:240–54.

Schlegel, H. 1837. *Essai sur la Physionomie Serpens.* Vol. 1. Leiden.

Schmidt, K. P. 1932. Stomach contents of some American coral snakes, with the description of a new species of *Geophis. Copeia* 1932:6–9.

Schroeder, B. 1986. Semi-annual report of the sea turtle stranding and salvage network Atlantic and Gulf coasts of the United States January–June 1986. Coastal Resources Division, National Marine Fisheries Service, Contribution Number CRD-86/87-5.

Schwaner, T. D., H. C. Dessauer, and L. A. Landry, Jr., 1980. Genetic divergence of *Nerodia sipedon* and *N. fasciata. Isozyme Bulletin* 13:102.

Schwartz, A. 1956. Geographic variation in the chicken turtle *Deirochelys reticularia* Latreille. *Fieldiana: Zoology* 34:461–503.

Scroggin, J. B., and W. B. Davis. 1956. Food habits of the Texas dwarf siren. *Herpetologica* 12:231–37.

Seidel, M. E., and H. M. Smith. 1986. *Chrysemys, Pseudemys, Trachemys* (Testudines: Emydidae): Did Agassiz have it right? *Herpetologica* 42:242–48.

Seifert, W. 1978. Geographic distribution: *Bufo americanus charlesmithi. SSAR Herpetological Review* 9:61.

Semlitsch, R. D., and G. B. Moran. 1984. Ecology of the redbelly snake (*Storeria occipitomaculata*) using mesic habitats in South Carolina. *American Midland Naturalist* 111:33–40.

Semlitsch, R. D., and C. A. West. 1983. Aspects of the life history and ecology of Webster's salamander, *Plethodon websteri. Copeia* 1983:339–46.

Sever, D. M. 1975. Morphology and seasonal variation of the mental hedonic glands of the dwarf salamander, *Eurycea quadridigitata* (Holbrook). *Herpetologica* 31:241–51.

Shealy, R. M. 1976. The natural history of the Alabama map turtle, *Graptemys pulchra* Baur, in Alabama. *Bulletin of the Florida State Museum, Biological Sciences* 21:47–111.

Shively, S. H. 1982. Factors limiting the upstream distribution of the Sabine map turtle. M.S. thesis, University of Southwestern Louisiana, Lafayette.

Shively, S. H., and M. F. Vidrine. 1984. Freshwater mollusks in the alimentary tract of a Mississippi map turtle. *Proceedings of the Louisiana Academy of Sciences* 47:27–29.

Shoop, C. R. 1960. The breeding habits of the mole salamander, *Ambystoma talpoideum* (Holbrook), in southeastern Louisiana. *Tulane Studies in Zoology* 8:65–82.

———. 1962. A comparative study of Louisiana *Necturus* populations. Ph.D. dissertation, Tulane University, New Orleans, Louisiana.

———. 1964. *Ambystoma talpoideum.* Catalogue of American Amphibians and Reptiles: 8.1–8.2.

———. 1965. Aspects of reproduction in Louisiana *Necturus* populations. *American Midland Naturalist* 74:357–67.

———. 1967. Relation of migration and breeding activities to time of ovulation in *Ambystoma maculatum. Herpetologica* 23: 319–21.

———. 1968. Migratory orientation of *Ambystoma maculatum*: Movements near breeding ponds and displacements of migrating individuals. *Biological Bulletin* 135:230–38.

Shoop, C. R., and G. E. Gunning. 1967. Seasonal activity and movements of *Necturus* in Louisiana. *Copeia* 1967:732–37.

Siekmann, J. M. 1949. A survey of the tadpoles of Louisiana. M.S. thesis, Tulane University, New Orleans, Louisiana.

Smith, H. M. 1938. A review of the snake genus *Farancia. Copeia* 1938:110–17.

Smith, H. M., and J. A. Slater. 1949. The southern races of *Eumeces septentrionalis* (Baird). *Transactions of the Kansas Academy of Science* 52:438–48.

Smith, P. W. 1951. A new frog and a new turtle from the western Illinois sand prairies.

Bulletin of the Chicago Academy of Sciences 9:189–99.

———. 1953. A reconsideration of the status of *Hyla phaeocrypta*. *Herpetologica* 9:169–73.

———. 1961. The amphibians and reptiles of Illinois. *Illinois Natural History Survey Bulletin* 28:1–298.

Smith, P. W., and J. C. List. 1955. Notes on Mississippi amphibians and reptiles. *American Midland Naturalist* 53:115–25.

Smith, P. W., and D. M. Smith. 1952. The relationship of the chorus frogs, *Pseudacris nigrita feriarum* and *Pseudacris n. triseriata*. *American Midland Naturalist* 48:165–80.

Smith, P. W., and H. M. Smith. 1952. Geographic variation in the lizard *Eumeces anthracinus*. *University of Kansas Science Bulletin* 34:679–94.

Stewart, M. M. 1983. *Rana clamitans*. *Catalogue of American Amphibians and Reptiles*: 337.1–337.4.

Strecker, J. K., and L. S. Frierson, Jr. 1926. The herpetology of Caddo and De Soto parishes, Louisiana. *Contributions from Baylor University Museum* 5:1–10.

Strecker, J. K., and L. S. Frierson, Jr. 1935. The herpetology of Caddo and De Soto parishes, Louisiana (second paper). *Baylor Bulletin* 38(3):33–34.

Stunkard, H. W. 1943. A new trematode, *Dictyangium chelydrae* (Microscaphiidae: Angiodictyidae), from the snapping turtle, *Chelydra serpentina*. *Journal of Parasitology* 29:143–50.

Taylor, E. H. 1935. A taxonomic study of the cosmopolitan scincoid lizards of the genus *Eumeces* with an account of the distribution and relationships of its species. *University of Kansas Science Bulletin* 23:3–643.

Telford, S. R., Jr. 1966. Variation among the southeastern crowned snakes, genus *Tantilla*. *Bulletin of the Florida State Museum, Biological Sciences* 10:261–304.

Thomas, R. A. 1974. Geographic variation in

Elaphe guttata (Linnaeus) (Serpentes: Colubridae). M.S. thesis, Texas A & M University, College Station.

Tinkle, D. W. 1952. Notes on the salamander, *Eurycea longicauda guttolineata*, in Florida. *Field & Laboratory* 20:105–108.

———. 1957. Ecology, maturation and reproduction of *Thamnophis sauritus proximus*. *Ecology* 38:69–77.

———. 1958. The systematics and ecology of the *Sternothaerus carinatus* complex. *Tulane Studies in Zoology* 6:3–56.

———. 1959. Observations of reptiles and amphibians in a Louisiana swamp. *American Midland Naturalist* 62:189–205.

———. 1961. Geographic variation in reproduction, size, sex ratio and maturity of *Sternothaerus odoratus* (Testudinata: Chelydridae). *Ecology* 42:68–76.

Tinkle, D. W., and E. A. Liner. 1955. Behavior of *Natrix* in aggregations. *Field & Laboratory* 23:84–87.

Trauth, S. E. 1983. Reproductive biology and spermathecal anatomy of the dwarf salamander (*Eurycea quadridigitata*) in Alabama. *Herpetologica* 39:9–15.

True, F. H. 1884. The useful aquatic reptiles and batrachians of the United States. In *The Fisheries and Fishery Industries of the United States*, by G. B. Goode, sec. 1, pt. II, pp. 137–62. Washington, D.C.

Valentine, B. 1962. Intergrading populations and distribution of the salamander *Eurycea longicauda* in the Gulf states. *Journal of the Ohio Herpetological Society* 3:42–51.

———. 1963. The salamander *Desmognathus* in Mississippi. *Copeia* 1963:130–39.

Viosca, P., Jr. 1923. An ecological study of the cold blooded vertebrates of southeastern Louisiana. *Copeia* (115):35–44.

———. 1926. Distributional problems of the cold-blooded vertebrates of the Gulf Coastal Plain. *Ecology* 7:307–14.

———. 1934. Principles of bullfrog culture. New Orleans, Louisiana (reprint, with revisions and additions, of article in *Transactions of the American Fisheries Society, 1931*).

———. 1944. Distribution of certain cold-blooded animals in Louisiana in relationship to the geology and physiography of the state. *Proceedings of the Louisiana Academy of Sciences* 8:47–62.

———. 1957. Have you a little gecko in your home? *Louisiana Conservationist* 9(4):20–21.

———. 1961. Turtles, tame and truculent. *Louisiana Conservationist* 13(7–8):5–8.

Vogt, R. C. 1978. Systematics and ecology of the false map turtle complex *Graptemys pseudogeographica*. Ph.D. dissertation, University of Wisconsin, Madison.

———. 1980. Natural history of the map turtles *Graptemys pseudogeographica* and *G. ouachitensis* in Wisconsin. *Tulane Studies in Zoology and Botany* 22:17–48.

Volpe, E. P. 1956. Experimental F1 hybrids between *Bufo valliceps* and *Bufo fowleri*. *Tulane Studies in Zoology* 4:61–75.

———. 1957. Embryonic temperature tolerance and rate of development in *Bufo valliceps*. *Physiological Zoology* 30:164–76.

———. 1959. Experimental and natural hybridization between *Bufo terrestris* and *Bufo fowleri*. *American Midland Naturalist* 61:295–312.

———. 1960. Evolutionary consequences of hybrid sterility and vigor in toads. *Evolution* 14:181–93.

Volpe, E. P., and J. L. Dobie. 1959. The larva of the oak toad, *Bufo quercicus* Holbrook. *Tulane Studies in Zoology* 7:145–52.

Volpe, E. P., M. A. Wilkens, and J. L. Dobie. 1961. Embryonic and larval development of *Hyla avivoca*. *Copeia* 1961:340–49.

Wake, D. B. 1966. Comparative osteology and evolution of the lungless salamanders, family Plethodontidae. *Memoirs of the Southern California Academy of Sciences* 4:1–111.

Walker, J. M. 1963. Amphibians and reptiles of Jackson Parish, Louisiana. *Proceedings of the Louisiana Academy of Sciences* 26:91–101.

———. 1965. Notes on two rare Louisiana serpents. *Herpetologica* 21:159–60.

Ward, J. P. 1980. Comparative cranial morphology of the freshwater turtle subfamily Emydinae: An analysis of the feeding mechanisms and the systematics. Ph.D. dissertation, North Carolina State University, Raleigh.

———. 1984. Relationships of chrysemyd turtles of North America (Testudines: Emydidae). *Special Publications, The Museum, Texas Tech University* (21):1–50.

Warwick, C. 1984. Wildtrack's terrapin investigation. *BBC Wildlife* 2:468–69.

Wasserman, A. 1968. *Scaphiopus holbrooki*. *Catalogue of American Amphibians and Reptiles*: 70.1–70.4.

Weaver, W. G., and F. L. Rose. 1967. Systematics, fossil history, and evolution of the genus *Chrysemys*. *Tulane Studies in Zoology* 14:63–73.

Webb, R. G. 1961. Observations on the life histories of turtles (genus *Pseudemys* and *Graptemys*) in Lake Texoma, Oklahoma. *American Midland Naturalist* 65:193–214.

———. 1962. North American recent soft-shelled turtles (family Trionychidae). *University of Kansas Publications, Museum of Natural History* 13:429–611.

———. 1973. *Trionyx spiniferus*. *Catalogue of American Amphibians and Reptiles*: 140.1–140.4.

Whitaker, J. O., Jr. 1971. A study of the western chorus frog, *Pseudacris triseriata*, in Vigo County, Indiana. *Journal of Herpetology* 5:127–50.

Williams, K. L. 1978. Systematics and natural history of the American milk snake, *Lampropeltis triangulum*. *Milwaukee Public Museum Publications in Biology and Geology* (2):1–258.

Williams, K. L., and L. D. Wilson. 1967. A

review of the colubrid snake genus *Cemophora* Cope. *Tulane Studies in Zoology* 13:103–24.

Wilson, L. D. 1970a. The racer *Coluber constrictor* (Serpentes: Colubridae) in Louisiana and eastern Texas. *Texas Journal of Science* 22:67–85.

———. 1970b. The coachwhip snake, *Masticophis flagellum* (Shaw): Taxonomy and distribution. *Tulane Studies in Zoology and Botany* 16:31–99.

Wood, J. T. 1955. The nesting of the four-toed salamander, *Hemidactylium scutatum* (Schlegel), in Virginia. *American Midland Naturalist* 53:381–89.

Wright, A. H. 1929. Synopsis and description of North American tadpoles. *Proceedings of the United States National Museum* 74:1–70.

———. 1932. *Life-histories of the Frogs of Okefinokee Swamp, Georgia.* New York.

Wright, A. H., and A. A. Wright. 1949. *Handbook of Frogs and Toads.* Ithaca, New York.

Wright, A. H., and A. A. Wright. 1957. *Handbook of Snakes.* 2 vols. Ithaca, New York.

Zeliff, C. C. 1932. A new species of cestode, *Crepidobothrium amphiumae*, from *Amphiuma tridactylum. Proceedings of the United States National Museum* 81:1–3.

INDEX